Pe... s

Slow Travel
Family Breaks

Jane Anderson   Holly Tuppen

EDITION 1

Bradt Guides Ltd, UK
The Globe Pequot Press Inc, USA

First edition published October 2022
Bradt Guides Ltd
31a High Street, Chesham, Buckinghamshire, HP5 1BW, England
www.bradtguides.com
Print edition published in the USA by The Globe Pequot Press Inc,
PO Box 480, Guilford, Connecticut 06437-0480

Text copyright © 2022 Bradt Guides Ltd
Maps copyright © 2022 Bradt Guides Ltd; includes map data © OpenStreetMap contributors
Photographs copyright © 2022 Individual photographers (see below)
Project Manager: Anna Moores
Editor: Samantha Cook
Cover research: Ian Spick

ISBN: 9781784778705

British Library Cataloguing in Publication Data
A catalogue record for this book is available from the British Library

Photographs © individual photographers credited beside images & also those picture libraries credited as follows: Alamy.com (A); iStock.com (iS); Shutterstock.com (S); Superstock.com (SS)

Front cover Children pond-dipping (SolStock/iS)
Back cover Tree-climbing on the Isle of Wight (Goodleaf Tree Climbing/Anna Fulford)
Title page A child in Liverpool's Walker Art Gallery (Gareth Jones/Walker Art Gallery)

Maps David McCutcheon FBCart.S
Typeset by Ian Spick, Bradt Guides and Pepi Bluck, Perfect Picture
Production managed by Zenith Media; printed in the UK
Digital conversion by www.dataworks.co.in

ABOUT THE AUTHORS

Jane Anderson has been a travel writer and editor for over 25 years, beginning her working life on a magazine for travel agents and heading off to Antigua for her first assignment. Once her kids came along, 18 and 15 years ago, her focus turned to enriching family travel experiences which landed her the job of editor of *Family Traveller* magazine. She is currently Travel Editor at *Prima* magazine and also contributes to *Good Housekeeping*, *RED*, the *Telegraph* and *iPaper,* among others. She is the author of the Footprint guides *Dorset, New Forest & Isle of Wight with Kids* and *Brittany with Kids*.

Jane is particularly interested in local adventures and how to travel sustainably, giving children life-enhancing travel experiences close to home. Having travelled around the world, from the Maldives to Vietnam, often with her two children, she genuinely feels that the UK is one of the best and most rewarding places to explore with youngsters – with the added benefit of no flying or jetlag.

Holly Tuppen's passion for travelling the world responsibly started in 2008 when she set off on an around-the-world-without-flying adventure. After sailing, cycling, walking and hitchhiking across oceans, deserts and mountain ranges, Holly returned to spread the word about sustainable travel through marketing for the *Green Traveller* website and editing *Green Hotelier* magazine.

Since her two boys came along, eight and six years ago, she's been continuing to travel slowly, but a little closer to home. Holly loves nothing more than discovering locally owned, independent experiences and places to stay, and believes that supporting these places is not only better for communities and the planet but also improves any holiday.

An expert in sustainable travel, working as a writer and consultant, Holly writes for the likes of *The Guardian*, *The Times* and *Condé Nast Traveller*. Her first book, *Sustainable Travel: The Essential Guide to Positive Impact Adventures*, was published in June 2021.

ACKNOWLEDGEMENTS

Thanks to: Louise Ferrall and the team at Visit England; Erin Hickey and the team at Visit Scotland; Jane Harris and Robert Jones at Visit Wales; Sara Whines, English Heritage; Eileen Rainsberry, Visit South West Scotland; Sarah Bolam, Sarah Bolam Communications; Jane Ellis, 1066 Country; Jilly Tyson, Hastings Country Park; Georgina Oakley and the team at Lotus PR; Mairi Thomson, Outer Hebrides Tourism; Paul Sharman, Hebridean Adventures; Victoria K Bond, Islands Partnership; Jonny Winter, Cumbria Tourism; Nici Hewitson, One Little Bird PR; Carol Rowntree & Richard Drakeley at The National Forest Company; Ana Ignatova, Make It York; Amanda Brown, AtoB Pr; Roddy Hamilton and Charlie at the Private Hill; Jenni Meikle, Northumberland Tourism; Aimee Rowe-Best PR; Lucy Jenner Brown, LJB PR; Susie Bowers, Visit Bristol; Fiona Reece, Travel Tonic; Coral Smith, Devon Wildlife Trust; Simon Clark, Visit Wight; Lana Croach, Visit Kent; Charlotte Goy, Visit Lincoln; Amanda Gore- Booth, Pilot PR; Sophie Sheilds, Visit Liverpool; Mick Thompson, Traveldog PR; Laurianne Chusseau, Experience Oxfordshire; Amy Noton, Marketing Peak District & Derbyshire; Julia Farish, Travel PR.

Also, a huge thanks to all the kind souls who hosted us on various trips and adventures in the making of this book. Travelling around these islands would be significantly less joyful without you!

FEEDBACK REQUEST & UPDATES WEBSITE

As well as taking you to places you may not be familiar with, we are aware that this book will be read by people who have specialist knowledge of the places we have explored, and although we have done our best to check our facts there are bound to be errors as well as some inevitable omissions of really special places. Please feel free to post your comments and recommendations, and read the latest feedback from other readers online at ⌂ bradtguides. com/updates. Alternatively, you can add a review of the book to Amazon, or share your adventures with us on social:

 BradtGuides   BradtGuides
 BradtGuides

CONTENTS

SLOW TRAVEL FAMILY BREAKS

The following is our personal selection of top family experiences in each location. Each chapter is also packed with suggestions in the local area for families wishing to experience Britain the slow way.

N

0   50 miles
0   100km

N O R T H   S E A

Shetland

Orkney

John o'Groats

Thurso

Fraserburgh

Aberdeen

Don

Spey

Inverness

Montrose

Dundee

Scotland

Perth

Forth

Tweed

Mallaig

Skye

Oban

Mull

Glasgow

Clyde

Arran

Ayr

Newcastle

Campbeltown

St Kilda

Outer
Hebrides

Stornoway

28 ISLE OF LEWIS
Whale- & dolphin-watching
liveaboard cruise
page 433

25 DUMFRIES & GALLOWAY
Guided Highland cow safari
page 385

22 THE LAKE DISTRICT
Walking with fell ponies
page 331

19 THE PEAK DISTRICT
Cycling the Monsal Trail
page 289

21 LIVERPOOL
The Beatles Story museum

27 THE CAIRNGORMS
Bespoke tour with Braemar
Highland Experience
page 417

26 EDINBURGH
Edinburgh International Film
Festival
page 401

24 NORTHUMBERLAND
Seabird safari, Farne Islands
page 371

23 NORTH YORKSHIRE
Fossil hunting on Whitby Beach
page 349

13 LINCOLNSHIRE
Exploring Lincoln's
12th-century castle

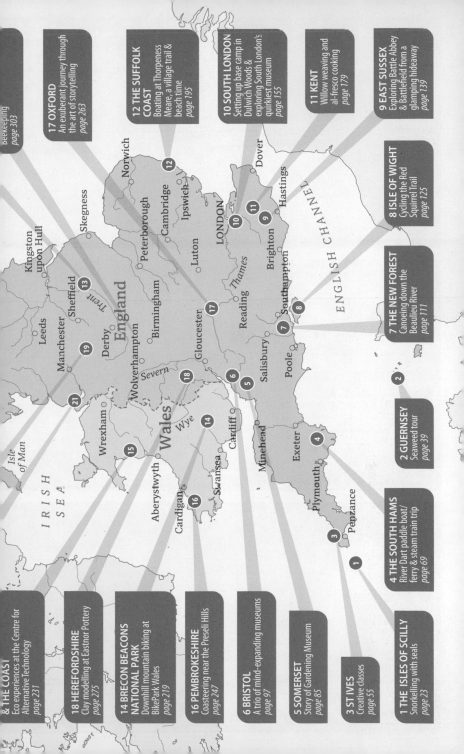

& THE COAST
Eco experiences at the Centre for Alternative Technology
page 231

17 OXFORD
An exuberant journey through the art of storytelling
page 263

12 THE SUFFOLK COAST
Boating at Thorpeness Meare, a village trail & beach time
page 195

10 SOUTH LONDON
Setting up base camp in Dulwich Woods & exploring South London's quirkiest museum
page 155

11 KENT
Willow weaving and al-fresco cooking
page 179

9 EAST SUSSEX
Exploring Battle Abbey & Battlefield from a glamping hideaway
page 139

8 ISLE OF WIGHT
Cycling the Red Squirrel Trail
page 125

7 THE NEW FOREST
Canoeing down the Beaulieu River
page 111

2 GUERNSEY
Seaweed tour
page 39

4 THE SOUTH HAMS
River Dart paddle boat/ ferry & steam train trip
page 69

1 THE ISLES OF SCILLY
Snorkelling with seals
page 23

3 ST IVES
Creative classes
page 55

5 SOMERSET
Story of Gardening Museum
page 85

6 BRISTOL
A trio of mind-expanding museums
page 97

16 PEMBROKESHIRE
Coasteering near the Preseli Hills
page 247

14 BRECON BEACONS NATIONAL PARK
Downhill mountain biking at BikePark Wales
page 219

18 HEREFORDSHIRE
Clay modelling at Eastnor Pottery
page 275

beekeeping
page 303

Norwich

Skegness

Cambridge

Ipswich

Peterborough

Luton

Dover

Hastings

LONDON

Brighton

Reading

Thames

Southampton

ENGLISH CHANNEL

Poole

Salisbury

Gloucester

Minehead

Exeter

Severn

Birmingham

Wolverhampton

Wye

Derby

England

Cardiff

Swansea

Wrexham

Aberystwyth

Cardigan

Wales

Trent

Sheffield

Leeds

Manchester

Kingston upon Hull

Isle of Man

IRISH SEA

Plymouth

Penzance

INTRODUCTION

When it comes to travelling with children, your instinct might be that everything speeds up. That travel becomes more frenetic with so much to consider. But this book offers a different approach. Going slow means getting under the skin of a place – taking time to experience nature and local culture with all your senses, meeting locals, from farmers to artists, who are passionate about their region, and opening up space for creativity and micro-adventures. Following the less obvious path may lead you to wild nature reserves in the heart of buzzing cities, quirky pottery workshops in grand country estates, sculpture trails hidden deep in the woods, and vast empty beaches where iridescent rock pools reveal miniature worlds.

Slow Travel Family Breaks explores the many special places in Britain, beyond the bucket-list showstoppers and tourist hotspots. It will lead you off the beaten track and connect you with local people eager to protect their communities and their landscapes so all can thrive. Each chapter features a number of talented individuals who extend a warm welcome to families – people keen to pass on their knowledge and enthusiasm for their patch and to create enriching, authentic experiences for you and your children.

As parents, we've found that it's often the small, local pursuits that engage children more than big, flashy, commercialised attractions. And ironically, it's often the free enterprises, those that give back to the community – from mini libraries along the Northumberland coast to children's workshops in community gardens in London – that work best for everyone.

◀ **1** Cycling adventures at the Scaladale Centre, Isle of Harris (page 446). **2** Children of all ages will love the Horniman Museum (page 158). **3** We've handpicked some fantastic activities for crafty children; see page 17 for some suggestions.

THE SLOW MINDSET

Hilary Bradt, Founder, Bradt Travel Guides

We shall not cease from exploration
And the end of all our exploring
Will be to arrive where we started
And know the place for the first time.
T S Eliot, 'Little Gidding', *Four Quartets*

This series evolved, slowly, from a Bradt editorial meeting when we started to explore ideas for guides to our favourite part of the world – Great Britain. We wanted to get away from the usual 'top sights' formula and encourage our authors to bring out the nuances and local differences that make up a sense of place – such things as food, building styles, nature, geology or local people and what makes them tick. Our aim was to create a series that celebrates the present, focusing on sustainable tourism, rather than taking a nostalgic wallow in the past.

So without our realising it at the time, we had defined 'Slow Travel', or at least our concept of it. For the beauty of the Slow Movement is that there is no fixed definition; we adapt the philosophy to fit our individual needs and aspirations. Thus Carl Honoré, author of *In Praise of Slow*, writes: 'The Slow Movement is a cultural revolution against the notion that faster is always better. It's not about doing everything at a snail's pace, it's about seeking to do everything at the right speed. Savouring the hours and minutes rather than just counting them. Doing everything as well as possible, instead of as fast as possible. It's about quality over quantity in everything from work to food to parenting.' And travel.

So take time to explore. Don't rush it, get to know an area – and the people who live there – and you'll be as delighted as the authors by what you find.

But going slow is also heaps of fun – tapping into our children's innate sense of play and unleashing it in adults, too. Once you've given it a go, we doubt you'll ever look back.

GOING SLOW, STAYING SUSTAINABLE

Sustainable travel means seeking experiences, places to stay, and ways to get around that have a positive rather than a negative impact on places and people. This means considering your environmental and social footprint when you head off on holiday. It may sound like a burden but in fact choosing the more sustainable option often leads to a more enjoyable experience.

Firstly, literally going slow often burns less carbon than going fast. Walking, cycling, riding, canoeing, kayaking and sailing are wonderfully low-impact ways to explore a destination without leaving a polluting trail behind you. Public transport also cuts carbon while investing in local services. Check out car-free options before travelling.

Supporting locally owned and run businesses not only means that your holiday pennies are going to local people, rather than big international brands, but locals are often more invested in the immediate area. What's more, smaller-scale businesses tend to be lower impact and better employers – aiming for loyalty and offering good service rather than always trying to cut costs. Buying local produce and goods also reduces your carbon footprint and can help educate children about where our food comes from.

Beyond going local, seek out experiences designed to give back to a community. These might be social enterprises, where profits go towards local benefit, like training disadvantaged people or offering low-cost services or experiences to those that need it. Or it may be an experience run by a community collective, where local people decide what they offer and where the profit goes. Sometimes it's possible to get involved in projects, like tree-planting, reviving ancient crafts or beach cleans. This can be a wonderful way to meet local people and to hear more about their perspective. What better way to encourage the next generation of changemakers than introducing kids to the many local heroes who are leading the way today!

Travelling sustainably also means thinking about when and where you travel. It often means avoiding overcrowded destinations or visiting popular places during the off-season or shoulder seasons (outside of summer holidays), to reduce pressure on infrastructure and the environment. This is particularly true where overtourism is a concern, in places like Pembrokeshire and St Ives – both of which are featured in this book. Here, second homes are damaging local economies, so ditch Airbnb and opt for hotels, campsites, or farm-stays instead. Better still, stay on the edges of the destination rather than in the thick of a tourist hub.

Most importantly, however, just like going slow, sustainable travel isn't about checklists or achievements – it's a mindset that we can take with us wherever we go.

GETTING AROUND

TRAINS

Trains are generally hassle free and add adventure to any holiday. They're also better for the environment than flying or driving. Trains work particularly well for city breaks, letting you enjoy the smug satisfaction of whizzing into a city centre without any concern about traffic or parking.

If you need a car in your destination, but don't want to do the long drive to get there, taking the train and then renting a car can be a good option. A relaxing five hours sitting, chatting and picnicking up to Scotland or across to Cornwall beats watching Google Maps' estimated time of arrival creep later and later. For a bigger adventure, try out the sleeper train routes from London to Penzance (Night Riviera Sleeper; ◇ gwr.com) and up to Scotland (Caledonian Sleeper ◇ sleeper.scot). Spending the night on a train is a brilliant introduction to overland travel for kids.

The problem with trains is usually the expense, but there are ways to cut costs. Invest in a Family & Friends Railcard (◇ familyandfriends-railcard.co.uk) to get a third off adult fares, 60% off children's. The Trainline booking service (◇ thetrainline.com) also offers a useful 'split fare' service, letting you know if it's cheaper to divide your trip into different tickets.

While researching this book we... Hopped up from London to Liverpool on the Avanti service (◇ avantiwestcoast.co.uk), to Edinburgh and York on LNER (London North Eastern Railway; ◇ lner.co.uk) and to Bristol and Totnes on Great Western Railway (◇ gwr.com). We also travelled by train all the way up to Llandudno from Cardiff (Great Western Railway) – a beautiful journey that snakes across the Welsh-English border.

COACHES & BUSES

Long-distance bus and coach travel is often overlooked but is often the most affordable and carbon-efficient way of getting around. National Express (◇ nationalexpress.com), Stagecoach (◇ stagecoachbus.com) and Citylink (◇ citylink.co.uk) are among the largest networks in Britain; look out for special offers, including £5 fares with National Express to over 50 destinations. Megabus (◇ uk.megabus.com) is one

---

1 Hiring a campervan is a great way to explore Britain with kids. **2** Taking the ferry to the Isle of Wight. **3** Kids will love the Dartmouth Steam Train (page 69). ▶

of the cheapest providers, with fares starting from £1 – trips between London and Glasgow provide the option to book a sleeper coach with a bed.

While researching this book we... Whizzed to Oxford from London on the Oxford Tube (⊘ oxfordtube.com), a private coach that offers a convenient ride up the M40. We also loved using the bus system around the Isle of Wight (⊘ islandbuses.info), and throughout the New Forest (⊘ newforestnpa.gov.uk).

FERRIES

Jumping aboard a ferry to cross the sea, however small the journey, adds a frisson of excitement to any trip! We love ferries, particularly with kids, since there's room to run about or sit and play games at a table, and plenty to see along the way. While longer crossings can take you out to islands – the Outer Hebrides (⊘ calmac.co.uk), the Channel Islands (⊘ condorferries.co.uk) and the Isles of Scilly (⊘ islesofscilly-travel. co.uk/scillonian-iii), for example – it's worth considering shorter ferry rides, by sea or river, wherever you are. It can be a great way to get a new perspective on the landscape.

While researching this book we... Jumped on a Wight Link (⊘ wightlink.co.uk) ferry to the Isle of Wight (we took our car, but the car-free option connecting with the train station in Portsmouth is brilliant). Smaller-scale ferries offered lots of fun and the chance to rest weary sightseeing legs in Bristol, Liverpool and the South Hams.

CAMPERVANS

Campervan travel has exploded in popularity of late, which is not surprising given the freedom it provides. Kids love cruising along in a mini home from home, and it can be really useful to have everything to hand while you're off adventuring – especially for those essential post-walk or -swim cups of hot chocolate.

Hiring a van is a sustainable and cost-effective option, and also relatively easy, thanks to a rise in Airbnb-style services for campervan owners. Yescapa (⊘ yescapa.co.uk), for example, will find you a campervan to rent pretty much anywhere in the UK, and offers insurance in case of mishaps.

Before you travel be sure to read up on regulations around campervans in your destination. Some places allow wild camping, while others have designated spots. Either way, always take all your rubbish away with you, only park up on tarmac in order to prevent landscape erosion, and be mindful of local communities. Factor in, too, that you'll need to pack up every time you drive off anywhere, unless you take a tent to store some things at the campsite while you head off during the day to explore.

While researching this guide we… Hired a converted VW Transporter campervan with Yescapa (⊘ yescapa.co.uk) in Kent and drove it up to Suffolk. It was exactly the wholesome, simple fun we all anticipated, particularly curling up to watch the sunset by the beach.

MAPS

OS Maps (⊘ osmaps.ordnancesurvey.co.uk) are a brilliant addition to any family adventure. If you're looking to take on some hefty walks, drives or cycling expeditions, bringing along a real-life map and getting kids to help plot the journey can make the whole experience more rewarding for them. For peace of mind, it's worth paying the yearly fee for the Outdooractive (formerly OS Maps ViewRanger) app (⊘ outdooractive.com), which provides access to handy offline OS maps on your phone wherever you are. It's saved our neck more than a few times…

A HELPING HAND...

The following organisations can help when it comes to getting around:

Byway ⊘ byway.travel. Bespoke car-free adventures.
Green Traveller ⊘ greentraveller.co.uk. Marvellous car-free and green adventures across the UK, including good accommodation reviews.
Guardian Travel ⊘ theguardian.com/travel/series/car-free-uk. *The Guardian's* series of car-free walks and adventures is a good source of inspiration for linking rail and bus networks.
Man in Seat Sixty-One ⊘ seat61.com. Rail expert Mark Smith offers an excellent online overview of ticket types and prices.

HOW TO USE THIS BOOK

This guide begins in the Isles of Scilly, as far southwest as you can get in the UK, hops south to the Channel Islands, and then snakes its way

WHO WE RATE

In addition to the resources we've detailed in *Getting around* (page 12) we rate the following organisations highly when it comes to planning or enjoying a slow family holiday:

English Heritage
⊘ english-heritage.org.uk
National Trust
⊘ nationaltrust.org.uk
RSPB ⊘ rspb.org.uk
Scottish National Trust
⊘ nts.org.uk

Sustrans ⊘ sustrans.org.uk
The Wildlife Trusts
⊘ wildlifetrusts.org
Woodland Trust
⊘ woodlandtrust.org.uk

The following are our favourite go-tos when searching for slow family travel accommodation:

Canopy & Stars
⊘ canopyandstars.co.uk
Cool Places ⊘ coolplaces.co.uk
Farm Stay ⊘ farmstay.co.uk
Feather Down Farms
⊘ featherdown.co.uk
Forest Holidays
⊘ forestholidays.co.uk

i-escape ⊘ i-escape.com
Luxury Family Hotels
⊘ luxuryfamilyhotels.co.uk
Pitch Up ⊘ pitchup.com
Sawday's ⊘ sawdays.co.uk
Under the Thatch
⊘ underthethatch.co.uk

back and forth across Britain, gradually heading north, and ends up in another awesome archipelago, the Outer Hebrides. We haven't tried to cover everywhere, but have carefully chosen places that we feel are of particular interest to families pursuing slow travel values. Some are well-known tourist destinations, but in the main we've tried to take you off the trodden path. In some chapters we've focused in on a very small area and in others we've zoomed out on the region as a whole, but we always pay close attention to the local, sharing our encounters with real people and their first-hand knowledge.

Each chapter opens with an at-a-glance information panel that details the top family experience for that destination, the best time to visit to enjoy that experience, and some indicators as to whether it's suitable for you and your family according to your kids' ages and their 'intrepid level':

① A very gentle activity that all ages and abilities can handle, such as exploring the site of the Battle of Hastings and glamping nearby (page 139).

② An experience or activity that requires a little more resilience, from a liveaboard whale- and dolphin-watch in the Outer Hebrides (page 433) to a scary interactive history experience in Liverpool (see box, page 326).

③ An activity with an extreme adventure element, which requires some skill and/or has a definite age requirement, such as snorkelling with seals in the Isles of Scilly (page 23).

The information box ends with a brief run-down of other highlights in the region and a suggestion of how long you might like to stay to do the destination justice.

Following the top family experience, the *Added Adventure* section covers the other slow travel family highlights of the region, usually arranged geographically, except in a few cases where a themed itinerary works best. Age restrictions for activities have been mentioned when necessary. Throughout the chapters, pull-out boxes hone in on local experiences – including age requirements and intrepid levels – plus various ways to support the community.

Each chapter concludes with a handy listings section covering where to stay and eat, along with details on how to get out to islands, some pre-departure tips, and websites for further information. All suggestions are in the spirit of slow travel, favouring local suppliers, small businesses and, of course, family-friendly facilities.

We haven't included prices for accommodation, eating or any of the activities we cover, as they vary so often according to the time of year and are always subject to change, but we believe that everything featured is good value for money, even at the pricier end of the scale, and we've tried to include a range of options for all budgets.

IF YOU'RE AFTER...

ARTS & CRAFTS

Guernsey: Guernsey-inspired art workshops, see box page 48

Herefordshire: Clay modelling, page 275

Kent: Willow weaving, page 179

The Lake District: Sculpture spotting in Grizedale Forest, see page 331
The Peak District: Egg-tempura painting, see box page 298
St Ives: Creative art classes, page 55

CAMPING & GLAMPING

East Sussex: Glamping at Battle Abbey, page 139
The Lake District: Family bushcamp, see box page 344
South London: Setting up base camp in Dulwich Woods, page 155

CULTURE & MUSEUMS

Bristol: M Shed, page 100; Where the Wall street-art tour, see box page 108
East Sussex: Battle Abbey and Battlefield, page 139
Edinburgh: Edinburgh International Film Festival, page 401
Liverpool: The Beatles Story museum, page 319
Newcastle: Seven Stories and the Baltic Centre for Contemporary Art, see box page 382
Oxford: The Story Museum, page 263
St Ives: Pirates, ghost and paper theatres, see box page 64
South London: The Horniman Museum & Gardens, page 158

CYCLING & OTHER OUTDOOR ACTIVITIES

Brecon Beacons: Downhill mountain biking at BikePark Wales, page 219
The Cairngorms: Bespoke tour with Braemar Highland Experience, page 417
Herefordshire: Walking in the Malverns, page 278; Apples for Autumn cycle trail, see box page 279
Isle of Wight: Cycling the Red Squirrel Trail, page 125; Tree climbing, see box page 132
Lake District: Family bushcamp, see box page 344
Northumberland: Beach school, see box page 372
The Peak District: Cycling the Monsal Trail, page 289
Pembrokeshire: Coasteering, page 247
South London: Den building, page 155

FOOD, FARMING & GARDENING

The Cairngorms: Woodland foraging for families, see box page 428
Edinburgh: The Royal Botanic Garden, see box page 414
Guernsey: Seaweed foraging tour, page 39
Herefordshire: Orchard tour, see box page 284
Kent: Al-fresco cooking, page 179
The Lake District: Family bushcamp, see box page 344
Lincolnshire: Bowthorpe Farm Park, see box page 216

◀ **1** Snorkelling with seals, Isles of Scilly. **2** A handful of foodie weekends are included in this book. **3** Exploring King Arthur's Cave, Herefordshire (page 280).

The National Forest: Beekeeping, page 303

North Yorkshire: Farm tour, see box page 362

Somerset: The Story of Gardening experience at The Newt in Somerset, page 85; The Community Farm, see box page 90

South London: Community Greenhouse Days in Brockwell Park, see box page 172

GEOGRAPHY & GEOLOGY

The Cairngorms: Bespoke tour with Braemar Highland Experience, page 417

East Sussex: Exploring the shore at Rye Harbour Nature Reserve, see box page 142

Gwynedd: Eco innovation at the Centre for Alternative Technology, page 231

Northumberland: Beach school, see box page 372

North Yorkshire: Fossil hunting on Whitby Beach, page 349

HISTORY

Bristol: SS *Great Britain*, page 97

East Sussex: Battle Abbey and Battlefield, page 139

Gwynedd: The National Slate Museum, see box page 242

Lincolnshire: Lincoln's 13th-century castle, page 205

Liverpool: The History Whisperer, see box page 326

North Yorkshire: Fossil hunting on Whitby Beach, page 349

St Ives: Guided ghost walk, see box page 64

ON THE WATER

Isle of Lewis: Liveaboard wildlife cruise, page 433

The Isles of Scilly: Snorkelling with seals, page 23

The National Forest: Canoeing on the River Trent, see box page 311

The New Forest: Canoeing down the Beaulieu River, page 111

Northumberland: Seabird safari, Farne Islands, page 371

Oxford: Punting on the River Cherwell, see box page 272

Pembrokeshire: Coasteering, page 247

The South Hams: Ferry and rail adventure on the River Dart, page 69

The Suffolk Coast: Boating at Thorpeness Meare, page 195

SCIENCE & SPACE

Brecon Beacons: Stargazing in the Dark Sky Reserve, see box page 226

Bristol: SS *Great Britain* and We The Curious science museum, pages 97 & 100

Dumfries & Galloway: Stargazing at Galloway International Dark Sky Park, see box page 396

Gwynedd: Eco innovation at the Centre for Alternative Technology, page 231

The Isles of Scilly: The COSMOS Community Observatory, see box page 30

WILDLIFE & CONSERVATION

Brecon Beacons Stargazing in the Dark Sky Reserve, see box page 226; Tree planting and maintenance, see box page 228

The Cairngorms: Bespoke tour with Braemar Highland Experience, page 417

Dumfries & Galloway: Guided Highland cow safari, page 385; Stargazing at Galloway International Dark Sky Park, see box page 396

East Sussex: Exploring the shore at Rye Harbour Nature Reserve, see box page 142

Edinburgh: The Royal Botanic Garden, see box page 414

Guernsey: Seaweed foraging tour, page 39

Gwynedd: Litter pick in Snowdonia, see box page 244

Isle of Lewis: Liveaboard wildlife cruise, page 433; Pony trekking on the sands, see box page 444

Isle of Wight: Rounding up goats, see box page 136

The Isles of Scilly: Snorkelling with seals, page 23; Guided walk, see box page 28

Kent: Birdwatching at Elmley Nature Reserve, see box page 188

The Lake District: Walking with fell ponies through Grizedale Forest, page 331; Family bushcamp, see box page 344

Lincolnshire: Bowthorpe Farm Park, see box page 216

The National Forest: Beekeeping, page 303

The New Forest A wild New Forest tour, see box page 116

North Yorkshire: Alpaca walk and farm tour, see box page 362; Micro-volunteering in the North York Moors National Park, see box page 364

Northumberland: Seabird safari, Farne Islands, page 371; Beach school, see box page 372

Pembrokeshire: Dolphin spotting in Cardigan Bay, see box page 256

The South Hams: Rock pool safari, see box page 80

South London: Exploring Dulwich and Sydenham Hills woods, page 155

The Suffolk coast: Wildlife tracking in the marshes, see box page 198

1
THE ISLES OF SCILLY

*You'll feel like you've journeyed halfway
around the world in this magical
archipelago with a touch of the Tropics.*

TOP FAMILY EXPERIENCE

SNORKELLING WITH SEALS

BEST FOR KIDS AGED: 8+	
WHEN TO GO:	April to October
INTREPID LEVEL:	③
ADDED ADVENTURE:	Wildlife walking, stargazing, botanic gardens, island art, gig racing
TIME:	One to two weeks

NOSE TO NOSE
WITH A SCILLIES SEAL

St Martin's TR25 0QL ⌀ sealsnorkellingadventures.com; children & adults must be confident swimmers in open water & be prepared to get straight off the boat into water that's deeper than standing depth. Trips are weather dependent. Under new management, booking via the website.

Staring into the big brown eyes of an Atlantic grey seal has to be one of the all-time highlights of my son Fin's childhood holidays. As we bob side by side in our buoyant wetsuits, masks down, in the glass-clear water off St Martin's, I can hardly stop grinning around my snorkel's mouthpiece when I see my son's saucer-like eyes as he connects with this sleek creature. Mammal to mammal. Young man to young seal. What different lives. What different species. And yet, a connection. Fin recognises that he's looking into the soul of an intelligent animal and, who knows, the seal possibly knows the same.

◀ Snorkelling with seals.

As quickly as it happens, it is over. The seal, so cumbersome on the rocks, is incredibly balletic in the water, darting away into the deep like an aqua dancer. This is their habitat, their awesome playground. We are merely visitors, literally out of our depth. I wonder if we appear as ungainly in the water to them as they do on the rocks to us. The playfulness of this young male gets the better of him as he swings back round to have a nibble on Fin's fin.

This is going to be my son's top holiday story for a long time to come, thanks to zoologist, diving instructor and marine mammal medic Anna Browne, who has been running seal snorkelling trips around St Martin's, one of the archipelago's wildest islands, for over 20 years. At the rustic gig shed on the white-sand beach opposite Higher Town Quay, where ten of us are kitted up in wetsuits, gloves, overjackets, masks and snorkels, she exudes the enthusiasm and confidence of the perfect guide. When we rang to book, she was clear in her advice: so long as children are confident in open water and up for meeting the seals, they will love the experience. But that confidence is essential. Some kids, she said, can be freaked out by the fact that you get straight off the boat into water where your feet don't touch the bottom, leading to tears and even aborted trips.

She tells Fin that the Isles of Scilly have a nationally important colony of wild Atlantic grey seals, which is partly why the islands are designated a Special Area of Conservation, and that the Latin name for these wonderful creatures is *Halichoerus grypus*, translated as 'hook-nosed sea pig'. She amazes all the kids by pointing out that these friendly souls, which live up to 45 years, could be older than their parents!

When we're all suitably awed, we jump in the RIB and whizz out to the nearby Eastern Isles, specifically Menawethan (seven acres) and Great Ganilly (34 acres). Anna has warned us that the water will be cold, and that because the seals are wild animals she can never guarantee what level of interaction you might get. Then she ups the excitement by saying that seals are generally very inquisitive and use their mouths to feel textures, and swim round in the water, often following you – as Fin is to experience later.

Along with the seals, we love seeing the Eastern Isles up close, with their kelp beds, and the occasional fish and sea urchin. Anna tells us to look out for peregrine falcons which nest there in May and June; there are also rare sightings, if it's a calm day, of puffins, dolphins and porpoises.

We see none, but with our head too full of seals we couldn't care less. Fin chats away to me about 'his' seal's expressive long whiskers and agility in the water. We hardly notice we are heading back to shore. As a parent wanting to give her child an educational yet thrilling encounter, this is job done!

ADDED ADVENTURE: ISLAND HOPPING

Every time my children and I step foot on the Scillies, we feel its magic envelop us. It's the feeling you get when you've left the everyday behind and found yourself in a place that forces you to gaze at the sea and the sky and to watch the way things are done. Typically this happens overseas, and yet this otherworldly archipelago is part of Cornwall, just 28 miles off the mainland. A UK Neverland which you can't quite place in the modern world.

The first time we touched down on the main island of St Mary's in our tiny Noddy plane (in reality, the Iles of Scilly Skybus, where kids can actually talk to the pilot and stare in awe at the unfathomable bank of controls), as far as my two tots were concerned, and possibly into their early teens, we could just as easily have landed on a Caribbean isle or a Maldivian atoll. These five inhabited islands, and around 135 uninhabited isles and craggy outposts, have their own microclimate, flora and fauna, not to mention mood. This is the kind of place where generations of families return year on year, and holidays turn into family folklore.

The Isles of Scilly are the very definition of slow travel. They demand perseverance because they are worth it. If you're coming from London or further afield, by the time you've taken the scenic coastal train to Penzance, overnighted in that delightful Cornish fishing town (including a dip in the UK's first geothermal heated lido), then journeyed on to your chosen island on the *Scillonian III* ferry or the plane from Exeter, Newquay or Land's End (at the mercy of the sea fogs), you might as well have travelled long-haul. The *Scillonian III* is more like a wildlife cruise than a ferry, and can offer glimpses of dolphins, Atlantic grey seals and epic sea birds: the captain may even yank the vessel round for a better view.

Arriving in St Mary's feels something like setting foot on a private island. Bags are labeled for those heading to an outer island by boat, with four to choose from: Tresco, Bryher, St Agnes and St Martin's.

Show your children a map and they will feel like explorers conquering new lands. And you'll soon discover that the freedom to roam safely could be the Scillies USP.

ST MARY'S

On St Mary's, you can spend a morning with the children horseriding across beaches and coastal paths with St Mary's Riding Centre (⚭ horsesonscilly.co.uk) while teens can cast aside their devices in favour of guided trail running, wild swimming and yoga with Adventure Scilly's Bryony Lishman (⚭ adventurescilly.co.uk).

If you're lucky, you'll spy a local gig race. These long colourful boats, with a crew of six rowers and a cox, are the Scillies' version of Cornish pilot gigs. Among the earliest known shore lifeboats, the gigs were originally used to take pilots out to vessels in the Atlantic, and would race to be the first to deliver pilots on to ships which were at risk of running aground. These days the races are for fun; local teams practise on Wednesdays and Saturdays in preparation for the World Pilot Gig Championships, which are held here (⚭ worldgigs.co.uk). Races begin just off St Agnes or at Nuts Rock and all finish at St Mary's Harbour.

In the tiny capital, Hugh Town, take children down the back streets to Rat Bags Canvas Shop (⚭ ratisland.net) to see the 'bag ladies', Helen and Carol, hard at work on their harbour-view sewing machines, creating hardwearing canvas bags in glorious sail colours – the perfect souvenir to take back to the real world.

TRESCO

The *Firethorn of Bryher* ferry takes you from St Mary's to Tresco, an island just two miles long and one mile wide, which the Dorrien-Smith family has leased since the 1830s from the Duchy of Cornwall. There are no cars here: just 130 permanent inhabitants, and many more puffins, Manx shearwaters, peregrines, gannets and curlews. It's best to hire bikes (⚭ tresco.co.uk/arriving) to explore the lanes lined with agapanthus and makeshift honesty stalls selling shell jewellery and potted succulents, bigger versions of which grow wild across the island.

---

1 Tresco Abbey Gardens. 2 Taking time out to paint, Tresco. 3 Gig racing, St Mary's.
4 Tresco's country lanes are lined with honesty stalls selling knickknacks. 5 At Ruin Beach Café, kids can make their own pizzas. ▶

ISLES OF SCILLY WILDLIFE TRUST: A GUIDED WALK WITH NIKKI BANFIELD

Tresco TR24 0PU ⊘ ios-wildlifetrust.org.uk; age: 3+ (children need to be able to walk or be carried on a parent's shoulders!); intrepid level: ①

The Isles of Scilly Wildlife Trust runs weekly beachcombing, rock pooling and wildlife walks for families during the holiday season. Nikki Banfield, a wildlife expert who works for the trust, has a Scilly heritage that dates back to the 1300s. Her mother's family were one of the last to leave the now uninhabited island of Samson in the 1800s.

Families assemble at the Ruin Beach Café, and set off following Nikki's capable walking-boot prints to Gimble Point where kids engage straight off the bat by listening to the birdsong. Nikki identifies tiny wren and explains how the male builds a few homes and – like a mini estate agent – shows a prospective mate around the 'houses' to see which one she likes best. Nikki will also get children right down in the grass looking at the bird's-foot trefoils (nicknamed eggs 'n' bacon for its egg-yolk yellow flowers and reddish buds) and hunting for bugs, and out into the bay overlooking the Golden Ball rocks searching for grey seals.

Nikki's a great advocate of the fight against plastic pollution. She shows me her multicoloured bag of beach debris – including a lobster pot tab from Maine dating back to 1995, a Smarties lid with the letter D on it from 1964, and Lego bricks that were spilled from a container lost off Land's End. She educates young ones about the islands' invasive species such as rhododendrons and what impact these have on the local wildlife, as well as its native species like ling and bell heather, vital to bee life. Alas the Scilly Bee, which looks like a little teddy bear, hasn't been seen on Tresco since 2012. Under Nikki's guidance, children and adults alike will begin to understand the fragility of Tresco's incredibly localised ecosystem.

Nikki and her bag of beach debris. ▶

If you had to create a fairy-tale island this would be it, with the remains of King Charles's Castle in the northeast, on the headland overlooking Cromwell's Castle on the mount (both ⊘ english-heritage.org.uk), and Ruin Beach on the west coast with its eponymous café where kids can make their own pizza during school holidays. Book in advance with the island office (⊘ tresco.co.uk) and devour the pizza on the al fresco deck before tearing back and forth across the beach and the rock pools.

In the south, Tresco Abbey Gardens (⊘ tresco.co.uk) should be firmly on your radar. These famous gardens are home to exotic species from 80 countries, from Myanmar to Brazil – including *Echium* with their

JANE ANDERSON

impressive blue spires, king protea and lobster claw – many of which wouldn't survive on the mainland. Children will delight in the crinkly moss-covered benches, the oversized bromeliads, the ancient ruins and shell mosaic follies. An outdoor Valhalla Museum is perfect for short attention spans, with its impressive collection of salvaged figureheads: cue much talk of shipwrecks, pirates and smuggling.

In the woods behind the Abbey Gardens, a beautiful old tree house built for the Dorrien-Smith children is just one of Tresco's hidden treasures, unveiled to families who are happy to wander off the track. Shhh, don't tell anyone…

BRYHER

Catch the early evening supper boat from Tresco across to Bryher for dinner – in the sea-faring Scillies this is perfectly normal – and head to the glorious summer pop-up, the Crab Shack at Hell Bay Hotel (𝒶 hellbay. co.uk). Here, in a cow barn adorned with fishing nets, everyone sits at trestle tables and is served oversized tureens of crabs, their impressive claws reaching over the sides as if to escape. After dinner, take a stroll to find the island's stone circles, like a mini maze for little ones.

SEEING STARS:
THE COSMOS COMMUNITY OBSERVATORY

St Martin's TR25 0QL 𝒶 cosmosscilly.co.uk; age: 5+; intrepid level: ①; drop-ins are possible, but booking in advance is recommended

COSMOS is the most southwesterly observatory in the UK. Located in the middle of the island of St Martin's, behind the Community Hall & Reading Room, it's the perfect place to gaze into the darkness and study the universe – there's virtually no light pollution here, and skies are inky black.

'How do we know what's out there? Where are the edges of space?' asks Charlie Payne, a COSMOS founder and local primary school teacher. 'These existential questions are the ones you often find younger children love asking and dealing with, hence why we enjoy welcoming families.

'Come on a Tuesday evening and – weather permitting – if the sky's getting dark, we'll head outside and chat about the stars as they emerge. We tailor it to whoever's there and then we'll use telescopes if there's anything to look at. We always make sure children are the first to have a look through.

'Friday afternoons are more relaxed drop-ins. We use a solar telescope through which children can have a look at the sun, and we talk about it being our newest star. Who knew that you could do astronomy during the daytime? Wow! Why is the sun important? What's so special about it? What is the sun? Astronomy isn't really covered by the school curriculum, so we try and engage the children. Kids always ask things like: Why is space so big? We don't know! Where does the moon go during the day? We can answer that one! No question is too silly.

'One evening we weren't expecting a great deal as it was fairly cloudy. We went outside at the end and as the clouds cleared we saw a lunar eclipse and the International Space Station pop over. We've also watched the Starlink satellites go across, which deliver high-speed internet access across our planet. Kids really love this!

'For me, the most magical thing is looking at Jupiter and Saturn. When children look at Saturn's rings through the telescope with their own eyes, it's just spinetingling. Twilight stargazing is nice for younger children. When you talk to children about the actual size of

During extreme spring tides, the 250yd watery barrier between Tresco and Bryher falls away and you will feel like you have conquered nature as you stroll across the seabed from island to island. Locals set up benches, a bar and fire pits on the sand with a feast of pasties, sausage rolls, fresh fish and paella for sale. Isles of Scilly Wildlife Trust guides regale visitors with wonderful seabed facts and set up impromptu games. Check on the day with Tresco Boat Services (✆ 01720 423373) or the Tresco Island Office (✆ 01720 422849) to make sure it's safe to do the walk.

COSMOS COMMUNITY OBSERVATORY

space, sometimes writing down what a light year is, it blows their mind. Six trillion miles. That's a six with 12 zeros after it. How many St Martin's do you think that is? St Martin's is one mile. What would it be like to walk a light year?

'We run walks in October where we map out the solar system to scale on St Martin's. We start with a beach ball at the end of the quay, and then you walk up the quay to Mercury, and that's a pinhead. After that you've got Venus represented by a pea, and a bit further on you've got earth, also a pea, and by the time you arrive at the shop which is almost half way round the island, you've got Saturn... and obviously we give little facts about each planet as we go. They are always well attended by families. It's all voluntary and a labour of love.'

"This is the kind of place where generations of families return year on year, and holidays turn into family folklore."

ST MARTIN'S

St Martin's is yet another idyllic island, slightly less manicured than Tresco, and more on the wild side. Its deserted beaches are blessed with fine sand and the turquoise water is beautiful. Families can snorkel with Atlantic grey seals (page 24), go on a paddling adventure with St Martin's Watersports (⊘ stmartinswatersports.co.uk), discover the UK's southwesternmost observatory (see box, page 30) or rummage around the island discovering local creatives such as jeweller Fay Page (⊘ faypage.co.uk) in her granite barn, whose gold- and silverwork – featuring everything from seashells to bees – is inspired by her home on the west of the island. Just a couple of minutes walk away, take time to munch on crab sandwiches at the Seven Stones pub (⊘ sevenstonesinn.com), with its views over St Lawrence's Flats.

ST AGNES

The island of St Agnes is the southernmost in the archipelago. Here, tiny commercial galleries include Pot Buoys (⊘ potbuoysgallery.co.uk), just a short walk along country lanes from where the ferry drops you. It is run by local artist Emma Eberlein, who sells artwork created by local schoolchildren alongside work from established artists. Make a beeline for the arcs of white sand at Periglis Beach, on the northwest side of the island, a boon for shell seekers, and make sure to stop at Troytown Farm (see opposite) for delicious ice cream served with a Flake and clotted cream.

St Agnes is the jumping-off point for boat trips that venture out towards the Bishop Rock lighthouse, four miles away. The treacherous Hancock Rocks surrounding the lighthouse accounted for the demise of four warships in 1707, one of the worse maritime disasters in the history of the British Isles. Sail with St Agnes Boating Wildlife Safaris (⊘ stagnesboating.co.uk) and your kids will enjoy a game of boating bingo, where cards are held up with wildlife to spot en route.

PRACTICALITIES

GETTING THERE

Scillionian III takes just under three hours from Penzance to St Mary's. Below deck you can purchase hot chocolates and snacks; bring extra woollies and waterproofs plus a picnic for extra fun

---

◀ Path to Great Bay, St Martin's.

on deck. You can also fly from Exeter, Newquay or Land's End to St Mary's on Skybus. See ⟳ islesofscilly-travel.co.uk for more. For details of the 15-minute flight from Penzance to Tresco or St Mary's see ⟳ penzancehelicopters.co.uk.

FAMILY-FRIENDLY SLEEPS

Overnight in Penzance at the Artist Residence (⟳ artistresidence.co.uk) or one of the family rooms at The Chapel House (⟳ chapelhousepz.co.uk).

St Mary's
Peninnis Farm Lodges
⟳ peninnisfarmlodges.co.uk. Cool self-catering wood cabins sleeping up to five, with log burners and outdoor areas with BBQs/fire pits. It's set on a working farm, so kids can collect eggs and help feed the animals.
Star Castle Hotel ⟳ star-castle. co.uk. This historic family-owned hotel is in an actual star-shaped castle with bungalows in the grounds and incredible island views.
Tregarthen's Hotel ⟳ tregarthens-hotel.co.uk. Perfectly located right next to the quay for off-island adventures, with a children's play area and family suites.

Tresco
Sea Garden Cottages ⟳ tresco.co.uk. These high-end self-catering houses are top-notch for families with stylish interiors and access to a beautiful indoor

pool, afternoon tennis sessions and dining options including the nearby Ruin Beach Café. The Sailing Centre is nearby, too.

Bryher
Bryher Campsite and Bell Tent Rental ⟳ bryhercampsite.co.uk. Tom and Jo, who run this camping and bell tent rental site, are given glowing reviews – they go above and beyond for families, with a warm welcome and a lack of unnecessary rules other than a healthy respect for your neighbours.

St Martin's
Churchtown Farm Cottage
⟳ scillyflowers.co.uk/holiday-cottage. Granite self-catering cottage with fabulous views across the islands and a beautiful garden.
Karma Hotel ⟳ karmagroup.com. Right on the beachfront, this luxury hotel has family rooms with connecting doors, plus board games and an outdoor games chest.

St Agnes
Troytown Farm Campsite and Cottages ⟳ troytown.co.uk. The UK's smallest dairy farm (there are just nine milking cows) also offers camping and holiday cottages, with fresh milk and ice cream on tap!
Westward Farm ⟳ westwardfarm. co.uk. The Cider Barn is a family-friendly self-catering lodge, sleeping four or five, with pretty interiors and a private garden with BBQ.

KID-FRIENDLY EATS

St Mary's

The Beach ⌂ scillybeach.com. This relaxed BBQ restaurant, in a converted boat shed overlooking St Mary's harbour, offers easy, tasty food and amazing sunset views.

Dibble & Grub Tapas ⌂ dibbleandgrub.co.uk. Kids will be excited to eat in a former real-life fire station, even if they've never heard of the TV series, *Trumpton*, from which the name is taken. Yummy tapas and beach views make this a winner.

On the Quay ⌂ onthequay.com. Come here for hearty, locally sourced food with harbour views. Kids are well catered for with a children's menu and a young adults' menu, not something you often come across.

Tresco

Ruin Beach Café ⌂ tresco.co.uk. This enchanting beachside café has shell mosaics on the walls and delicious pizzas and seafood on the menu. Bag a table on the deck and parents can relax and take their time while kids play in sight on the sands.

Bryher

Fraggle Rock ⌂ bryher.co. Much-loved café with outside space and gorgeous views. Go on Friday night for the local fish and chips.

Island Fish ⌂ islandfish.co.uk. The Pender family have been fishing out of Bryher for centuries and their outdoor café is an island institution – enjoy a lobster sandwich with plenty of space for children to roam safely.

St Martin's

Polreath Tea Rooms ⌂ polreath. com. No family can resist the wonderful cream teas served in the tea room of this cosy guesthouse where anyone is welcome to stop by.

Seven Stones Inn ⌂ sevenstonesinn. com. This local stone-built pub serves family favourites from burgers to locally caught lobster and has a terrace and huge grassy play area.

St Agnes

Coastguards Café ✆ 01720 423747. Welcoming island café serving tasty sandwiches and cream teas using fresh Cornish produce from nearby Troytown Farm (page 35).

BEFORE YOU GO

Become a friend of the Isles of Scilly Wildlife Trust (⌂ ios-wildlifetrust.org. uk) and help protect the natural beauty of the islands.

MORE INFO

Isles of Scilly Tourist Board

⌂ visitislesofscilly.com
Isles of Scilly Travel ⌂ islesofscilly-travel.co.uk

The award-winning Slow Travel series from Bradt Guides

Over 20 regional guides across Britain.
See the full list at bradtguides.com/slowtravel.

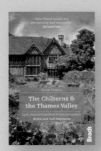

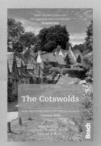

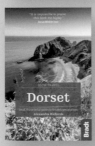

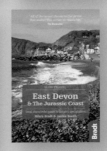

AURORA GSY/S

LIZ SEYMOUR/S

2
GUERNSEY

*Go-slow Guernsey and its tiny outer
islands offer adventures from tidal pool
dips to real-life wartime tales.*

TOP FAMILY EXPERIENCE

SEAWEED TOUR WITH GUERNSEY SEAWEED

BEST FOR KIDS AGED:	2+
WHEN TO GO:	May to October
INTREPID LEVEL:	①
ADDED ADVENTURE:	Fairy rings, wild food foraging, WWII history, puffin patrols
TIME:	One to two weeks

SEAWEED SUPERPOWERS

Meet at Port Soif in the upper car park above the kiosk, GY6 8JT ⚲ guernseyseaweed.com;
seaweed foraging tours last around 1hr 30mins & take place at low tide. Children under 15
go free (one per paying adult).

Ben Trustin, aka Vraic Man, is a bit of a superhero. Or should I say
seaweed hero. As Guernsey's only seaweed farmer, he's a passionate
campaigner for this wonder plant. With our wellies firmly on, my kids
and I meet him on Guernsey's wide and accessible Soif Beach at low tide
when the rock pools are at their best, wondering what on earth to expect
from a seaweed foraging tour. After all, seaweed is usually something
that's associated with smelly beaches and slippery rocks, isn't it?

On this stunning arc of white sand, with the Port Soif/Portinfer Dunes
Nature Reserve at its far end, Ben greets us with a wide smile and an
infectious enthusiasm that soon has us wading through crystal-clear rock
pools searching for seaweed. It's hands-on from the word go as we start

◄1 & 3 Foraging for seaweed. 2 Port Soif.

by picking one of the best-known varieties: the one with the poppers and the brilliant name, bladderwrack! Once we've given it a quick rinse in the clean rock-pool water, he encourages us to take a nibble.

There's much kerfuffle and screwing up of noses, but eventually we all have a chew on this surprisingly tasty leaf. Ben assures us that, unlike mushrooms or other foraging favourites, there are no poisonous seaweeds and no-one has ever had an upset stomach after one of his tours.

Next up, Ben gets the kids to squeeze the rubbery bladderwrack poppers and out squirts a clear gel. There are shrieks of 'erghhh!', especially when he gets us to rub the gel on our faces. This part of the proceedings is interesting to us mums as it turns out bladderwrack gel is packed full of vitamins and minerals and is probably just as good as any fancy, overpriced face serum. Ben confirms it's incredibly moisturising for your skin and the kids think it's hilarious when I suggest decanting it into our water bottles.

"There's much kerfuffle and screwing up of noses, but eventually we all have a chew on this surprisingly tasty leaf."

Now that we're all enthralled, Ben explains that seaweed was incredibly important to Guernsey for around 500 years and that it was only after the occupation during World War II that it went off the radar. 'Before then,' he says, 'it was the most important industry on the island, predominantly for fertiliser. They used to burn it and sell off the potash to farmers in the spring.'

It's not only a fabulous fertiliser, but it could also be one of the answers to the climate crisis. 'The general consensus is that around 70% of the world's oxygen is created by seaweed. And that 70% of the world's CO_2 is absorbed by seaweed. There are lots of people looking at growing seaweed and sinking it in deep trenches in the Atlantic and Pacific to lock in the carbon. But another extremely effective way is to use it as fertiliser like we did before the war, locking it into the soil and subsequently into plants.'

Seaweed absorbs more CO_2 than every blade of grass, plant and tree on the planet, according to Ben who also informs us that if you put 10% of a cow's diet to seaweed it reduces methane emissions by 90%. Ben says he's talking to the local government with the aim of doing just that with the Guernsey cows that produce the island's famous dairy milk, butter and ice cream.

It's all eye-opening stuff. My kids' enthusiasm for seaweed is growing by the second, and we're amazed by how many different varieties we've come across simply exploring the rock pools of this picturesque bay on Guernsey's northwest coast. Sea lettuce is the one that looks most like normal lettuce as it bobs about in the water, and is one of the easiest to cook; Ben recommends frying it on a high heat. He tells us that seaweeds taste very different depending on whether they are eaten raw, steamed or fried. 'Those seaweeds that people don't like fresh and raw tend to be the ones that are really nice cooked. Cooking brings out completely different flavours.'

We all find it hard to verbalise how our seaweed tastes. Ben explains this is because seaweeds hit your umami taste buds. 'What on earth are umami taste buds?', ask the kids. Ben explains that along with salty, sweet, sour and bitter taste buds we also have buds for umami. 'A Japanese guy in the 1920s noticed that eating kelp was affecting a part of his mouth that felt unusual. It wasn't something he could describe with the taste buds we knew about. It wasn't until 1996 that the existence of umami taste buds was proven. Umami is what we taste in Marmite or the bottom of the steak when it hits the pan.'

Finally, Ben tells us about one last seaweed superpower – the creation of bioplastic. It may be in its infancy, but seaweed can be used to create a plastic-like membrane (used in the London Marathon for drink pouches, according to Ben), or hard plastics when mixed with corn starch. 'It could revolutionise food packaging. If sandwiches go off after three days, the wrapping could degrade on the fourth day, leaving no waste. Genius!' he smiles.

As we stand on this pretty Guernsey beach, surprisingly deserted even in the school holidays, the tide begins to turn. We leave with a new respect for nature, which, as usual, has had the answers all along. A superpower indeed.

ADDED ADVENTURE: GO-SLOW ARCHIPELAGO

At 24 square miles, Guernsey is the second largest of the dinky Channel Islands, which sit 80 miles south of England and just off the coast of France. Guernsey itself comprises a group of islands: Alderney, Sark, Brechquou, Herm and Jethou, along with many uninhabited islets.

Wherever you are in Guernsey's ten parishes, nothing is too far away. With its French influences, jade waters, rocky outcrops and exotic *Echium* plants, as far as kids are concerned you could be on a tropical island. Yet Guernsey is also steeped in old English traditions. Come in summer and you're sure to stumble across a scarecrow competition or a village fête with maypoles and Punch and Judy shows. Happily, many of the island's roads are designated Ruettes Tranquilles – lanes with a speed limit of 15mph – where walkers, cyclists and horseriders have right of way, making this the perfect place for a slow family holiday.

WEST COAST GUERNSEY

Guernsey is justifiably much loved for its beaches. **Cobo Bay** is one of the most popular for families, while neighbouring **Vazon Bay** is the largest, its rocky inlets the perfect place for first-time kayakers to explore. It's also home to **Guernsey Surf School** (⊘ guernseysurfschool. co.uk) which offers Mini Summer Camps to get kids aged six to 16 catching the waves.

Rock pooling is another of Guernsey's specialities. The island is gifted with one of the largest tidal ranges in the world, at 33ft, which means that magnificent rock pools are revealed twice a day: bring your wellies, buckets and nets.

Just off the west coast, **Lihou Island Nature Reserve** (⊘ lihouisland. com) is one of Guernsey's uninhabited islets. Managed as a charitable trust, this tidal island is only accessible via a quarter-mile causeway at low tide. Once there, families can explore the ruins of a Benedictine Priory, founded in the 12th century, and discover the Venus Pool, an in-the-know swimming spot which traps water at high tide.

Back on the mainland, **WildGuernsey** (⊘ wildguernsey.wordpress. com) near Fort Grey offers wild food workshops, foraging from the island's edible land and seascapes. Activities are designed to engage families in earth education and fireside camp craft.

At **Pleinmont Headland**, on the island's southwest tip, families can see a fairy ring linked with local folklore relating to fairies, witches and elves. Enchanting stuff for young minds. You can also explore World War II fortifications dating back to the German Occupation of

---

1 Rock pooling is especially good on Guernsey. 2 Cobo Bay is popular with families.
3 Surfing at Vazon Bay. ▶

the island – which lasted from 30 June 1940 to 10 May 1945. Families can download self-guided walking routes at ☉ guernseytravel.com/things-to-do/guernsey-activities, while for a structured guided tour, Soo Wellfair of **Guernsey Guided Tours** (☉ guernseyguidedtours.com) offers family tours using pictures and treasure hunts en route. Soo brings the Occupation and Liberation Day to life for kids and you can join her BYO picnic day out visiting Vale Castle, a site of fortification that dates back to the Iron Age, as well as Jerbourg, a stunning southeasterly lookout point from which France is visible, and the west coast.

Head slightly inland to find **Golden Guernsey Goat Farm** (◼ guernseygoatscheese.co.uk), where children can feed Peter and Mandy Girard's pretty goats and discover how goat's cheese is made.

ST PETER PORT & SURROUNDS

Guernsey's historic harbour capital, St Peter Port – known simply as 'town' by locals – is often called the prettiest capital in Europe with its spectacular views out to the neighbouring islands of Herm and Sark, its grand mercantile architecture, its colourful hanging baskets and summer bunting.

Guarding the harbour is **Castle Cornet** (☉ museums.gov.gg) dating back to the 12th century, where kids can dress up as knights and princesses, cartwheel on the lawns and learn about the castle's history. The noonday gun is fired daily by soldiers decked out in red Royal Guernsey Light Infantry uniforms, straight out of the 19th century. Under strict supervision, kids can gaze down the barrel of the cannon and are given a thorough briefing on how to light a fuse. Most days throughout the season, the **Guernsey History in Action Company** (☉ ghiac.org) re-enacts stories from the island's past.

Just south of the castle, **La Vallette Underground Military Museum** (☉ lavalette.tk) occupies a set of complex tunnels built by German forces as a store for U-boat fuel during their occupation of the island. The museum covers Guernsey's military history and gives children an insight into what it must have been like to pack one small suitcase and wave goodbye to your parents for five years on the mainland.

---

1 Pleinmont Headland. **2** Guernsey History in Action re-enact scenes from the island's past. **3** Castle Cornet. **4** Exhibits at La Vallette Underground Military Museum. ▶

AURORA GSY/S

VISIT GUERNSEY

GUERNSEY HISTORY IN ACTION COMPANY

RICHARD SOWERSBY/A

Opposite the underground museum are the **Victorian Bathing Pools** (⊘ thebathingpools.com). In Victorian times, gentlemen were permitted to swim nude here, while ladies, clad in elaborate bathing suits, were limited to their own pool. Today the beautifully restored saltwater pools offer families a lovely day of splashing around right next to the sea, for free. The café is well worth a look too; don't miss a luxurious Guernsey ice cream.

A trip on the **Petit Train** (⊘ petittrain.gg) around St Peter Port is a good way for families with younger children to explore the capital.

HERM & SARK

The tiny islands of Herm and Sark lie just 20 and 45 minutes by boat respectively from the east coast of Guernsey. Kids love the sense of adventure that comes with jumping on a ferry to an even smaller island, and exploring the laidback charms and peculiarities of a car-free destination. In-the-know families return annually and the few places to stay are booked up way in advance.

Whether you come for the day or decide to stay on **Herm** – just a mile and a half long and half a mile wide – the hardest decision you'll have to make is which beach to go to. It's a place where kids have time to think and digitally detox as they amble down sandy lanes bordered by lush brackens, bamboo and fluttering butterflies, stopping to buy a fishing net en route to idyllic **Shell Beach**, which even in August is far from crowded. Made up of millions of tiny shell fragments, this is the perfect swimming beach (under parental supervision, of course) as it gently shelves away. A host of scenic strolls from Shell Beach include the walk to Belvoir Bay, with lovely views of Sark; on the way pop into St Tugual's, Herm's quaint 11th-century church.

Herm is home to Europe's most southerly **puffin** breeding colonies. Between March and July families can join Puffin Patrol, a kayaking excursion for ages five and up (under-14s must be accompanied by an adult) with **Outdoor Guernsey** (⊘ outdoorguernsey.gg); it starts at Shell Beach and travels south past Belvoir Bay down to Puffin Bay. Between March and September, Outdoor Guernsey also runs family kayaking trips to the Humps Archipelago, just off Herm, which is

---

1 La Coupée connects the islands of Big and Little Sark. **2** Spot beautiful wildflowers along Herm's rocky coastline. ▶

GUERNSEY-INSPIRED
ART WORKSHOPS WITH FRANCES LEMMON

Croix, Plaisance Rd, St Peter Port GY7 9SJ & guernseyartworkshops.com; age: 5+; intrepid level: ①; maximum 8 children.

'I realise that I am almost on a crusade against some of the art teachers in primary school, quashing the dreams and abilities of children, who consequently turn into adults who own the belief that they can't draw – criminal!' says Frances as I hand over my kids to her for a morning of art in her light-filled studio. Outside she has a gorgeous garden surrounded by three fields so there's plenty of space to run around between creating. She's also happy for parents to chill out there too, or take the opportunity to head off and have some me time in town.

Frances is a practising artist who paints in acrylic, oil and watercolour. She also sketches regularly and, having moved to Guernsey at the age of 12, finds inspiration in reinterpreting local folkoric stories in her work.

'In my kids' art sessions, I always do one section of drawing each day, and without the children realising it, they're upskilling themselves. I bring in objects for them to draw, like skeletons of fish, fossils, seaweed and shells. We've even had rabbits, chickens and donkeys as models!' says Frances as she encourages my kids to look at basic outlines and add depth, using different media such as ink or wax pastel, or even dropping things on to the page to see what happens. 'I think art is a transformative process. You see something and put it there and then you do something to it. It's not set in stone,' she says.

Many of Frances's fun art sessions are beach themed, using the wealth of inspiration from Guernsey's stunning coastline. 'We do a lot of printing with seaweed, dipping it in paint.. We also make sand clay pots by drizzling sand and glue and Polyfilla over balloons which set hard. This tends to be really popular with children as they get to take something beautiful away with them.'

teeming with wildlife – including a local colony of **seals** who often come and say hello.

On neighbouring Sark, which spreads across just two square miles, horse-drawn carriages and tractors carry guests' luggage to hotels on arrival, or take day-trippers on tours of the island. Bring your own bike or hire one locally for the cycle along La Coupée, a 262ft-high natural causeway joining Big Sark with Little Sark, or visit the Boutique Caves, a long tunnel-like cave network with side entrances. Thanks to its lack of light pollution, Sark is the world's first designated Dark Sky Island. Ferry schedules mean that even day-trippers can visit the Dark Sky Observatory (& sark.co.uk) on a clear evening for stargazing.

She also makes great play of the island's notorious pirate history. 'Thinking about bad people always appeals to children!' she comments. 'We look at the legacy of pirates – in our local church, which is about five minutes away, there's a pirate gravestone with skull and crossbones on it. The children go and have a look at this living history and then we might build a model boat, or create a map using different materials. I give them lots of resources and offer them the freedom to use their imaginations.'

FRANCES LEMMON/FRANCESLEMMON.COM

PRACTICALITIES

GETTING THERE

Guernsey can be reached by **car or passenger ferry** (⌂ condorferries. co.uk; daily departures all year) from Poole (three hours) or Portsmouth (seven hours). **By air**, Guernsey sees direct flights from airports across the UK, including year-round services from London Gatwick, Manchester, Birmingham, Bristol, East Midlands, Southampton and Exeter, and seasonal services from Leeds Bradford and Norwich.

FAMILY-FRIENDLY SLEEPS

Camp de Rêves ⌂ guernseyglamping. com. Camp de Rêves ('field of dreams') offers back-to-nature glamping for families looking for adventure. The site has five safari-style tented cottages sleeping up to six, and shepherd's huts sleeping two – perfect for grandparents. Communal areas include a playground, firepit, pizza oven, petanque pitch, ball games and woodland, plus a games barn. The two-acre field overlooks the beautiful western bays, and it is just a ten-minute wander to sheltered L'Eree, a Blue Flag beach with kayaking and great fish and chips.

Cobo Bay Hotel ⊘ cobobayhotel.com. Long a family favourite, this beach hotel has a great location, with balconies and sea views over Cobo Bay, one of Guernsey's best family beaches, just three miles from St Peter Port. Family and interconnecting rooms are available.

Farmhouse Hotel ⊘ thefarmhouse.gg. This family-run boutique hotel in the rural parish of St Saviours has a modern-meets-country house vibe. Junior suites and superior rooms come with sofa beds and travel cots are available. The pretty gardens have an outdoor pool and cosy little covered cabanas for dining.

Fauxquets Valley Campsite ⊘ fauxquets.co.uk. A family-run campsite, right in the centre of the island, offering glamping-style log cabins and safari tents (sleeping four to six); you can also pitch your own tent or park your motorhome or caravan. There's a heated outdoor pool, games room, TV room, playground and play field with goal posts and a volleyball net.

Herm self-catering cottages and camping ⊘ herm.com. Herm's 20 family-friendly self-catering cottages and barn conversions (sleeping three to seven) are dotted around this small island. Book early, as they get snapped up in the school holidays. For camping, eight- or six-person tents are available for a minimum of three nights in peak season; food and extra camping cots can be pre-ordered.

Rocquaine Bay Apartments ⊘ rocquainebay.com. These eight self-catering apartments and two holiday bungalows on the west coast are perfect for families, with a children's play area, swimming pool, sauna and games room and family-friendly beaches nearby.

St Pierre Park Hotel, Spa & Golf Resort ⊘ handpickedhotels.co.uk. Located in St Peter Port, Guernsey's only 'resort' hotel offers generous family rooms and suites, a spa and indoor pool, gardens and mini golf. Children love the VIP mini dressing gowns and complimentary milk and cookies before bed.

White House Hotel Herm ⊘ herm. com. Herm's one and only hotel, the White House welcomes families who have been returning for generations: it's one of those old-school places that do everything well. Family accommodation comes with separate rooms for the children and there are eight dog-friendly rooms, too. Facilities include an outdoor pool, croquet and tennis.

WildGuernsey ⊘ wildguernsey. wordpress.com. This pretty eco-camping site, a stone's throw from the sea, is an extension of the owner's passion for the environment and care of the

ISLAND PRODUCE

Guernsey attracts a lot of creative makers and individuals who take pride in the island's wealth of local produce. In St Peter Port, check out **Seafront Sundays** – held on select Sundays between May and August – when the harbourfront is closed to traffic as local producers set up stalls selling food, drink, arts and crafts.

Other local markets and summer festivals are listed on ⌁ visitguernsey.com.

You might also want to embrace an island tradition by looking at **Hedge Veg** (⌁ hedgeveg.gg), a list of places where islanders sell their homemade and home-grown goods from wooden crates set out on rural lanes. Honesty boxes are used to pay for everything from home-roasted coffee beans to fresh Guernsey crabs as well as the more familiar fruit and veg. Why not give your children some cash, and see what they choose to buy?

earth, aiming to offer family stays with the lowest possible impact on the land. Choose from the Woodsman Ger yurt (sleeps six), Seashore Safari Tent (sleeps four) with nearby paths and tunnels for kids to explore, or the Barefoot Forager Tipi (sleeps four). All have field kitchens, and you can order home-cooked veggie meals. Woodland workshops are available (page 42).

KID-FRIENDLY EATS

Beach House ⌁ beachhouseguernsey. com. On the north coast of Guernsey, with stunning views overlooking Pembroke Bay, the Beach House offers informal dining in a family-friendly setting. A tasty children's menu is available, as well as burgers, bar meals and seafood. The outside terrace is perfect for an afternoon coffee or scenic evening meal and parents can keep an eye on kids while they play on the sand below.
The Boathouse ⌁ thechristiesgroup.gg. The Boathouse, sitting on St Peter Port's bustling harbour, has a sunny deck for

dining with a view, and serves breakfast, lunch and dinner with a focus on local seafood. A children's menu is available, as are vegetarian options.
Cobo Fish & Chip Bar ✆ 01481 254276. Join the locals who head down to Cobo Bay on a sunny Guernsey evening, order your fish and chips from the Cobo shack and perch on the sea wall or beach below to watch the infamous west coast sunset.
Crabby Jack's Restaurant ⌁ thechristiesgroup.gg. This lively restaurant, on Guernsey's west coast, alongside Vazon Bay, serves homemade family favourites from burgers to pizzas, seafood to salads. There's a large rooftop terrace for evening dining with a beach view, and a kids' play area.
Dix Neuf ⌁ liberationgroup.com. In St Peter Port Arcade, just off the main shopping street, this bustling French brasserie-style restaurant offers a 'Good Food for Little People' menu, listing hearty dishes such as breaded chicken

schnitzel, Malaysian seafood curry and Guernsey ice cream for dessert.

Gusto ⌀ gusto.gg. Classic Italian cuisine from brothers Peppe and Sabino in central St Peter Port, with plenty of child-pleasing pasta and pizzas.

Patois Brasserie ⌀ patoisbrasserie.gg. A pretty brasserie, not far from Guernsey Airport, where you can try local specialities Guernsey Gâche (fruit loaf) and bean jar (cassoulet), or a Guernsey crab sandwich. It also serves Bean 14, Guernsey roasted coffee. Smaller portions from the main menu are available along with a dedicated kids' menu featuring ham and fried eggs and breaded fish goujons.

Saltwater ⌀ saltwater.gg. Located at Beaucette Marina, on the northern tip of the island, Saltwater has a distinctly Mediterranean feel. Tuck into fresh fish and seafood specialities, or opt for a meat or vegetarian option. The children's menu comes with a few puzzles.

Terrace Garden Café
⌀ terracegardencafe.com. Relaxed al fresco dining any time of the day with views over St Peter Port's Victoria Marina. You can order anything from light bites to main meals, including children's options and an extensive list of Thai dishes.

MORE INFO

Visit Guernsey ⌀ visitguernsey.com
Visit Guernsey Walking App Free to download from Google Play and the App Store.

Camp de Rêves Glampsite is set in one of the most beautiful parts of the island, boasting fabulous panoramic west-coast sea views and stunning sunsets over the Atlantic Ocean.

Each safari tent sleeps 6 and has 3 bedrooms, a shower room, kitchen, lounge area and decking with BBQ and gated garden. The shepherd huts each sleep 2 adults and offer wonderful sunset views from a private deck

Camp de Rêves is the perfect base whether you're looking to relax or stay active and, with just 5 safari tents and 3 shepherd huts on a 3 acre site, you can be sure of a peaceful retreat.

www.guernseyglamping.com
enquiries@guernseyglamping.com
07781 415640

3
ST IVES

St Ives has been attracting artists and adventurers for centuries – come and explore your inner creative.

TOP FAMILY EXPERIENCE
CREATIVE CLASSES AT BARNOON WORKSHOP

BEST FOR KIDS AGED: 5–18
WHEN TO GO: Easter to October half term
INTREPID LEVEL: ①
ADDED ADVENTURE: Art galleries, sculpture gardens, surfing, storytelling walks
TIME: A long weekend to a week

UNLEASH YOUR INNER ARTIST AT BARNOON WORKSHOP

Unit 6, The Harbour Galleries, Wharf Rd, TR26 1LF ⚭ barnoonworkshop.co.uk; classes can cover abstract art, watercolours, oils, beach craft, resin jewellery making, portraits, decoupage, soap & candle making. Groups of up to ten people, with classes tailored to kids of all ages.

A former public toilet block by a car park is an unlikely setting for an art class, but here I am with my teenage daughter and her boyfriend, sitting, paintbrush in hand, in the studio of local artists Zoe Eaton and Peter Giles. This unassuming white slab of a building is perched up on the clifftop between the architecturally honed Tate St Ives roof and ancient Barnoon Cemetery. When it came up for tender, Zoe and Peter jumped at the chance to turn it into an art studio, ripping out the toilets and making it a minimalist white space.

Here for a two-hour abstract art session, we begin by looking at the bold work of locally inspired abstract artists, including Terry Frost who

---

◀ Creative classes at Barnoon Workshop.

lived and worked in nearby Newlyn. Cornish light, colours and shapes lay at the heart of his work, and once you've visited this southwest tip of the country you can see how it became, and continues to be, an artistic touchstone for so many creative souls. We flick through art books about Wilhelmina Barns-Graham, a member of the influential Penwith Society of Arts, and Patrick Heron who lived in the neighbouring Cornish hamlet of Zennor and was recognised as one of the leading British painters of the 20th century.

Both my accompanying teens are studying art A-level and are keen to get stuck in. Zoe pitches the session to their age, telling us that abstract art is as much about what the paint does on the canvas as the shapes and motifs used. She suggests we cover our A4 canvases in a scrubby layer of paint first and go from there. Before any of this, we create a prototype abstract collage with paper card. Zoe advises us to go with our instincts and not think about it too much, even using shapes that are already cut out in her box of coloured card. It's fascinating how we all go in such different directions with colours and forms, and it's incredibly satisfying to see how motivated my teens are and how experimental they are with colours and shapes. Zoe encourages bold decisions and reinforces the idea that experimentation is the only way to go with art, especially abstracts.

After the session, which goes by in a flash, we all end up with an A4 abstract on canvas that – while they may not win a place on the wall in the Tate – are pretty good, nonetheless. Inspired by past masters and the light and colours of this pretty Cornish enclave, we've definitely caught the St Ives bug.

ADDED ADVENTURE: WHERE PAINTBRUSHES MEET SURFBOARDS

The little Cornish town of St Ives is well known for its Instagram-friendly harbour, its cute pasty shops and the grand surf beach at Porthmeor, but slow the pace down and linger longer with your children and you'll begin to appreciate why so many artists and creatives have gravitated here over the years. It could be the constantly changing light, or the appealing combination of tight streets and vast landscapes. Somehow, St Ives manages to feel cosy while also retaining an epic quality.

If your children are at all interested in art, this is a wonderful place to holiday. You should begin, of course, with a trip to the mighty Tate St Ives, and the Barbara Hepworth Museum and Sculpture Garden, but there are many other small independent art galleries to browse. St Ives doesn't disappoint when it comes to traditional Cornish holiday beach pursuits, either. It's a well-known surf spot and a good place for children to learn to ride the waves. All in all, though, it's fun just to take it slow, taking in the details – a wander through the narrow streets reveals names such as Salubrious Place, Teetotal Street and Wheal Dream. For children who love trains, the ten-minute jaunt on the cute St Ives Bay branch line to Carbis Bay via Lelant is a must. And for the gentlest of pursuits, watch the stone balancer on Lambeth Walk Beach behind the Lifeboat Station create seemingly impossible structures until the tide comes in and knocks them down with a satisfying plonk as they fall.

ART BY THE SEA

The unusual circular design of **Tate St Ives** (tate.org.uk), created in 1988 by architects Eldred Evans and David Shalev, and opened in 1993, echoes the former gasworks overlooking Porthmeor Beach and the Atlantic Ocean. This regeneration via art is something us adults are used to, but for children it may still come as a revolutionary idea. Looking at the gallery from the beach, it's at the same time hidden in the sprawl of white houses and a bold statement, like a mighty seashell.

The first art kids see here is the gloriously bold stained-glass window by Patrick Heron. Devoid of the usual black leading, it instantly lifts the mood and piques interest. The gallery's permanent exhibition explores Modern Art and St Ives itself, looking at the histories and ideas of modern artists working in and around the town during the 20th century, including Patrick Heron, Dame Barbara Hepworth, Ben Nicholson and Peter Lanyon. Depending on the age of your child, these works can spark valuable conversations. My 13-year-old said it made him so cross that someone could get famous for painting abstracts like Patrick Heron's *Green and Purple Painting with Blue Disc*, which led to a discussion about how the Modernists were doing something new, something no-one had done before.

Local art is mixed with international works including from the mighty Picasso, whose *Bowl of Fruit, Violin and Bottle* illustrates clearly to children the literal deconstruction of conventional images on the canvas. My son was drawn to the surrealist Sir Roland Penrose's *Le Grand Jour*, enthusing about the many worlds that were going on in one painting.

And of course, you need to have a discussion about naïve artist Alfred Wallis, a former fisherman and marine stores dealer who took up painting in 1922, aged 67, for 'company', he said. He was self taught and never had an art lesson. Although he died in poverty, Wallis has an elaborate gravestone in **Barnoon Cemetery**, right next to Tate St Ives, possibly one of the prettiest cemeteries you're ever likely to see. It's a revelation for children to read the old names and work out how old people were when they died. If you don't find it too morbid, set your kids the task of finding Wallis's grave, which depicts a tiny mariner at the foot of a huge lighthouse, a popular motif in his paintings.

If your children are inspired to paint and draw, check out also the gallery's **Tate Create** – a programme of school holiday events aimed at engaging families through open studios exploring current exhibitions. Each holiday focuses on a different theme and materials – you can use the Tate's learning studios to make your own art, and any work created can be shared in an open gallery or taken home. Other seasonal events organised by the gallery include **Beach Art Explorers** in the summer, encouraging families to create art on the beach, and the **Winter Festival**, with light installations, choirs and festive activities.

Hidden away behind the high stone walls of the steeply inclined Barnoon Hill, the **Barbara Hepworth Museum and Sculpture Garden** (⊘ tate.org.uk) feels like a secret enclave and offers a tantalising look into how an artist works. The museum is set in Trewyn Studio, bought by Hepworth in 1949 and where she lived until her death, aged 72, in a house fire in 1975. Visiting the museum and garden is an especially empowering experience for young girls as Hepworth was one of the few women artists of her day to achieve international prominence, and her legacy has endured. In the subtropical vegetation of her lush garden, the immense stone carvings and bronzes have a size and heft that might usually be associated with male artists; here, however, we see a woman taking control of mighty forms, many of them managing to convey very tender feelings of protection. The highlight for many children is peering into her workshop, which stands exactly as she left it: rows and rows of well-used chisels; heavy hammers and dusty goggles; a turntable; stone plinths topped with circles of marble and half-formed shapes; shelves holding rusty containers and brown glass bottles – all revealing the grit and hard work that goes into the artist's alchemy. Kids can enjoy a special 'Tate Shapes' activity as they explore the garden, where there are also Toddle Tate sessions in summer.

If your kids are enchanted by this sculpture garden and you feel they'd like to see more, consider a short hop (six miles) across the neck of the narrow Penwith Peninsula to the **Tremenheere Sculpture Gardens** (⊘ tremenheere.co.uk) near Penzance. Here kids can climb trees, wander through woodland, discover subtropical plants and experience nature through a series of art installations, including a camera obscura and an elliptical domed chamber by renowned American artist James Turrell. While here, don't miss a swim in Penzance's glorious Art Deco seawater lido, **Jubilee Pool** (⊘ jubileepool.co.uk). The geothermal pool is the first of its kind in the UK, with natural salt water heated to 35°C by a geothermal well. Just remember to book an all-ages session when coming with kids.

Back in St Ives, there are a host of commercial **galleries** to inspire children. The **St Ives Society of Artists** (⊘ stisa.co.uk), housed in a former church in Norway Square, is worth a look. You could also sneak in a little art appreciation in between playing at the amusements arcade and eating ice cream on the harbourfront by taking an easy detour into **Harbour Galleries** (∎). Seven shop spaces here display the work of local artists, including Zoe Eaton and her husband Peter Giles. The art is all very accessible, and Zoe and Peter sell paints and paper as well as a beautiful hand-drawn *Colour St Ives* colouring book.

Another creative place to take children is **Leach Pottery** (⊘ leachpottery.com), founded in 1920 by Bernard Leach and Shoji Hamada. Scores of potters from across the world have trained here, and the studio is well geared up to encourage children of all ages to engage with the art form. Options might include 'Baby Clay', a sensory experience that allows very small children to explore what clay feels like on their hands and feet, or short creative sessions during the school holidays for children between six and 12, focusing on themes such as coil pots, tropical fish or monsters. Even if you don't join a session, you can take the family museum trail and learn about the pottery itself.

For more artistic inspiration, the **St Ives School of Painting** (⊘ schoolofpainting.co.uk) runs an **activity trail** for families and offers painting courses for children seven and over in its evocative studios

overlooking Porthmeor Beach. CAST, the Cornubian Arts & Science Trust (⌀ c-a-s-t.org.uk) in Helston at the northern end of the Lizard Peninsula, a 15-minute drive from St Ives, also has a lovely programme of free family workshops during the school holidays that encourage you to be creative together.

OUTDOOR LIFE: SURFING, WILDLIFE & SCENIC WALKS

Porthmeor Beach is one of the West Country's most sought-after surf beaches, home to the **St Ives Surf School** (⌀ stivessurfschool.co.uk), which has another site on neighbouring **Porthminster Beach**. Both offer surfing lessons, coasteering, paddleboarding and guided sea kayaking sessions for all ages. And as long as the lifeguard is on Porthmeor Beach giving you the go ahead, surfing is often better in squally conditions, so don't let the unpredictable English weather put you off getting out there.

For a spectacular family walk, head west from Porthmeor Beach along the **South West Coast Path** (⌀ southwestcoastpath.com) around Clodgy Point, following wild cliffs and moorland along a six-mile stretch of dramatic coastline to the hamlet of Zennor where writer D H Lawrence lived during World War I. Enjoy a pub lunch at the **Tinners Arms** (⌀ tinnersarms.com) and, if little legs are tired, catch the 300 bus (summer only) back to St Ives.

You could also take a four-mile walk out of St Ives, above Carbis Bay, to **Trink Dairy** (⌀ trinkdairy.co.uk), run by the local Knowles family who really do care for their grass-fed herd. After watching the cows being milked, you can head to the Parlour Shop for a drink of the fresh white stuff, and stock up on delicious Cornish cheeses, giant chocolate buttons and raw chocolate pie.

Alternatively you can take the coastal route five miles east to the town of Hayle. En route, on the most southwesterly estuary in the UK, you'll discover the **Hayle Estuary Nature Reserve** (⌀ rspb.org.uk). Winter is one of the best times to come here, when the wetland is home to vast flocks of teal and wigeon. The reserve is good for walking and has pushchair-friendly paths. It's also on the National Cycle Network (⌀ sustrans.org.uk), and perfect to reach by bike.

◀ **1** The geothermal Jubilee Pools. **2** Exhibition at Tate St Ives. **3** Decorating pots at Leach Pottery. **4** Barbara Hepworth's workshop.

In Hayle, **Paradise Park Wildlife Sanctuary** (⊘ paradisepark.org.uk) is an easy day out for parents of younger children, who will get to meet colourful birds including parrots, Humboldt's penguins, Caribbean flamingos, red-billed Cornish choughs and golden eagles. You might also glimpse rare red squirrels, red pandas and playful Asian otters. Many of the species are in conservation breeding schemes.

Another great place to interact with nature in the raw is **Godrevy**, some 12 miles from St Ives (⊘ nationaltrust.org.uk). The sandy beach leads on to wildlife-rich headlands and the dramatic coves of the North Cliffs where you can peer down Hell's Mouth as the birds soar, or scan the ocean for seals. Just take care of children near cliff edges.

SHOPPING FOR KIDS

Bijou St Ives is the sort of place you can give your kids the thrill of going off on their own for a wander around the shops with a little bit of cash – depending, of course, on your own judgment as a parent. Children of all ages adore **Emjems** (🛇 emjemsofstives) on St Andrews Street, a family-run treasure trove of gemstones, crystals and fossils. Gems cost as little as a £1 and each is labelled with its properties – rainbow moonstone, for example, is said to increase creativity, compassion and confidence. The **St Ives Slate Co**, tucked away on Cyril Noah Square, off Fore Street, is another find with its quirky slate fish and impressive swords that look like something out of *Lord of the Rings*.

PRACTICALITIES

FAMILY-FRIENDLY SLEEPS

21 The Digey ⊘ 21thedigey.co.uk.
In the centre of St Ives and just a minute from Porthmeor Beach, this traditional fisherman's cottage, with two bedrooms, is both quaint and contemporary.
Beersheba Farm ⊘ beersheba.co.uk.
This hilltop farm overlooking St Ives Bay offers off-grid glamping in woodland-set 'landpods' (sleeping up to five) and the self-catering Brea Cottage (sleeping up to six), which has a private hot tub. Standing Stone Stables, adjacent to the wood, offers pony rides and hacks for all ages, including little ones – they will even deliver you back to your landpod on horseback.

◀ **1** Porthmeor Beach – one of the West Country's most sought-after surf beaches.
2 Paradise Park gives kids a chance to meet some colourful birdlife. **3** Learning to bodyboard at Porthmeor. **4** Dunlin flock at Hayle Estuary Nature Reserve.

ST IVES STORIES:
PIRATES, GHOSTS & PAPER THEATRES

Westcott's Quay, TR26 2DY *shantybaba.com*; age: 5–18; intrepid level: ①

The age-old tradition of story telling is alive and well in St Ives thanks to Shanty Baba. A chartered accountant in a previous existence, Shanty now brings the creepy atmosphere of spooky local legends and tall tales to life on his story-telling walks around the town's offbeat nooks and crannies. Younger kids enjoy his St Ives Pirate Walk, with much audience participation, as well as the summer-holiday Twilight Zone Ghost Walk. Everyone gathers at Westcott's Quay just behind the St Ives Lifeboat Station, where Shanty waits by the water, lantern in hand, ready to lead you round the back streets. Dressed as a natty old-fashioned mariner, he launches into tales of men who encountered their own horse-drawn coffins turning up in the night, mass plague pits in the Trewyn Gardens and terrible dares, coffin diving and blood sucking rats in Barnoon Cemetery.

Shanty also runs a tiny museum in his St Ives terraced house about maverick and anti-establishment figure Captain Sir Richard Francis Burton. While this is not aimed at children, he does open up his library for impressive Victorian paper theatre shows such as *Robin Hood* and *One Thousand and One Arabian Nights*; these are intimate family performances, with sometimes just four people in the audience.

STEPHEN R JOHNSON/A

Carbis Bay Holidays

⟡ carbisbayholidays.co.uk. A reliable selection of luxury holiday cottages in and around St Ives, many with enclosed gardens, BBQs, table tennis and sheds full of beach toys and games.

Carbis Bay Hotel ⟡ carbisbayhotel. co.uk. Set on Carbis Bay beach, this five-star hotel offers family rooms in the main house or gorgeous beach lodges right on the sand. Kids love the heated outdoor pool and gardens, the film nights and hosted activities; mums and dads can enjoy the C Bay Spa while children are entertained at the C Bay Kids Club.

Enys House ⟡ cornishgems.com. This five-bedroom family house, up a steep road from town and just around the corner from the Barbara Hepworth Museum, is the perfect place for two families or a multi-gen stay. With beautiful white interiors, it is filled with thoughtful touches for kids including bunks and twin beds with pretty cushions and Tintin images, a snug with board games and kids' books, and plenty of bathrooms including an outdoor shower on the back decking. The views over the town, beaches and harbour and out to sea are epic and uplifting – they can also be enjoyed from the landscaped front garden with its palm trees and chunky wood seating.

Three Mile Beach ⟡ threemilebeach. co.uk. A collection of 15 have-it-all beach houses on the northern Cornwall coast just four miles from St Ives, designed to evoke carefree fun and nostalgia for childhood seaside holidays. Hidden among the sand dunes and coastal grasses, the three- and four-bedroom houses have kitchen-diner-loungers, log burners, wraparound terraces with sunken cedar hot tubs, and barrel saunas. You can book a chef, order hearty homemade oven dishes, or nip out to the Three Mile Beach street food truck. Four luxury tented suites are also available for glamping.

Una St Ives ⟡ unastives.co.uk. This ecolodge resort is a good one for parents seeking a wellness angle to their family holiday. Along with morning yoga sessions, a spa and gym there's a 49ft indoor infinity pool for all the family, plus wood-fired pizzas from Una Kitchen.

KID-FRIENDLY EATS

Café at Tate St Ives ⟡ tate.org.uk. For awesome views over Porthmeor Beach, head to the top floor of the Tate: perfect for a cake or cream tea. Alternatively, the gallery's Loggia is a great place for an outdoor, but covered, picnic.

Godrevy Beach Café 📷 @godrevycafe. This extremely cute café, hidden away in the dunes behind Godrevy Lighthouse, offers home-baked cakes, hearty breakfasts and doorstep sandwiches.

Hub Box ⟡ hubbox.co.uk. Located on The Wharf in St Ives, Hub Box serves American-inspired street food including award-winning burgers using 21-day dry-aged Cornish rare breed beef.

Hungry Horsebox Co ⟡ hungryhorsebox.co.uk. This outstanding mobile food truck on

Gwithian Beach serves Cornish beach picnics, beach BBQs and homemade cakes. Try to get to one of their sunset cookouts, and take your own blanket.

Lula Shack ⟨⟩ lulashack.co.uk. A hit with hungry families, this fresh seafood and ribs shack overlooks the Hayle Estuary's tidal waters and is definitely a place where you can kick off your shoes and relax.

Norway Stores ⟨⟩ @norway_stores. If you're self-catering you should check out this great local grocery store, on Back Road West, housed in allegedly the oldest shop in St Ives. Pick up general groceries including fresh fruit and veg, tasty deli staples and delicious homemade cakes.

Porthgwidden Beach Restaurant ⟨⟩ porthgwiddencafe.co.uk. Gorgeous restaurant right by the beach of the same name, with lovely sea views. Sustainable fish is served in everything from classic fish and chips to international offerings such as smoked haddock chowder.

Porthmeor Beach Café ⟨⟩ porthmeor-beach.co.uk. A popular restaurant located on the spectacular surf beach. Kids love the private outdoor booths. Downstairs on the prom, a more casual daytime café serves pasties, chips and hot drinks. It's the perfect post-surfing hangout.

Porthminster Beach Café ⟨⟩ porthminstercafe.co.uk. Nestled right on the beach with uninterrupted views across St Ives Bay to Godrevy Lighthouse, this reliably good seafood restaurant serves family-friendly plates such as crispy fried squid and smoked salmon tacos.

St Ives Bakery ⟨⟩ stivesbakery.co.uk. Buy some of the best takeaway pasties in town at this little place on Fore Street to munch on the beach or harbour wall. Kids will love the lamb and mint, steak and stilton, or cheese and veg varieties.

Trevaskis Farm ⟨⟩ trevaskisfarm.co.uk. Combine a family day out picking your own fresh produce with a meal in the gorgeous Farmhouse Kitchen Restaurant with healthy kids' menus and satisfying Sunday roasts. Located a 10-mile drive east of St Ives near Connor Downs.

BEFORE YOU GO

Check out **Kidz R Us** (⟨⟩ kidzrus.net), a brilliant local theatre and social

SURFING AS THERAPY

The result of a successful crowdfund, **SurfHouse St Ives** (⟨⟩) is a clifftop clubhouse for a girls-only surf club run by pro-surfer Tassy Swallow. Its summer programme is packed with workshops, courses, exhibitions, talks and music events that anyone is welcome to attend. Meanwhile, **St Ives Surf School** (⟨⟩ stivessurfschool. co.uk) has partnered with The Wave Project (⟨⟩ waveproject.co.uk), a surf therapy charity for young adults and children which strives to change lives through surfing.

enterprise which works with around 100 young people a year to put on highly professional shows including a celebrated panto. Book in advance.

MORE INFO

St Ives Tourist Board
⌀ stives-cornwall.co.uk
Visit Cornwall ⌀ visitcornwall.com

A mindful journey through Britain's special places

4
THE SOUTH HAMS

Life in this unspoilt pocket of south Devon revolves around its rivers, which plummet from moor to estuary to sea leaving a myriad of ecosystems and histories in their wake.

TOP FAMILY EXPERIENCE
RIVER DART FERRY AND STEAM TRAIN TRIP

BEST FOR KIDS AGED: 3+
WHEN TO GO: March to November
INTREPID LEVEL: ②
ADDED ADVENTURE: Wild swimming, rock pool explorations, canoeing trips, coastal walks, catching breaks on sweeping, sandy beaches
TIME: Five days to one week

STEAMING THROUGH BY RIVER & RAILWAY

South Embankment, Dartmouth TQ6 9BH dartmouthrailriver.co.uk

Dartmouth Steam Railway and River Boat Company's combination of ferries/paddle steamers and steam trains provides numerous options for days out, whether you want to head on to the moor or out to sea, or take a circular adventure. We're eager to get on the water, so we opt for a circular link from Totnes to Paignton, Dartmouth and back.

Leaving the best (the boat) until last, we first head to **Paignton** by bus. There's a frisson of excitement at the prospect of a day without the car and on the move. At Paignton, the atmosphere livens as we approach the station; the boys (big and small) gaze at the info boards to guess which of the many vintage steam trains will be our iron horse. The top pick is

---

◀ **1** Boarding the River Dart ferry. **2** Dartmouth Steam Train.

the oldest of the four, *4277 Hercules*, built in 1920 and left rusting in a scrapyard in Barry, Wales, for 22 years before being rescued by a train enthusiast. As memories of hours of *Thomas the Tank Engine* flood back – with mixed emotions – the station hums with excitement and 'toot toots' as our ride arrives in clouds of smoke. 'It's the *Hercules!*' bellows someone's granddad as the lean, green machine chugs alongside us.

From Paignton, the steam train trundles for 30 minutes along the coast and into the Dart Valley to Kingswear, just across the river from Dartmouth. Seascapes dominate the first part of the journey, and we gaze at colour-popping beach huts and a horizon that bobs up and down in time with the train's clickety-clack rhythm. Beyond Goodrington and Churston stations, the line heads into the slopes of Long Wood to Greenway Halt, a 30-minute woodland walk from Agatha Christie's much-loved house, **Greenway** (⊘ nationaltrust.org.uk). The mansion gracefully lords over a particularly picturesque bend in the river, so we can't resist stopping for a quick coffee. With longer, there are hours' more adventure to be had. The house is full of old-fashioned games and Christie's prized knick-knacks and ornaments from all over the world, while the garden boasts more than 2,700 tree species. A small ferry also chugs back and forth to **Dittisham** – a renowned crabbing spot and home to the much-sought-after (book ahead) **Anchorstone Café** (⊘ anchorstonecafe.co.uk). But, eager to get back on track, we leave that for another time.

Back on board another steam train, and it's a quick ten-minute journey through the woods and along the water's edge to Kingswear. Despite numerous proposals to build a bridge from here to **Dartmouth** over the years, cars and foot passengers still rely on the short ferry hop to reach the home of all things sailing, naval and maritime. 'It's like we've stepped into the olden days,' my youngest exclaims as we stumble on to the cobbled twists and turns of Tudor-built **Bayard's Cove Fort** (⊘ english-heritage.org.uk). He's not wrong – humans have used the Dart's deep-water harbour here for thousands of years.

After weaving among Dartmouth's brightly painted houses and boutiques, we order crab sandwiches from a window in a wall and dodge seagull dives and crabbing lines on the worn-down harbour wall. Beyond an eclectic mix of vessels bobbing gently as the tide ebbs and flows, the *Kingswear Castle* steals the show. In her heyday, this coal-fired paddle steamer was the lifeblood of the river, carrying almost 500 passengers between Totnes and Dartmouth until the 1960s. Although she occasionally chugs up the river to Totnes, today we hop on the more functional-looking *Dart Explorer* for our voyage.

The **River Dart**, which starts on Dartmoor and flows 46 miles through moors, woodland, riverside villages and market towns to Dartmouth, is awash with stories and folklore. A good place to dive into its history is Alice Oswald's award-winning poem, *The Dart*, which is the product of over three years of listening to stories of those that lived and worked on the river. Its name descends from the Cornish and Welsh word *Dar*, meaning oak, and after a few minutes cruising along its tidal waters, it's clear why. Towering ancient oaks line large chunks of the river, sitting atop the water at high tide and revealing a gnarly, squelchy, rocky shoreline at low. Here, on the quieter stretches, kingfishers flash electric-blue plumage, egrets bedazzle emerald treetops with their snowy white feathers, and crabs scuttle for shelter as mud, seaweed and rocks bubble and squeak in a constant state of flux.

We see the round, shiny heads of grey seals among buoys and boats, which seem to scatter from Dartmouth and Dittisham like iron filings. There's even a rewilded estate in one of the river's prettiest bends at Sharpham, where a few brave souls are swimming in the swirling currents. On the *Explorer's* vast outside deck, our heads dance from side to side like meerkats soaking up life on the river and waving to passers-by.

Once in **Totnes**, we make a beeline for **The Curator** café (*⌀* thecurator. co.uk) to quell the river's chilly breeze with hot chocolates and brownies. Gobbled at record speed, the fuel feels well deserved. We may not have hiked or kayaked, but our slow travel hat-trick has offered enough excitement and variety to leave our minds and bodies in a happy state of exhaustion.

ADDED ADVENTURE: WATER-BASED FUN & MARITIME HISTORY

Stretching from the wild edges of Dartmoor to the coast, much of the South Hams (derived from the old English word 'hamme', which means enclosed or sheltered space) is a designated Area of Outstanding Natural Beauty. Warren-like lanes weave through steep-sided valleys to estuaries and beaches abundant with wildlife and centuries-old naval traditions.

"Towering ancient oaks line large chunks of the river, sitting atop the water at high tide and revealing a gnarly, squelchy, rocky shoreline at low."

This patch of Devon also abounds in local-produce champions in bustling market towns like Totnes. There's so much to enjoy here beyond bucket-and-spade fun at the beach.

TOTNES & SURROUNDS

Totnes, sitting at the point where the River Dart becomes the Dart Estuary, was one of the UK's first 'transition towns' (a grassroots community project that aims to increase self-sufficiency). Residents lead fierce rebellions against any inkling of a chain; Starbucks was scared off a few years ago. While there's a healthy dose of the hippy (Friday markets are a good place to bask in the Fairtrade vibes), the High Street is also a treasure trove for interiors, quirky clothes brands and second-hand goods. The classic motte-and-bailey **Totnes Castle**, in the middle of town (⌂ english-heritage.org.uk), offers the finest viewpoint, while a mile-long footpath along the river from Steamer Quay to Longmarsh is ideal for kids that want to let off steam.

"Residents lead fierce rebellions against any inkling of a chain; Starbucks was scared off a few years ago."

Water activities are plentiful, although most start further downstream. **Red Equipment** (⌂ red-equipment.co.uk) suggests a Totnes to Dartmouth itinerary that's good if you have your own SUPs. Otherwise, group tours and kayak, canoe and SUP rental are offered by **Totnes Kayaks** (⌂ totneskayaks. co.uk), based in the pretty village of Stoke Gabriel about five miles downriver from town.

On the other side of the estuary from Stoke Gabriel, in the tiny hamlet of Tuckenhay, **Canoe Adventures** (⌂ canoeadventures.co.uk) organises 'By the Seat' group canoe trips from the Maltsters Arms pub on Bow Creek. A day trip involves team-building, chanting, canoeing, and building a fire for tea and biscuits. Canoeing and bushcraft trips with **Winding River Canoe** (⌂ windingrivercanoe.co.uk), in a variety of locations along the river, are a little pricier and focus more on foraging and wildlife.

North of Totnes, the **River Dart Country Park** (⌂ riverdart.co.uk) and **Dartington** (⌂ dartington.org) are two standout destinations on the way up to Dartmoor. The former offers an active experience: 90 acres of swimming, playgrounds and adrenaline-fuelled activities including rock climbing and high ropes in Ashburton. The latter is more genteel. A series of free family concerts take place on the estate's Great Lawn each summer. There's a toy shop at the Cider Press Centre and an Earth Wrights (natural materials) playground. The 1,200-acre estate is free to explore via a Deer Park and other trails, including a Children's Trail featuring den building and bug hotels. The **Dart Valley Trail** (⌖ southdevonaonb.org.uk) is an off-road bike route covering about 10 miles from Dartington to Sharpham Estate.

FROM BEESANDS TO MATTISCOMBE

The **South West Coast Path** (⌖ southwestcoastpath.org.uk) is the UK's longest National Trail, stretching 630 miles from Minehead to Poole. A great chunk in these parts starts in the coastal village of **Beesands** and heads southwest beyond Start Point – a lighthouse and the most southerly tip of Devon – to the tucked-away beach of **Mattiscombe**, from where it's possible to cut cross-country and be back in Beesands in time for lunch or dinner. It's a total walk of about eight miles. In Beesands, the much-loved **Britannia at the Beach** (⌖ britanniaatthebeach.co.uk) serves simple, local seafood, while the **Cricket Inn** (⌖ thecricketinn. com) has a more comprehensive menu (and indoor seating for when the weather doesn't play ball).

Highlights along the way include the gentle cove and deserted village of **Hallsands**, half of which fell into the sea in 2012. The **Start Point Lighthouse** visitor centre (⌖ startpointdevon.co.uk) runs 45-minute tours of the lighthouse, although simply standing on one of the most exposed peninsulas on the English coast, jutting almost a mile out to sea, is enough of a thrill. Look out for seals that often swim in the pools just beyond Start Point, and pack your swimmers so you can make the most of Mattiscombe's white-sand beach.

If you're looking for more organised fun, check out the activity days run by **Forest and Beach** (⌖ forestandbeach.co.uk), which operates from a field just above Beesands. Full- or half-day camps for kids include marine and coastal flora and fauna identification, shelter-building and learning about tides.

SALCOMBE & BIGBURY BAY

Salcombe is one of the most popular spots along the south Devon coast and in peak season can feel more like Piccadilly Circus than a lazy backwater. That said, it doesn't take long to get off the beaten track. A ferry (and sometimes accompanying tractor) runs trips from town to **North and South Sands**: the former is popular with younger kids thanks to its shallow, clear water; older children might prefer adventuring with **Sea Kayak Salcombe** (⊘ seakayaksalcombe.co.uk) on South Sands.

Across the river, **Mill Bay** (⊘ nationaltrust.co.uk) is a good base for shorter walks: it's just 300yds across the sand to **East Portlemouth** beach when the tide is out, or two miles along the coast to **Gara Rock** – a sandy cove fringed by rock pools that is home to the luxurious **Gara Rock Hotel** (page 79), which offers refreshments and lunch to walkers (book ahead).

Heading north from Salcombe, a series of much-loved beaches and less-known coves line the coast up to Mothecombe. Hotspots like **Thurlestone** and **Bantham** can get busy in summer, so if you're looking for solitude, it's worth visiting off-season or finding beaches that are only accessible by foot. Steep footpaths down to the sea put most visitors off **Soar Mill Cove** and **Sunny Cove**, but the effort is always worth it. Half a mile from Bigbury-on-Sea, **Burgh Island** is a tidal island with its own Art Deco hotel. Although getting stranded is part of the fun, a water tractor comes into use when the tide is in – that is, if the old-world Pilchard Inn doesn't persuade you to stay. The mile-long swim around the island is one of Britain's iconic open-water swims: **SwimTrek** (⊘ swimtrek.com) offers a day trip to help guide you (and older kids) around. For other water pursuits, Bigbury's **Discovery Surf School** (⊘ discoverysurf.com) holds surf lessons for kids (aged seven or over), and rents out kayaks and stand-up paddleboards.

Just north of Bigbury, **Ayrmer Cove** is a good choice for younger families looking for a bit of an adventure – it's less than a mile's walk from the National Trust car park at **Ringmore**, making it a short and easy stroll. Four miles northwest of Ayrmer, **Wonwell** is one of the region's most atmospheric beaches, sitting at the mouth of the Erme Estuary, flooded at high tides and glimmering with wet sand at low when it's possible to wade across to **Mothecombe**. Both beaches sit within the huge, privately owned **Flete Estate** (⊘ flete.co.uk), much of which is open to the public.

Keen swimmers will want to check out the infamous **Bantham Swoosh** (⊘ outdoorswimmingsociety.com). Every year, starting at Bantham, swimmers of all ages and abilities swim down four miles or so of the River Avon, culminating in a 'swoosh' when the tide ebbs through a narrow section of the river. The MiniSwoosh is a shorter activity especially for kids older than six.

PLYMOUTH & PLYMOUTH SOUND

Located at the mouth of the River Tamar, the maritime city of Plymouth offers a good variety of family attractions that appeal to all ages, from historical sites to boat trips and wildlife.

The largest of its kind in the UK, the **National Marine Aquarium** (⊘ national-aquarium.co.uk) is in the harbour in the heart of town. Run by the Ocean Conservation Trust, it has been designed to help people understand seas both at home and further afield. Four zones explore Marine Protected Areas around the world, from Maldivian seagrass meadows to the Eddystone Reef near Plymouth. Events and activities include aquarium late nights, ocean documentary screenings, ranger beach days and snorkel safaris from Mount Batten Beach, just across the estuary.

"Events and activities include aquarium late nights, ocean documentary screenings, ranger beach days and snorkel safaris."

Plymouth has a real knack for fusing its naval history with contemporary arts and culture. The 19th-century naval **Royal William Yard** (⊘ royalwilliamyard.com), for example, is now an arts hub, with regular outdoor family-friendly theatre productions and artists in residence. **The Box** (⊘ theboxplymouth.com), meanwhile, is a relatively new museum and arts venue – kids will love the figurehead exhibition and the model boats.

Plymouth's Art Deco saltwater **Tinside Lido** (⊘ everyoneactive.com) overlooks the sea at the tip of Plymouth Hoe. If you'd rather take to the sea, consider Plymouth Boat Trips' **Fish 'N' Trips** (⊘ plymouthboattrips. co.uk), which take families (no children younger than seven) mackerel fishing; you can cook your catch with a BBQ on the boat. **Devon Sailing Experiences** (⊘ devonsailingexperiences.co.uk) has starter day sails for beginners (eight plus).

In the Plymouth Bay area, ten miles south of the city, **Noss Mayo** (⊘ nationaltrust.co.uk) is a picturesque village close to the mouth of the River Yealm. Surrounded by creeks, so wooded that they feel utterly secret, it's a great base for days messing about on the water or heading out on coast-path walks.

PRACTICALITIES

FAMILY-FRIENDLY SLEEPS

At the Beach ⏣ luxurycoastal.co.uk/ developments/at-the-beach-torcross. Occupying the former Torcross Hotel, this collection of 13 modern apartments (sleeping up to six), lies a 15-minute drive from Dartmouth between Slapton Ley's wetlands and the sea. There's a café, fish-and-chip restaurant and a pub within moments from the front door, along with the most sheltered section of Torcross Beach. Kids will love clambering over the rocks and there are coastal walks towards Dartmouth and Start Point.

Fingals ⏣ fingals.co.uk. Children love the freedom at this rambling collection of six self-catering properties sleeping between two and six with ample gardens on a pretty lane near Dittisham. There's a tennis court and indoor pool, but best of all is the homely feel – the apartments and rooms are decorated with antiques collected over the years. There's an honesty bar in the communal lounge.

Flete Estate Cottages and Glamping ⏣ flete.co.uk. A number of self-catering properties, including a gamekeeper's lodge in the woods and coastguard cottages moments from the sea, are peppered around the vast Flete Estate. Each place, sleeping between two and 12, is within a ten-minute walk of the Erme Estuary and beaches. If you're not able to book into a cottage, consider their glamping options, available in summer, or the Mothecombe Beach House, built into the rocks overlooking the sea, which is available for day hire.

Gara Rock Hotel ⏣ gararock.com. Perched on a bluff moments from Salcombe, Gara Rock has all the feel of a contemporary luxury hotel with a welcome wallop of wilderness. The blingy Land Rovers ferrying guests around set the tone. It's pricey, but that's thanks to the sea views, indoor and outdoor pools, spa and cinema. The two- and three-bedroom apartments are probably best suited to families.

Mount Folly Farm ⏣ bigburyholidays. co.uk. What you see is what you get here, and, in Mount Folly Farm's own words, this is 'no-frills camping in the South Hams that's all about the view' – overlooking Bigbury-on-Sea, it's one of the finest views around. Not one for late night parties, this campsite is all about tranquillity and nature. If sleeping under canvas doesn't appeal, check out the bunkhouse, which sleeps up to 20 in three bedrooms.

KID-FRIENDLY EATS

Hope Cove House ⏣ hopecovehouse. co. It can be hard to bag a room at

---

◀ **1** Totnes Castle. **2** The High Ropes at River Dart Country Park. **3** The South West Coast Path near Start Point.

ROCK POOL SAFARI AT
WEMBURY MARINE CENTRE

Church Rd, Wembury, Plymouth PL9 0HP ⬙ wemburymarinecentre.org; age: 4+;
intrepid level: ①

Down by our feet, several inches of the clearest water glimmers with pink sea fans, green seaweeds and the maroon stripes of a jellyfish nonchalantly bobbing between rocks. The scene ahead is just as vibrant, as 30-odd kids between three and 14, along with a number of Wildlife Trust volunteers, scatter across the rocks and pools like crabs dashing for the surf beyond.

We're on a rock pool safari with the Wembury Marine Centre, a treasure trove of 'infotainment' for kids and adults alike, and one of only a handful of dedicated marine centres in the UK. Other events include a rock pool safari after dark, toddler safari, snorkel safari and identification sessions, but the centre alone is worth a visit. Here

you can learn about the staggering amount of wildlife in Wembury Bay and the offshore reef; kids will love learning how to spot the difference between ray and shark eggs and seeing photos of the basking sharks that sometimes grace these waters.

'Today we'll be following the Seashore Code,' Matt, our group leader, explains before clambering from beach to rocks. 'Use hands, not nets, keep one creature in the bucket at a time, and after a good look replace each creature where you found it.' We're not the only ones to wince at the thought of numerous irresponsible rock pooling expeditions in the past.

Identification charts in one hand, white tubs in the other, it's clear the adults are as

into it as the kids. 'Pipefish!', a man in his late 40s hollers, tub thrust into the sky, eager to confirm his identification with a volunteer, who tells the group that these slender fish are paired up at this time of year, which is why it's so important to put them back where you find them. Every spot sends a ripple of excitement across the pools as kids bury their heads and hands a little further into the squelch, sand and shells to pull out a top find.

Hermit crabs, velvet swimming crabs, common prawns, cushion starfish, beadlet anemones, rock gobby and blennies are all excitedly spotted, inspected and discussed. The netless, hands-on approach is a revelation, leading to an altogether more enjoyable experience with no eyes poked, creatures scraped or arguments about whose turn it is with the net. It also encourages you to get up close into nooks and crannies that

the net can't reach. In one, a five-year-old spots a light-bulb sea squirt – a tiny floating structure clinging to the rocks like a miniature filament, and from another, a volunteer pulls out a star ascidian. 'It looks like a clump of daisies but is, in fact, a colony of bottoms connected by one mouth,' she explains to a ripple of giggles.

A couple of hours flies by, and we hand back our tubs to explore beyond the rocks. The sky has cleared, and the tide is still retreating, leaving in its wake a sandy cove ideal for bodyboarding, swimming and splashing. Seaweed floats around our ankles, and someone spots a jellyfish mulling about by the rocks. Rather than the usual squeamish response, we linger, enjoying the sensation of the swirling water, sand and whatever else lies below, feeling that bit more bonded with the sea and all the weird and wonderful creatures that call it home.

HOLLY TUPPEN

this small, accoladed and much in demand boutique B&B in quaint Hope Cove, three miles south of Bantham. But fear not, because the food on the terrace is worth a visit alone. Lunch and dinner menus are simple – think rock oysters, crab linguine, brill and chips – but probably suit older kids rather than toddlers.

River Shack ⚲ therivershackdevon. co.uk. This Stoke Gabriel place is so bedded into the fabric of its pretty, laid-back millpond and riverside setting that it's hard to believe it is relatively new. Serving brunch, coffee, cream teas, ice cream, local beers and ciders, seafood like Brixham crab, and wood-fired pizza (check timings beforehand), this is the perfect place to sit back and relax while the kids go crabbing or mess about on the river.

Rockfish ⚲ therockfish.co.uk. With restaurants in nine locations across Devon, including Plymouth, Salcombe and Dartmouth, Rockfish might be dismissed on first sight as a conventional chain. In fact, this locally run fish-and-chip restaurant and take-away business is responsible to the core. Fish is locally and sustainably sourced, kids get welcome packs about native fish species, and the group participates in plastic clean-ups and local charitable work.

Schoolhouse ⚲ schoolhouse-devon. com. The kind of place where coffee drifts into brunch and drinks drift into dancing, Schoolhouse on the Flete Estate near Modbury serves some of the finest locally sourced grub around. Friday-night themed feasts might include 'Fish & Fizz', tapas, BBQs with live music, or pizza.

BEFORE YOU GO

Unlike other parts of the southwest, south Devon, and particularly the South Hams, is well set up for car-free travel. This is partly thanks to the Great Western train line from London stopping at Dawlish, Totnes and Plymouth, and the availability of local services from those stations. Perhaps more excitingly, there's a comprehensive ferry network up, down and across rivers, too. Most are for foot passengers

THE RIVERFORD REVOLUTION

'Leading the veg revolution since 1986', **Riverford Organic** (⚲ riverford.co.uk) delivers seasonal organic veg all over the country. The company is not only employee-owned and B Corp certified (proving serious sustainability creds), but it has donated over a million portions of veg to charities. It's also handily on the main road into Totnes, providing the perfect opportunity to stock up or order a box to be delivered to your holiday home or campsite. Visitors are welcome to wander around the farm, where the Riverford Field Kitchen cooks up a 'vegcentric' feast each day.

only, so it's a good idea to investigate bus and train routes to the rivers before you travel and factor that into where you stay. **Hello Kingsbridge** has a good guide to getting to and around the area, including the South Hams Bus Timetable (⊘ hellokingsbridge.co.uk/getting-around).

5
SOMERSET

Bucolic landscapes and countryside communities lend themselves to slow pastimes in southern England's most rural county.

TOP FAMILY EXPERIENCE
STORY OF GARDENING EXPERIENCE AT THE NEWT IN SOMERSET COUNTRY ESTATE

BEST FOR KIDS AGED: 3+	
WHEN TO GO:	April to October
INTREPID LEVEL:	①
ADDED ADVENTURE:	Dramatic gorges, hill walking, historic gardens, mysterious legends
TIME:	One week

FROM VIPER TO VR: AN INTERACTIVE GARDEN ADVENTURE

The Newt in Somerset, Hadspen, Bruton BA7 7NG ⌁ thenewtinsomerset.com

'Is this a show?' the youngest asks, as we meander from The Newt in Somerset's gatehouse towards the entrance foyer along a lit-up boardwalk. It's quite the welcome to this curiously named, rambling country estate, also home to a luxury boutique hotel, orchards and gardens. The theatrical approach makes the surrounding ancient woodland feel exotic – birdsong fills the air and a breeze dances among summer-green oak leaves. The foyer is an attraction in itself. The vast converted threshing barn offers a sneak peek of the gardens beyond from floor-to-ceiling glass panels. Studio Drift's 'Amplitude' sculpture pulses up and down, symbolising the pulse of living nature. The boys run to touch a giant wood-carved apple. Thankfully, no-one seems to mind their hands-on enthusiasm.

◀ Exploring the gardens at The Newt.

The gardens are open to day visitors via an annual membership scheme. It's not cheap, but guest tickets are available, kids go free, and membership includes entrance to other gardens in England. Once inside, it's possible to while away a full day wandering and wondering around the 30-acre farm, gardens and woodland.

The threshing barn opens on to a courtyard – the main hub of the estate and the entire visitor experience. From here, paths lead to cultivated gardens, cafés, restaurants, shops and the cider press, and five marked walkways spiral out into the wilder enclaves.

Eager to visit the Story of Gardening Museum, we meander through woodlands towards The Viper – an elevated walkway that leads into the museum. 'It's this way! Wow, look at this! Let's go this way!' The boys' cries bounce between the trees as they dart from dragonfly-filled pond to woodland den, and debate which signposts to follow.

We're all distracted by the Marl Pit along the way, created by the ancient practice of 'marling' – digging out lime deposits to improve agricultural soil. In the gaps and mounds left behind by the digging, islands and ponds spill over with greenery, designed to 'evoke a sense of Avalon'; apt, given we're in Arthur country, with the supposed site of Camelot not far away. We look out for crested newts – after all, the garden is named after the 2,000 or so resident amphibians – but make do instead with an epic frogspawn pile.

"Eager to visit, we meander through woodlands towards The Viper – an elevated walkway that leads into the museum."

'Wheeeeeeeeee!' We whizz around the 425ft The Viper walkway, high in the treetops, colliding with various other flying creature impressions from kids coming in the other direction. The walkway dips just before reaching the heights of the canopy, diving into a green-roofed building, almost hidden from view. 'It's a hobbit hole!', one of the kids remarks enthusiastically, bounding into the museum.

'LEAVE SHOES HERE', a big signpost indicates as we walk into the Story of Gardening Museum's atrium – a sun-drenched communal spot with tree-trunk benches and living walls. 'It's all part of the immersive experience,' a host mentions, noticing our perplexed looks. Shoes tucked away, we pick up audio guides and kids' activity packs before embarking on the journey. The museum was designed using interdisciplinary techniques from the worlds of lighting, film, audio and virtual reality.

One great feature is that rather than prescribing a staid route around static info boards, the audio guide follows your lead, identifying where you are in the museum – ideal for kids that like to hop from one thing to the next, following heart rather than head.

On one side of the building, a series of interconnected gardens offer a walk through 2,000 years of gardening history. The other side explores the science of plants. The boys leap at the chance to push mud around and sniff the artificially created smells of all kinds of flowers. Buttons, drawers, spyholes and video footage keep everyone thoroughly enthralled, whether learning about the philosophy of Japanese gardens or why poo is a fertiliser. The finale comes with a series of virtual reality headsets that transport us to Rome's Tivoli gardens and the Babylonstoren wine estate in South Africa. 'Don't look down!' the kids screech, loving their first VR experience. After 90 minutes we tear ourselves away, but could happily spend longer here.

Leaving the museum, full of excitement, we stop at a viewpoint by an old Roman road. An unassuming bench offers one of the best views of the gardens and from here the boys plot our way around from patchwork kitchen gardens to a walled labyrinth. Running from one spot to the next, we take in highlights include the egg-shaped parabola, home to over 500 varieties of apple, and a cheeky frog that sprays hysterical kids with water as they leap about its giant lily pad. After a farm-to-fork feast from the café, eaten in the laid-back 'winter garden' greenhouse, we laze about in hanging straw pods imagining what it would be like to be a family of dormice. Filled with hyper-local produce and garden inspiration, we've come to the perfect end of a thoroughly immersive day.

ADDED ADVENTURE:
MOORS & HILLS, GORGES & SEA

Sandwiched between Bristol and Exmoor, Somerset is a huge and varied county, offering everything from fossil-filled beaches to hill walking, awe-inspiring gorges to country gardens. Rather than spend all holiday in the car, pick a chunk to explore and go slow. That might mean heading west, where Victorian seaside towns like Minehead and Watchet rub alongside wild moors and coast; exploring the gentle rural communities and hilly Quantocks around Taunton; or journeying further north, where the Mendips are home to dramatic gorges and centuries of legends. Wherever you are, you're sure to find all manner of community farms and orchards offering visitors a slice of quiet country life.

EXMOOR NATIONAL PARK & SURROUNDS

The medieval village of **Dunster** is the gateway to Exmoor National Park, which spreads across 267 square miles from northwestern Somerset to Devon. In addition to a useful visitor centre, offering maps and wildlife guides for the park, the village has over 200 listed buildings beneath towering **Dunster Castle** (⊘ nationaltrust.org.uk). The castle, which has seen 1,000 years of history, includes a working mill, walled garden, subtropical gardens and an outdoor theatre; it's easy to spend a whole day here. Although pretty, the high street can get a little choked with cars, so for a quieter explore veer off towards the priory and dovecote. And for something even more peaceful, seek out the **community orchard** just above the village, accessible only by footpaths. Complete with picnic benches, it offers beautiful views across the Bristol Channel. A highlight of the year in these parts, and a splendid snapshot of rural life, is the **Dunster Country Fair** (⊘ dunstercountryfair.co.uk), held every July. From horse trials to bird of prey shows and brass bands, there's something for everyone.

"A highlight of the year in these parts, and a splendid snapshot of rural life, is the Dunster Country Fair."

Three miles west, **Minehead** is a busy beach resort with faded Victorian mansions and a huge Butlin's. The beach's sweeping sands are ideal for little ones and family games of football and cricket. **Hidden Histories of Minehead** (⊘ minehead.storywalks.info) offers a series of self-led walking tours, which is a great way to explore beyond the beach. Alternatively, the **Maritime Mile Heritage Trail** (⊘ mineheadbay. co.uk) celebrates Minehead's myths and legends via a mile-long open-air gallery and app.

Minehead is also the start of the epic 630-mile **South West Coast Path** (⊘ southwestcoastpath.org.uk) which skirts up and down cliffs along the coast to Poole. The first stage, from Minehead to Porlock Weir, comprises 8.9 miles of ups and downs along steep clifftops and through wooded combes.

---

1 Porlock Weir. **2** Dunster community orchard. **3** The Tarr Steps, Exmoor National Park. **4** Exmoor Pony Centre. ▶

HELEN HOTSON/S

ADRIAN BAKER/S

EXMOOR PONY CENTRE

SS

THE COMMUNITY FARM

Denny Ln, Chew Magna BS40 8SZ *&* thecommunityfarm.co.uk; age: all; intrepid level: ①

'It's a comma!' Leah says excitedly as a huddle of kids and grown-ups gather around. A few of the kids mark another tick in their wildlife sheets. The bright-orange jagged winged butterfly is hovering around a patch of nettles, oblivious to its new-found fame. 'We haven't seen any for a while, so it's good to have one back,' she continues. Having never seen one before, we share in the joy; its large, delicate wings are unmissable.

We're on a wildlife tour around The Community Farm, a 15-acre site overlooking Chew Valley Lake north of the Mendips. Owned by 200 shareholders and relying on volunteers, the farm was established on the back of local needs – to deliver healthy food to the local community using local suppliers. Its seasonal veg boxes deliver around Bath, Bristol, the Chew Valley and Frome.

We're visiting as part of **Valley Fest** (*&* valleyfest.co.uk), Yeo Valley Farm's annual music and local produce festival, which is taking place in the neighbouring field, but the farm is open to visitors year-round. Community Farmer Days are a great introduction to the farm, and children are welcome as long as they're willing to get their hands dirty!

Leah is one of the volunteers showing us around today, evidently proud of every living thing that's thriving among the farm's organic produce. 'Remember to get up close, kids!' she reminds the group as kids and adults immerse themselves in the micro, spotting everything from ladybirds to cardinal beetles and dragonflies.

Our tour weaves between polytunnels, greenhouses and patches of wildlife-friendly flowers, shrubs and trees. The boys decide they'd like to pack up and move into The Roundhouse, a grass-roofed eco-hut on the edge of the farm.

'Why do you think it's important to encourage birds?' Leah asks some of the children, pointing out bird boxes along a row of trees on the farm's perimeter. 'Because

Porlock Weir itself is one of Exmoor's most idyllic coastal spots. Ancient woodland towers above a tiny harbour and thatched cottages, unchanged for centuries. The surrounding wild coastal landscapes include a submarine forest, salt marsh and exposed stony beach. There's a hotel, a tea room, a couple of pubs, a few crafting shops and the **Porlock Bay Oysters hut** (*&* porlockbayoysters.co.uk) selling locally farmed oysters (ring ahead to find out about experience days when you can farm and shuck your own oysters). Beyond that, Porlock Weir is all about exploring the untouched landscape and the beach.

Moments outside Porlock Weir, **Exmoor Adventures** (*&* exmooradventures.co.uk) has heaps of family fun on offer including

they eat the insects!' one pipes up. 'Yes, and we plant flowering plants in the polytunnels so the butterflies head in there and eat the aphids,' she continues. Leah tells us about the farm's organic status, which means no pesticides (the birds and butterflies do that job), and regular checks from the Soil Association. Thanks to efforts to improve biodiversity through a pond, wildflowers and hedgerows, the farm is home to skylarks, woodpeckers, yellowhammers and badgers.

It's the mini beasts that steal the show today, however. Despite the funfair rides, music and circus games enticing us back to the Valley Fest, the kids linger on the farm long after the tour, counting and marking down insect finds. It's tough to compete with nature on an English summer's day.

MAHTOLA EAGLE-LIPPIATT

stand-up paddleboarding, kayaking and mountain biking – there's something for all ages and abilities. Back towards Porlock village, you can step back in time at **Allerford Museum** (⊘ allerfordmuseum.org. uk), a Victorian school building housing the **West Somerset Rural Life Museum** and a photographic archive.

Exmoor National Park (⊘ exmoor-nationalpark.gov.uk) is an International Dark Sky Reserve where heather-clad hills drop down to a dramatic coastline and deer and ponies roam wild. The **Exmoor Pony Centre** (⊘ moorlandmousietrust.org.uk), operated by the Moorland Mousie Trust, which has given 500 Exmoor ponies a home since 1998, is a wonderful experience for kids of all ages. Seasoned riders will want to trek out onto the moor, but for beginners there are muck-out sessions and arena rides, led by the most patient and passionate staff. The centre is near the famous **Tarr Steps** – an ancient bridge – and the market town of **Dulverton**.

TAUNTON & THE QUANTOCK HILLS

Given its extensive rail links to London and the Midlands, the market town of **Taunton** is a popular base for exploring the **Quantock Hills** (∂ quantockhills.com). Market days and summer festivals liven up the otherwise sleepy town, while the **Museum of Somerset** (∂ swheritage. org.uk), housed in the town's 12th-century castle, is a good rainy-day option, offering regular family activities, historical re-enactments and story-time sessions.

For a slow railway adventure, check out the **West Somerset Railway** (∂ west-somerset-railway.co.uk), the longest heritage railway in England. From Taunton, you can travel by bus to the first stop at Bishops Lydeard, where the train rolls 20 miles through the Quantocks towards the coast all the way to Minehead. A Rover Pass lets you hop on and off along the route: **Crowcombe Heathfield** is the best place to jump off for a walk around the Quantocks; **Watchet** is a pretty harbour town with a boat museum and plenty of fish and chips; and **Blue Anchor** is a sleepy beach and village.

A few miles north of Taunton, **Hestercombe House & Gardens** (∂ hestercombe.com) offer a wonderfully slow day out, particularly in spring and summer when the gardens buzz, hum and flutter with wildlife. The garden's known history starts in the 13th century, when a medieval document references 'my Lord of Hestercombe's garden'. Since then, the gardens have become the main attraction, and visitors are invited to explore 50 acres of formal plantings, lakes and wildflower meadows. Nature is king throughout; kids will love the bat cam, stepping stones and the Charcoal Burner's Camp, a natural play area hidden in the woods. Follies are a big attraction, too, from the Witch House to the Gothic Alcove. Look out for holiday camps and outdoor theatre in the holidays, and take a rug and picnic for the ultimate slow day in beautiful surrounds.

1 Hestercombe Gardens. **2** Looking for clues on the Glastonbury Treasure Trail. **3** Cheddar Gorge. ▶

GLASTONBURY,
THE MENDIP HILLS & SURROUNDS

Northern Somerset is dominated by the limestone plateau of the Mendip Hills, where the soft rock creates an impressive landscape of steep-sided hills, gorges and caves. On the southern side of the Mendips, at **Wookey Hole** ($\mathcal{O}$ wookey.co.uk), one of England's largest cave networks, a huge visitor experience gives you access to 20 caves, including a rare rock formation chamber. Eight miles north, **Cheddar Gorge and Caves** ($\mathcal{O}$ cheddargorge.co.uk), some three miles long and 400ft deep, is the UK's largest limestone landscape, its grassy banks giving way to plummeting cliffs. Here, the **Museum of Prehistory** is crammed with cave paintings and archaeological artefacts, but the dramatic ravines and folds speak for themselves. It's possible to walk through the gorge (which is managed by the National Trust) without paying to enter the official attraction. Arrive early in the morning if you can, to avoid the crowds. The **Cheddar Gorge Cheese Company** ($\mathcal{O}$ cheddaronline.co.uk) invites visitors to watch cheese-making and sample the favourite English staple.

Fourteen miles south, legend and mysticism pervade every inch of **Glastonbury**, which has been a magnet for pilgrims both Christian and Pagan for centuries. Tale upon tale will fuel little and large imaginations alike – telling of the cave under the Tor that leads to the fairy realm of Annwn, for example, or of the site of King Arthur's last battle, the Isle of Avalon. Given the Tor's unusual geology, towering 520ft above the flat-as-can-be Somerset Levels, it's hard not to get swept up in the mysticism, which is of course part of the appeal.

Roads surrounding the Tor are narrow and parking is forbidden, so it's best to walk up. The four-mile **Glastonbury Tor and Abbey Circular Walk** is a great option and includes the chance to romp around the abbey ruins. More adventurous is the eight-mile pilgrimage route from **Wells Cathedral to Glastonbury Abbey** ($\mathcal{O}$ britishpilgrimage.org), which follows country lanes and footpaths. Glastonbury town is worth a stop, teeming with curious shops and characters. The **Glastonbury Treasure Trail** (purchase from $\mathcal{O}$ treasuretrails.co.uk), on which kids solve clues linked to architecture and history, is a good way to keep kids busy while exploring.

If crowds at Glastonbury Tor are off-putting, try **Burrow Mump**, a smaller version ten miles southwest, where a similar tower stands atop a mound surrounded by the Levels. Also just a few miles outside Glastonbury, the **RSPB Reserve at Ham Wall** (⬦ rspb.org.uk) is an accessible place to get a sense of the waterlogged Levels and the wildlife that thrives there, including kingfishers and bitterns.

Fourteen miles east of Glastonbury, market town **Bruton** is an arty enclave of crafts and makers with a healthy dollop of brunch and bakeries. Although some of the contemporary art may be lost on younger kids, the **Hauser & Wirth gallery** (⬦ hauserwirth.com) welcomes kids with hands-on activities on the first Saturday of every month – call ahead to check age requirements.

PRACTICALITIES

FAMILY-FRIENDLY SLEEPS
Burcott Mill Guesthouse
⬦ burcottmill.com. This guesthouse sits in a pretty Grade II-listed Victorian flour mill beneath the Mendip Hills five miles north of Glastonbury. The play area, chickens, orchard and guinea-pig run keep kids happy. There's also a self-catering cottage across the road, next to the pub, the Burcott Inn, which is handy for evening meals. The owners of Burcott Mill are happy to listen to baby monitors in both the guesthouse and the cottage if you want a night off.
Middlestone Farm ⬦ middlestonefarm. com. A family-run all-singing, all-dancing glamping site in the far west of Somerset, close to the Devon border. Huge safari-style tents, with private bathrooms and kitchens, come kitted out with children's crockery and cutlery, trugs of toys and snug-as-can-be cubby-hole beds. Alongside farm tours and ample space for running around, there's an on-site play area and ride-on tractors.

Old Rectory House
⬦ oldrectoryhousesomerset.com. Moments from Kilve, in the Quantocks, an uncrowded beach famous for fossil hunting, Old Rectory House is a luxury self-catering farm stay offering two shepherd's huts and The Coach House. The latter sleeps eight, and comes with a private heated pool and access to a walled garden, wildflower meadow and croquet lawn. There's a games room with table football, board games and Nintendo Switch (shh, don't tell the kids).
Somerset Yurts ⬦ somersetyurts. co.uk. Across three acres of fields on a working dairy farm in the Quantock Hills, Somerset Yurts is a simple site with far-reaching views and ample space. A communal barn provides a kitchen, hot showers and flushing toilets. Local favourites The Monkton Inn and The Maypole Inn are both within walking distance for a break from campfire cooking.

KID-FRIENDLY EATS

Driftwood Cafe
driftwoodblueanchor. This quaint wooden chalet serves seafood, sandwiches, fish and chips, breakfasts, cakes and coffee overlooking the sea, moments from the Blue Anchor steam railway station. It's quite small and can get busy in peak season, so it's worth arriving early to bag a table in the sunny garden. The sheltered veranda is ideal for sea views on colder days.

Old Tannery Restaurant and Bar
redbrickbuilding.co.uk. Situated on the ground floor of the Red Brick community hub in Glastonbury, this restaurant is all about local produce and suppliers. The friendly atmosphere is thanks to the building's community ethos, with events and workshops running throughout the year. The restaurant is open all day and children are welcomed with a kids' menu and colouring-in kit.

The Stables betterfood.co.uk. Occupying a converted stable block at the entrance to the Hestercombe estate, The Stables feels like a treat while welcoming families in a relaxed and spacious setting. Most dishes are sprinkled with a touch of garden colour, be it from fruit or petals, and the afternoon tea is particularly in keeping with the English garden surrounds. There's a courtyard for sunnier days.

Ziangs Workshop ziangsworkshop.com. A handy spot if you tire of fish and chips, this is a brilliantly unexpected option with take-away-only picnic benches overlooking Porlock Weir. The family here has been cooking Southeast Asian street food since the 1950s; today, a noodle-bar-style menu makes it easy for kids to create their ideal dish.

BEFORE YOU GO

Somerset is packed with local produce – it's hard to come across a pub or eatery that doesn't offer it, even if only the cider and beer. If you're self-catering and would rather cook up your own Somerset storm, check out **Local Food Direct** (localfooddirect.co.uk), a Community Benefit Society that delivers produce from small-scale farms to addresses across the county. Weekly deliveries take place on Thursday and Friday.

MORE INFO

Somerset Tourist Board
visitsomerset.co.uk

6
BRISTOL

England's most eco-minded city bursts with enough green innovation, engineering feats and urban nature to set little minds awhirl.

TOP FAMILY EXPERIENCE

A TRIO OF MIND-EXPANDING MUSEUMS: SS GREAT BRITAIN, M SHED & WE THE CURIOUS

BEST FOR KIDS AGED:	6+
WHEN TO GO:	Year-round
INTREPID LEVEL:	①
ADDED ADVENTURE:	Boat trips, art galleries, green parks, cycling trails, nature reserves, a mighty bridge, street art
TIME:	Three days

HANDS-ON DISCOVERIES: ENGINEERING FEATS, COOL SCIENCE & LOCAL CHANGEMAKERS

SS *Great Britain*: Great Western Dockyard, Gas Ferry Rd, BS1 6TY ⌀ ssgreatbritain.org;
M Shed: Princes Wharf, Wapping Rd, BS1 4RN ⌀ bristolmuseums.org.uk;
We The Curious: 1 Millennium Square, Anchor Rd, BS1 5DB ⌀ wethecurious.org

Although three quite separate attractions, these Bristol museums are world-class when it comes to engaging kids, putting a wonderfully contemporary slant on history and society in Bristol and beyond. There's no traipsing through stagnant info boards or displays unchanged since the 1980s: SS *Great Britain*, M Shed and We The Curious offer families a fully immersive journey through science, engineering and Bristolian history. They are also within easy walking distance from each other, each hugging the canal that meanders past

Millennium Square – a focal point of the city, thronging with visitors and locals – and Bristol Marina. This makes it convenient to dart between all three if energy levels are good, or pick one for a more relaxed meander.

We start our voyage on Isambard Kingdom Brunel's **SS *Great Britain***, which is moored up next to Bristol Marina. Arriving by boat is fun; it's a 30-minute boat trip from the back of Temple Meads train station. 'Discover the ship that changed the world,' a man dressed in Victorian clothing cries to anyone milling around the museum entrance as we make our way in. It sounds hyperbolic, but there's some truth in it. The SS *Great Britain* was the world's first ocean liner, and Brunel's clever engineering, using a propeller on an iron ship for the first time, made her famous. In 1845 she took her maiden voyage as the first iron steamer to cross the Atlantic Ocean; the crossing took only 14 days.

The museum focuses in part on these engineering feats. We begin under the ship's hull in the Dry Dock, which sits below glass, creating an underwater feel. The huge propeller is a highlight, as is spotting repaired holes and cracks in the hull – damaged during her final voyage around Cape Horn in the early 1880s, the ship was retired to the Falkland Islands and used as a wool store for nearly 50 years before being left to rot. Rescued in the 1970s, SS *Great Britain* was towed 8,000 miles back to Bristol, a trip which took 87 days. The boys have to be torn away from an interactive drawing game, using a computer program to design their own ships and testing whether they sink or float.

Back upstairs and it's time to wander below deck, through dining rooms, doctor's rooms, kitchens and dorm spaces. There's much hilarity when an automated voice shouts 'Oi!' as the kids try to enter the toilet. But besides from soaking up the atmosphere, much of this part of the museum is about the characters that travelled on SS *Great Britain*. A passport-sticker-collection game gets kids to identity certain people, from Yot, one of a group of Chinese men who boarded in St Helena and sadly died on his way to Australia, to Hester Elizabeth Baird, one of the first women to work on board. Themes such as identity and immigration are cleverly woven throughout.

Off the ship once more, a 'Being Brunel' exhibition explores the life and work of the famed engineer. Though it's designed for older kids,

◄ The Dry Dock, SS *Great Britain*.

my six-year-old still enjoys it, particularly the 'draw a perfect circle' test and a bone-rattling ride on a broad-gauge carriage. The final section of the museum explores what our world would look like without Brunel's propeller, which now helps us move people and goods all over the world, as well as generate electricity from wind.

A 15-minute walk further along the canal, past houseboats and disused rail tracks, **M Shed** is a huge modern block sandwiched between the canal and shipping containers repurposed to house cafés and independent shops. You can't miss the huge electric cranes lined up like robots outside the museum; these are relics of the port's 1950s heyday. At certain times of the year, it's possible to tour the cranes and head out from the museum on historic boat trips – the 'Pyronaut' fireboat, which helped to put out the blazes of the Blitz in the 1940s, is a highlight.

"Inside, M Shed leads visitors through Bristolian history but with a pleasing focus on the contemporary."

Inside, M Shed leads visitors through Bristolian history but with a pleasing focus on the contemporary. There's heaps to do and see, from listening to the Bristolian accent on headphones to a dedicated exhibition on Bristol's links with the slave trade and the city's various communities today. 'There's John!' one of the boys shouts as we spot John Nation, our street art guide (see box, page 108), on the walls in an exhibition of unsung Bristol heroes.

Back out into fresh air and it's time to cross the water (we opt for the bridge, but you can hop on the ferry again) to Millennium Square, where **We The Curious** sits next to a huge mirrored dome (hours of fun in itself!). A merry band of 'Bristol pirate' buskers sing sea shanties while we eat a picnic lunch in the sunshine. Inside, We The Curious blows little and big minds alike. This vast science museum is entirely hands-on; you could easily spend days absorbing all there is to learn and play.

With the six-year-old in tow, we make a beeline for the more playful aspects: running in a human hamster wheel to power enough water to make sand from rock; moving sand to reflect the contours of a projected map; watching parachutes float down on to a huge

---

1 SS *Great Britain*. **2** Exhibits at the M Shed. **3** We The Curious. **4** Being Brunel exhibition, SS *Great Britain*. ▶

trampoline. Upstairs, there's a planetarium, along with opportunities to experiment with computer animation and explore the inner workings of musical instruments.

Older kids may get more out of the opening exhibition space, which explores themes like colour and our bodies through a medical, scientific and sociological lens. How are rainbows created? Why are humans drawn to colours? What do rainbows mean in different societies? The curation is refreshingly holistic and relevant; exactly what's needed to stimulate the creative and scientific minds of the future.

ADDED ADVENTURE: GREEN SPACES, COMMUNITY SPIRIT & STREET ART – A VIBRANT CITY ON A MANAGABLE SCALE

England's most populated southwestern city, bordering Gloucestershire and Somerset, Bristol is connected to the Severn Estuary and Bristol Channel via the River Avon – a shipping route that has shaped much of the city's history. The city centre isn't the prettiest; it has suffered from poor post-war planning and a heavy focus on roads and traffic that seem to slice it in half. But dig beneath the surface and you will find a place buzzing with intriguing and unexpected green spaces, community hotspots and contemporary culture. There are 12 nature reserves dotted throughout and around the city, so a dose of wilderness and respite from concrete is never far away – and, since 2015, when Bristol was awarded the title of European Green Capital, it's become a poster child for eco innovation, home to the likes of The Soil Association, Sustrans and Triodos Bank. It's a city that's happy to go deeper than picture-postcard moments, and visitors are rewarded for doing the same.

CITY CENTRE

Besides its trio of superb museums (page 97) and street art (see box, page 108), Bristol's busy city centre offers pockets of green, culture and history that are well worth exploring.

One of the best ways to understand the city's geography is to take to the water. **Bristol Packet Boat Trips** (⊘ bristolpacket.co.uk) run popular 45-minute harbour tours from Gas Ferry Road (close to SS

Great Britain) on pretty *Tower Belle*. They also run an hour-long **Avon Gorge Cruise**, which heads into the tidal part of the Avon to admire the gorge and suspension bridge.

Also by the water, on Bristol harbourside, the **Arnolfini** (⊘ arnolfini. org.uk) is packed with contemporary art and has free family film screenings and activities on the last Saturday of every month. A ten-minute walk away, in the middle of town, there's something for everyone – from retro records to a spice emporium – at the quaint **St Nicholas Market** (**f**); on Saturdays, neighbouring **Corn Street** turns into a lively flea market. The market extends indoors into the **Corn Exchange**, where cafés and craft stalls spill into one another beneath beautiful 18th-century ceilings.

Further west, **Bristol Museum and Art Gallery** (⊘ bristolmuseums. org.uk) has nine galleries hosting art from around the globe and an art-themed play area for under-sevens called Curiosity. Nearby, **Brandon Hill** is the oldest park in Bristol, with beautiful vistas across the waterways and city. There's a play area and a mini nature reserve and, when it's open, you can climb the 105ft **Cabot Tower** to get the best views.

For a little more activity, the 13-mile off-road **Bristol to Bath Cycle Path** (⊘ sustrans.org) conveniently connects Temple Meads Station with Bath Spa Station, so it's possible to ride to Bath one way and take the train back. **Bristol Cycle Shack** (⊘ bristolcycleshack.co.uk), five minutes from Temple Meads Station, at the start of the path, rents bikes.

MONTPELIER & SURROUNDS

North of the city centre, the **Gloucester Road** and **Montpelier** areas, where Victorian terraced houses line leafy residential streets, offer a laidback contrast. The main high street, Gloucester Road, is strung with independent boutiques, charity shops and cafés; ideal for a sunny Sunday brunch and browse. A couple of roads east, **St Andrews Park** has a lot going on for its size. The Victorian landscaped gardens include a large playground and paddling pool and, a testament to Bristol's community spirit, a café that has been serving hot drinks to the neighbourhood for years and which locals recently rallied to save.

A little further east, **St Werburghs City Farm** (⊘ swcityfarm.co.uk) has been connecting people and nature since 1980. There's an adventure playground, organic café in a crazy hobbit-style building, community garden and smallholding with pigs, sheep, goats and chickens. Just

103

LIFE CYCLES

FOOD CHAINS

ALGAE

MAKE AN ANIMAL

south of the farm, **The Church** (⊘ theclimbingacademy.com) is an indoor climbing and bouldering centre popular with families (ring for age restrictions).

CLIFTON & THE DOWNS

West of the city, perched on a hillside above the spectacular Avon Gorge, the smart suburb of **Clifton** and the surrounding green space, known as the **Downs**, hug the Avon River as it meanders through chalky cliffs and steep-sided woods. While there is much to enjoy in Clifton's upmarket shopping arcade, leafy Georgian streets and spacious parkland, the main reason to head out here is to admire Brunel's epic **Clifton Suspension Bridge** (⊘ cliftonbridge.org.uk). It's amazing to consider that Brunel was just 24 when he was commissioned to design a structure that could span the gorge. Before crossing the bridge, explore the **Clifton Observatory** (⊘ cliftonobservatory.com) a former mill that sits on top of a Celtic fort. There's a 360° observatory, a small museum covering the history of the bridge, a huge camera obscura, and tunnels down to the Giant's Cave, a secret lookout over the gorge.

The crossing itself entails a thrilling five-minute walk 331ft above the gorge. Afterwards, pop in to the visitor centre to see displays on the work of Brunel and the mechanics of suspension bridges. Also on this side of the bridge, **Leigh Woods** (⊘ nationaltrust.org.uk), a huge bank of forest tumbling down to the Avon, is criss-crossed with footpaths, while the 850-acre **Ashton Court Estate** (⬛) is another popular big green space with natural play areas and woodland trails, mountain-bike tracks (and rental) and a miniature railway. The estate is particularly popular in summer for the **Bristol International Balloon Fiesta** (⊘ bristolballoonfiesta.co.uk), a sight to behold as hundreds of hot air balloons ascend into the sky.

Back on the Clifton side, following the Avon north for a couple of miles brings you to **Old Sneed Park Nature Reserve** (⊘ oldsneedparknaturereserve.org), which is a brilliant place for bug hunting. It borders the Woodland Trust's **Bishop Knoll Wood**, all crumbling follies and ancient trees, where there are plenty of opportunities for den building.

◄ **1** Taking in the views from Cabot Tower. **2** Interactive fun at Windmill Hill Farm. **3** Exploring Bristol by bike. **4** St Nicholas Market.

PRACTICALITIES

FAMILY-FRIENDLY SLEEPS

Brooks Guesthouse

⊘ brooksguesthousebristol.com. Brooks Guesthouse has a wonderfully easy-going and welcoming feel thanks to an honesty bar, lounge area, huge breakfast buffet and courtyard. Rooms are a little tired and small, but given its central location, just off the cobbled streets of St Nicholas Market, it's very affordable and has various family rooms. The Rooftop Rockets, converted airstream campers, offer the chance to glamp on the roof – a particular hit with teens.

Mollie's ⊘ mollies.com. Sitting slap bang on the motorway north of the city, Mollie's shouldn't appeal as much as it does for a city break, but that's the skill of the Soho House team. Rooms are huge and surprisingly quiet, beds are comfy, and Mollie's Diner next door will fill the whole family up with waffles, eggs and pancakes in the morning. There's a large lounge area and pretty courtyard garden with help-yourself snacks and hot drinks.

Paintworks Apartments

⊘ paintworks-apartments.bristol-hotels-uk.com. These one- and two-bed flats in a former paint factory on Bath Road, close to the River Avon, make up for being a little out of town with all the comforts of self-catering luxury. Indulgent touches include giant TVs, walk-in wet rooms and surround sound systems, and décor is quirky – huge murals abound and one loft apartment has a fixie bike hung to the wall. There's free parking, plus cots, highchairs and plenty of board games and puzzles.

YHA Bristol ⊘ yha.org.uk. Housed in a former waterfront grain house, this large youth hostel is moments from all the main sites, just across the water from Millennium Square. It has several private en-suite rooms and self-catering kitchens, and a large bar and café serves meals throughout the day, including breakfast. Bike storage, high chairs and baby-changing facilities are on offer.

KID-FRIENDLY EATS

Aqua ⊘ aqua-restaurant.com. Aqua is a small Bath and Bristol Italian restaurant chain committed to local, organic food. The waterside restaurant, Aqua Welshback, is a great central spot for lunch or dinner, with a no-fuss kids' menu and large outdoor terrace.

Better Food Company ⊘ betterfood.co.uk. Organic, local and ethical, the Better Food Company encapsulates Bristol's green ethos while serving up simple lunches and baked snacks. The plastic-free shop, deli and café has branches in Gloucester Road and Clifton, and a newer store in Wapping Wharf with outside seating between waterways.

◀ **1** Clifton Suspension Bridge. **2** Leigh Woods.

'WHERE THE WALL' STREET ART TOUR WITH JOHN NATION

City Hall, College Green, BS1 5TR ⟨⟩ wherethewall.com; age: 8+ (no age restrictions but younger children may find it tricky to keep up with the group); intrepid level: ①

'I'm John, and these devices only come in Bristolian so I hope you can all hear and understand me OK,' our guide soundchecks, booming into our earpieces with a distinct Bristol twang. 'It's like we're undercover police,' I joke to the six-year-old, hoping he'll keep up with a two-hour commentary about Bristol's buzzing street art scene.

'We've got two hours and I've been part of the street art scene for over 35 years, so there's a lot to get through – let's get started,' John sets off as we follow on. He's not wrong; later that day we spot him in M Shed – Bristol's brilliant local history museum (page 100) – celebrated as a local champion for his commitment to the street art movement.

It's a cold January day but spirits seem high as we kick off with a Banksy, just across the road from City Hall, where the tour starts. 'Without Banksy, lots of people wouldn't know about Bristol's street art, but he's just a part of it. This piece, *Well Hung Lover*, nicely sums up his relationship with the city – and the police,' he continues as we huddle on the pavement just yards from the monochrome stencil image.

The image shows a naked man hanging out of a window while an angry-looking man, with an anxious woman behind him, leans out of the window (wondering where he's gone?). Blue paint is splattered across the picture and other faded splodges to the side reveal where the blue paint has been scrubbed off – revealing attempts to both ruin and save the artwork.

'This was painted illegally in broad daylight in 2006. Banksy hired scaffolders and dressed in decorating clothes. At the time, councillors were meeting in that room just opposite to discuss regulating where artists can spray. It's never been about regulation and control, so Banksy brought that argument to their front door,' John explains.

'Sneaky,' observes the eight-year-old, who seems to be following OK. We learn that this was a watershed moment in the city because Bristol City Council decided to allow the artwork to remain – the first time they had not removed a Banksy piece from a public space.

We wander on, weaving between back streets to avoid traffic and see more examples

No 1 Harbourside 🔲. Vegan and veggie dishes alongside children's favourites like fish-finger sandwiches and pasta at this central, Sustainable Restaurant Association-approved restaurant. Kids are so welcome they're given colouring pads and toys on the way in.

Pieminister ⟨⟩ pieminister.co.uk. Although it is now a nationwide chain, Pieminister began its days in Bristol, flinging open its doors to pie

of legal and illegal street art along the way. John talks non-stop, keeping everyone's minds off the drizzle and in a cocoon of creative thinking. Stops include Nelson Street, where the kids delight in being the first to spot huge murals that stretch up the sides of mid-century concrete blocks. This is a city where looking up pays off.

'This is all legal,' John explains, as he talks us through the work produced during the See No Evil spraying festival that he and street artist Inkie put on in Bristol in 2012. The kids are fully absorbed, pointing out bits of art all over the buildings, even between church archways, where Andy Council has painted a scene of the city skyline composed of his signature fantastical creatures. Nelson Street feels like the heart of the action, but that's before we step into Stokes Croft – a haven of independent shops and music venues. Barely a building here is left untouched.

'Woahhhh,' my eight-year-old cries as we approach the The Full Moon pub, painted head-to-toe in a spacescape. Around the corner, we stumble upon some people spraying. 'Is that legal?' the kids whisper, kickstarting a little group discussion about what's acceptable and what's not. Rather timely, our final stop, Banksy's *The Mild Mild West* (1998), more explicitly demonstrates

tensions with police – a teddy bear figure fights back at a trio of riot police. We all walk away with more questions than answers, which I think is exactly what Banksy would want.

HOLLY TUPPEN

lovers in Stokes Croft in 2003. The menu is simple as can be, offering a variety of veggie, vegan and meat pies with sides of mash and peas and gravy. The ice-cream sundaes are hard to resist, too.

BEFORE YOU GO

The toppling of Edward Colston's statue in Bristol in 2020 sparked nationwide debates about the links between heritage, history and the slave trade. Since then, **Bristol Museums** has been working with local history teachers, academics and black teenagers from Bristol and London to create a book explaining the city's link with the slave trade. It's a great resource to help kids understand the past and the impact it has on people today. *Bristol and Transatlantic Slavery* is available to buy at ⊘ shop. bristolmuseums.org.uk.

MORE INFO
Bristol Museums
⊘ bristolmuseums.org.uk
Bristol Tourist Board
⊘ visitbristol.co.uk

7
THE NEW FOREST

The New Forest, designed by a conqueror,
is perfect for young explorers looking
for their first slow adventures.

REVERIE ON THE RIVER

Bailey's Hard, Bailey's Hard Lane, Beaulieu SO42 7YF ⏣ newforestactivities.co.uk; enquire which sessions are best suited to the age of your children before you book

'Seal!' squeaks my eldest, with binoculars in one hand and paddle in the other, making his attention-grabbing arm-waving somewhat treacherous for the rest of us trying to balance our four-person canoe. Within seconds, eight or so kids, some striking out in solo vessels and others with nervous parents sitting akimbo, have swung heads to catch a glimpse of a big old grey seal wallowing no more than six yards away. Also angling for a peep, a stand-up paddleboarder comes splashing down into the water, sending the seal on his way to ripples of laughter as kids and parents alike ease into the new watery surroundings.

We're moments into New Forest Activities' 90-minute family canoeing trip, a wonderfully accessible way to get all ages and abilities on to an exclusive chunk of the Beaulieu River – one of the world's very few

private waterways. The seal sighting is a testament to how well protected the river is. The brackish estuary, which meets the Solent just four miles downstream, is a Site of Special Scientific Interest and teeming with wildlife carefully monitored by Natural England. 'From May to September, thousands of moon jellyfish float down the river on tidal currents. They're completely harmless, so if you see one, it's fine to scoop it up, have a good look, and carefully put it back,' Joe, our guide, explains as we paddle in circles close to the shore.

We, a group ranging from 18 months to about 70 years old, soon realise how foolproof the Canadian-style open-top canoes are and feel confident enough to venture farther. 'The tide dictates our trips,' Joe explains, 'and today we'll be heading upstream to the heart of Beaulieu village where we'll turn around.' If we'd travelled downstream, we would have reached Buckler's Hard, the working hub of the river, once home to Admiral Nelson's shipbuilding yard. Beyond that, the river dribbles out into the sea at Needs Ore, one of the UK's finest birdwatching spots.

Joe continues, 'Everyone can go at their own pace, but I'll point out a few meeting places so we can concertina up and down the river and stay in touch.' Having canoed before, my boys bolt off at a pace more suited to an Olympic training session than a gentle meander. Thankfully, Joe's suggested wildlife-spotting slows things down. Before setting off, each child

"Having canoed before, my boys bolt off at a pace more suited to an Olympic training session than a gentle meander."

gets a pair of binoculars, a bucket and a magnifying glass to set the nature-spotting tone. 'Our first meeting point will be just around the bend, where I want you to look for a huge nest,' he explains just before we glide out of earshot.

Beaulieu means 'beautiful place' in French, and it doesn't take long to see why the river's name was changed from the River Exe many years ago. Below the village of Beaulieu, the river is tidal, coursing through reeds and ancient woodland undisturbed but for the occasional mansion with manicured lawns tumbling down to the water's edge. A couple of *Swallows and Amazons*-style traditional wooden sailing boats flutter by and, besides a few kayakers and our motley crew, the river is tranquil as can be.

◄ **1** The village of Beaulieu. **2** Canoeing along the Beaulieu River.

'Slow down, boys, you're in kingfisher territory there,' Joe calls as we tuck in close to the shore where the heavy lower boughs of 100-year-old oaks kiss the water. Everyone stops paddling to marvel at the silence and set beady eyes on the low-hanging branches, hoping to spot dashes of brilliant blue darting between the greenery – often the only glimpse of a kingfisher you get, Joe had explained before we left. Alas, no kingfishers today, but another canoe claims the first sighting of the incongruous, giant nest.

Beyond a cluster of redshanks, chattering and picking at the river's boggy edge, a dead oak trunk soars up to a vast, artificial nest. 'The river is a bit like a service station for ospreys on their way from Scotland to winter in West Africa. They're always happy to use a ready-made eyrie for hunting or breeding from,' Joe explains, as we crook our necks looking out for the raptors' vast wingspan soaring above. Although we don't manage to spot an osprey, a buzzard provides much excitement ruffling its feathers in a nearby tree, totally unphased by a sea of binoculars turning for closer inspection.

The remainder of the trip drifts by in a similar state of reverie. The river's natural world is so compelling that the boys forget about their canoe race as we glide back alongside the mansions, the redshanks, the pretty wooden sailing boats, and all the nooks and crannies of the river we now know a little more intimately.

ADDED ADVENTURE: BACK-TO-NATURE FUN

Spanning some 200 square miles from Southampton to Bournemouth, the New Forest is neither new nor just a forest. The patchwork of heathlands, river valleys and deciduous woods were lumped together as a royal hunting estate for William the Conqueror almost 1,000 years ago. Today, it's somewhat more accessible, with over 125 miles of marked walking and cycling paths, in the national park, ideal for families itching to explore. Whether you end up encountering free-roaming ponies on Whitefield Moor or seals on the River Beaulieu, the gentle landscape gives way to never-ending, back-to-nature fun.

Some say that the New Forest holds Western Europe's largest chunk of ancient woodland – defined as a woodland habitat that has existed since AD1600. So, if you're after some forest bathing and tree appreciation, this is the place. There are several treasured spots where you can fully appreciate the age and diversity of the trees, including Blackwater Arboretum, Rhinefield Ornamental Drive and Bolderwood Arboretum. From heritage trails to picnic spots and den-building, there are hours of fun in these special places to be had for free.

BROCKENHURST & SURROUNDS

Slap bang in the middle of the New Forest, **Brockenhurst** is a small village brimming with options to amuse youngsters, from bike-hire and pony-ride outlets to old-fashioned sweet shops. Served by mainline trains from London Waterloo, Southampton and Bournemouth, it's also an excellent base for car-free fun.

Cyclexperience (⊘ cyclex.co.uk) will kit the whole family out with bikes, helmets, trailers and even a guiding app to make the many surrounding trails that bit easier to navigate. With cycling routes fanning out from the village in all directions, there's something for all ages and abilities. The Hawkhill Trail offers nine miles of traffic-free tracks across World War II airfields, while the seven-mile **South Taste Trail** (⊘ thenewforest.co.uk) takes in pit stops at New Forest Cider (⊘ newforestcider.co.uk), Burley Fudge (⊘ burleyfudge.co.uk) and Setley Ridge Farm Shop (⊘ setleyridgefarmshop.co.uk). Another family favourite is the disused railway known as Castleman's Corkscrew, which tears nine miles across fields to Burley village.

In **Burley**, **PEDALL** (⊘ pedall.org.uk) provides inclusive cycling sessions for people that need extra support. The project uses a variety of adapted bikes with three or four wheels for extra stability and specialist guides. Also encouraging a wider range of people to get out on two wheels in the New Forest is **Southern Ebike Rentals** (⊘ southernebikerentals. co.uk), which will deliver e-bikes right to your door or help organise one-way rides.

If a slower pace beckons, contact **Brockenhurst Donkey Walks** (⊘ brockenhurstdonkeywalks.com), based a mile outside the village, where you can get to know the donkeys while taking them on a gentle stroll through the surrounding heathland and woodland.

LYNDHURST

Four miles north of Brockenhurst, Lyndhurst is often referred to as the 'capital' of the New Forest and has the bustle to prove it. The **New Forest**

A WILD NEW FOREST TOUR

Pig Bush Car Park, between Beaulieu & Lyndhurst, SO42 7YQ ⊘ wildnewforest.co.uk; age: 6+; intrepid level: ②

'This is some of the cleanest water in the UK, despite its muddy appearance,' Russell tells us as we peer into the copper-tinted stream coursing through one of the New Forest's many bogs. Much to everyone's delight, Wilf, my eldest, spots a raft spider gliding on the water's surface. While the boys squeal with excitement (the floating spider is a Top Trumps and *Deadly 60* favourite), Russell and our other guide Marcus jot down the time and location. 'It's the first we've seen this year – thanks, boys.'

Rather than slogging around the New Forest's many touristy animal parks in order to meet the local wildlife, we've headed out on a three-mile walk with Marcus and Russell, founders of Wild New Forest, a Community Interest Company whose profits go back into community or environmental projects. After leaving careers in science and conservation in 2016, the duo wanted to do something to 'inform, involve and inspire' people living in and visiting the New Forest to protect its incredible flora and fauna. We're only 15 minutes in, and already we've stumbled across one of the species Wild New Forest would like more people to understand. In addition to the spider, other pin-ups include red deer, pine marten, otter, smooth snake, sand lizard, Emperor moth and goshawk.

'Although the park is protected, it's under increasing pressure from urban development and pollution, so more people need to understand what's here and why and how to protect it,' Russell explains so earnestly that even the kids stop in their tracks to take it on board. Throughout our tour, we learn that there are over 15,000 species of insect (two-thirds of the UK's total), 2,700 species of fungi, 44 species of mammal, and at least 12 species of reptile and amphibian. The New Forest is also a UK hotspot for rare birds like the honey buzzard and Dartford warbler. 'Most people living or visiting have no idea what this ecosystem is home to, but we want to change that via guided tours and talks,' Russell continues.

The sense of wilderness increases as we stride out further from the cars, which we left at the car park. Gravel paths peter out, and I'm grateful for our guides as they set off on an interesting route through the scrub, bog and ancient oaks. There doesn't seem to be a set path; instead, Russell and Marcus follow their instincts for keeping the kids engaged.

Heritage Centre (⊘ newforestheritage.org.uk) here, a free museum and information centre with interactive displays and art exhibitions, is a good reason to visit. The local information on everything from wildlife to history is brilliant for kids on a rainy day.

About a mile outside town, the **Foxlease Activity Centre** (⊘ girlguidingactivitycentres.org.uk) offers a whole host of activities for

We spot narrow-leaved lungwort's colour-popping blues, the pansy-like dog violet, pungent bog myrtle and even round-leaved sundew, a wild carnivorous plant that will eat up to 2,000 insects in summer. On sniffing out a half-collapsed oak tree's climbing potential, we learn that the tree leans its lower branches down to the ground to prop itself up in old age. 'Now we know it's an ancient tree; it's best to leave it be,' Marcus urges the kids, distracting them with the promise of mould: 'Who likes fungi?'. We soon linger around puffball fungi, and Russell explains how to identify species including bearded lichen and chicken of the woods.

Before returning to the mêlée of people and cars at Pig Bush, we pause for a snack. As the adults sink into the soft, mossy earth underfoot, savouring the dappled sunlight creeping through the forest canopy above, the kids get busy carefully lifting logs with Russell and Marcus to check out what creepy crawlers are in residence below. A wolf spider darts out into the light. Marcus explains, 'It's a sprinter that chases its prey, eventually leaping on it like a wolf.' There's a chorus of 'coooool!' from the kids who instantly start mimicking the spider's wily ways. If any place in the UK demonstrates how deeply our native flora and fauna can surprise and delight, this surely is it.

WILD NEW FOREST

children over five years old, including archery, bushcraft, climbing, raft building and abseiling, scattered among a 65-acre chunk of woodland.

BOLDERWOOD ARBORETUM

Between Brockenhurst and Lyndhurst, in the heart of the national park (⊘ forestryengland.uk) is home to the 'Queen of the Forest', a

500-year-old oak which, at 24ft wide, is the oldest, largest and most famous in the region. At the heart of an enclosure, reached by a level gravel track that passes other-worldly redwoods and the remnants of dens and hideouts made by previous little visitors, it's a magical spot for a picnic. Bolderwood is also home to an Information Unit, open every weekend or every day in the school holidays, which answers questions about the New Forest's history and ecology. Herds of wild fallow deer can be spotted from an elevated platform overlooking a large meadow in the neighbouring Bolderwood Deer Sanctuary.

For a more hands-on and interactive experience, get in touch with **Wild Heritage** (⌀ wildheritage.co.uk) about group and private activities at Bolderwood and throughout the New Forest that promote nature awareness through crafting and fun.

BEAULIEU & BUCKLER'S HARD

Six miles east of Brockenhurst, Beaulieu's extensive history (it was founded in 1204) makes it a bit of a tourist hotspot, but that's no reason to stay away. The **National Motor Museum**, **Palace House** and **abbey** comprise the main hub of activity (one ticket provides access to all three: ⌀ beaulieu.co.uk). Home to 250 vehicles, a monorail connecting gardens with the museum, a play area, go-karts and a 1930s bus ride, the motor museum alone offers a big day out. Add to that the pretty Palace House with its Victorian gardens and working kitchen, and there's something for the whole family, motoring enthusiasts or not.

If you'd rather avoid the crowds, head off on a two-mile riverside walk (part of the 60-mile **Solent Way**; ⌀ solentway.co.uk) to **Buckler's Hard** (⌀ bucklershard.co.uk). The path meanders along some of the prettiest sections of the tidal Beaulieu River, a Site of Special Scientific Interest that is awash with wildlife including kingfishers, redshank and seals (page 111). Budding **birders** can book a guided tour with local ornithologist Graham Giddens (⌀ grahamgiddens.co.uk). Once at Buckler's Hard, you'll find an array of activities depending on the time of year. There's a living museum, which you pay to get into, or you can follow the public footpaths in for free. Daily **Living History Tours** (⌀ bucklershard.co.uk) take visitors back in time to meet Nelson's

◄ **1** Bolderwood Arboretum. **2** Exploring the New Forest by bike. **3** The National Motor Museum.

Navy shipbuilders, and there are hands-on knot-tying and boat-building exhibitions in the **Buckler's Hard Museum**.

LYMINGTON, MILFORD-ON-SEA & KEYHAVEN

If market town buzz is what you're after, make a stop in **Lymington**, the national park's southern gateway, on a Saturday, when the pretty Georgian High Street springs to life with market stalls selling everything from doughnuts to second hand toys. Dive off into cobbled side streets or head down to the old harbour, popping into indie shops and cafés along the way. Look out for the **Lymington Seafood Festival** (⊘ lymingtonseafoodfestival.co.uk) every July that floods the streets and waterfront with live music, craft stalls and, of course, mountains of local seafood.

For water-based fun, towards the port you will find the UK's oldest sea baths; built in 1833, the **Lymington Seawater Baths** (⊘ lymingtonseawaterbaths.org.uk) swimming pool is still open today, and in the summer hosts inflatable watercourses and stand-up paddleboard lessons. For families with older kids, sunset cruises with **Escape Yachting** (⊘ escapeyachting.com) offer a civilised sailing experience, or if you're up for doing the hard work, **Calshot** (⊘ hants. gov.uk/outdoors) has a series of group and private sailing courses for children over five. While in town, look out for Sir Ben Ainslie's gold postbox, painted in 2012 to celebrate his Olympic Gold medal for sailing.

On the way to the coast, **Milford-on-Sea** is a good place to stock up on supplies and check out more activities. In the summer, the village green often hosts events and has picnic benches. With excellent fish and chips and a couple of pubs, the village also boasts Holland's, a treasure trove of a food store stocked with local produce. On the village green, the **New Forest Paddle Sport Company** (⊘ thenewforestpaddlesportcompany. co.uk) is a good bet for equipment hire or SUP tours (all under-18s must be accompanied).

Rather than heading straight to Milford's never-ending beach, skirt east towards **Keyhaven** for a geography- and history-packed five-mile loop by ferry and foot. Kick-start the adventure by hopping on the **Hurst Castle ferry** (⊘ hurstcastle.co.uk) which putters a mile across Kayhaven Lake every 30 minutes or so (check timetable). If you're lucky, you might catch sight of kitesurfers leaping overhead or Brent geese and black-tailed godwit swooping into the water. Once on dry land, explore the

TASTE THE NEW FOREST

The **Taste the New Forest** campaign (⊘ thenewforest.co.uk) celebrates local food and drink producers, makers and growers by signposting visitors towards the New Forest Marque symbol (the sign of 'true local provenance'), where to purchase local goods, how to order a local hamper, and what produce to expect throughout the seasons. Shops to stock up in include Hockey's Farm Shop in South Gorley (⊘ hockeys-farm.co.uk), Sunnyfields Farm Shop in Totton (⊘ sunnyfields.co.uk), and the New Forest Cider Shop in Burley (⊘ newforestcider.co.uk). Local hamper businesses such as The Forest Foodie (⊘ theforestfoodie.com) are a wonderful alternative to a supermarket shop on arrival, or simply save space for spontaneous purchases as you go.

original Tudor fort and catch glimpses of the Isle of Wight from **Hurst Castle** (⊘ hurstcastle.co.uk). A two-mile walk along Hurst Spit, with the wild, pebbly beach to one side and mudflats on the other, takes you back to Keyhaven, just in time for a drink or lunch at the Gun Inn (page 122).

A little inland, in New Milton, children of all ages can muck in at the **Burley Villa stables** (⊘ burleyvilla.co.uk). While older kids can head out on a forest ride, little ones can take part in the Kidz Brush n Ride – a grooming session before a short amble along the lane.

PRACTICALITIES

FAMILY-FRIENDLY SLEEPS

Camping in the Forest

⊘ campingintheforest.co.uk. A collection of ten campsites in the heart of the New Forest where ponies stroll between tents and beneath towering oaks. Matley Wood has miles of car-free cycling routes, and the Ashurst site is a field away from the family-friendly New Forest pub (⊘ newforestashurst.co.uk).

Green Hill Farm Holiday Village

⊘ lovatparks.com. To the north of the New Forest, Green Hill is a Lovat Holiday Park that offers guests everything from glamping bell tents with hot tubs, showers and fully stocked kitchens, to static caravans, camping pods and a camping field. Activities on-site include archery, crazy golf and scheduled pursuits from nature crafts to wildlife walks.

Hucklesbrook Farm

⊘ newforestholidaycottages.com. Hucklesbrook is a pretty 17th-century farm with three self-catering cottages each sleeping five plus a baby. Hens and ducks keep kids amused, as do the games room with table tennis and table football, and the mini adventure playground with sandpit. You'll find it just outside the national park near Fordingbridge.

Muddycreek Farm ⏾ muddycreekfarm. co.uk. A couple of miles outside Milford-on-Sea, Muddycreek offers no-nonsense camping in July and August only. There are hot showers and toilets on-site, firewood for sale, pizza nights, 15 acres of fields – and little else.

New Park Manor

⏾ newparkmanorhotel.co.uk. This luxury hotel, close to Brockenhurst, is surrounded by paddocks and woods and has been designed with families in mind. There's a listening service, kids' club, kids' tea, toys, games, and a spa with a swimming pool big enough for a family splash.

Tree Tops ⏾ newforestliving.co.uk/ cottages/treetops. Found along a single-track road, Bailey's Hard is a secluded waterside location on the River Beaulieu where a handful of exclusive homes are available to rent. Tree Tops is a modern cabin sleeping five, surrounded by the sights and sounds of the forest.

Warborne Farm ⏾ warbornefarm. co.uk. Home to eight lovingly restored barns and farmhouses of all shapes and sizes, sleeping between four and 12, this working farm lies just north of Lymington. Kids will love roaming free among the hay bales and farmyard and are invited to feed the resident chickens, ducks and often several friendly pigs.

KID-FRIENDLY EATS

Exbury Gardens Mr Eddy's Restaurant & Café ⏾ exbury.co.uk. It's worth travelling to pretty Exbury Gardens – a 200-acre garden with a steam railway, across the river from Buckler's Hard – for Mr Eddy's sustainably minded food alone. There are several food outlets on-site, but this is the best for kids and local produce.

Ferndene Farm Shop Ⓕ. Buy local at this busy farm shop in the south of the forest at New Milton, which sells everything from flowers to homemade cakes and beef from grass-fed cows. The kids may even get the chance to feed some of the animals.

Gun Inn ⏾ theguninn.co.uk. This olde-worlde pub in the heart of Keyhaven, moments from the coast, is a perfect spot for a warming roast in the naval-themed dining area or a cold drink in the large, grassy garden.

Needles Eye Café ⏾ needleseyecafe. co.uk. Near Milford and Keyhaven marshes, this unfussy beachfront place offers simple grub, cakes, coffees and hot choc, as locally sourced as possible, with ample space for kids to romp around outside.

Old Station Tea Rooms

⏾ stationhouseholmsley.com. This converted railway station on the Castleman's Corkscrew cycle path offers mountains of cakes, sandwiches and cream teas, surrounded by historic train memorabilia.

The Pig ⏾ thepighotel.com. The Brockenhurst branch of The Pig, a chain of hotels and restaurants famed for local sourcing and casual dining, is the original. It's much loved by families looking for an indulgent dinner or lunch; kids are made to feel welcome and there's lots of outdoor space.

Rainbow Fish Bar ⊘ rainbowfishbar. co.uk. One of the New Forest's most-loved fish and chip shops, Rainbow has been serving up sustainable fish and freshly cut chips in Brockenhurst since 1983. Take-away only; ring ahead or drop in.

BEFORE YOU GO

Reliant on donations, the **Love the Forest** campaign, run by the **New Forest Trust** (⊘ newforesttrust. org.uk), funds 600 or so volunteers to maintain the national park's footpaths and car parks in order to keep it open to the public while protecting wildlife and ecosystems. Head over to their website to check on local projects and ways to donate.

MORE INFO

New Forest National Park Authority
⊘ newforestnpa.gov.uk
New Forest Tourist Board
⊘ thenewforest.co.uk

8
ISLE OF WIGHT

Although visible from the mainland, this bijou island can feel worlds away thanks to its sunny disposition, hidden coves and rare wildlife.

TOP FAMILY EXPERIENCE

CYCLING THE RED SQUIRREL TRAIL, COWES TO SANDOWN BAY

BEST FOR KIDS AGED: 6+

WHEN TO GO: March to October

INTREPID LEVEL: ①

ADDED ADVENTURE: Tree-climbing, watersports, botanical gardens, farm visits, and beaches galore

TIME: Three days to one week

CYCLING WITH THE SQUIRRELS

Various locations redsquirreltrail.org.uk

'I'm completely out of controlllll!' is all we hear as Barney speeds up and over the brow of a gravel track, leaving the rest of us wobbling in the dust under the stately Freemantle Lodge Gateway. The huge arch is part of now-deserted Appuldurcombe House, one of Hampshire's most impressive English Baroque-style mansions – epitomising the excesses of 18th-century nobility. Today, the house and gardens (owned by English Heritage but free to enter) are a wonderful playground for little imaginations; crumbling and roofless staircases and walls set the stage for hide and seek and ghost stories. It's late spring, and clumps of daffodils and primroses look luminous against the grey Portland stone.

The mansion is one of many intriguing stops on the 31-mile Red Squirrel Cycling Trail from Cowes on the north of the island to Sandown

---

◀ **1** Appuldurcombe House. **2** Look out for red squirrels along the cycle route.
3 Cycling the Isle of Wight.

Bay on the south. Mostly traffic-free, the trail makes excellent use of old railway lines and bridleways. Various offshoots create circular and shorter routes, so there's something for all ages and abilities. Having hired bikes from RouteFifty7 (⌀ routefifty7.com) – a jolly outfit in Lower Hyde Holiday Park, right next to a traffic-free chunk of the trail – we take on a 14-mile loop from Shanklin via Wroxhall, Merstone and Sandown.

Having spent longer than we intended marvelling at Appuldurcombe House's dramatic ruins, we're now back on the bikes with another nine miles or so to go. After weaving through pretty fields peppered with ancient farm buildings and the occasional grand farmhouse (this is the Isle of Wight's rural interior, which so many visitors miss), we arrive in the quaint village of Godshill, where a model village and handful of tea rooms have drawn in visitors for generations. We load up with sandwiches and scones for lunch and bypass the touristy distractions to get back on track.

"Hawthorn-fringed paths meander from Godshill to Merstone Station – a community orchard and attractive picnic spot."

Hawthorn-fringed paths meander from Godshill to Merstone Station – a community orchard and attractive picnic spot with benches, tables and BBQ pits. A mound here, which was once a busy railway junction, is now sprouting cowslips – much to the delight of several dancing red admirals. The boys absorb themselves with an information board listing all the species that live here before commencing on a mini-beast hunt of their own. In summer, it's possible to spot pyramidal orchids – the Isle of Wight's county flower, which thrives in this chalky landscape.

Back on the bikes, we follow the route along the River Yar down straight and flat paths to the Pedallers Cafe, a well-trodden Red Squirrel Trail pit stop which offers everything you need to keep going, including cake and a sunny garden. Aware the day is slipping away, we double down efforts to spot the trail's namesake. Extinct in most parts of the UK, partly due to their larger, more aggressive grey relatives, the native red squirrel has one of its last few strongholds on the Isle of Wight.

Unfortunately, Barney's enthusiasm for freewheeling at volume dashes our chances – until we reach the 30-acre Alverstone Mead Nature Reserve's marshy splendour (mead is an ancient word for water meadow). Here, after whizzing through a near-deserted web of boardwalks, streams and footpaths, we spot a blur of reddish-orange fur scurrying up a gnarly oak tree, closely followed by a second. 'Mission accomplished!' celebrates Wilf, just as a Spitfire roars overhead. Wildlife and planes all in one moment; we can't believe our luck.

Wildlife thrives in the nature reserve. Thanks to local conservation efforts, this unique ecosystem is flourishing under the care of grazing Highland cows, wildlife-friendly farming and an increasingly engaged local community (it was saved from development 20 years ago). As clouds thicken and spots of rain begin to fall, we make a dash for the reserve's raised hide where binoculars and wildlife charts invite everyone to get spotting. Information boards tell us that kingfishers, herons, kestrels, and barn owls live here but alas the rain seems to have kept them away today, although we do spot two buzzards soaring high overhead.

Back on the trail, the bustle of Sandown marks an abrupt end to Alverstone's wildlife haven. At the top of town, you might be lucky enough to spot glass-blowing in action at Glory Art Glass or at least browse their collection of locally made, colourful creations. Before descending to the pier, we dive into Jurassic Jim — a ramshackle collection of fossils, skeletons and gems.

The last chunk of the ride is along the Sandown promenade, between the vast sandy beach and soaring sandstone cliffs. Aware we must get back up to the top of those cliffs before the end of the day, we make one last stop at Fins Beach Cafe, a quiet beachside spot where we could happily while away hours with our sundowners while the boys play on the sands. Instead, we begin the long, slow climb back to Shanklin before RouteFifty7 shuts up shop and we have to reluctantly hand back our steeds.

ADDED ADVENTURE: RETRO FUN & GREEN DELIGHTS

The Isle of Wight has long charmed holidaymakers with its winning combination of old-fashioned seaside fun, 500-plus miles of footpaths, and a fascinating history that punches well above its size, from dinosaurs to Osborne House. A growing commitment to long-term nature conservation and a slow travel ethos has also improved the visitor experience — things are greener, more accessible and more wildlife focused than ever. Half the island is an Area of Outstanding

SS

ENGLISH HERITAGE

ENGLISH HERITAGE

VISITISLEOFWIGHT.CO.UK

Natural Beauty and it's also a UNESCO Biosphere Reserve, recognised for bringing nature and humans together in harmony. For ease, we've divided the island into four geographical chunks but it's all very accessible. The longest journey time will be approximately 40 minutes by car.

NORTH WIGHT

The waterside town of Cowes, centrally located on the north coast, is most famous for its annual regatta, one of the largest in the UK, which floods the town for a week every summer with boating enthusiasts and Pimms (⊘ cowesweek.co.uk). For a taste of the fun, check out the town's **UK Sailing Academy** (⊘ uksa.org), which runs watersports fun days for eight to 15-year-olds or a four-day Dinghy Start course accredited by the RYA. Younger kids can find inspiration at the **Classic Boat Museum** (⊘ classicboatmuseum.com) – home to more than 85 boats including Ben Ainslie's 2017 America's Cup test boat.

Cowes is divided by the River Medina, which heads 17 miles inland to Newport. Between the two towns, a former railway line now acts as an off-road cycling track: pick up bikes at **Two Elements** in Cowes (⊘ twoelements.co.uk). If real trains are more appealing, you may want to book a ride on the **Isle of Wight Steam Railway** (⊘ iwsteamrailway.co.uk), which trundles along a gentle track just outside Newport.

On the east side of the River Medina, just a mile or so from the centre of town, sits Queen Victoria's island getaway, **Osborne House** (⊘ english-heritage.org.uk). Kids will particularly love the Swiss Cottage, which is a palace in miniature, built by Prince Albert as a place where his children could learn good life skills: growing fruit and vegetables, and play fighting in the fort. Today you can wander around the rooms of the Swiss Cottage to get a sense of what life was like for young royalty in the 19th century and peruse their collectables. There's also an adventure playground and a short walkway to the estate's beach: Osborne Bay, a nice, sheltered spot for families. Nearby, another English Heritage property, **Carisbrooke Castle**, is particularly worth a visit in the summer holidays when events include medieval fayres and

---

◀ **1** The pretty town of Yarmouth. **2** Carisbrooke Castle. **3** Swiss Cottage garden at Osborne House. **4** Tapnell Farm.

jousting days. Sitting on the edge of Newport, surrounded by footpaths meandering into surrounding countryside, it's a great car-free option.

Heading west from Cowes, the coast stretches beyond the village of Gurnard to the wilder **Hamstead Heritage Coast** (heritage coast status is awarded to parts of the UK that are particularly unspoilt). Five miles west of Cowes, Thorness Bay can be reached by a coast path that passes through salt marshes and woodland. You'll be rewarded with rich fossil finds on the beaches, and you might spot teal, snipe, curlew and little egrets. Further along the coast, at **Newtown**, an abandoned medieval settlement, the National Trust hosts birdwatching walks and other events, including fungi trails (⊘ nationaltrust.org.uk).

WEST WIGHT

With its sailing boats, waterside George Hotel, cobbled streets and views across The Solent to the New Forest, **Yarmouth**, in the far west of the island, is the Isle of Wight's prettiest port. On the southern edge of town, converted railway station café **Off The Rails Yarmouth** (⊘ offtherailsyarmouth.co.uk) makes a good base from which to explore. As well as serving up locally sourced food, they have compiled a list of five local walks ranging from one to five miles – these include a route along the River Yar, one that takes in coastal forts including Golden Hill Fort, and another around Rofford Marsh.

At the point where the English mainland plunges towards the Isle of Wight at Hurst Point, **Colwell Bay** is best visited at low tide and sunset when the wet sand glows orange. **Sup Dog** (SupDogRentals) rents paddleboards from a pretty beach hut on the seawall.

Further south, drama prevails on the 28-mile-long **Tennyson Heritage Coast** – named after Alfred, Lord Tennyson, the Poet Laureate, who lived at **Freshwater Bay** – which runs from the striking chalk stacks known as **The Needles** all the way around to Ventnor. Beyond Freshwater Bay the path skirts plunging cliffs and windswept beaches along the Military Road to **Chilton Chine**, a series of waterfalls dropping into the sea. There is loads to see and do at The Needles, albeit all slightly touristy; bypass the rides and sweet stalls for the rickety chairlift down to Alum Bay, where it's possible to walk away from the crowds to explore caves and swim at the southern end of the bay. The National Trust's Victorian **Old Battery** offers one of the best viewpoints across The Needles as well as shedding light on the area's wartime and historical significance.

A few miles inland from Yarmouth, **Tapnell Farm** (⊘ tapnellfarm. com) is an increasingly popular attraction for families. Once a rough-around-the-edges farm attraction, it is now an all-singing, all-dancing affair, with pillow trampolines, an animal park, archery and axe throwing, football golf and an aqua park. Although busy, it's a beautiful site with views across The Solent.

Further east towards Newbridge, **Chessell Pottery Café** (⊘ chessellpotterycafe.co.uk) offers pottery painting workshops for kids and substantial cream teas, while nearby **Mottistone Gardens** (⊘ nationaltrust.org.uk) has a playful flowerpot model trail and den building area.

A fun way to get around this part of the island is on the Breezer open-top bus that travels between Yarmouth, Freshwater, Alum Bay and Colwell (⊘ islandbuses.info/days-out-bus).

EAST WIGHT

On the northeast tip of the island, **Ryde** has a huge beach that's ideal for building sandcastles, running races and playing beach games. As you walk south, after half a mile or so the beach and towpath runs into the landscaped **Appley Park** where red squirrels leap between giant oaks. In the park, Dell Café (⊘ dellcafe.com) is a lovely spot for breakfast overlooking the sea, and **Goodleaf** runs a splendid tree-climbing and orienteering course (see box, page 132).

A few miles south of Ryde, the villages of **Seaview** and **Bembridge** represent the prettier parts of the east coast. Seaview's Edwardian houses tumble down towards the sea, where wooden boats and a sailing club lend the place an upmarket feel. Beaches here are a mix of rocks and sand – leave the crowds behind and walk a couple of miles to privately owned **Priory Bay** where soft sands meet the National Trust-owned Priory Woods (access from Seaview only possible at low tide).

A mile south, **Bembridge Harbour** is a large inlet with **St Helens Duver** (an Isle of Wight term meaning sandy spit) and **Fort** (⊘ nationaltrust.org.uk) on one side and **Bembridge Beach** on the other. The St Helens side is one of the best spots on the island for rock pooling. Operating out of Woodnutts Yard in St Helens, **Tackt-Isle Adventures** (⊘ tackt-isle.co.uk) is a wonderful outfit for families, offering two-hour SUP experiences – including a Mega SUP for up to eight people – and bushcraft sessions on the beach. On the Bembridge side,

TREE CLIMBING WITH GOODLEAF'S PAUL MCCATHIE

Appley Park, Garden Walk, Ryde PO33 1QX ⟨⊘⟩ goodleaf.co.uk; age: 8+; intrepid level: ③

'You'll find us at the big oak tree in Appley Park,' Paul had told us the day before. It sounded ridiculously vague but sure enough, there in front of us, moments inland from the park's seafront walk, towers a 69ft-high oak tree with branches spinning off into every direction. When we notice the snaking green and orange ropes hanging down to the ground, it's clear we're in the right place. 'Are you excited, boys?', I utter quietly, trying to conceal my nerves.

Goodleaf is run by Paul McCathie, a Kiwi who moved to the Isle of Wight in 2010 after marrying an Islander. Increasingly unsatisfied with tree surgeon work, which often involves stunting a tree's growth, Paul wanted to do something to help people appreciate the awe-inspiring wonder of trees. 'We won't be able to protect them unless we have the chance to love them,' he tells us.

Although big in the US, recreational tree climbing is relatively unknown in the UK so Goodleaf is something of a pioneer. The response has been overwhelming. On Paul's three-day course, people come from all over the UK to learn how to set up a rope system so they can do it themselves – even a few environmental protesters and tree

sitters have come along to learn the ropes. Families like us, however, get just a taster on a two-hour climbing session. 'It's as much about getting to know the tree as it is doing something you wouldn't usually do together – switching off from everyday life and focusing on nature,' Paul says.

Pushing nerves aside, we get our helmets on and make our way over to the 200-year-old tree. 'It's magnificent, isn't it?' Paul starts, inviting a pause to appreciate the natural structure we're about to climb. With the rope system in place, we concentrate on learning knots – how to tie them and when to tighten up or loosen ropes. After a steady explanation and demonstration, we test our knots on the ground before heading up towards the sky. Paul explains that standing in the middle of the tree, clinging on to the trunk is the ultimate tree hug, so we set our sights on that. After a few false starts, we steadily make our way up. Everything slows down and the whole experience soon feels calming rather than alarming.

It's possible to get up to 50ft or so, but we stick in the middle of the tree for a good 20 minutes. Only just old enough to join in

Sally's Riding School (⟨⊘⟩ sallysridingschool.com) offers gentle horseriding experiences along the coastline's soft sands. The island's only surviving windmill, **Bembridge Mill** (⟨⊘⟩ nationaltrust.org.uk), is interactive enough to entertain little ones.

From Bembridge Harbour the Eastern Yar floods **Brading Marsh**, which, managed by the RSPB, is one of the most important wetlands in

(he's eight), Wilf is happy to follow my lead – some teenagers in the session before us had bolted up to the top in minutes leaving parents scrambling down below. Blue tits chitter chatter in the outer branches, as if perplexed by our presence, and it's funny to see the people wandering past down below. Middle is enough of a new perspective for us.

After we have descended, Paul gives us a couple of Goodleaf orienteering packs. After getting to grips with the concept of map reading, the kids scamper off into the woods in search of hidden number plaques. Another hour ticks by with the children doing nothing but playing in and among the trees: enjoying nature's playground in all its simple glory.

ANNA FULFORD/GOODLEAF TREE CLIMBING

southern England. Several trails are accessible from Brading Station at one end or Bembridge Windmill at the other. Avid birdwatchers might be lucky enough to spot the rare hobby falcon here.

Further south, **Sandown** and **Shanklin** are the island's most popular beach resorts – think big beaches, arcades, crazy golf and a bustling pier. These sandy bays are also ideal for watersports: **West Side Beach**

1

2

3

(⌀ westsidebeach.co.uk), **Bayside Beach Hire** (⌀ baysidebeach.co.uk) and **Sandown Bicycle and Beach Hire** (⌀ sandownbikeandbeach. co.uk) all rent sea kayaks, surfboards and stand-up paddleboards by the hour. Also based in Sandown but able to move around the island to seek out the best conditions, **iSurf** (⌀ iowsurf.com) offers hourly lessons in surfing and SUPing (eight years and above).

SOUTH WIGHT

Claiming some of the hottest and longest spells of sunshine in the whole of the UK, the Isle of Wight's southern coast has been loved by holidaymakers for hundreds of years. **Ventnor Beach**, flanked by grand Victorian villas, is particularly vibrant during the **Ventnor Fringe** (⌀ vfringe.co.uk) held at the end of July and featuring open-air performances from *A Midsummer Night's Dream* to *Treasure Island*. Four miles east of Ventnor, **Devil's Chimney** is an incredible natural chasm in the rocks that leads to a number of short circular wooded walks.

On the other side of town, just a 15-minute stroll along the cliffs, **Steephill Cove** is one of the island's prettiest bays. Only accessible by a steep footpath, its rickety beach huts, piled-up lobster pots and sun-bleached beach houses are bursting with seaside charm. The Crab Shed serves up ice creams and crab pasties just above the lapping water. It's easy to while away hours doing nothing but enjoying the cove's sheltered sunshine – visit early or late in the day for a more tranquil atmosphere.

Above Steephill Cove, **Ventnor Botanic Garden** (⌀ botanic. co.uk) packs in heaps of 'infotainment' for the whole family among its 22 acres and 33,000 rare plants and trees. The garden path weaves through different 'geographical' zones, from Australasia to Japan and the Mediterranean. Kids' entertainment includes a series of trails highlighting everything from dinosaur plants to champion trees, and a lizard safari pack for recording sightings of the garden's infamous wall lizards. There's a small playground, too, and the Plantation Room Café has a large terrace.

Above the hustle and bustle of the coastal towns, the Ventnor and St Catherine's Downs are home to some spectacular walks. Head to

◀ **1** Steephill Cove. **2** Ventnor Fringe Festival. **3** Taking to the water with Tackt-Isle Adventures.

ROUNDING UP GOATS ON VENTNOR DOWNS

Every October, volunteers support National Trust rangers in rounding up the goats that preserve the unique chalk grassland on the Ventnor Downs. Kids and adults scramble across the hills and scrub to herd the often-stubborn goats into a pen for their annual health check. The 50-odd goats have roamed Ventnor Downs since the early 1990s, naturally controlling the spread of trees, particularly the holm oaks that were introduced several centuries ago from the Mediterranean. Although pretty, the oaks threaten native flora and fauna, smothering the yellow horseshoe vetch, for example, which is important for the survival of the Adonis blue butterfly. It can take up to 70 volunteers to help get them into a pen.

For more information, visit the National Trust website: ⟲ nationaltrust.org.uk.

St Catherine's Lighthouse, aka St Catherine's Oratory – a medieval lighthouse on one of the highest points of the island, affectionately nicknamed the Pepperpot.

PRACTICALITIES

FAMILY-FRIENDLY SLEEPS

Camp Wight ⟲ campwight.co.uk. This low-key, family-run woodland campsite in the heart of West Wight, just two miles from the ferry port at Yarmouth, is ideal for families looking for 'back to basics' fun. A qualified Forest Schools practitioner takes groups of kids on woodland adventures throughout the day and firepits warm the cockles under dark skies by night.

Nettlecombe Farm
⟲ nettlecombefarm.co.uk. Just above Whitwell village in South Wight, Nettlecombe is the kind of place where families return year after year. What it lacks in trendy interiors, it more than makes up for in farmyard fun – kids can feed the animals and even cuddle the sheep every day. There's a football pitch, playground and fishing lake, and heaps of walks right from the doorstep. There are nine self-catering properties in total.

Tiny Homes ⟲ tinyhomesholidays.com. Cabins of all shapes and sizes welcome families to Tiny Homes – a collection of places to stay in a beautifully protected meadow and ancient woodland close to Cowes harbour. Owners Helen and Frazer Cunningham ran a glamping business (Vintage Vacations) for years; Tiny Homes offers an even more environmentally sound and wholesome experience.

Tom's Eco Lodge ⟲ tapnellfarm.com/ stay/toms-eco-lodge. Tom's Eco Lodge is one of the island's longest running green accommodations. Once a handful of safari tents, it now offers wood cabins and eco pods. Sitting on the downs above Freshwater, next to Tapnell Farm (page 131), this is a brilliant base from which to explore the island – if you can drag yourselves away from the views and Tapnell Farm's extensive menu of fun. Tapnell Farm also offers self-catering accommodation.

KID-FRIENDLY EATS

Best Dressed Crab in Town
⊘ thegoodsshed.co.uk. The Isle of Wight is awash with waterside chefs serving up the freshest seafood; one of the most sought-after is the Best Dressed Crab in Bembridge Harbour. The menu is shellfish heavy, so this is for kids that are happy to tuck into crab, lobster and prawns. With tables right on the water, it's a great place to watch boats come and go.

Garlic Farm ⊘ thegarlicfarm.co.uk. This family-run farm ten miles east of Newport has been growing garlic and making garlic-infused goods (from cheese to beer) for over 60 years. The restaurant serves up a suitably garlicky menu, including light bites including soup, bread and cheese and family favourites like burgers. Walk off your lunch with a farm tour or a stint in the play area.

The Hut Colwell ⊘ thehutcolwell. co.uk. Tucked away on one end of Colwell Bay, with views across The Solent to Hurst Point and Castle, The Hut is surrounded by blue at high tide and sand at low. A vast glass atrium makes the most of the view whatever the weather. Although relaxed, The Hut is a sit-down restaurant – ideal for long, lazy seafood feasts.

Lady Scarlett's Tea Parlour
⊘ ladyscarlettsteaparlour.co.uk. Right on the seafront promenade in Ventnor, this 1940s-themed tea parlour serves up the finest cream teas on the Isle of Wight, along with a huge dollop of nostalgia. It's a brilliant spot to watch the world go by, too.

BEFORE YOU GO

The Isle of Wight tourist board, a huge advocate of slow travel, has curated the digital **Slow Wight guide** (⊘ slowwighttravelguide. co.uk) to promote car-free fun on the island. The guide features 22 walking and eight touring routes that use a combination of walking, bike, bus or train, pinpointing highlights such as lesser-known wildlife, archaeological sites and local heritage. Meanwhile the island's Sustainable Travel Scheme allows accommodation owners with the highest green rating, including Nettlecombe Farm and the Seaview Hotel, to offer free bus travel for their guests (details on the same website).

MORE INFO
Isle of Wight Tourist Board
⊘ visitisleofwight.co.uk
Isle of Wight UNESCO Biosphere Reserve ⊘ iwbiosphere.org

9
EAST SUSSEX

From the hillforts and artists' houses of the South Downs to the fishing fleets of Hastings, East Sussex offers educational fun in spades.

TOP FAMILY EXPERIENCE

EXPLORING BATTLE ABBEY & BATTLEFIELD FROM A GLAMPING HIDEAWAY

BEST FOR KIDS AGED:	4–12
WHEN TO GO:	Year-round
INTREPID LEVEL:	①
ADDED ADVENTURE:	Seaside fun, quirky towns, arty sights, mighty chalk cliffs, ancient woodlands
TIME:	Three days to one week

TRAVEL BACK TO 1066 FROM A 21ST-CENTURY GLAMPSITE

Battle Abbey, Butter Cross, High St, Battle TN33 0AE ⟨⟩ english-heritage.org.uk; Feather Down Great Barn Vineyard, Battle TN33 0RB ⟨⟩ featherdown.co.uk

I'm on the Battle battlefield with my diminutive warriors. We're armed with wooden swords from the gift shop and a makeshift bow and arrow that we fashioned ourselves from bendy conifer sticks found in the woods near our glampsite. They've learnt about the Battle of Hastings in their Year 4 classroom, and now they're ready to take part. My son Fin claims the role of Harry, King of England, while his sister Scarlett is the French upstart William the Bastard. Heady stuff indeed! I wonder if this might be the most cathartic way of allowing warring siblings to have it out.

As we set out on the trail around the actual site of the Battle of Hastings, which looks tranquil in the late spring sunshine, it's a leap of

---

◀ **1** Re-enacting the Battle of Hastings. **2** Cupboard bed at a Feather Down Farm.

the imagination to conjure up the dramatic reality of what took place on this land. English Heritage has armed us with an easy-to-use audio guide giving context and lots of exciting dramatisations and sound effects. We're told about the personalities of both leaders and the journey both armies made before meeting – the Saxons in good spirits after their victory at Stamford Bridge, the Normans taking the arduous journey across the Channel. Wooden sculptures dotted around the battlefield, depicting soldiers from both sides, help us to conjure up the scene. When we get to the crux of the commentary about what really happened on that October day, a day that changed the course of British history, it's suggested that William tricked the Saxon front line, pretending to retreat so that the English broke their shield wall. And then there's the knotty question of whether Harold really was shot in the eye with an arrow – that iconic historic image so memorably captured in the Bayeux Tapestry. The commentary puts a case instead for William having sent in a hit squad of his four best knights to decapitate and disembowel Harold on the battlefield. This disruption of what my kids have learnt at school provokes an interesting discussion about how history is recorded, who records it, and how myths and legends become so powerful.

This 1066 experience also challenges kids to examine the aftermath of the battle. We hear that people were stunned at the bloodshed that day, and William, being a God-fearing Catholic, built the mighty abbey on the site as penance. We stand in the abbey's huge upper storey, now roofless, originally the monks' dormitory, and try to imagine sleeping there in winter with no heating. Nearby is the grand Abbot's House, now Battle Abbey School. The abbey at Battle was one of the richest in the country, with plentiful supplies of food and wine. We're told that novice monks were made to ride a donkey the 14 miles from Battle to Hastings and back to bring mackerel for the friar, reminding kids that there was a time before cars, let alone computers.

Stopping off in the village of Battle to pick up supplies, we wander back through Battle Great Woods to our Feather Down Farm glampsite, knowing that this is the very route fleeing Anglo-Saxon soldiers may have taken at the moment of defeat. Instead of October, we're here in early May, and the ground is carpeted with bluebells. We collect dry sticks for our wood-burning stove and massive outdoor hot tub.

Our site has just three safari-style tents. There are woods – perfect for a spot of den building – behind us and a lovely wide grassy valley in front, where the kids can run free with the rabbits while I enjoy a glass of wine produced from the owner's on-site vineyard from my deckchair. While the tent is luxurious, there is no electricity. Light is provided by by candles, oil lamps and the central wood-burning stove, which gets us all toasty and is hot enough to cook our Battle bangers and Pevensey bacon. It's a pure digital detox – and perhaps a tiny glimpse into what life might have felt like here in the 11th century.

ADDED ADVENTURE: FROM ANCIENT FISHING FLEETS TO ICONIC CHALK CLIFFS

East Sussex is often counted as part of the commuter belt and, as such, frequently overlooked – with the exception of Brighton – as a family holiday spot. There's plenty to entice families who want to slow down the pace, however, from the glorious South Downs to the medieval town of Lewes, renowned for its wild Bonfire Night celebrations, and the dynamic south coast with its arty enclaves and spectacular clifftop walks.

HASTINGS & SURROUNDS

The coastal town of **Hastings** is a cool one to explore with kids. Begin on the shingle beach, home to the largest remaining beach-launched fishing fleet in the UK. The colourful boats and fishing nets are there for all to see up close: go early and you may see a catch being landed. It's well worth popping into the **Hastings Fishermen's Museum** (ohps. org.uk), in the former Fishermen's Church of St Nicholas, for a peek at the history of this arduous profession. Even in this tiny space, you can climb on deck of a former fishing boat and get a sense of what it was like to earn a living from the deep.

Back out on the beachfront, kids can't help but be struck by the tall black wooden huts, originally used to dry fishing nets. Their striking design is echoed in the black walls of the seaside **Hastings Contemporary art gallery** (hastingscontemporary.org) which allows up to four children to go free with an adult ticket. Every year the gallery runs a programme of new work created by local artist and patron Sir Quentin Blake, loved for his endearing kids' book illustrations, most notably for Roald Dahl. Blake is also patron of the **Hastings Storytelling Festival** (hastingsstoryfest.org.uk) a week-long autumn celebration of storytelling through music, dance and film; previous guests have included Benjamin Zephaniah and Lauren Child.

Alongside the fishing heritage and art, beachfront Hastings has no shortage of kiss-me-quick seaside attractions – crazy golf, trampolines, sweet shops selling stripy rock and a miniature railway line that rattles along the coast.

Spreading back from the sea, **Hastings Old Town** is a warren of twittens (narrow passageways) and historic houses, some dating back to Shakespeare's day. Take a stroll down George Street for its cosy cafés and artisanal sweet shops – check out **Only Coco Chocolates**

EXPLORING THE SHORE
AT RYE HARBOUR NATURE RESERVE

Rye Harbour Discovery Centre, Rye Harbour Rd, Rye Harbour, Rye TN31 7FW
rye.sussexwildlifetrust.org.uk; age: 4–11; intrepid level: ①

We've come to Rye Harbour Nature Reserve in the late May sunshine. It's a brilliant time to visit according to wildlife officer Lucy Bowyer, because the shingle plants are in flower. And sure enough, the sea kale sticking out of the pebbles like giant cabbages are covered in delicate white flowers smelling sweetly of honey. Lucy points out a lovely blue and pink flower brilliantly named viper's bugloss, and a more familiar looking yellow horned-poppy, which has such vibrant sun-coloured petals you can't help but smile.

'This patchwork of colour on the shingle blossoms in May and June,' says Lucy as she guides us on an 'Explore the Shore' event. Soon we're hearing the screeches of the breeding birds who also arrive at this time of year. There are five bird hides on the reserve, and even without binoculars you can spot blackheaded gulls, common terns and sandwich terns on their nests with their chicks.

It's amazing to think we're on a manmade, managed piece of land, once ripped up for quarries. With skilled management, it now comprises a mix of picturesque coast, salt marsh, grass and wetlands, and is the place to come to be introduced to all sorts of interesting new wildlife.

Soon we're dipping our nets into the low tide, looking for shrimp and crabs. Lucy tells us that most of the guided activities are aimed at families with primary-school children. 'We do wildlife tracking, planting and setting up camera traps to look at parts of the reserve people don't usually go to, where we might see small mammals like mice, shrew and voles. We can put cameras close to the wetlands where people can't really walk – we recently spotted jacksnipe, a very shy bird.'

It's well worth booking a tour with a professional guide who knows everything about the local area, but if you don't manage

(⊘ only-coco.co.uk). Turn on to the old High Street for a rummage around the **Hastings Antique Warehouse** (⊘ hastingsantiques.co.uk), which always has something to wow: old funfair lighting, perhaps, or a Victorian rocking horse. And don't miss a visit to **Hendy's** (⊘ aghendy.com) – an upmarket hardware/kitchenware store that is more art installation than interiors shop. Proprietor Alastair Hendy also owns **135 All Saints Street**, just around the corner, a medieval merchant's house that he opens twice a year in summer and winter. It's quite an experience for kids to explore this historic house all candlelit before Christmas.

to get on to a tour and want to wander around yourself, there are some very good resources available. Download trail maps from the website, or pick one up from the impressive Rye Harbour Discovery Centre, which has tons of information about how to explore, plus a lovely café. High-spec information panels dotted around the reserve include QR codes, and there are numerous metal plaques on which you can make rubbings of native flora and fauna. Armed with paper and crayons, we're soon furiously crayoning away to reveal cream-spot tiger moths, ringed plovers, delicate sea pea plants and cuttlefish – and ending up with brilliant keepsakes of an awesome day.

TONY SKERL/S

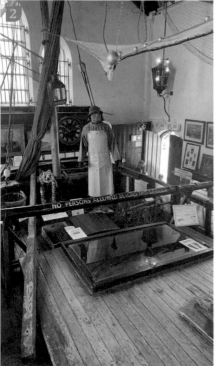

JANE ANDERSON

JANE ANDERSON

Hastings Old Town, flanked by high ground, has two Victorian funiculars to choose from, complete with steep inclines and historic wooden carriages. The **West Hill Lift** unusually takes you through a tunnel and out again to emerge on to the West Hill where views stretch as far as Beachy Head. Once at the top, take a look at the 12th-century ruins of **Hastings Castle** and **Smugglers Adventure** (⊘ smugglersadventure. co.uk) where you can explore underground tunnels in the company of Hairy Jack the smuggler.

The **East Hill Lift** takes you up the cliff face to **Hastings Country Park Nature Reserve** (⊘ hiddenhastings.org.uk) where rolling grassy plains dive down into wooded glens, all with panoramic sea views. The park has a fascinating history involving smugglers, secret bunkers, poets and artists. In summer, family-friendly nature projects include bug hunts, bat walks, moth nights and volunteering sessions to remove invasive plants such as dock. There is also an impressive straw bale visitors' centre called The Bale House at the eastern end of the park, at Firehills. Here you'll find a sandpit for kids to excavate for fossils and shells, seasonal touch tables with birds' nests, animal bones and the like, plus trail maps for rewarding family walks. Firehills is also the starting point for an accessible walk along the heathland where tiger beetles, wasp spiders and butterflies can be seen. There are three glens, Ecclesbourne, Fairlight and Warren, with ancient woodlands to explore, and rocky beaches for a swim. Ecclesbourne Glen even has a cave where a real-life hermit used to live.

Keep heading east and you come to the medieval town of **Rye** and **Rye Harbour Nature Reserve** with its discovery centre (⊘ rye. sussexwildlifetrust.org.uk; see box, page 142). Further east still is the bleak but bewitching shingle landscape of **Dungeness** in Kent (page 181).

To the west, Hasting merges into **St Leonards-on-Sea**, a happening little seaside enclave attracting many creatives with its small independent galleries and vintage shops. It's a scenic cycle along the coastal path west to **Bexhill-on-Sea,** passing colourful beach huts on the way to the **De La Warr Pavilion** (⊘ dlwp.com), an iconic Art Deco arts centre built as a prototype for London's South Bank in 1935. This beacon of culture right on the seafront is worth a visit for the building alone – all curves and straight lines – with art exhibitions often championing local

◄ **Hastings**: **1** Old Town. **2** Fishermen's Museum. **3** The shingle beach.

artists and family shows such as Julia Donaldson's *Stick Man* or Michael Morpurgo's *I Believe in Unicorns*. Check out too for the LOOK-THINK-MAKE workshops, usually held on the first Sunday of the month, which explore themes found in the galleries.

LEWES

A great slow alternative to Brighton, the ancient market town of **Lewes**, often used as the gateway to the South Downs, is a perfectly formed treat for families, offering history, culture, nature and a little bit of gothic witchery all rolled into one. Its twittens and old cobbled streets, lined with ancient timbered houses, give way to South Downs vistas and chalk cliffs beyond.

The town's bite-sized historic attractions are easy to digest (and walkable from the train station). **Lewes Castle** (⊘ sussexpast.co.uk) has a Norman keep and opportunities to dress up in medieval costumes, learn about historic recipes for Sussex pie and gingered bread, and enjoy a picnic in the gardens. It's not far to the **Anne of Cleves House** (⊘ sussexpast.co.uk), owned (but not lived in) by the fourth wife of Henry VIII, who escaped with a divorce settlement and her head intact. Rooms have been beautifully preserved and there's a Tudor garden with traditional plants.

Carry on to the **Priory ruins** (⊘ lewespriory.org.uk) and try to piece together what they must once have looked like before being razed to the ground by Henry VIII. And if your kids have had enough of history, the ruins are simply great for climbing.

It's fun to wander Lewes High Street for cute shops such as **Closet & Botts** (⊘ closetandbotts.com) and **Wickle** (⊘ wickle.co.uk) which sell thoughtful toys, clothing and accessories for babies and younger children as well as grown-up gifts and homeware. Just off the High Street, the **Needlemakers** (⊘ needlemakers.co.uk) is an interesting collection of independent shops housed in a 19th-century candle factory, its old cobbled floors, stable doors and deep well all intact. You can lose a few happy hours here browsing books, toys, Fairtrade gifts and exotic house plants. A fifteen-minute walk to the east, crossing the River Ouse, brings you to **Bags of Books** (⊘ bags-of-books.co.uk) children's bookshop.

---

1 Lewes is a great slow alternative to Brighton. **2** With older kids, consider timing your visit for Lewes Bonfire Night. ▶

GIANLUCA FIGLIOLA FANTINI/S

REBECCA FITZGERALD/S

On a hot summer's day you'll want to head to **The Pells** (⌁ pellspool. org.uk), the oldest public freshwater/spring-fed swimming pool in the UK, dating back to 1861. Handily, it's next to an outdoor play park where there's plenty of space to run around or picnic under the shady trees.

Lewes literally comes alight on **Bonfire Night**, when, in a tradition rooted in the Middle Ages, pagan torchlit processions through the streets bear effigies from shamed politicians to Guy Fawkes himself. It's a bit too full-on for small kids, but exciting for older ones under supervision. The event is so popular you have to be in town before 5pm, as roads and rail stations close to prevent overcrowding (⌁ lewesbonfirecelebrations.com).

BEYOND LEWES:
THE SOUTH DOWNS & SEVEN SISTERS COAST

Heading out of Lewes at the foot of the High Street, climb Chapel Street to **Mount Caburn** (480ft) to discover the remains of an Iron Age hillfort; archaeologists suggest Neolithic people may have used the hill as a sacred place. Today it's a popular spot for hang gliders with spectacular views back over Lewes, the Downs and south to Newhaven.

For a scenic family walk, follow the River Ouse from Lewes to Virginia Woolf's **Monk's House** (⌁ nationaltrust.org.uk), a leisurely 90-minute stroll. Or drive out towards West Firle and visit **Charleston** (⌁ charleston.org.uk), the former home of Virginia's sister Vanessa, with its inspiring craft interiors, beautiful gardens, modern galleries and a great café and outdoor entertainment space.

More easy wins with children include the gentle **Drusillas Park** (⌁ drusillas.co.uk), just north of Alfriston, a ten-minute drive from Lewes, with its Hello Kitty Secret Garden and farmyard encounters, and **Blackberry Farm Park** (⌁ blackberry-farm.co.uk), around 15 minutes' drive from Lewes, which has llamas, alpacas and Highland cattle, plus rabbits and guinea pigs. The half-day 'Farmer' and 'Pony' experiences allow children to feed and groom the animals.

For a slow and uplifting family day out from Lewes, pull on your walking boots and catch a boxy little branch line train for the 15-minute ride to the terminus seaside station of **Seaford**. The train passes through Newhaven – where you can catch the ferry over the channel to Dieppe

◀ **1** Paddleboarding on the Cuckmere River. **2** Getting up close with the wildlife at Drusillas Park. **3** Crafting at Charleston.

– and Tide Mills, a working town long since abandoned when the river silted up. Jump off the train at Seaford and wander down through town to the esplanade with the English Channel before you. Head east along the seafront past the **Seaford Museum** (⊘ seafordmuseum.co.uk) in the Martello Tower, and on to **Splash Point**, a section of the pebbly beach protected on two sides by manmade breakwaters; it's the perfect place for a swim within sight of the mighty chalk cliffs that dominate this coastline.

From Splash Point, you can scramble up the headland in front of the golf course and up on top of the cliffs for the scenic 90-minute walk to **Cuckmere Haven**, where the meandering Cuckmere River meets the sea. The mighty **Seven Sisters** dominate views here: seven white cliff faces, undulating their way around the coast, that have inspired painters, writers, photographers and filmmakers for centuries. The highest cliff is Haven Brow (253ft); its siblings are named Short Brow, Rough Brow, Brass Point, Flagstaff Point, Baily's Brow and Went Hill Brow. If your children are at all interested in art, bring along pencils, paper and watercolours so they can have a go at capturing this iconic view.

Stop by the pretty **Cuckmere Haven Coastguard Cottages** that stand sentinel over the bay; these were originally home to coastguards who would combat smuggling, perform salvaging and lifesaving duties, and guard against invasion during the World Wars. Now severely at risk from cliff erosion, they're some of the most picturesque cottages you're likely to encounter, and have featured in many films including *Harry Potter and the Goblet of Fire*.

Just beyond Cuckmere Haven, the coastal route dips down to **Hope Gap** beach – at the foot of the Seven Sisters cliffs and only accessible at low tide – which is a great place for rock pooling and fossil hunting. The gullies and ridges at the foot of the cliffs are a haven for marine life such as sponges and sea anemones, and you might even spot a seal or two. Shore walks along here also reveal evidence of shipwrecks past.

Instead of walking along the coast from Seaford, you could walk or cycle a mile-long track which follows the Cuckmere River through **Seven Sisters Country Park** (⊘ sevensisters.org.uk). More intrepid families can canoe or stand-up paddleboard down the river, along the languorous ox bows that meander through the wide valley bed. Operating locally, the non-profit **Buzz Active** (⊘ buzzactive.org.uk) offers accompanied kayaking or SUP trips down the river to the sea or upriver towards

Litlington and Alfriston, along with raft-building courses (suitable for over-eights) and multi-activity days for kids during the school holidays that combine kayaking, raft building, team games, SUPing, orienteering and bivouac building. **Pied A Terre Adventures** (⌀ patadventures.com) is another locally run adventure company offering family-friendly self-guided and guided tours of the area.

PRACTICALITIES

FAMILY-FRIENDLY SLEEPS

Alfriston Camping Park

⌀ alfristoncamping.com. With a designated family field, this camping park is surrounded by the natural beauty of the South Downs and is just two miles away from Drusillas Park. Special events usually include a Faerie Festival in May.

Blackberry Wood ⌀ blackberrywood. com. Set at the foot of the South Downs National Park in Streat, this gloriously inventive collection of camping, glamping and treehouses brings families closer to nature with creative touches including a Grand Bugapest Hotel bug house! Transport-mad kids will particularly adore staying in the 1964 double-decker Routemaster bus (with underfloor heating), Angus the Fire Engine and the 1965 Wessex Search and Rescue Helicopter.

Burning Heart River Camp

⌀ canopyandstars.co.uk. Burning Heart, with one riverside yurt, a couple of caravans, a campervan, trailer tent and three bell tents, is perfect for a large gathering of family and friends – there's even a disco caravan for a silent disco! Alternatively, you could simply book the family-friendly yurt (sleeps four) – they rent out either the entire site or just the yurt – set in the middle of a water meadow with a river running close enough to gaze upon from the king-sized bed. There's an outdoor bath or shower and you can swim or fish straight from the jetty, play on the bench swing and light a firepit.

Deans Place ⌀ deansplace.co.uk. This pretty family-run hotel in Alfriston offers family rooms for up to five. Dogs are welcome, too. The outdoor heated swimming pool, with South Down views, is a big draw.

Flint Barns, Rathfinny Estate

⌀ rathfinnyestate.com. The ten en-suite bedrooms at the Flint Barns, on an award-winning South Downs vineyard that overlooks the Cuckmere Valley to the sea, provide a beautiful and relaxing place to stay with children (cots available). In summer the Flint Barns Dining Room serves picnics of local produce, presented in a natty wooden box to eat on the grass outside. Vineyard tours include their state-of-the-art gravity-powered presses and vats that can store four million bottles of wine.

Oakey Koakey Treehouse

⌂ downashwoodtreehouses.co.uk. This ultra-luxurious, family-sized treehouse in Ticehurst – north of Battle up the A21, in an area of Outstanding Natural Beauty – is reached by rope bridge. With its modern rustic interiors, the place evokes serious Swiss Family Robinson for the 21st century vibes.

Original Hut Company ⌂ original-huts.co.uk. Two clusters of four shepherd's huts near Bodiam, just outside Battle, offering a great chance to get off grid. The huts sleep up to five, snugly, and has a gas hob inside and a firepit for cooking outside; each cluster of four shares one wash hut. There's also an on-site café.

Palm Beach House

⌂ cabinsandcastles.co.uk. Just a minute's walk from the shingle Pett Level beach, six miles from Hastings, this five-bedroom Scandi-chic home offers contemporary interiors and a beautiful decked terrace for al-fresco dining.

Secret Campsite ⌂ thesecretcampsite. co.uk. Hidden away between the villages of Mount Pleasant and South Chailey, just north of Lewes, this pretty campsite offers honest-to-goodness camping pitches along with a tree tent that sleeps three adults and a child, and a gridshell sleeping up to five.

Seven Acre Woods Camping

⌂ sevenacrewoods.co.uk. With tent pitches and five log cabins with pretty front porches, this campsite is near Sedlescombe village near Battle. Thoughtful extras include a coffee station, a book swap and a log store, and for kids there are woodland swings, a squirrel lookout and pygmy goats to feed.

Skoolie Stays ⌂ skooliestays.co.uk. Kids will love the irony that they're not off to school but on holiday when you book this big old yellow American school bus parked in a field near Beachy Head. This ultra-cool glamping option was created by Guy and Ruth, who, inspired by their year travelling around the US with their young kids, brought a bus back to the UK and set it up here. It sleeps a family of four, with trendy wooden bunks for the kids, a wood-burning stove and a pretty deck.

The Star ⌂ thepolizzicollection. com. This Grade II-listed 16th-century building has been renovated by renowned hotelier and interior designer Olga Polizzi with her daughter, TV presenter Alex, in the village of Alfriston. Of the 30 rooms, there are eight sets of interconnecting rooms for families with extra beds and cots available. Kids will love the fact it's just a three-minute drive to Drusillas Park, or you can explore the wonderful Much Ado Books in the village. Olga will direct you to her favourite Italian ice-cream parlour, Fusciardis, in Eastbourne.

Sustainability Centre

⌂ sustainability-centre.org. This former Ministry of Defence building turned ecolodge offers B&B family suites sleeping four, an eco hostel for those who are happy to bunk up with others, yurts and camping. There's a vegetarian café on-site and a drop-in Wood Mouse Forest School for young kids. Family holiday workshops include activities such as shelter building, foraging and woodcrafts.

YHA South Downs ⌂ yha.org.uk. The dorm rooms in this refurbished Sussex farmhouse offer a low-cost way to enjoy Lewes and the South Downs National Park. You can also use the hostel facilities if you book a camping pod, bell tent, landpod or camping spot. Cots, drying room, laundry and cycle store available.

FAMILY-FRIENDLY EATS
Bathing Hut Café
⌂ thebathinghutcafe.com. Located on the seafront outside St Leonards towards Bexhill-on-Sea, this mainly meat-free al-fresco café serves delicious halloumi or katsu tofu burgers and dirty fries with bean chilli and cheese. Parents can watch their kids play on the pebbles from beachside tables.

Battle Deli & Coffee Shop 🄵. On the High Street opposite the 1066 Battlefield and Abbey, this attractive deli is a relaxed place for families to come for all-day breakfasts, jacket potatoes, toasted paninis and cake. The outdoor terrace at the back is a good spot in the sunshine and dogs are welcome too.

Bill's ⌂ bills-website.co.uk. Lewes was the site of the first Bill's restaurant,

which retains its cosy, wholesome vibe from its humble origins as a greengrocer's. Kids' menus feature yummy buttermilk pancake stacks and Little Bill's hamburgers. The baby-changing facilities are good, too.

Café Bar & Kitchen ⌂ dlwp.com. The De La Warr Pavilion's bright and airy restaurant, with sea views and balcony dining, is a lovely place for a family meal before or after a show or exhibition. The children's menu is more creative than most, listing such dishes as pea and mint risotto or a mini vegan summer bowl.

Goat Ledge ⌂ goatledge.com. Families adore this relaxed beach bar and fish hut on the Lower Promenade in St Leonards for its tasty fish baps and William the Cone-queror ice cream. There are tables on the beach or you can reserve a themed beach hut for sheltered dining by the sea. Summertime sees a number of fun events here, including live music.

Maggie's ⌂ maggiesfishandchips. co.uk. You won't get fresher fish 'n' chips than at Maggie's, a family-run restaurant right on Hastings fishing beach near the tall black net huts. Specials depend on the morning's catch. Generous kids' portions are good value for money.

Middle Farm ⌂ middlefarm.com. This working family farm in West Firle near Lewes sells fresh local produce in its farm shop, butcher's, bakery, cheese shop and cider barn. It's a great place to stock up for picnics and self-catered stays, and the kids can take a look at the pigs, llamas, ponies and donkeys. There's even a play barn with hay bales. **Tibbs Farm** ⌂ tibbsfarm.com. Stop by for breakfast, brunch or lunch – the menu lists everything from homemade pancakes to ham and cheddar ciabattas – in the picturesque Tillingham Valley, just west of Rye. In summer you can pick your own strawberries, raspberries or gooseberries. Children will love the maze, visiting the pigs and, in October, the pumpkin patch.

Tommy's Pizzeria ⌂ tommyspizzeria. co.uk. This St Leonards pizzeria serves wood-fired soughdough pizzas both inside and in its courtyard. There's also a take-away shack out front for sausage rolls, cakes and coffee. The staff here are particularly friendly and accommodating, especially with children.

Trawlers ☎ 01323 892520. A seaside classic in Seaford, this traditional fish and chip restaurant and take-away is a favourite for families. Eat in or take your box of cod 'n' chips to eat in the nearby St Leonard's Church graveyard (not as weird as it sounds) or down on the beach.

BEFORE YOU GO

The **Sussex Dolphin Project** (⌂ sussexdolphinproject.org) inspires and educates young people about the dolphins off the Sussex coast. You can support them by booking a Sunset Wildlife cruise or a Windfarm and Wildlife cruise from Brighton or Newhaven, both of which run from May to September. It's also possible to volunteer for projects such as beach cleans, or simply make a donation.

MORE INFO

1066 Country Tourism & Travel Information ⌂ visit1066country.com
South East England Tourist Board ⌂ visitsoutheastengland.com

10
SOUTH LONDON

From the bank of the Thames to the ancient woods of Dulwich, London's south side is a surprisingly wild adventure playground for families.

TOP FAMILY EXPERIENCE
SETTING UP BASE CAMP IN DULWICH WOODS &
EXPLORING SOUTH LONDON'S QUIRKIEST MUSEUM

BEST FOR KIDS AGED: 2–11
WHEN TO GO: June to September
INTREPID LEVEL: ①
ADDED ADVENTURE: River explorations, big-hitting galleries, offbeat museums, gardens, Olympic-style cycling, bookshops, parks
TIME: Long weekend to a week

BACK TO NATURE IN THE BIG CITY

South London Scout Centre: Grange Lane, Dulwich SE21 7LH, nearest train station Sydenham Hill ⚲ southlondonscouts.org.uk. Dulwich Woods & Sydenham Hill Wood: free to explore; Horniman Museum, 100 London Rd, Forest Hill SE23 3PQ ⚲ horniman.ac.uk; the museum & gardens are free to enter but there are admission fees for the Aquarium, Butterfly House & temporary exhibitions; book online in advance.

It's sunset and we've set up camp. There's that satisfying feeling of having created a snug home in nature after all the palaver of tent poles, blow-up mattresses and fairy lights. Our metal firepit and logs are all ready and waiting under the ebbing rays. I send my kids out to scavenge for kindling among the nearby trees, even though I've cheated and brought a dry backup bag with me. They return with armfuls of damp sticks and twigs, heady with the success of their haul. As the sun disappears and the frenzy of camping excitement turns to happy exhaustion, they at last gaze out at the view, myriad

lights catching their attention on the horizon. We spy the pretty yet formidable pink spike of the Shard standing proud, the rounded dome and criss-cross of the Gherkin, and the four white towers of Battersea Power Station – London landmarks that seem incongruous with our rural campfire setting. It's heartening, and a little magical, that even in the metropolitan spread of south London there are still mini pockets of wilderness waiting to be explored. We're here at the **South London Scout Centre**, where the private-school playing fields of Dulwich meet the affluent houses of Sydenham Hill. With its three large camping fields and indoor facilities for ablutions and cooking, it feels like a delicious secret. A slow and affordable way to stay in the capital, with easy access routes into its heart – whether that's jumping on the train at Sydenham Hill station to be whisked into London Blackfriars, right on the River Thames, in under 20 minutes, or bringing your bikes and exploring via the city's growing number of cycle lanes and low-traffic neighbourhoods.

This campsite is particularly precious. Not only does it sit next to a leafy golf course and sprawling allotments, but also, more significantly, to **Dulwich Woods** (75 acres), which segues into **Sydenham Hills Wood** (61 acres), both of which are now privately owned and managed by the Dulwich Estate. Together they form the largest surviving parts of the ancient Great North Wood – a living social geography lesson for children. I blow my kids' minds over their campfire sausages with the information that back in the Middle Ages this woodland, rich with mighty sessile oaks, common hornbeams and hazel, would have stretched right up to the Shard.

After our first night of urban camping, we set off to explore the woods, checking the **Wild London website** (⊘ wildlondon.org.uk) for species of rare fungi, insects, birds and woodland mammals to spot en route. On our list of birds are tawny owl, kestrel, firecrest, nuthatch and green woodpecker. What we actually spy are the psychedelic flashes of green parakeets that have flooded the capital, sparking a discussion about how they got here, how they survive and integrate, and whether they might put native birds at risk. These imported pets turned escapees have flourished owing to the heartening fact that 47% of London consists of

---

◀ **1** The Sunken Garden, Horniman Museum and Gardens. **2** Woodland den building. **3** Getting up close with moon jellyfish at the Horniman Aquarium.

green space, with 35,000 acres of parks, commons, woodlands, wetlands, cemeteries, allotments and gardens.

As we wander deeper into the woods, we spot fenced-off areas designed to let ancient woodland flowers like wood anemone and English bluebell thrive, and to give threatened wildlife such as hedgehogs a chance to survive. There's a Victorian folly, previously a garden ornament, to climb on, uprooted trees to investigate, and evidence of den building to inspire you to build your own. We stumble upon a glade, perfect for sun-loving plants and pollinators, and spy a family having a teddy bears' picnic.

When we've completed our morning's woody exploration, we head towards Cox's Walk, an 18th-century oak-lined avenue with a footbridge over an old railway track, and find signs to Green Chain Walk and the Horniman Museum, just half a mile away. Once out of the woods, we walk through a small housing estate to **Horniman Triangle Park**, a kids' playground with wood-and-rope climbing frames over a large sandpit.

After a five-minute walk up the busy London Road (A205), a main artery south out of the city, we come to the **Horniman Museum and Gardens**, an off-the-beaten-track treasure beloved of local children. The museum is a quirky place: originally built in Arts and Crafts style in 1901, it now features a 1996 'eco extension' with a living grass roof. Before we even enter, the outdoor bee garden is the first thing to catch my children's attention. Inside, meanwhile, this largely free museum offers an insightful and sometimes hands-on experience of global cultures and natural wonders. Its natural history gallery is like a mini version of London's Natural History Museum with its impressive taxidermy, skeletons and fossils, and feels generally a little more digestible. There will be oohs and ahhhs over the colossal mounted walrus that greets you, and gasps of revulsion at the pickled specimens. My son Fin reminisces about a series of books he loved called *An Awfully Beastly Business* about a werewolf boy who works for the Royal Society for the Protection of Cruelty to Beasts, battling against a baddy who's after rare specimens. Such is the charm and intelligence of this museum.

Down in the basement we discover a pint-sized aquarium, perfect for small children who tire easily of massive displays. The size helps you focus

"As we wander deeper into the woods, we spot fenced-off areas designed to let ancient woodland flowers thrive."

on the minutiae. From Fijian coral reefs to simulated wave action on a British shore, we are offered an exciting glimpse of life beneath the waves.

Back out in the fresh air, there's plenty to explore in the Horniman Gardens. Right by the café is the most exquisite Victorian glasshouse your kids are likely to encounter, and racing up the hill they're greeted by one of the best London views. Test your London knowledge and educate the family by spotting Wembley Stadium, Dawson Heights Estate, Strata SE1, St Paul's Cathedral, the Shard, the Walkie Talkie, the Cheese Grater and the Gherkin. A plaque reveals the geology of the capital, explaining that London was once attached to Europe and that the Thames was a tributary of the Rhine before glaciers diverted it into a new valley. My kids hoot out loud when we discover that hippos, lions and hyenas used to roam the city.

Next, we head up the hill to the Butterfly House, where we get a taste of what it's like to be in a tropical forest. A malachite butterfly is polite enough to land on my daughter's head. Outside there are alpacas, goats, sheep, guinea pigs and rabbits on the Animal Walk and plenty of grass for a tumble or a picnic. Who knew there was so much exotica to be found in south London?

ADDED ADVENTURE: FROM DINOS TO LIDOS – A CAPITAL CAPER

London can be an exhausting and stressful experience for families, with pressure to cram in all the iconic sights and get a quick handle on this heaving metropolis. Take the slow and local approach, though, and you relieve much of this intensity. Having lived in London most of my adult life, I've come to know and love it as a series of villages – a cosmopolitan patchwork of communities to dip in and out of while also taking in the big sights. South London has many not-to-be-missed family attractions, from the Imperial War Museum (⊘ iwm.org.uk), which questions rather than glorifies conflict, to the Royal Observatory and Royal Museums Greenwich (⊘ rmg.co.uk) where children can literally straddle east and west and learn about time zones. Mix these biggies up with homespun parks, smaller museums, offbeat historic attractions, artisanal markets and scenic cycle routes (check on ⊘ tfl.gov.uk), and you'll get that more authentic feeling of experiencing a place through the eyes of a local.

CRYSTAL PALACE

The **Crystal Palace Dinosaurs** (∂ cpdinosaurs.org) have been rocking south London since 1854. And though these impressive sculptures created by Benjamin Waterhouse Hawkins now have a few cracks here and there – the megalosaurus is in urgent need of a nose job – they are still much loved by families. This unlikely and free Jurassic encounter in the lower reaches of **Crystal Palace Park** (∂ crystalpalaceparktrust. org) brings to life the mind-blowing notion that creatures such as this roamed these parts millions of years ago. Check out the iguanodon that sprawls on the trunk of a cycad, a tropical plant whose fossils have been found nearby.

Kids will have fun running around the fenced-in ponds and islands, spotting the dinosaurs they know and love, though there may be some confusion as dino knowledge has come on somewhat since Victorian times. Some of the sculptures combine several animals that we now know about – a lesson in how knowledge evolves.

As you head around to the **boating lake** (∂ parkboatslondon.co.uk), you can set sail on the blue pedalos or perhaps task your children with finding the sculptures of Irish elk, an animal that died out thousands rather than millions of years ago.

Crystal Palace's 200 acres of rolling parkland feature many other eccentric attractions. The **Crystal Palace transmitter**, erected in 1956 to increase TV coverage across south London and the southeast, is quite literally a beacon for the area. At 700ft high it stands sentinel like a mini Eiffel Tower, and is a sight to behold at night with its red illuminations.

Just down the hill is the former site of the original glass-and-iron structure which gave the area its name. Three times the size of St Paul's Cathedral, the extravagant palace was moved here from the Great Exhibition in Hyde Park in 1851 and was initially loved as the 'Palace of the People' before falling into disrepair, ending in a blaze in 1936. All that remains are the incongruously grand stone steps and gargantuan stone lions guarding what is now a grassy expanse with city views.

The nearby **Crystal Palace National Sports Centre** (∂ better.org. uk) offers a mighty indoor pool and running track – the country's first rubberised and all-weather track – and beach volleyball on the 3,000

---

1 Book a ticket for Art Sundays at Dulwich Picture Gallery for family-friendly fun.
2 Crystal Palace Dinosaurs. ▶

tons of sand shipped over from Horse Guards Parade after the Olympics. Activities are bookable in advance. Nearby is an impressive and non-intimidating skate park which is free to use and suitable for all levels.

Head down the hill to the **maze**, also free and open to all. It is one of the largest in the country, with towering hedgerows just made for kids to charge around. Close by is the extraordinary RIBA Stirling Prize-shortlisted **stage**. Made from pre-weathered Corten steel and nicknamed 'the rusty laptop', it has been fraught by bad acoustics and flooding and now stands unused. Mischievous teens take delight in trying to breach the moat around it and clamber on.

DULWICH

It's an easy and largely downhill cycle or bus ride from Crystal Palace to **Dulwich Village**, a well-to-do area of south London that can leave you feeling like you've stepped into a little bit of the English countryside. Wander down the main street and you'll find old-school shops including Mr Green's art stationers, with a toy shop in the back, much loved by locals.

Across the road from Dulwich Park is **Dulwich Picture Gallery** (∂ dulwichpicturegallery.org.uk), England's first purpose-built public art gallery, founded in 1811. While the permanent collection of Old Masters may not ignite children, the special exhibitions are often thought-provoking and accessible and bijou enough so as not to tire kids out. Book a ticket for Art Sundays – interactive sessions for families on themes such as nature-inspired art. The pretty gardens are a good place to sit with a snack or an ice cream, and home to a different immersive installation each summer.

HERNE HILL & BRIXTON

Bike-mad families will adore the **Velodrome** (∂ hernehillvelodrome. com), which dates back to 1891 and hosted the 1948 Olympic cycling events. Just a ten-minute walk north of Dulwich, this revamped 1,475ft-banked track is available for kids' track cycling tasters and learn-to-cycle sessions. Be sure to book online two weeks in advance. Race evenings in summer (Wednesday, Friday and Saturday) are free to watch.

---

1 Brockwell Park Lido. **2** Tales on Moon Lane bookshop, Herne Hill.
3 Community greenhouses at Brockwell Park. ▶

Herne Hill itself is a cool enclave for families. Here you'll find **Tales on Moon Lane** bookshop (⌀ talesonmoonlane.co.uk), owned by children's author Tamara Macfarlane, who wrote the *Amazing Esme* series. A regular winner of Children's Bookseller of the Year at the British Book Awards for its creative window displays, fun interiors and fabulous book selections for all age groups, it's the perfect place for a rummage. School holidays see children's author readings and events in the storytelling cabin.

Nearby **Brockwell Park** is one of those London parks so loved by residents but which also has loads for visitors. Here you'll find community greenhouses (see box, page 172), a walled secret garden, a water play area, a pond with resident heron and swans, a large play park, BMX track and a miniature steam railway which makes you feel like a giant as you sit on the diminutive carriages for a ride. The Art Deco **Brockwell Lido** (⌀ fusion-lifestyle.com) is heaven for a family dip on a hot summer's day.

"Here you'll find Tales on Moon Lane, a regular winner of Children's Bookseller of the Year at the British Book Awards."

The **198 Contemporary Arts & Learning** (⌀ 198.org.uk), a five-minute walk from Brockwell on Railton Road, is a great space for children to encounter art that focuses on social inclusion and diversity. Stroll down to the other end of Railton Road – site of the Brixton Riots in 1981, now a gentrified, low-traffic neighbourhood – and you're in the heart of **Brixton**, with its covered markets, historic **Ritzy Cinema** (⌀ picturehouses.com) and the **Black Cultural Archives** (⌀ blackculturalarchives.org) in Windrush Square, where displays teach kids about the histories of African and Caribbean people in Britain.

THE SOUTH BANK

There's something primal about following a riverbank, even if it is the mighty Thames ebbing and flowing its way through its ever-insistent urban jungle. Kids can get a handle on a river, and on a sunny day there are few places more uplifting in London than the South Bank. It's a ready-made thoroughfare for families to follow, packed with attractions big and small in a metropolis that has the potential to overwhelm. At low tide, there are a number of accessible riverbank beaches and mudflats for supervised mudlarks with inquisitive ducks, gulls and even cormorants – most notably in front of Tate Modern and Gabriel's Wharf. There's usually a buzz to the place, with buskers, pedal-powered rickshaws and street-food stalls lining your route, and in school holidays there's a definite festival atmosphere.

While we have laid out the following route as an itinerary, it would not be possible to tackle it all in one go – there is far too much to see and do, and a large part of the pleasure is in meandering by the water, cherry picking your attractions and activities and taking spontaneous, unhurried breaks.

For the ultimate vantage point the **Shard** is a must. Disembark the train at London Bridge Station and crane your necks to view this mighty structure that looks like something out of a Marvel movie. It's interesting to discuss what might have inspired architect Renzo Piano. Was it London's church spires, perhaps? Try guessing how tall Western Europe's tallest building really is. Spoiler – 1,016ft! The **View from the Shard** (⌀ theviewfromtheshard.com) is the platform above the 72nd floor, reached by a bullet lift which shows the evolution of London from primordial swamp to 21st-century city as you pulse up through the different levels. From the top, kids get a great perspective over London with spectacular toy-town views of everything from the Tower of London to the London Eye.

Behind the futuristic Shard runs St Thomas Street, its old buildings juxtaposing with the new, not least the 18th-century church of the old St Thomas' Hospital, home to the **Old Operating Theatre Museum & Herb Garret** (⌀ oldoperatingtheatre.com). Climbing up a narrow spiral staircase to the garret, kids step back in time to an era before anaesthetics and antiseptics. Alarming instruments, pickled specimens, ancient skeletons, old-fashioned scales and dried herbs intrigue the most cynical of young people.

If you're with older teens, the nearby **Science Gallery London** (⌀ london.sciencegallery.com) is worth a visit for its free exhibitions, live experiments, open discussions and festivals on topics from gender to anxiety.

When you're done delving into the history of medicine or the future of science, cross busy Borough High Street by London Bridge to **Borough Market** (⌀ boroughmarket.org.uk; page 176), the original artisan market, dating back to the 11th century when fresh produce was brought up from the south coast ports. Ask your children to imagine a life before you could pop out to the supermarket and how when, before we had fridges, live cattle and goats would be brought to market, causing havoc. These days, you can wander around the inviting stalls, ranging from East Sussex cheesemakers Alsop & Walker ($\oslash$ alsopandwalker. co.uk) to Iraqi street food at Juma Kitchen ($\oslash$ jumakitchen.com), taking advantage of the many free samples en route. The delicious breads and pastries from **Bread Ahead** ($\oslash$ breadahead.com) are a hit with families, and children over six can attend their hands-on courses, including a two-hour doughnut workshop, so long as they are accompanied by an adult. Book well in advance.

The **Low Line Commons** ($\oslash$ lowline.london) is a four-mile walking trail that runs along the base of disused Victorian rail viaducts, celebrating the heritage of the railway arches and reanimating forgotten sites near Borough Market, Southwark Cathedral and London Bridge station. It aims to increase eco-diversity with tree planting, community gardens and new wildlife habitats and is well worth seeking out.

Back on the riverfront, wind your way via the mighty Southwark Cathedral to the riverside and explore the **Golden Hinde** ($\oslash$ goldenhinde.co.uk), a reconstruction of the galleon originally called the *Pelican*, captained by Francis Drake as he circumnavigated the globe between 1577 and 1580.

And if you love a bit of crime and punishment, make for the **Clink Prison Museum** ($\oslash$ clink.co.uk) just a little further along the river. Housed in a real prison dating back to 1144, making it the oldest gaol in Britain, the Clink today offers a chilling demonstration of a brutal penal system, and is suitable for kids aged seven and up only.

One of the stars of the South Bank is without doubt **Shakespeare's Globe** ($\oslash$ shakespearesglobe.com), reconstructed in 1997 near the original site of the 1599 amphitheatre. If ever you wanted to bring Shakespeare's England and the theatrical world he created to life, this is the place to come. At its heart is an icosagon, a 20-sided polygon structure built from oak beams, lime-plaster walls and water-reed thatched roof (the only thatched roof in London), which forms the roofless theatre. Prams are not allowed in, but babies in slings and carriers are very welcome. Guided family tours, aimed at children aged between seven and 11 (though all ages are welcome), get down to the nitty-gritty of theatre-going in Elizabethan England in a time before

---

1 The Golden Hinde. **2** Old Operating Theatre Museum & Herb Garret. ▶

"Ask your children to imagine a life before you could pop out to the supermarket and how when, before we had fridges, live cattle and goats would be brought to market, causing havoc."

mobile phones, computers and television (gulp!). Kids will get a sense of how impactful theatre was, and learn how poor people, named 'penny groundlings', would pay a penny to be crammed into the standing-only pit to watch a play. Check out the website for children's workshops and events such as a Midsummer Night's Dream puppetry workshop for children aged three and above.

Moments away from the Globe is a literal giant of Bankside – **Tate Modern** (⊘ tate.org.uk). Since my kids were very little, the Turbine Hall has been a place of joy and wonder with its sloping entrance for tumbling down and its temporary interactive creations such as Carsten Höller's large stainless-steel slides. The Tanks, huge spaces previously used to store oil in the days when the gallery was a power station, sometimes host live performance art, and there are always kids' workshops during the school holidays. The Blavatnik Building Viewing Level in the Tate Modern extension is an awesome and free way to gaze over the city, and you can pause for a drink and a snack.

"Check out the website for children's workshops and events such as a Midsummer Night's Dream puppetry workshop."

Right outside Tate Modern is the **Millennium Bridge**, otherwise known as the Wobbly Bridge owing to its lateral suspension which did cause it to actually wobble when it first opened. Stand on it with kids for the epic view to St Paul's Cathedral – an optical illusion makes it seem as if the bridge connects with the church.

Further along the South Bank, **Gabriel's Wharf** (⊘ southbanklondon. com) is a great pit stop for food, independent shops, and a run around the landscaped Bernie Spain Gardens for little ones.

Nearby are the big hitters of the **National Theatre** (⊘ nationaltheatre. org.uk), **BFI Southbank** (⊘ whatson.bfi.org.uk), **Hayward Gallery** and **Royal Festival Hall** (⊘ southbankcentre.co.uk). All four mighty arts institutions are a real draw for families in search of culture. The Royal Festival Hall is particularly accessible for families with its free exhibition spaces, cafés and gift shops, which always have a kids' section. The architecture of this part of the South Bank invites exploration: the sun-bright yellow spiral steps outside the Queen Elizabeth Hall Purcell

---

◀ Borough Market. **1** The Globe theatre. **2** Summer fun in the fountains on the South Bank. **3** Breathtaking views from the London Eye. **4** South Bank's Skate Park. ▶

Rooms; the hidden fountains just outside the RFH, where kids squeal with delight and inevitably get soaked in summer (top tip – pack swimsuits and a towel); the neon-red benches in crazy shapes, including a smile, for families to cram on for a selfie; and the covered skate park where skater boys and girls do their thing among the graffiti.

Slightly further upriver, beyond the Hungerford Bridge, **Jubilee Park & Gardens** (⊘ jubileegardens.org.uk) has a proper playground for little ones and makes a good place to while away some time before a ride on the **London Eye** (⊘ londoneye.com), a big wheel that offers panoramic city views. The nearby **SEA LIFE Centre London Aquarium**

COMMUNITY GREENHOUSE DAYS IN BROCKWELL PARK

Brockwell Park Community Greenhouses, Brockwell Park, SE24 9BJ ⊘ brockwellgreenhouses. org.uk; age: 4–16; intrepid level ①; small fees charged for workshops: booking advised

Brockwell Park's Community Greenhouses are a great place to visit with children, even if you're just passing through and spending an afternoon in the park. There's an unsupervised mud kitchen for families to play in, a Sound Trail, an orchard, vegetable and herb gardens, and a fern gulley.

Best of all, though, are the special events. We arrive at the greenhouses just in time for Story Stompers, a gentle nature-based activity for preschoolers which begins with a picture-book story. 'We always have a theme that ties in with something like vegetable growing, nature, or plants and creatures that we find in the garden,' says volunteer Beth Barber. After the story, a tale about a rabbit discovering spring, the children set off with Beth to hunt for spring flowers, blossom and leaf buds in the plantings around the greenhouses. We then regroup to make bunnies out of gathered twigs, flowers and leaves, plus recycled materials.

'We sometimes sow tomato seeds and the children decorate the pots and take them home to grow,' says Beth. 'We might make toilet-roll squirrels, or stick twigs on a piece of MDF and decorate it with tissue paper to celebrate *hanami*, the Japanese cherry blossom festival.'

Beth also runs weekend community events. 'Our most popular is when we fire up the outdoor clay pizza oven. Families can choose what herbs from the garden they want to include on their pizza topping. We also have themed seasonal events such as the popular wassailing day in January, and the May Day fête where the children make Jack o' the Green masks.'

The school holidays, too, see a wealth of workshops. These might range from rag weaving using local materials to science-based sessions – an exploration of microbes, for example, in which children can use a microscope to peer at pond water

(⌖ visitsealife.com) is well worth a look, but you might want to carry on upriver where the mood alters to something altogether less touristy, despite the awesome view of the Houses of Parliament and Big Ben across the river.

A hidden delight of the South Bank is **Archbishop's Park** behind Lambeth Palace, with its beehives, ping-pong tables, five-a-side pitches and nature trails. And don't miss a visit to the unassuming **Garden Museum** (⌖ gardenmuseum.org.uk) in the former St Mary-at-Lambeth church by Lambeth Bridge, the perfect place to show children the power of gardening. Hands-on exhibits include an interactive Plant

BROCKWELL PARK COMMUNITY GREENHOUSES

and some of the creatures that live in it. 'We have a look at the composting process and go on a garden search looking for fungi in the log pile which kids are always fascinated by. And we might make felt microbes for the children to take away with them.'

It's a wonderfully broad spectrum. Whether your kids – and you! – want to learn about flatbreads or wood preserving, medicinal herbs or woodworking, willow weaving or fermenting, you'll find something to inspire you at this special place.

Quest where kids assume the role of a young plant hunter heading off into the world to find new species. There's also the added bonus of climbing the ancient church tower, up 131 narrow winding stairs, for breathtaking views over the Thames, Westminster and the Harry Potter-esque rooftops of Lambeth Palace – like your very own, ancient mini Shard.

September 2022 saw the reopening of the iconic **Battersea Power Station** (⊘ batterseapowerstation.co.uk) following a £9 billion investment which has transformed this 1935 behemoth into a new district of London with its very own tube station, children's play park, shops and restaurants and riverside park. Families can take the elevator 360ft up the North West chimney for a 360° view of the London skyline.

To explore the Thames by boat, kids, especially teens, will love a bit of high-octane fun aboard the **Thames Rib Experience** speedboats (⊘ thamesribexperience.com). If you want something more sedate, local and cheap, simply catch one of the many public transport river buses operated by **Thames Clippers** (⊘ thamesclippers.com). For example, you could go from the O2 at North Greenwich to Battersea Power Station, sightseeing as you go.

PRACTICALITIES

FAMILY-FRIENDLY SLEEPS

Abbey Wood Caravan Club Site
⊘ caravanclub.co.uk. Family-friendly campsite near Greenwich, open to caravans, motorhomes and campers. Trains link into central London in just 35 minutes or take a river cruise between Greenwich, Tower Bridge, Westminster, Kew, Richmond and Hampton Court.

Alma Hotel ⊘ almawandsworth.
com. This Wandsworth pub with pretty, contemporary bedrooms is stylish and cosy with a country kitchen feel. Two bedrooms with a private connecting hallway suit families, and kids can play in the private garden terrace.

citizenM London Bankside
⊘ citizenm.com. A slick, futuristic hotel just a two-minute walk from the River Thames and Tate Modern. Kids will love the huge beds, mood lighting, rain showers, free films and soft drinks.

Half Moon, Herne Hill
⊘ halfmoonhernehill.co.uk. This attractive pub with rooms, just by Brockwell Park, offers a real taste of south London but is also close to Herne Hill train station so you can be whisked into central London in just ten minutes. The spacious Grand Suite has a large king-size bed and sofa bed for up to two children. Or if you're staying with teens,

book them into the fun Cabin Room. The restaurant has tasty kids' menus, and al-fresco dining, too.

Hilton London Bankside ⬙ hilton. com. You'll feel the excitement of staying right on London's South Bank at this chic urban hotel. Interconnecting family rooms include a goodie bag with crayons and a children's city map, child-sized bathrobes and slippers and a onesie for kids up to the age of three! There's also a heated indoor pool.

Hoxton Southwark ⬙ thehoxton. com. This buzzy hotel near the river has rooms inspired by the tanneries and factories that once populated south London. Roomy and Biggy rooms sleep two adults and a child. Some are dog friendly. Kids who don't like sitting down for formal breakfasts will love the option of having a breakfast bag hung on your door in the morning.

InterContinental London – The O2 ⬙ iclondon-theo2.com. This Greenwich Peninsula hotel offers a great family package including a studio or suite for up to four guests, breakfast in the on-site Market Brasserie, complimentary parking, late checkout, children's TV channels and dedicated children's swim times. It's fun to arrive at the hotel by the Thames Clipper service (⬙ thamesclippers.com) to North Greenwich Pier.

London Marriott Hotel County Hall ⬙ marriott.co.uk. This imposing hotel in the former City Hall has a great river location next to the London Eye, with family rooms, babysitting services, a kids' concierge, games, an indoor pool, bike hire and complimentary cookies. Book family afternoon tea in the Library, with views across to Big Ben and Westminster.

Native Bankside ⬙ nativeplaces.com. Formerly a Victorian tea warehouse, this aparthotel beside Shakespeare's Globe and the River Thames offers families stylish modern apartments for up to four guests, with fully equipped kitchens including washing machines. You'll all get a buzz from the boutique hotel feel and cool location – perfectly placed to food shop at Borough Market.

Pestana Chelsea Bridge Hotel & Spa ⬙ pestana.com. Located between Battersea Park and the new Battersea Power Station development, this modern four-star is a solid choice for families, with a selection of family rooms and suites and an indoor pool.

Sea Containers London ⬙ seacontainerslondon.com. This magnificent building, which feels like an ocean liner locked on the banks of the River Thames, sits close to Tate Modern and Shakespeare's Globe. Kids will adore its playful modern style, awesome river views and in-house cinema. Book a large suite or an apartment.

Shangri-La The Shard ⬙ shangri-la. com. This five-star hotel is a show-stopper. Exiting the lift into the reception on floor 34, families get a breathtaking panorama over London. If budget allows, book the family package and receive a second room at 50%

discount for guests up to the age of 15. Children also receive a plush stuffed toy, while the whole family can enjoy a private shopping trip at Harvey Nichols and a dip in the infinity Sky Pool, the highest hotel pool in the Western world, on level 52.

South London Scouts

 southlondonscouts.org.uk. Camping right next to Dulwich Woods (page 155). **Tulse Hill Hotel** tulsehillhotel.com. This cosy boutique hotel has just nine bedrooms including large, family-sized doubles. Its friendly restaurant serves British seasonal food and has a garden bar in the summer months. Close to Herne Hill, Dulwich and Brixton.

Victoria Inn victoriainnpeckham. com. Close to the Horniman Museum, this boutique pub with rooms offers cool Scandi interiors and has a feature double room with a sofa bed that sleeps four. The pub restaurant serves seasonal British food with a good children's menu, too.

KID-FRIENDLY EATS

Battersea Power Station

 batterseapowerstation.co.uk. The food offerings at Battersea Power Station are still evolving, but rest assured there are plenty of choices for families. Gordon Ramsey Street Pizza specialises in sourdough pizzas, whilst Megan's At the Power Station serves Mediterranean cuisine with riverside views and a bottomless brunch at weekends. Dogs are very welcome too. Japanese cuisine from Tonkotsu.

Borough Market boroughmarket. org.uk. A great place to browse with kids and pick up a take-away meal, from Italian pasta and gnocchi to salt beef, falafel and classic deli foods.

Four Hundred Rabbits 400rabbits. co.uk. This small southeast London chain offers a tried and tested formula of sourdough pizza, gelato and beer (or soft drinks for kids) in a fun atmosphere. Its Herne Hill restaurant is by Brockwell Lido, with outdoor seating overlooking the pool. It's a great place to come after a swim. There's another branch in Crystal Palace.

Gabriel's Wharf (southbanklondon. com). South Bank enclave with a good choice of places to eat with kids, some of them take-away only. Good choices include the Gourmet Pizza Company (gourmetpizzacompany. co.uk), The Wharf, Hola Guacamole (holaguacamole.com) and The Big Melt Toastie Shack.

Herne Hill Sunday Market

 weareccfm.com. Step off the train at Herne Hill station and you're at the top of Railton Road, home of Herne Hill's Sunday market (10am to 4pm). Here you can pick up tasty take-away food including tartiflette, hot sausage rolls and popcorn – all crowd-pleasers for young palates.

Minus 12° Craft Ice cream

 minus12.co.uk. This glorious ice-cream stand, housed in an avante-garde black box in Herne Hill Station, serves the most inventive gelato and sorbets around. Try the Green Eyed Monster (peppermint gelato with homemade chocolate brownie pieces) and Joker (cheesecake gelato with homemade chuckleberry ripple). Top marks, too, for biodegradable and compostable packaging.

Pavilion Café. In the centre of Dulwich Park, just near the boating lake, this inviting café has indoor and outdoor seating and a cute inside play area with toys and books for young children. They serve a hearty café menu of soups, salads, pastries and cakes.

Pop Brixton *⊘* popbrixton.org. Teens will love a mooch round Pop Brixton, a market created out of shipping containers, for secondhand clothes and street food with a hip vibe. Feast on plant-based burgers at Halo Burger, modern Caribbean street food at Mama's Jerk, churros from Love Churros and more. This is also the HQ of Reprezent, south London's youth radio station.

Rocca Di Papa *⊘* roccarestaurants. com. This Dulwich Village institution is a big hit with local families for its consistently good pizzas and pastas in a relaxed atmosphere.

Swan Bar & Restaurant at Shakespeare's Globe *⊘* shakespearesglobe.com. The theatre restaurant has river views, comfy leather banquettes, bespoke children's menus and highchairs. It's breastfeeding friendly and they can warm up bottles or baby food and provide hot water for formula. Great for afternoon tea, weekend brunch or a Sunday roast. Book ahead.

Wahaca Southbank *⊘* wahaca. co.uk. Housed in cantilevered shipping containers right by the River Thames, this South Bank Mexican restaurant is a hit with kids for its playful construction and fresh burritos, tacos, nachos and salads. Kids can build their own mini tacos. Just make sure you book in advance.

BEFORE YOU GO

Staying in south London with your children, you owe it to yourself to check out what's on at the **Unicorn Theatre** (*⊘* unicorntheatre.com), a performance space on Tooley Street, not far from Tower Bridge, dedicated to productions for kids from six months old right up to teens.

MORE INFO

Londontopia *⊘* londontopia.net
Visit London *⊘* visitlondon.com

11
KENT

Between Weald and beach, Downs and sea, the Garden of England is home to enterprising producers, makers and creators delighted to share their purpose and patch.

TOP FAMILY EXPERIENCE

WILLOW WEAVING & AL-FRESCO COOKING AT COWSHED WORKSHOP, TENTERDEN

BEST FOR KIDS AGED: 6+

WHEN TO GO: Year-round

INTREPID LEVEL: ①

ADDED ADVENTURE: Arty seaside resorts, canoe trips, country walks, foraging, cycling, birdwatching, wilderness camps, beaches

TIME: Three days to one week

GETTING CREATIVE IN A COWSHED

Reader's Bridge Rd, St Michaels, Tenterden TN30 6TH ⊘ cowshedworkshop.co.uk

Off a winding country lane near the quaint town of Tenterden in the Kentish Weald, surrounded by towering oaks and laden hedgerows, family-run Cowshed Workshop is an evolving enclave of creativity on a former hop farm. Having worked in tourism for years, owner Seren knows a thing or two about delivering experiences that exude a sense of place. Local artisans run courses for beginners on everything from pewter and copper jewellery-making to ceramics, in two beautiful spaces – a cosy indoor room and a converted cowshed, where the family activities take place.

Within moments of arriving for our willow weaving and outdoor cooking session, free-range animals steal the show. 'He just wants a stroke,' Seren's daughter Summer explains, as one of three nosy turkeys

---

◀ Willow weaving at Cowshed Workshop.

plops itself down by our ankles. It doesn't take long to make friends: 'It's purring!', beams Barney. Once it's clear the boys are receptive to curious creatures, Summer takes them off on a mini farm tour to meet 'the world's smallest chicken' and resident donkeys Daisy and Doris. Meanwhile, I enjoy a coffee in the workshop before we delve into weaving. A giant willow and dried hop chandelier hangs from the vaulted ceiling, mountains of willow are piled to one side, and a glowing wood-burning stove is a happy reminder that autumn is coming. It's a calming space.

"The boys can pick what they'd like to make – a game of quoits, a mouse, a fishing line or a wand, perhaps."

Our weaving experience starts out in the fields, where we meander around the farm to spot wildlife and forage for foliage that might be useful. Seren likes everything to relate to the seasons and the land, and so heading outside is a natural place to start. Seren explains, 'It was on a walk a few years ago that I spotted the waste from a vine prune at Biddenden Vineyard just down the road. It got me thinking: there must be so much of this wasted foliage in Kent, especially near here, where there are eleven vineyards – we should work it into our courses.'

Back at the workshop, we pile a random collection of finds on the huge oak table to start making. Luckily, Seren has a stack of willow ready and waiting (I was concerned our twigs and leaves wouldn't amount to much). The boys can pick what they'd like to make – a game of quoits, a mouse, a fishing line or a wand, perhaps. We settle for a game of quoits and a fishing line; both handy for the beach, where we're heading next. The willow is surprisingly stiff to work with, and while Seren whips up a mouse in no time at all, it takes the three of us a while to get used to it. Once we do, we're happily lost in the rhythmic winding, twirling and occasional chopping for almost an hour. 'What's great, boys, is that now, whenever you're on a country walk, you can find some twigs and do some weaving along the way,' explains Seren enthusiastically. I find the image hard to imagine but appreciate having another long walk distraction technique up my sleeve.

Willow hoops for quoits on the beach and a swirling fishing line in hand, it's now time for lunch. For this part of the session, Seren has teamed up with local outfit **Wild Classroom** (wildclassroom.co.uk), which delivers 'cooking stripped bare', educating people about traditional cooking techniques in the great outdoors. We wander from the cowshed to a cooking station beneath a 300-year-old oak tree. A huge cauldron hangs over a pile of logs while head chef Scott talks us through the chosen ingredients – a mêlée of seasonal fruit and veg – and what we're going to make. The cauldron is called a 'Dutch Oven' (yes, there were some sniggers) – a camper's dream bit of kit that can boil, stew, roast, fry and bake foods over an open fire. The kids look startled and delighted in equal measure at the prospect of both chopping *and* fire.

First, the chopped squash, pepper, potatoes and onions go in to make a warming soup. Next, we head to Seren's orchard to pick ingredients for the second course; a sweet apple pizza, baked on the fire – much to the amazement of the kids, who are hanging off Scott's every word – and loaded with crème patissière and icing sugar. Once the feast is complete, it's time to dig in. None of us can quite believe we made something so tasty with nothing but a cauldron and fire. With bellies full of joy and a car full of willow, it's time to head on to the next adventure.

ADDED ADVENTURE: CASTLES, CLIFFS & CRAFTING

Long known as the 'Garden of England', the southeastern county of Kent is awash with fresh produce, and there are plenty of opportunities to taste, pick and explore. Its orchards are home to 2,200 apple varieties, more than 45 vineyards churn out fine wines, and 90% of England's cherries weigh down the boughs of the county's cherry trees. Browse dozens of listings on Produced in Kent ($\oslash$ producedinkent.co.uk) to find delicious and imaginative food and drink to buy and experience. Kent's Area of Outstanding Beauty, comprising the chalky Kent Downs and largely wooded Kent Weald, carves a line across the county from Surrey and Sussex to the eastern shores of England. Check out the Kent Downs site ($\oslash$ kentdowns.org.uk) to find out more about outdoor adventures and the geography here. And then there's the sea: beyond the farmland, the long-distance North Downs Way carves a chalky path from Sevenoaks to the white cliffs of Dover, while the coastline – more than 350 miles of it – has as much historical and cultural interest as it does wildlife.

DUNGENESS & ROMNEY MARSH

Dungeness, the desolate 12-square-mile stretch of shingle between the sea and Romney Marsh, is often cited as the UK's only desert. Although this is not technically true – the area has too much rainfall for that to be the case – the other-worldly headland (the name derives from the Norse for headland, 'nes', and the Denge Marsh inland) certainly has that feel. As one of the largest expanses of shingle in Europe, it's a fiercely protected national nature reserve and Special Protection Area. Unique vegetation, including yellow flowered broom bushes, white-tipped sea kale and viper's bugloss (as vibrant as it is intimidating), attracts butterflies, moths and other insects. Porpoises sometimes feed off the point, and kids will love scouring the high-tide mark for crab skeletons, shells and hagstones (stones with holes running through the middle). It's a treat for children to run about in this vast open space, pulled in all directions by creative and natural attractions.

So huge is the beach, it would be easy to get lost if not for a few key landmarks. Dungeness' two decommissioned nuclear power stations provide a bleak industrial backdrop to the **Old Lighthouse** (⊘ dungenesslighthouse.com), built in 1901. The 169-step climb (not suitable for toddlers) rewards visitors with incredible sea views. All the other buildings are low rise, and the whole place has a frontier feel about it. **Prospect Cottage**, once home to filmmaker Derek Jarman, is the most famous of Dungeness's much sought-after beach houses. Since there are no boundaries in the nature reserve, visitors can wander around the artistic garden surrounding the cottage, although the house itself is private. Similarly intriguing, **Open View Studio** (⊘ ocean-view-studio.com) and **Dungeness Open Studios** (⊘ paintings-for-sale.net) both welcome visitors into their workspaces to browse art. **Dungeness Lifeboat Station** is also worth a visit, to see the RNLI at work and admire the boats – ring ahead for opening times or to book a tour (⊘ dungenesslifeboat.org.uk).

A little inland, kids can pick up a Wildlife Explorer rucksack (free of charge) before embarking on mini-beast hunting, birdwatching and pond dipping at the **RSPB Dungeness Nature Reserve** (⊘ rspb. org.uk). Lade Pits, a former quarry used to extract sand and gravel for construction, makes up part of the reserve and features the bizarre **Denge Sound Mirrors**, three concrete structures, 195ft tall, that were used to pick up the sounds of enemy aircraft in the early 1930s. You can

1 *Holiday Home* is one of 74 artworks dotted across Folkestone. **2** Prospect Cottage, Dungeness. **3** Romney, Hythe and Dymchurch Railway. ▶

see the sound mirrors from the nature reserve, but to get a closer look walk up to them from the coastal Seaview Road, half a mile from the reserve. About five miles up the coast, **Romney Marsh Visitor Centre** (⊘ theromneymarsh.net) is a community-run haven of attractions and nature trails, including the Marsh Community Garden, the Art Shack with regular exhibitions by local artists, and the Looker's Hut – one of the original shepherd huts on the marsh. Ring ahead to book experiences from sheep shearing to wood whittling.

One of the most enjoyable ways to experience this section of the coast is on the **Romney, Hythe and Dymchurch Railway** (⊘ rhdr.org.uk). Using steam and diesel trains that are one-third the standard size, the line has a wonderfully old-fashioned, seaside fun feel about it – larger knees poke out of cabins, picnics sprawl, and everyone gives passers-by a wave. Visitors can hop on and off at seven stations along a 13-mile track between Dungeness and Hythe. Don't miss the huge **Model Railway Exhibition** at New Romney Station.

FROM FOLKESTONE TO WHITSTABLE

Heading north from Dungeness, the Kent coastline hugs the English Channel via Dover and Deal up to Ramsgate, Broadstairs and Margate on the Isle of Thanet, and then curves around to Whitstable. It's an area of varied attractions. From the white cliffs of Dover to sandy Botany Bay, from Margate's **Turner Contemporary** to the Roman **Reculver Towers** (⊘ english-heritage.org.uk) near Herne Bay, there's enough on this patchwork coastline to fill weeks of exploration.

Twenty miles up the coast from Dungeness, the arty town of **Folkestone** may not be as pretty as the likes of Whitstable or Deal, but there's plenty on offer if you know where to look. The **Lower Leas Coastal Park** (⊘ visitkent.co.uk), a short walk from the town along the seafront, has lots of interest for kids including one of the largest and best-designed adventure playgrounds in the region and an amphitheatre that hosts live music and theatre. On the other side of town, Cornelia Parker's bronze sculpture *The Folkestone Mermaid* sits on rocks beside the aptly named Sunny Sands beach. It's one of 74 permanent and temporary outdoor **artworks** throughout Folkestone, including a cast-iron human statue by Antony Gormley, that date from the town's highly acclaimed **Triennial art festival** (⊘ creativefolkestone.org.uk). Down by the harbour, **Folkstone Harbour Arm** (⊘ folkestoneharbourarm.co.uk), a former railway terminal, now hosts a collection of food trucks. Back in town, older kids will enjoy the ingenuity of **The Upcycled Trading Company** (⏀ tutco.co.uk), which runs a series of arty workshops – painting old tea trays, for example.

Another ten miles up the coast, just beyond Dover, **Wild Kitchen's Edible Seashore** (⏀ thewildkitchen.net) foraging experiences offer a wonderful experience. The meeting place is a boat-shaped wooden beach hut on the north side of St Margaret's Bay, where wildflower-topped white cliffs plummet down to the sea. Tours start on the clifftops, with scissors and baskets in hand, to gather edible berries and herbs, and then descend to the sea for a session on identifying coastal vegetables and seaweeds.

"Tours start on the clifftops, with scissors and baskets in hand, to gather edible berries and herbs."

Back at the hut, guests enjoy a vegan wild food feast – learning more about the tastes and flavours of the landscape as they eat – including seaweed crisps, seaweed and dock seed bread, and botanical mocktails.

Beyond the handsome historic resort of **Deal**, which is worth a visit for its Tudor castles, ice-cream parlours, and pier, **Chequers Kitchen Cookery School** (⏀ chequersdeal.co.uk) offers families more conventional foodie experiences with pasta- and bread-making lessons that get kids understanding and handling ingredients from scratch. If history is more appealing, try one of Deal's family-friendly **History Project** (⏀ thehistoryproject.co.uk) tours on subjects such as 'The Smugglers' Trail' and 'Piers over the Years'.

The **Viking Coastal Trail** (⏀ sustrans.org.uk), a 30-mile cycling route that starts at the village of Cliffsend near Ramsgate and takes in the resorts of Ramsgate, Broadstairs and Margate, is a wonderful way to experience the Isle of Thanet – Kent's coastal 'hump'. The inland loop passes **Minster Abbey**, dating back to AD670, which is not far from **Monkton Nature Reserve** (⏀ monkton-reserve.org), home to rare orchids. Other good sections for families include the stretch from Ramsgate to Broadstairs, which runs through the wooded, clifftop King George VI Memorial Park, and a largely traffic-free five-mile chunk from Margate harbour to Minnis Bay, which takes in a series of sandy coves. **Wider Experience** (⏀ widerexperience.co.uk) organises bespoke bike tours around the coast, as well as bike and e-bike hire and a passenger drop-off and pick-up service.

ENGLISH HERITAGE

HOLLY TUPPEN

RON ELLIS/S

VISIT KENT

As for the Thanet resorts, the pretty Victorian town of **Broadstairs** boasts a big sandy beach, as does arty **Margate** – the latter is a haven of creativity, and is home to the **Turner Contemporary** (⊘ turnercontemporary.org), which has free drop-in family workshops, and kiss-me-quick seaside fun. A mile east of the centre, the **Walpole Bay** tidal swimming pool is great for a splash and surrounded by rock pools at low tide.

Fifteen miles along the coast from Margate, the pretty seaside town of **Whitstable** is particularly popular during its annual summer **Oyster Festival** (⊘ whitstableoysterfestival.co.uk). Besides (literally) mountains of the oysters, there are lifeboat shows, Morris dancing, crafts and live music. For a closer understanding of natural and human history in the area, the **Salt Marsh Walking Company** (⊘ thesaltmarshwalkingcompany.co.uk) peppers local guided walks with locally sourced picnics; if you prefer to go it alone, try the **Whitstable Maritime Coastal Trail and Oyster Walk** (⊘ whitstablecoastaltrail.org.uk), a flat three-mile walk manageable with little legs, or the **Crab and Winkle Way** (⊘ explorekent.org), a path along a disused Victorian railway line that runs 7½ miles between Whitstable and Canterbury.

Whitstable's winding high street, back-to-back with independent shops, including several toy shops, is worth a browse. If the main beach, a sloping stretch of shingle backed by a seafront path, is a little busy, head east to the quieter **Tankerton**, another shingle beach, which sits below **Whitstable Castle** (⊘ whitstablecastle. co.uk) – not a castle but in fact a mansion. The castle has a small café and toilets.

CANTERBURY & THE KENT DOWNS

Kent's **River Stour** carves its way from the edge of the North Downs via **Canterbury** to the coast at Pegwell. Some claim it's England's most historic river, thanks to its heavy use in Roman and medieval times, particularly by pilgrims. A relaxing way to get a sense of this history is on a 45-minute rowing expedition through the city centre with **Canterbury Historic River Tours** (⊘ canterburyrivertours.co.uk). The humorous

◀ **1** Reculver Towers. **2** Cookery class at Chequers Kitchen. **3** The Turner Contemporary, Margate. **4** Preparing oysters, Whitstable.

BIRDWATCHING AT ELMLEY NATURE RESERVE

Elmley, Isle of Sheppey ME12 3RW ⊘ elmleynaturereserve.co.uk; age: 3+; intrepid level: ①

It's possible to explore the reserve at your own pace, but today we've got Abbie Burrows, the reserve's engagement officer and guide, to show us around. Decked out with binoculars, we meander towards the seawall to one of the reserve's four bird hides. It's late October, and although the sun is out, there's a nip in the air. Golden grasses shimmer in the breeze, broken by channels of water slithering like snakes across the landscape to the Swale's churning inky chop just below the seawall.

'It's the start of the overwintering period,' Abbie explains, 'so more birds are joining us all the time. From now until February, the wildfowl and wading birds, including curlew, teal, wigeon, Brent geese and ducks, will eventually reach the tens of thousands on the Swale Estuary. This brings in the birds of prey to the reserve, such as merlin, peregrine and short-eared owls.'

Within moments we spot the distant V-formation of a flock of greylag geese and a marsh harrier hovering nonchalantly right above the gravel track. 'We have 12 breeding pairs at Elmley, which is pretty incredible given the species was nearly extinct only 40 years ago,' says Abbie. We also marvel at a green sandpiper on the water's edge, as Abbie explains how far it must still go on its journey to winter in Africa, and babbling brent geese that have flown in from the Arctic. A mini geography lesson soon unfurls as the boys try to get their heads around the distances involved.

The three-mile walk across Elmley is peppered with stops; Abbie helps the boys use the binoculars and survey bird charts along the way. Before we know it, we're at the far end of the reserve where the final hide, aptly named Spitend, sits on the edge of the salt marsh with views out to sea. Surrounded as it is by water and marsh, it's easy to see how significant this site is for wildlife. 'The Thames Estuary is one of the biggest migratory stopovers in the southeast,' Abbie tells us. 'What would the birds do without it?' one of the boys asks. We all agree that we hope to never find out.

After a picnic at Spitend, we head back, this time to talk bugs, critters and pond life to keep the kids engaged as we retrace our steps. No

commentary keeps little ones entertained and there's a dry-land version if the boating doesn't appeal. **Punting tours** (⊘ canterburypunting. co.uk) are also available for those that want to take to the river in a little more style.

While the main sight in town is the lofty **Canterbury Cathedral** (⊘ canterbury-cathedral.org), there are a number of other child-friendly experiences. Check out **Canterbury Ghost Tours** (⊘ thecanterburytours.com), which bring the city's darker history and

chemicals have been used on the site for over 50 years, so insect life is plentiful. On closer inspection, we notice web after web hanging between grasses, and it doesn't take long before we spot the culprit: a wasp spider. A migrant hawker – one of 12 species of dragonfly on the reserve – hovers above a pond. It's sometimes possible to spot marsh froglets and the greater pond snail, too, Abbie tells us.

Back at the café in the reserve's central hub, Kingshill Barn, a tiny murmuration of starlings is a sign of things to come and the last of the year's swallows swoop and dive between the rafters as if to compete. Windswept and brimming with new wildlife facts, it feels like we've been around the world and back in just six miles; the perfect nature rush for sponge-like little minds.

REBECCA DOUGLAS PHOTOGRAPHY/ELMLEY NATURE RESERVE

legends to life (better for older kids), and the **Sherlock Official Live** (𝒪 thegameisnow.com) game that gets children to follow clues around the streets.

Just moments from the city you will find ample green space, woodlands and waterways. **Canoe Wild** (𝒪 canoewild.co.uk) offers guided or self-guided canoeing or kayaking adventures between Grove Ferry (seven miles from Canterbury) and the village of Fordwich. These three-hour trips are a good way to experience how wooded and secretive the river

can become. The river at **Fordwich** is a popular wild-swimming spot, as is the nearby **Westbere Marshes Lake**.

Held in various woodlands around Canterbury, the activities organised by **Natural Pathways** (⊘ natural-pathways.co.uk) are an ideal choice for families looking to hone their bushcraft and wilderness skills. Options include a weekend-long Family Wilderness Adventure, a Bushcraft Day and a Children's Mini Survival Adventure, a three-hour event where kids work together to build a survival camp.

The chalky paths that criss-cross the **Kent Downs**, an Area of Outstanding Natural Beauty, offer walks for all ages and abilities. Some top spots include Devil's Kneading Trough with its sweeping views, the Wye Crown carved into a hillside above the medieval village of Wye, and Denge and Pennypot Wood. Cutting through the Downs, the **Pilgrim's Way** (⊘ ldwa.org.uk), which stretches some 150 miles from Winchester to Canterbury, is one of the most storied walks in Britain, an ancient route taken by medieval pilgrims visiting the shrine of Thomas Becket in Canterbury Cathedral. To help plan longer expeditions and self-guided walks with accommodation along the way, contact **Coast and Country Rambles** (⊘ coastandcountryrambles.co.uk).

PRACTICALITIES

FAMILY-FRIENDLY SLEEPS

Bloom Stays ⊘ bloomstays.com. Kent locals Rowena and Nicky set up Bloom Stays to curate a collection of beautiful holiday homes, taking the stress out of letting and renting. Their collection of properties, from cleverly converted bungalows on the seafront in Dungeness to historic rural idylls in the Weald, are characterful, beautiful and kitted out with everything you could ever need. You pay a little more for the privilege of not having to trawl through Airbnb reviews.

Cabü ⊘ holidays.cabu.co.uk. Moments from the beach at St Mary's Bay, near Deal, Cabü by the Sea provides a slick and trendy slice of cabin life on a patch of private scrubland where rabbits play hide and seek in marram grass and thistles. In addition to the well-appointed holiday cabins, an outdoor heated pool, communal lounge and BBQ area, free bicycles and outdoor hot tub provide a proper holiday vibe.

Canterbury Cathedral Lodge ⊘ canterburycathedrallodge.org. Sitting at the foot of Canterbury

◀ Exploring the Quire at Canterbury Cathedral.

MADE IN ASHFORD

Made in Ashford (🖱 madeinashford.com) is a quirky craft shop selling everything from handmade soap to hand-painted vases. It's also a workshop space and a community centre. As a Community Interest Company and social enterprise, every penny of profit is reinvested back into its mission: to create an inclusive crafts hub and in particular help those feeling isolated or excluded. It hosts pop-up galleries, community groups and a revolving programme of workshops, including block painting, that are open to all.

Cathedral, this sensitively designed 29-room hotel, using local stone and materials, is a great option for those that only have a night or two in the city. Cots can fit into the larger doubles, and the Burgate annexe apartment, with a double and twin room, is perfect for families. Access to the cathedral and discounted tours are included in the rates.

Leeds Castle 🖱 leeds-castle.com. From falconry to fireworks, Leeds Castle, near Maidstone and the M20, doesn't do things by halves (it's supposedly the most visited historic building in Britain), and its accommodation is no exception. Seven holiday cottages, including Battle Hall, which sleeps ten, are dotted throughout the 500-acre estate, but the most novel option is Knight's Glamping, where eight striped tented pavilions (sleeping four) come complete with flame-effect stoves, furry throws and four-poster beds.

Whitstable Fisherman's Huts 🖱 whitstablefishermanshuts.com. About 3yds from the shingle and the oyster beds, these 150-year-old converted fisherman's huts could not be closer to the beach and the bustle of Whitstable. Each comes with a kitchen and communal area, and most have more than one bedroom. Four are dog friendly. Right in the heart of the action, the huts are best suited to those that enjoy people watching.

KID-FRIENDLY EATS

Dungeness Snack Shack
🖱 dungenesssnackshack.net. This is one of those places best found by accident for the sheer joy of stumbling upon the best meal of the holiday. It's hard to believe that the fresh-as-can-be scallop rolls, mackerel flatbreads and triple-cooked chips come from a regular food van. Right on the beach, it's a windy spot but that's all part of the charm. A hut next door, owned by the same people, sells fresh bread and fish so it's an ideal place to stock up if you're self-catering.

Goods Shed 🖱 thegoodsshed.co.uk. Canterbury's finest food emporium, this covered food market showcases the best local produce Kent has to offer. Seasonal veg comes from within a six-mile radius, 40 cheeses are on offer from Cheesemakers of Canterbury, and

Docker sells craft ales and sourdough loaves made in a shipping container in Folkestone. Gill's Café is an equally local outfit, serving coffee from a local roastery in Woodchurch.

Zetland Arms ⌀ zetlandarms.co.uk. This traditional pub (it's over 100 years old) almost looks out of place perched on the pebble beach in Kingsdown, near Deal, where it offers spectacular views in summer and a cosy break from the elements in winter. The menu offers standard pub grub with something for everyone.

BEFORE YOU GO

With so much coastline, going plastic-free and keeping beaches clean is a big deal in Kent; it is important visitors do their bit. Top tips from the **Kent Wildlife Trust** (⌀ kentwildlifetrust. org.uk) include cutting out the big four – plastic bags, straws, bottles and take-away cups – by carrying reusables everywhere you go, switching shampoo and shower gels to bars, taking your own Tupperware or containers when visiting farm shops, using natural fibre sponges when washing up to avoid sending microplastics down the drain (and into the sea), and trying beeswax wraps rather than cling film. **Surfers Against Sewage** (⌀ sas.org.uk), the **Thanet Coast Project** (⌀ thanetcoast. org.uk) and **Marine Conservation Society** (⌀ mcsuk.org) all run beach cleans in Kent, so check dates if you want to join in.

MORE INFO

Kent Downs AONB
⌀ kentdowns.org.uk
Kent Tourist Board
⌀ visitkent.co.uk

12
THE SUFFOLK COAST

*An enchanting blend of nostalgic seaside fun,
timeless waterways and lonely nature reserves.*

TOP FAMILY EXPERIENCE
BOATING AT THORPENESS MEARE FOLLOWED BY A VILLAGE TRAIL & BEACH TIME

BEST FOR KIDS AGED:	5+
WHEN TO GO:	April to October
INTREPID LEVEL:	①
ADDED ADVENTURE:	Hands-on nature reserves, forgotten waterways, an Anglo-Saxon hoard, quaint seaside villages
TIME:	Two days to one week

THORPENESS MEARE: BOATING ADVENTURES IN NEVERLAND

The Meare, Thorpeness IP16 4NW ⊘ thorpenessmeare.com

'You'll be alright. Just have fun!' the kayak handler shouts from the shore, as the boys (ages five and seven) both float off in their own kayaks for the first time. Having begged to be allowed to go alone, the youngest now looks a little uncertain. The glass-fibre streamline boat wobbles one way, then the other, but within a few strokes they're off, gliding past swans and ducks under a bright blue sky. 'Freedom!' I shout, holding back the tears that come when you see your kids taking another step towards independence. I hop in a third soggy kayak and paddle furiously to catch up.

There are plenty of places around the UK offering boating fun, but the Meare is a boating lake like no other. From the air, the 60-acre landscape is a patchwork of blue and green as the Hundred River weaves between islands just a few yards from the beach. It was this setting that in 1913

◀ Kayaking, Thorpeness Meare.

inspired Glencairn Stuart Ogilvie, a local landowner, to create a fantasy holiday village in Thorpeness.

The boating lake was hand-dug out of a former shipping haven, and many of the brightly painted wooden rowing boats that launched then, over 100 years ago, are still in use today. Family friend J M Barrie, author of *Peter Pan*, named the islands that boaters can hop off to explore: the Pirate's Lair, Wendy's Home and Captain's House, among others.

But best of all for families, the entire lake is only three feet deep, creating a wonderfully safe environment for kids to run, row, sail and paddle. Whenever the boys look unsure, I hastily remind them of the shallow water: it's a steamy July day, and a quick dip would be more than welcome anyway.

'Argh!' scream a pack of dishevelled older kids on kayaks coming the other way, paddles splashing each other as they race towards ice creams back at the boating hut, not an adult in sight. Tiny fish jump in their wake, like silver bullets leaping into the air, soon greeted by terns flocking and diving to join the action. A mini feeding frenzy for a miniature world.

We paddle into a slither of water between the trees. 'Is this a mangrove?' the youngest asks, as we duck to avoid spindly willow branches dipping into and sprouting out of the channel in all directions. A moorhen overtakes us, and sleepier mallards watch on nonchalantly from Wendy's House on the water's edge. Blues and silvers fade and green prevails as we glide deeper into the woodland. The boys point out the weird and wonderful props that pop up along the way – the Magic Pavilion and the House of the Seven Dwarfs – as we enter the Blue Lagoon. Surrounded by wooded islands, it feels worlds away from reality. Wilf takes the lead, searching for a good spot to disembark: we follow him to the outer edges of the adventure, around the North West Passage towards a 'secret' crocodile area. Luckily the croc isn't ticking. Time slows and the sun dips as we cool our feet in the water eating melted Kit Kats, looking out for kingfishers.

As we make our way back to the boathouse, the House in the Clouds, a curious cladded house atop a disguised water tower, looms overhead, guiding us back towards civilisation. Back on dry land, with soggy bottoms and smelling a little of pond water, we're welcomed with a hubbub of families juggling ice creams, fishing nets, beach gear and boating kit. We dodge the busy boathouse café and the Dolphin Inn and instead explore Thorpeness village's heritage trail. Starting at the Meare, the trail weaves between small passages and lanes to explore historic fishing-village dwellings and enviable holiday villas built in the 1900s, many of them mock Tudor – or 'Tuna Houses', the youngest announces.

The mile-long circuit takes us to the shingle beach, backed by pastel-coloured villas and stretching as far as the eye can see in both directions – to Sizewell in the north and Aldeburgh in the south. The boys skim stones while I swim before an evening shadow guzzles the warmth and it's time for fish and chips. English summer fun at its finest.

ADDED ADVENTURE: WATERY WONDERLANDS & CREATIVE ENCLAVES

Saturated with waterways, mudflats and marshes, and exposed to the wild North Sea, the Suffolk coast is quiet, understated and less populated than many coastal areas in the UK. Beyond the A12, which snakes through inland forests, narrow country lanes link villages unchanged for centuries, eventually reaching dead ends in nature reserves of rolling heath and woodland that tumble into the sea. This is a place to lose track of time and go slow in the simplest of ways.

FELIXSTOWE & RIVER DEBEN

At the southern end of the **Suffolk Coast and Heaths AONB** (⊘ suffolkcoastandheaths.org), the bustling town of **Felixstowe**, often overlooked for Suffolk's prettier seaside villages, is more charming than its reputation as a North Sea container port suggests. In the north of town, the fishing village of **Felixstowe Ferry**, on the banks of the River Deben, is particularly enticing with its beach huts, mudflats and fresh fish shacks. A ferry (⊘ felixstoweboats.co.uk) hops from the boatyard here over to sandy **Bawdsey beach**, and a footpath runs upstream along the river.

On the Bawdsey side, a 30-minute walk from the ferry, **Bawdsey Hall** (⊘ bawdseyhall.com), dating back to the 16th century, is a hotel whose grounds feature a series of wildlife hides that are open to the public. The nearby **Bawdsey Radar Transmitter Museum** (⊘ bawdseyradar.org. uk) tells the story of the world's first operational radar, which helped win the Battle of Britain. Local beachcombing expert Kate Osborne runs **Beach Bonkers** (⊘ beachbonkers.org.uk) trips from Bawdsey and

WILDLIFE TRACKING IN THE MARSHES

Carlton Marshes Suffolk Wildlife Trust, Burnt Hill Ln, Carlton Colville, Lowestoft NR33 8HU
⊘ suffolkwildlifetrust.org; age: 5+; intrepid level: ②

'Detectives at the ready! First, we're going to go tracking,' Jo Shackleton, Carlton Marshes' Wild Learning Officer, instructs 20 or so under-ten-year-olds kitted out with water bottles and animal footprint guides. 'Are we going to see bears?' one of the younger members of the group asks. 'What about tigers?' echoes another. The older kids laugh. 'No, today we're looking out for species that live here in Carlton Marshes. Who can tell me what some of those might be?' Jo throws the questioning back to the kids. There's a ripple of suggestions, including a marsh harrier, raft spider, barn owl and field mouse, giving away the fact that many of the kids have been on this activity day before.

I'm tagging along on what would usually be a strictly kids-only event, one that offers affordable and educational respite for families that might need childcare or space for the day. There's a nice mix of local and holidaying kids, and although shy at first, within half an hour the group is one big rabble of friends. The pace is gentle so that no-one gets left behind.

After a briefing on what species to look out for, including a staggering 28 types of dragonflies, we head into the reserve.

Carlton Marshes is part of the Suffolk Broads, a few miles inland from Great Yarmouth. The landscape isn't as pretty as the coast, but with miles of boardwalks weaving between reeds and woodland, it's a wonderful place for kids to get close to nature. 'It's a bit like the Broads but in miniature,' Jo explains, as we weave past waterways dancing with dragonflies and popping with the brilliant pink of ragged robin wildflowers. She continues, 'It's too late in the year now, but a month or so again we had a brilliant display of marsh orchids. Last week's group spotted a water vole, too.'

Conscious of the hot midday sun, Jo leads the group into the reserve's woodland. 'The softer ground is better for tracking,' she says, as kids gather on logs in the shade and prod around at the mossy ground. Jo explains what signs to look for – not just footprints, but bite marks, scratch marks, fur or feathers, signs of eating and nibbling, and, even, poo. The group erupts with laughter before heading off in all directions.

Exclamations echo around the oak trees and shrubs. 'A badger! A deer!' kids squeal, guessing at what may have caused various footprints and other signs of life. Under a

other spots along the coast; spoils might include 50-million-year-old fossilised sharks' teeth, sea wash balls and hagstones – stones with holes through the middle, which are believed to be lucky.

Eight miles upstream from Bawdsey, on the edge of the market town of Woodbridge, is **Sutton Hoo** (⊘ nationaltrust.org.uk), the site of one

hazelnut tree Jo explains how we can tell which animal has been nibbling the nuts: 'If it's got a hole in the middle, it's a mouse, if it's been split in half, it's a squirrel.' We find a feeding site of a blackbird or a thrush, snail shells scattered all around after having been whacked on a tree trunk, and learn that the chicken-pox-like marks on leaves are galls — caused by mite eggs.

Getting into pairs, the kids make tree identification dials with cardboard and scissors and start learning which leaves belong to which trees. 'Can we keep it?' one pipes up, rather attached to his creation.

Peering over the boys' shoulder, I'm eager to keep one, too — it's not just kids that need to learn more about our native wildlife.

Satisfied with the crafting, wildlife spotting and leaf identifications, the group heads back to base for lunch. Wandering back alongside the waterways, we spot an egret and great diving beetle. 'What's that?' a kid shouts, staring at a pair of huge green eyes hovering above the water. The group crowds around to learn, in amazement, that it's a Norfolk hawker dragonfly. Who needs bears when there are such mysterious critters so close to home?

ADRIAN MUTTITT/A

of the greatest archaeological discoveries of our time: an undisturbed Anglo-Saxon ship burial, filled with extraordinary treasures, unearthed in the 1930s. Today the estate has three main visitor attractions: the burial grounds themselves; Tranmer House, celebrating the life and work of Edith Pretty, who owned the estate and instigated the digs that uncovered the hoard; and the High Hall, exhibiting a life-sized model of the burial chamber and objects found within it. Being able to explore the site and see the hoard brings history alive for kids of all ages.

On the outskirts of Woodbridge, **Kyson Hill** (⊘ nationaltrust.org. uk) provides views and grassy slopes for kids to play on, along with accessible walks around the marshes and wetlands. If you're travelling without a car you can walk to the hill from Woodbridge train station via The Tea Hut in about 25 minutes.

ALDEBURGH TO SOUTHWOLD

Aldeburgh and Southwold are the most popular holiday destinations along the Suffolk coast, for good reason. **Aldeburgh** is the smaller of the two, with a shingle beach. Older kids with creative leanings may well be drawn to its artistic attractions, including Maggi Hambling's controversial **scallop sculpture**, towering 13ft above the shingle, and the unusual **Aldeburgh Beach Lookout** (⊘ aldeburghbeachlookout.com), which hosts a different artist every week – if you're lucky, you may catch them at work. A little inland, the **Red House** (⊘ brittenpearsarts. org), the former home of composer Benjamin Britten and singer Peter Pears, documents their life and work among preserved 1950s interiors; there's a garden discovery trail for families, and a Mini Music Makers session for under-fives every Friday.

"The best way to truly understand the landscape, however, is to explore on the water."

The River Alde meanders for six miles from Aldeburgh inland to Snape; you can walk between the two on the the 100-year-old Sailor's Path trail, following the river and crossing marshes. At Snape, the former brewery complex **Snape Maltings** (⊘ brittenpearsarts.org) houses galleries, shops, a concert hall and cafés – look out for family-friendly outdoor concerts in summer. The best way to truly understand the landscape, however, is to explore on the water. **Iken Canoe** (⊘ ikencanoe.co.uk; ages seven and up) rents out Canadian canoes, kayaks and paddleboards; maps, safety briefings and dry bags are included in two-hour slots. Less strenuous are the 45-minute **boat trips** along the River Alde from

1 Aldeburgh scallop shell sculpture. **2** Exhibits at Sutton Hoo. **3** Pond dipping, Minsmere. **4** Looking for sharks' teeth with Beach Bonkers. **5** Beach huts on Southwold Beach. ▶

DAVID CALVERT/S

SS

HOLLY TUPPEN

BEACH BONKERS

PHILIP ELLARD/S

Snape Maltings aboard converted fishing boats *Sea Trader* and *Hagar* (⊘ brittenpearsarts.org).

Between Aldeburgh and Southwold, **RSPB Minsmere Reserve**, home to coastal lagoons and ancient woodland, and the huge shingle beach at **Dunwich** offer even wilder, quieter coastal adventures. Dunwich beach can be accessed via the **National Trust Dunwich Heath and Beach car park** (⊘ nationaltrust.org.uk), from where footpaths dart in all directions through woodland (there's a dedicated den building area) and heath. Dunwich village itself has a pub, a beachside café and the clifftop ruins of **Greyfriars Medieval Friary** (⊘ dunwichgreyfriars.org.uk), ideal for a quiet picnic. Tiny **Dunwich Museum** (⊘ dunwichmuseum. org.uk) tells the story of how the medieval port was claimed by the sea.

Eight miles north, much-loved **Southwold** is bigger than Aldeburgh, with a pier – don't miss the eccentric collection of slot machines in the Under the Pier show – a lighthouse (the only one open to the public in Suffolk), the Adnams brewery, and a healthy dose of kiss-me-quick seaside fun alongside smart boutiques and hip coffee shops. The soft sandy beach is a big draw for families – much of the rest of the coast along here is shingly – and it gets quieter towards the dunes at **Denes Beach**, south of town.

LOWESTOFT & RIVER WAVENEY

Lowestoft is a North Sea fishing port on the most easterly point in the UK. Although the town is run-down in parts, its sandy beaches are ideal for younger kids; south of Claremont Pier, sand stretches three miles to Kessingland dunes. A few miles inland, **Carlton Marshes Nature Reserve** (⊘ suffolkwildlifetrust.org) welcomes families with a visitor centre, nature cams (to spot marsh harriers and barn owls), a natural play area and boardwalks. During school holidays, rangers take kids of all ages on full- or half-day holiday camps, where activities include 'tracking' wildlife in the woods and bird box building (see box, page 198).

Inland from Lowestoft, the River Waveney marks the border with Norfolk. **Somerleyton Hall and Gardens**, six miles west of Lowestoft (⊘ somerleyton.co.uk), is particularly idyllic in late spring when butterflies dance around a maze, walled garden and arboretum surrounded by rewilded parkland. Ten miles southwest of Somerleyton, the market town of **Beccles** is a southern hub for the Norfolk and Suffolk Broads. **Big Dog Ferry** (⊘ bigdogferry.co.uk) runs trips along three quiet miles of the river from **Beccles Lido** ($\oslash$ beccleslido.com), a heated outdoor pool in the middle of town, and **Hippersons Boatyard** ($\oslash$ hippersons.co.uk) has electric boats, canoes and kayaks available for day hire. **Waveney River Centre** ($\oslash$ holidaysforallseasons.co.uk) is another hub for river-based fun; there's a foot ferry from here to Carlton Marshes. Lucky wildlife spotters may see otters, Chinese water deer and water voles.

PRACTICALITIES

FAMILY-FRIENDLY SLEEPS

Applefields Campsite $\oslash$ 01728 833501. This small, family-run campsite, close to the town of Leiston inland, but well situated for the Suffolk coast, has no frills to boast of, but that's exactly the point. The flat field is surrounded by woodland with ample space between pitches. A toilet, kitchen and washing block has warm showers, and firewood is available. Best of all, prices are fixed, so there are no crazy costs in school holidays.

The Crown & The Swan
$\oslash$ thecrownsouthwold.co.uk &
$\oslash$ theswansouthwold.co.uk. A local brewery doesn't sound like an obvious choice for a family holiday, but family-run Adnams not only has a selection of brilliant pubs across the county, but two hotels – The Crown and The Swan. Both have family suites and are slap bang in the heart of Southwold, ideal for stress-free exploring. The Swan has been recently renovated and is a little smarter than The Crown.

Hippersons Boatyard $\oslash$ hippersons. co.uk. Offering a variety of houseboats, floating pods and cabins on the River Waveney, Hippersons is a great base for families wishing to explore the Suffolk Broads. The nearby Beccles Station café can provide picnic hampers and breakfasts, and a 'Sparrows and Amazons' package includes self-drive boat hire, a guided canoe trip and dinghy sailing.

Minsmere Holidays
$\oslash$ minsmereholidays.co.uk. Scattered throughout a twelve-acre rewilded woodland on the edge of the Minsmere RSPB Nature Reserve, this collection of chalets provides families with back-to-nature fun. There is a huge communal field for kids to run free, and plenty of bird and bat boxes in the surrounding woods.

Secret Meadows $\oslash$ secretmeadows. co.uk. Horsebox Hideaway and Gypsy's Rest are two of the glamping options nestled within the 115-acre White House Farm site, preserved and protected since the 1990s by the Sinfield Nature Conservation Trust. There are wildflower meadows, a turf labyrinth and tree circles to explore, and on-site activities include whittling and bushcraft. All profits are ploughed into conservation efforts.

KID-FRIENDLY EATS

Flora Tea Rooms

⬦ floratearoomsdunwich.co.uk. This huge, no-nonsense café, serving everything from rosé to ice cream, cake to fish and chips, makes a trip to remote Dunwich Beach even more enticing. The afternoon teas are a treat during the colder months.

Old Dairy ⬦ olddairy.restaurant. Occupying Beccles' former grocery and dairy, this family-run restaurant and café – owned by Jo and Ryan, whose local heritage goes back three generations – prides itself on serving wholesome food from breakfast through to dinner. Food is locally sourced and there are plenty of no-nonsense options for kids.

Pizza & Live Music Tipi

⬦ brittenpearsarts.org. It's easy to while away hours at Snape Maltings and, on a sunny day, the Pizza Tipi is an ideal spot for a family lunch. Live music accompanies stone-baked pizzas throughout the summer holidays.

Two Magpies Bakery

⬦ twomagpiesbakery.co.uk. Queueing down Southwold High Street is commonplace in the height of summer for baked goods and coffee at this much-loved local chain; Saturday is pizza night. There's also a cookery school, which offers classes on everything dough related.

MORE INFO

Suffolk Tourist Board

⬦ visitsuffolk.com

Suffolk Wildlife Trust

⬦ suffolkwildlifetrust.org

13
LINCOLNSHIRE

*With its wild coast, expansive horizons
and wealth of history, lesser-visited
Lincolnshire is ideal for great escapes.*

TOP FAMILY EXPERIENCE
EXPLORING LINCOLN'S 13TH-CENTURY CASTLE

BEST FOR KIDS AGED: 5+
WHEN TO GO: April to October
INTREPID LEVEL: ①
ADDED ADVENTURE: Historic city strolls, quaint foodie villages, wildlife-rich
                         coastal landscapes, boat trips, active fun
TIME: Two days to one week

STEPPING BACK THROUGH TIME

Lincoln Castle, Castle Square, Lincoln LN1 3AA ⊘ lincolncastle.com

'Race you to the top,' the kids shout as they charge up the worn, stone steps on to the walls of Lincoln Castle. Despite taking the lift, the adults are left for dust. Since a huge refurbishment in 2019, it's possible to walk (or run) the whole way around Lincoln Castle's walls to experience one of the finest Norman strongholds in all of England.

The audio guide kick-starts at the top of the stairs: 'You'll soon walk in the footsteps of kings, courtiers, soldiers and criminals through 1,000 years of history. Battles and sieges and pomp and pageantry. You'll learn how successful these castle walls have been, keeping prisoners in and invaders out.'

There's a bit of everything on offer in Lincoln Castle. Built on the site of a significant Roman fortress and settlement, the walls and ruins represent a microcosm of English history from the Roman invasion and the disintegration of the Roman empire to the English Civil War and

Victorian penal system. The castle's many uses make it a brilliant place to visit for shorter attention spans — there's even an Observatory Tower used by prison governors for stargazing in the 19th century.

'Welcome to Lindum Colonia,' one of my boys sniggers, announcing Lincoln's Roman name. 'Urghhhhhh – someone was beheaded right here!' they both scream, before whizzing off to the next numbered spot that takes their fancy. By the end it becomes apparent that, between the running and screeching, some history does seep in. The youngest proudly recalls that, 'If not for the lady that guarded Lincoln Castle, we might be speaking French.' He's referring to the crucial role Royalist and castle protector Nicola de la Haie played in overcoming King Louis of France's army in the 13th century.

Though the dramatic stories are never-ending, the appeal of the castle walls is not purely historic. It's rare to get such a magnificent and undisturbed view of a city. To the east, quaint cobbled streets meander down to the river and across to Lincoln's Cathedral Quarter. 'You're looking across Bailgate, a confused jumble of slopes, beams, thatch and plaster,' the audio guide tells us, setting the scene of what it would have been like in the 1100s, when it was a lively, thriving marketplace. Funnily enough, it doesn't feel that different today, as people gradually fill the streets in search of lunch, beer and ice cream. Straight ahead, the impressive Lincoln Cathedral today towers 272ft above the city. Although disputed by historians, in 1311 it was thought to be the tallest building in the world, before falling victim to earthquakes, fire and storms in the 16th century.

In the other direction the boys point out the International Bomber Command Centre monument — a huge rusty spire soaring above the trees on the hill opposite the castle and cathedral. Having visited earlier, we know that below the spire 23 walls list the names of 57,861 men and women who lost their lives serving Bomber Command. The placing of the spire so near the cathedral is deliberate – for the bomber forces the view of the cathedral was either the welcome back or the last glimpse of home.

Beyond the walls, there's plenty on offer at the castle, including a tour of the Victorian prison and an exhibition dedicated to one of the four surviving original copies of Magna Carta. We bypass the prison and head straight for the Magna Carta vault; Lincoln Castle is the only place

◀ Lincoln Castle.

in the world where an original 1215 Magna Carta and 1217 Charter of the Forest (a charter that gave people free access to royal forests) can be seen side by side. Although some of the details are lost on the kids, the vault's suitably important air leads us to discuss how the document changed the course of history. 'So, was it to stop the kings lying like Boris Johnson?' one of the boys asks, indicating that some understanding has sunk in.

Back out in the fresh air, we head into the huge grassy hill and park inside the castle walls. It feels quiet and calm, despite being in the middle of the city; the perfect spot for a picnic and hill rolling before heading into the cobbled streets to compare life today with what we now know it was like through the centuries.

ADDED ADVENTURE: HANDS-ON HISTORY, BUCOLIC HILLS & A DUNE-BACKED COAST

It's not difficult to slow down in Lincolnshire. Even the county's capital, Lincoln, is dominated by big green views, its mighty cathedral visible from miles around. Well known for its aviation heritage, having played a significant role as an air base in World War II, the county also has some wonderful rural history. And while the county is known for its plane-like landscape, it's not all flat; whether cycling in the Wolds between market towns brimming with local produce and crafts, or wildlife spotting on one of the UK's wildest coasts, there's plenty of variety to enjoy.

LINCOLN

After exploring the castle walls (page 205), head across to **Lincoln Cathedral** ($\mathscr{O}$ lincolncathedral.com) for even more spectacular views (tower climbs only available to children over 14). Even without climbing the tower, the huge cathedral is worth a visit, often hosting a kids' trail to get them exploring all sorts of intriguing nooks and crannies. It's fun, too, to spot fossils in the limestone slabs in the nave floor. There's a café, and the visitor centre juts out into pretty gardens.

---

1 Hartsholme Country Park. **2** Lincoln Cathedral. **3** & **4** International Bomber Command Centre. ▶

Check out **Visit Lincoln** (⊘ visitlincoln.com) for kids' adventure trails – they might involve quests for knights, fairies or imps – and download a map; older children in particular may enjoy the self-guided mystery treasure trail around the cathedral quarter. Leave plenty of time to meander down aptly named Steep Hill from Bailgate, which is packed with independent shops and intriguing alleyways. At the bottom, you can veer off down Danes Terrace to **Temple Gardens**, a hillside park, and **The Collection** (⊘ thecollectionmuseum.com), a purpose-built archaeology museum.

On the south side of town is **Brayford Pool**, where the River Witham meets the **Fossdyke Canal**. It's a hive of activity both beside and on the water. For a relaxing tour, hop on board the **Brayford Belle** (⊘ lincolnboattrips.co.uk) for a 50-minute river cruise with commentary; alternatively, you can get active on the ten-mile lock-free canoe trail along the Fossdyke Canal, which connects Lincoln with the River Trent at Torksey. Heading south, the 15-mile **Water Rail Cycle Trail** (⊘ sustrans.org.uk), a flat track along the River Witham, follows the route of an old railway line to Boston. There are sculptures along the way and two viewing platforms with views across the flat, waterlogged landscape of the Fens. A pleasant stop or destination is **Bardney Abbey**, the remains of a Benedictine monastery founded in AD697.

There's plenty of green space to explore on foot around Lincoln, too. To the south, on a prominent hill surrounded by fields and gardens, the **International Bomber Command Centre** (⊘ internationalbcc.co.uk) is a moving and very accessible memorial to Bomber Command and the 57,861 people who died in its service (page 207). A few miles west of the city, **Hartsholme Country Park** offers woods, dens, a lake and nature trails to explore in its 100-acre green space. And a few miles beyond that, still heading west, **Doddington Hall & Gardens** (⊘ doddingtonhall. com) is a family-run 16th-century mansion with heaps to entertain families. The walled gardens and grounds are full of intrigue, from bug hotels to willow sculptures and fields set aside for rewilding. Converted outbuildings are home to a bike-hire outlet, a cycling-themed café and a huge farm shop. Pick up bikes (or bring your own) and head out on to the estate's mountain-bike jump trail or the tarmacked, traffic-free **Georgie Twigg Track**, which weaves through the surrounding fields. For a longer ride, the track links with the National Cycle Network Route 64, which goes all the way to Lincoln.

LINCOLNSHIRE COAST

Bulging out into the cold North Sea between The Wash and the River Humber, Lincolnshire's coast offers a wonderful mix of wild and desolate beaches and traditional seaside resorts. The chunk of coast framing the Wolds (page 213) is the prettiest, a 40-mile-odd stretch from **Gibraltar Point** in the south to **Donna Nook** and **Horse Shoe Point** in the north. Salt marsh and sand dunes protect much of the coastline from human development, creating unique wildlife habitats ripe for exploration by budding David Attenboroughs.

Gibraltar Point Reserve (⊘ lincstrust.org.uk) feels so secluded, it's hard to believe it's just a mile or so south of the hustle and bustle of **Skegness**. The reserve is home to extensive dunes, wetlands and salt marsh, which all eventually lead to the sea via a maze of channels and spits. Avid birdwatchers have four hides from which to admire the likes of terns, skylarks, brent geese, snow bunting and redwing, depending on the season. The surrounding beaches are only accessible by foot and mostly deserted; a visitor centre provides maps, nature tick lists for kids, snacks and sheltered picnic benches for when the North Sea wind howls.

"The reserve is home to extensive dunes, wetlands and salt marsh, which all eventually lead to the sea."

Six miles north of Skegness, the **North Sea Observatory** (⊘ lincsnaturalcoast.com) runs crafting events for families during holiday times, and an art gallery showcases rotating local and marine-themed art. Further up the coast, at **Anderby Creek Beach**, a huge stretch of sand backed by dunes, you can check out the **Cloud Bar**. This small, unexpected installation, featuring sky-facing mirrors and a raised platform, was built after the site was designated an official cloud-spotting area by the Cloud Appreciation Society. A few hundred yards south is another curious structure – the plywood **Round and Round House**, used for bird- and marine life watching.

At Lincolnshire's northern tip, **Donna Nook Nature Reserve** (⊘ lincstrust.org.uk) is home to one of the UK's largest grey-seal-breeding colonies; from late October to the end of December you can watch them lolling about on the sand and rocks. The **Lincolnshire Wildlife Trust** recommends checking its website for 'pupdates', since the reserve can get very busy at peak times (and there are no on-site facilities) and the reserve is keen to keep visitor numbers low for the well-being of the animals.

NORTH SEA OBSER

For active holidays, the 166-mile **Humber to The Wash cycle route** (⌗ cycle-england.co.uk) combines coastal roads and country lanes, travelling through some beautiful coastal estates and landscapes. Pitchup (⌗ pitchup.com) is a good place to search for campsites along the route.

LINCOLNSHIRE WOLDS & SURROUNDS

Spreading north to south parallel with the coast, halfway between Lincoln and the sea, the **Lincolnshire Wolds AONB** (⌗ lincswolds.org. uk) is a welcome pocket of wooded hills and winding country lanes in a landscape otherwise dominated by flat agricultural lands and long straight roads. Life here feels slow, and there's heaps to explore.

Criss-crossed by footpaths, the Wolds have many walks to choose from. The 69-mile **Lindsey Trail** spans the area from Market Rasen to Horncastle, and is suitable for riders, cyclists and walkers. The 69-mile **Lincolnshire Wolds Walk** celebrates Lincolnshire's greatest literary figure – Alfred Lord Tennyson – and passes through his home village, Somersby, where you can refuel in the poet's 16th-century local, the White Hart Inn. For less hiking and more wildlife, **Snipe Dales Country Park and Nature Reserve** (⌗ lincstrust.org.uk) is a great place for families to explore woodlands and wetlands on the southern edge of the Wolds.

The market towns of Alford and Louth sit on the eastern edge of the hills. Both are worth a visit for their food and craft markets and make great bases for walking and cycling adventures. **Louth**, once described by Rick Stein as 'the finest little market town in Britain', is a foodie haven, with many independent shops selling and serving Lincolnshire's abundant local produce, from speciality sausages to cheeses. When the sun shines, take your Louth goodies to **Spout Yard** community park (⌗ spoutyardpark. org.uk) for a picnic – there are benches, a play area and even an art gallery. A mile west of town, **Hubbard's Hill** is a good walking spot. The steep-sided chalk valley is filled with butterflies in summer.

The craft market at **Alford** is the largest in the county, sprawling around **Alford Manor** (⌗ alfordmanorhouse.co.uk), a large, thatched 17th-century house with pretty gardens and the Hackett Barn Museum, a treasure trove of rural history. Organic flour is still churned out by the town's working five-sailed windmill.

◀ **1** Gibraltar Point. **2** Grey seal at Donna Nook Nature Reserve. **3** North Sea Observatory.

Between the Wolds and Lincoln, the market town of **Woodhall Spa** is home to **Jubilee Park** (⊘ jubileeparkwoodhallspa.co.uk), which has an outdoor lido, the **Kinema in the Woods** (⊘ thekinemainthewoods. co.uk) vintage cinema, and **Petwood Hotel** (⊘ petwood.co.uk), once home to the famous World War II 617 Squadron, the Dambusters. You can hire bikes at the hotel to ride along the 147-mile **Viking Way** (⊘ ldwa.org.uk), a cycling and walking trail so named because it follows the route of 9th-century Norse invaders, which passes through the town.

PRACTICALITIES

FAMILY-FRIENDLY SLEEPS

Bainland ⊘ bainland.co.uk. Bainland's luxury wooden chalets and treehouses, sleeping from two to 24, are spread around a quiet wooded site just outside Woodhall Spa. There's on-site archery, mini Range Rovers for kids to drive around a track, and tennis, alongside heaps of space to cycle and simply run about. Some of the bigger chalets have their own pools, and many of them come with hot tubs.

Brackenborough Hall Coach House ⊘ brackenboroughhall.com. The Bennett family have lived at Brackenborough, on the eastern edge of the Wolds, for over a hundred years and today combine environmentally friendly farming with holiday accommodation. Three apartments, run on renewable energy, sleep between four and eight, and guests are welcome to pick produce from the kitchen gardens.

Branston Moor Campsite ⊘ branstonmoorcampsite.co.uk.

Very affordable, low-key and peaceful campsite between the Wolds and Lincoln – the cathedral tower can be seen in the distance. It's on the Water Rail Cycle path (page 210) so makes a good base for multi-day cycling adventures.

Lincoln Hotel ⊘ thelincolnhotel. com. Just opposite the cathedral, this mid-range hotel is a great place to stay for a day or two when exploring the city. Interconnecting rooms are ideal for families and there's a garden at the back. The hotel restaurant, bar and terrace have leafy views across to the cathedral gardens.

Seaside Lodge ⊘ seasidelodge.co.uk. Two minutes from Anderby Creek Beach, this two-bedroom chalet-style holiday lodge offers a wonderfully simple but comfortable retreat for families. It's surrounded by a sunny garden overlooking a fishing lake, and there are pubs, cafés and shops just a short stroll away.

◀ **1** Lincolnshire Wolds AONB. **2** The farmers' market, Alford. **3** The Viking Way.

LINCOLN REDS & A LEGENDARY OAK

Bowthorpe Park Farm, Manthorpe, Bourne PE10 0JG ⊘ bowthorpeparkfarm.co.uk; age: 3+; intrepid level: ①; the farm is only open to the public during lambing season & holidays, hosting special events on various weekends, so check the website before visiting; the shop, selling field-to-fork meat, milk, eggs & other local produce, is open year-round.

'It's always been part of family life,' comments George Blanchard, fifth-generation farmer at Bowthorpe Park Farm near Manthorpe village in south Lincolnshire. Despite the Blanchards' passion for farming traditional breeds, including Lincoln Red cattle, which graze the surrounding fields, George is in fact talking about a tree.

We are staring at the Bowthorpe oak, thought to be the oldest oak tree in the UK. With a girth of 44ft, its sheer size is staggering. 'We think it's about 1,000 years old,' he continues, as we contemplate all it has witnessed over the years. There's a fence separating the tree from visitors today, but in the past people have celebrated the majestic specimen by sleeping, and even having parties, inside its hollow trunk: one account tells of the Squire of Bowthorpe entertaining 20 guests for supper inside the tree in 1760.

'We're eager to protect it for future generations, so the Woodland Trust is providing expert care, and the fence keeps it from harm,' George tells us. Despite the fence, we're close enough to marvel at the gnarly trunk and enjoy watching blue tits flutter in and out. My six-year-old recalls Nick Butterworth's books about a collection of animals and their huge home within the trunk of an oak tree, and I wish we'd brought some paints or pencils

Thorganby Hall ⊘ thorganbyhall. co.uk. These three self-catering cottages, sleeping between two and 16 each, make a brilliant base in the heart of the Lincolnshire Wolds. There's an on-site tennis court, and one of the properties has an indoor pool and sandpit. Welcome packs are stuffed with local produce, and high chairs and cots are available.

KID-FRIENDLY EATS

Cheese Society Café

⊘ thecheesesociety.co.uk. Just off Steep Hill in Lincoln, the Cheese Society Café serves up artisan cheeses, both local and European, in every possible shape and form. Kids will particularly love the loaded macaroni. There's a shop, too, so you can stock up for picnics and self-catering.

Daisy Made Farm ⊘ daisymadefarm. co.uk. One of Lincolnshire's top ice-cream makers, Daisy Made Farm, in the village of Skellingthorpe on the western outskirts of Lincoln, has a drive-through ice-cream shop and an on-site café offering a staggering 60 flavours. There's a play area, crazy golf and small farm on-site, too.

Doddington Hall Coffee Shop

⊘ doddingtonhall.com. On a lane by the side of the Doddington Estate (page 210),

– the tree is a wonderful source of creative inspiration and there's no-one else around. I bet even the most hardened adolescent imaginations would be inspired.

Beyond the tree, Bowthorpe Park Farm educates visitors about traditional breeds and farming. There are Berkshire pigs, pedigree Lincoln Reds and Jacob sheep. Unlike at many overly commercial and hectic farm parks, here the animals are clearly healthy, and the enclosures are spread out, making it a much more enjoyable experience all round. Local farming on local terms – just how it should be.

HEATHER DRAKE/A

the Doddington Hall Coffee Shop has a large patio area and indoor seating. Hot food includes fish-finger sandwiches and locally sourced burgers. Coffee and cake is available all day.

Greyhound Inn ⊘ greyhoundlouth. co.uk. This pub is a renowned foodie spot in the pretty market town of Louth, with ample space inside and out. The lunchtime menu includes flatbreads and burgers, and there's a full vegan menu, too.

Kings Head ⊘ thekingsheadtealby. co.uk. Sitting on the edge of the Wolds in the pretty village of Tealby, this relaxed pub is the oldest thatched building in Lincolnshire, dating back to the 14th century. There's a large beer garden and a extensive home-cooked menu, and dogs are welcome.

BEFORE YOU GO

Local, seasonal food is a big part of Lincolnshire life so it's good to support local producers when you visit. If you're self-catering, rather than default to supermarket shops, check out Visit Lincolnshire's **Taste Lincolnshire** initiative (⊘ visitlincoln.com/taste-lincolnshire), which lists and maps shops, restaurants and suppliers selling local produce. For an even more immersive experience, book one of the hands-on courses for young people run by farmer Fiona Lucas at **Lincolnshire Cookery School** (⟰ lincolnshirecookeryschool. com), surrounded by countryside halfway between the Wolds and Lincoln.

MORE INFO

Lincolnshire Tourist Board
⟰ visitlincolnshire.com
Visit Lincoln ⟰ visitlincoln.com

14
BRECON BEACONS
NATIONAL PARK

*Wales' adventure heartland offers nearly 50 miles
of accessible outdoor fun from east to west.*

TOP FAMILY EXPERIENCE
DOWNHILL MOUNTAIN BIKING AT BIKEPARK WALES, MERTHYR TYDFIL

BEST FOR KIDS AGED: 8+
WHEN TO GO: March to October
INTREPID LEVEL: ②
ADDED ADVENTURE: Stargazing, hill walking, mine explorations, canal trips, waterfalls, quarries, caverns
TIME: Two days to one week

A DOWNHILL ADRENALIN HIGH

BikePark Wales, Gethin Woodland Centre, Abercanaid, Merthyr Tydfil CF48 1YZ
⊘ bikeparkwales.com

'There's nothing to worry about – this is our beginner run; it'll be fun!' says Nick Pole, our mountain-biking guide for the next few hours, as we run through a diligent safety briefing. He's looking at the kids, but I suspect he's talking to the trepidation that's creeping across my face. Nerves settle deep in my gut. 'It's good to get out of your comfort zone,' I tell myself while padding up knees and elbows and lifting an enormous helmet over my head. We certainly all look the part.

Nick demonstrates the automatic seat lift function on our rented Shimano and Trek bikes, and a chorus of giggles takes the edge off the nerves as we practise moving our seats up and down. 'Let's do this,' the kids enthuse as we follow Nick on to the trails.

We're at BikePark Wales, the newest and most accessible in a series of mountain-bike parks across the country. At the foot of Gethin Woodland Park, 20 miles north of Cardiff, the 2,100-acre site lures beginners and pros alike. We've come to try out the three-mile Kermit Trail, the longest downhill in the UK, ideal for beginners and kids, and have opted for the 'Ticket to Ride' – a four-hour guided ride with induction, bike hire and uplift access (page 219). It's the priciest of the BikePark options, so families with a little more experience and their own kit might want to opt for one of the other packages.

Wales has long been a major centre for mountain biking, and the sheer number of opportunities on offer can be overwhelming. In the Brecon Beacons alone there are 12 recognised mountain-biking spots – route maps are available from visitor centres or online (⊘ breconbeacons. org). The towns and villages of Brecon, Sennybridge and Talybont-on-Usk are particularly good bases for beginners, and outfits such as Drover Holidays (⊘ droverholidays.co.uk) offer bike hire, delivery and guided experiences across the region. BikePark Wales, however, is ideal for those looking to boost confidence on the downhills or to try mountain biking for the first time.

A meandering chunk of the trail takes us from the BikePark base to the 'uplift' station. Here, minibuses ferry bikers and their bikes up to the summit. It feels a little like skiing as we pile in and embark on a long and winding ascent, catching glimpses of Brecon Beacon views through rows of pine trees.

At the top, the pros make a dash for the hardcore trails. 'Can *we* do AC DC?' one of my kids pipes up as we follow the green markers to Kermit, only to be met with a chorus of 'Errr – no – not yet…' When we reach the trail Nick continues, 'OK, here we go. It's a single track so you'll feel the thrill of the downhill, but it's been carefully designed to manage speed – so just enjoy the ride.' He reassures us that we'll be making plenty of stops to take in the views and check everyone's doing OK. Then 'Wheeeeeeeee!' – the boys are off before any of us can think again.

After the initial shock of the speed, and having to remember when to brake, when to turn, and how to stand up on the bike (with a little encouragement from Nick), the ride is pure joy. Unlike so many mountain-bike trails, which tend to be in monocrop pine plantations,

◀ **1** & **2** Cycling with BikePark Wales.

Gethin Woodland Park is refreshingly varied. After weaving through dark, foreboding sections of pine, we enter an almost mythical kingdom of lichen- and moss-draped oak trees. 'The bluebells here are amazing in spring,' Nick tells us. If properly managed, mountain-bike trails are a good way to access the forest without trampling all over it. And within Gethin Woodland Park, the Woodland Trust has created more than 13 miles of trails for those who prefer horseriding and walking instead.

The sheer beauty of the place helps to slow everyone down – critical for the speed-junkie youngsters. 'Try to slow before the turns but not in them,' Nick keeps reminding the boys as they skid and slide across the trail. Pit stops every few hundred yards make it easy to rest when needed. About halfway down, we refuel at a picnic bench overlooking the Valleys of south Wales with Pen y Fan, the Brecon Beacons' highest peak, looming in the distance.

'Again, again, again,' everyone cheers at the bottom of the trail, glowing with that intoxicating mix of relief and adrenalin that adventuring in the great outdoors is all about. Luckily, the uplift service means we can do it all over again, this time with the confidence to whizz pass pit stops and around burns without a second thought.

ADDED ADVENTURE: FROM EERIE MINES TO THE MILKY WAY

The Brecon Beacons National Park (Parc Cenedlaethol Bannau Brycheiniog, in Welsh; ⊘ breconbeacons.org) is an area of more than 500 square miles, containing four distinct areas – the Black Mountain in the west, Fforest Fawr and the Brecon Beacons mountain range in the middle, and the confusingly named Black Mountains in the east. The Black Mountains are clearly separated from the rest by the Usk Valley, but the other landscapes form one massif, home to undulating moorland and woodland. Just a hop, skip and a jump across the English border, the region is famous for its wealth of accessible outdoor adventures; thanks to being one of the UK's four International Dark Skies Reserves and a UNESCO Global Geopark (a site recognised for geological importance), the park is also a wonderful outdoor classroom for budding astrologers, geologists and geographers.

THE BLACK MOUNTAINS

On the eastern side of the park, the sandstone **Black Mountains**, carved by six rivers, are sandwiched between two much-loved market towns: Abergavenny to the south, and Hay-on-Wye to the north. **Hay-on-Wye** is known as the 'Town of Books' thanks to 30-odd secondhand bookshops and the world-famous annual **literary festival** (⬦ hayfestival.com) at the end of May. Many of the hundreds of talks by authors and activities to inspire imaginations are aimed at kids. **Outdoors@Hay** (⬦ outdoorsathay.com) and **Drover Cycles** (⬦ drovercycles.co.uk) are the go-to outfits for anyone wanting to book an organised cycling, walking or bushcraft expedition from town. Ten miles south, the ruins of the 12th-century **Llanthony Priory** (⬦ llanthonyprioryhotel.co.uk; page 230) – one of the earliest Augustinian priories in Britain – and the surrounding Vale of Ewyas make magical picnic and play spots.

Abergavenny, just a 40-minute train ride from Cardiff, is an ideal base for families travelling by public transport. The Black Mountains loom into view around every corner and, from town, the three spectacular peaks of Sugar Loaf (1,955ft), Blorenge (1,841ft) and Skirrid (1,594ft) are all climbable with kids. If possible, time your hike to correspond with the town's legendary **farmers' market**, on the fourth Thursday of the month, and pick up a feast of local goods to picnic on at the top. Further south, in the Welsh Valleys, just outside the national park, **Big Pit National Coal Museum** (⬦ museum.wales) is a free, hands-on place for kids to learn about the region's mining heritage; the Underground Tour takes visitors 300ft down into the mineshaft.

On the western side of the Black Mountains lies charming **Brecon**, a pretty Georgian town with Norman history. Following the wooded Usk Valley from north to south, the **Monmouthshire & Brecon Canal** (⬦ canalrivertrust.org.uk) travels 35 miles from here down to Pontypool. The 48-mile **Usk Valley Walk** and 55-mile **Taff Trail**, a popular cycle route, both pass by the canal, and narrowboats can be hired for self-catering holidays from **Country Craft Narrowboats** (⬦ countrycraftnarrowboats.com) in Llangynidr (12 miles south of Brecon) and **Brecon Park Boats** (⬦ beaconparkboats.com) at Llangattock (17 miles south of Brecon). Day boats, canoe hire and boat trips available from various outlets at Brecon and **Goytre Wharf**, 28 miles to the south.

Around ten miles east of Brecon, Llangorse Multi Activity Centre (𝒹 activityuk.com) sits close to the shores of Llangorse Lake, the largest lake in Wales, and leads horseriding and climbing experiences for kids aged four and above.

BRECON BEACONS & FFOREST FAWR

The middle of the national park is dominated by the Old Red Sandstone ridge below Brecon. Softened by weather and time, the ridge's heather-clad escarpments and grassy moorlands create an undulating landscape. Here, former pit ponies graze 20 miles of common land, keeping vegetation in check and creating a landscape ideal for running wild.

The highest peak in this part of the park is Pen Y Fan (2,900ft), which offers views all the way to the Severn Estuary and mid Wales. Most visitors hike to the mountain top from the Storey Arms activity centre (𝒹 storeyarms.com), eight miles south of Brecon, but the path up from Taf Fechan Forest just beyond Neuadd Reservoir is quieter. A less challenging climb is to summit Craig Cerrig-gleisiad (2,060ft) on a 2.7-mile walk from a car park (Libanus, Brecon LD3 8NH) on the A470. Thanks to its steep, stony sides, sheep haven't managed to graze in this area, making the flora more spectacular than in other parts of the national park. The peak borders a nature reserve of the same name, so it's possible to see rare species like peregrine falcons, redstarts, ring ouzel and brown hairstreak butterflies as you walk.

In the south of the Brecon Beacons range, the Four Waterfalls Walk is a 4½-mile out-and-back from a car park near Ystradfellte. Each of the falls – Sgwd Clun-Gwyn, Sgwd Isaf Clun-Gwyn, Sgwd y Pannwr and Sgwd yr Eira – has its own character, but Sgwd yr Eira is the most dramatic, with a pathway behind the curtain of tumbling water. For a more immersive experience, Adventures Wales (𝒹 adventureswales. co.uk) organises wet and wild canyoning days in waterfalls throughout the national park for children over ten years old.

In the west of the Brecon Beacons range, Fforest Fawr Geopark (𝒹 fforestfawrgeopark.org.uk) is a park within a park: one of some

◀ 1 Llyn y Fan Fach lake. 2 Llanddeusant Red Kite Feeding Station. 3 Dan-yr-Ogof National Showcaves Centre for Wales. 4 Time a visit to Hay-on-Wye for its famous literary festival. 5 Big Pit National Coal Museum. 6 Llanthony Priory.

STARGAZING IN THE DARK SKY RESERVE

Brecon Beacons National Park Visitor Centre, Libanus, Brecon LD3 8ER
⊘ darkskywalestrainingservices.co.uk; age: 6+; intrepid level: ②

'Are we looking at aliens right now?' one of the kids in our group asks, to a ripple of laughter. 'Well, you may laugh,' explains Allan Trow, founder of Dark Sky Wales and our galaxy guide for the next couple of hours, 'but we might well be. The Orion Nebula is up there so we're looking at stars being born, and therefore planets being born, and who knows what's on those planets.' Allan later tells me that kids always ask the questions that grown-ups want to but steer clear of for fear of looking silly.

We're staring through a portable telescope, which Allan has set up on a patch of grass at the National Park Visitor Centre. There's an observatory here, too, but setting up outside makes the stargazing season accessible to more people. There's not an electric light in sight; the darkness makes you realise how rare that is. Trees sway in the breeze and Pen y Fan looms to the south. The odd sheep bleats. Above, the night sky is ablaze with other worlds.

The Brecon Beacons is one of two official Dark Sky Reserves in Wales (Snowdonia is the other). To become certified was a two-year process involving stakeholders across governments, communities and the national park to lessen light pollution and put plans in place for education and outreach. The impact is net positive. 'Dark skies not only help astronomy, but they are also critical for nature and the health and wellbeing of people,' Allan enthuses. The highest level of Dark Sky Reserve is called a 'Sanctuary', and there's only one of those in the world – in the middle of the Pacific Ocean.

Allan is from the Valleys, just down the road, and got into astronomy by chance. 'My grandfather had racing pigeons and they weren't very reliable, so we spent lots of nights staring into the sky waiting for them to come home. That's when I started to learn about the stars.'

So far, we've toured the sky spotting constellations and learning their Greek and Celtic meanings. 'To us, Orion is a Greek hero, but in Japan it's a Geisha girl and also a drum,' Allan continues, explaining some different cultural interpretations of the stars across time and geography. For example, in ancient days the only people who had access to astronomy were from the Church, so they embedded moral meaning into everything

150 geoparks worldwide recognised by UNESCO for their unique geology and history. Hiking these storied hills comes to life when you consider people have lived in the landscape for over 8,000 years, and the mountains were sculpted by ice over 20,000 years ago. Within the geopark, the **Cribarth Geotrail**, a 3¼-mile circular walk starting at **Craig-y-nos Country Park**, passes crags and folds created in the Ice Age

they saw. The Seven Sisters is the only constellation that seems to have the same meaning everywhere in the world.

Once we've explored the constellations, Allan talks through other phenomena, like Andromeda – the most distant thing that can be seen with the naked eye. At first, we try to spot it with no equipment, then we look through the telescope, and then, the finale, we take photos through the telescope. 'Wowwwww,' the group exhales as colours and patterns come to life through the camera. 'It's the same with the northern lights, when we get them,' Allan explains. 'You can only see the colours through a camera lens.'

Speaking of the legendary northern lights raises questions about the most spectacular thing Allan's ever seen. He captivates young and old with tales of a huge solar storm in 2016 and light pillars – a rare phenomenon where light reflects off hexagonal ice crystals close to the Earth's atmosphere. While listening, no-one can take their eyes off the night sky. 'It's compulsive,' Allan says. 'There's always something new to notice, if only we all looked up.'

CHARLES PALMER/S

and dramatic scars of quarrying. Younger children might find Craig-y-nos Country Park itself easier to manage. Here, 40 acres of woodlands, meadows and rivers blend with Victorian gardens. Just down the road, the **Dan-yr-Ogof National Showcaves Centre for Wales** (𝄐 showcaves. co.uk) has more than ten miles of underground rivers, waterfalls and tunnels to explore, while further to the west, **Herbert's Quarry** is an

STUMP UP FOR TREES

Stump up for Trees (⌖ stumpupfortrees. org) is a community-based charity that hopes to improve the biodiversity of the Brecon Beacons by planting a million trees across the uplands. It's an example of landscape management for 'Public Goods' – providing benefit for everyone through better air and water quality and public access to the outdoors. The pilot project, led by local farmers, took place at Bryn Arw Common near Abergavenny and saw 135,000 native broadleaf trees planted. Some local accommodation providers support the initiative by donating for every room booked – these include the Angel Hotel in Abergavenny (⌖ angelabergavenny. com) and Gliffaes Country House Hotel (⌖ gliffaeshotel.com). Older children accompanied by adults are also welcome to join volunteering days either planting trees in winter or carrying out tree maintenance across the summer months.

abandoned limestone quarry just off the Brynaman to Llangadog road. Given the unguarded sheer drops this is probably one to explore with older kids only.

BLACK MOUNTAIN

The remote village of **Llanddeusant**, which sits near the remote **Sawdde Valley** – a chunk of the 95-mile **Beacons Way** – and the spectacular **Llyn y Fan Fach lake**, is a pretty base in the western part of the national park (not to be confused with the Black Mountains in the east). You may well see red kites soaring overhead in this area, thanks to more than 20 years of conservation efforts to bring the species back from the brink. At the **Llanddeusant Red Kite Feeding Station** (⌖ redkiteswales.co.uk), you can watch the birds divebombing for food from bird hides at various feeding times throughout the week.

A mile away from the feeding station, **Arc Adventures** (⌖ arc-adventures.com) uses funds from their activity days and holidays to subsidise activity weeks for young people struggling in mainstream education. There are more than 20 activities to choose from: crafts might include making Druid amulets (wands), while outdoor fun includes axe throwing, gorge walking and abseiling.

On the western edge of the national park, **Carreg Cennen Castle** (⌖ carregcennencastle.com) is not only a brilliant example of how a castle has changed hands throughout time, but also has a farm park and tea room on-site. Kids will enjoy lamb feeding in the springtime.

PRACTICALITIES

FAMILY-FRIENDLY SLEEPS

Tyn Y Coed Cottage ⬦ tynycoed-cottage.co.uk. This 300-year-old cottage, picture-perfect with its whitewashed Welsh-stone walls and climbing wisteria, is a couple of miles from Brecon in a remote spot surrounded by mature woodland. Renovations have been sensitive to the building's history, maintaining a large open fireplace, inglenook and exposed wooden beams. There are rope swings and dens for kids to explore in the garden, and a hot tub to make the most of clear skies. It sleeps six.

Wildman Woods ⬦ thewildmanwoods.com. As the name suggests, holidays are all about getting back to basics at this five-acre campsite on the fast-flowing River Sawdde a mile from Llanddeusant. Footpaths meander past the farm's geese and chickens towards Llyn Y Fan Fach lake and the Fan Brycheniog mountain range. There's a compost loo and toilet shed, and firewood can be bought on-site. Contact the site to find out about bell tents, plus pop-up suppers, foraging and bushcraft.

Ysgubor Y Ffin ⬦ underthethatch.co.uk. Slap bang on the Welsh-English border (the name means 'border barn' in Welsh), this 18th-century barn conversion sleeps ten in a beautifully remote spot near Hay-on-Wye and Abergavenny. There's a main house and an annexe, making it ideal for multigenerational groups or two families. Views stretch over to the Black Mountains in the east of the national park.

KID-FRIENDLY EATS

Angel Bakery ⬦ theangelbakery.com. Coffee, cake, pastries and sandwiches are served in this much-loved bakery on Abergavenny's Lower Castle Street, which specialises in long-fermented sourdough bread and pastries using entirely local and British ingredients. There are only a few tables so it's best to plan a takeaway picnic or arrive early to grab a spot.

The Bear ⬦ bearhotel.co.uk. This 500-year-old pub in the heart of Crickhowell, in the east of the national park, has an atmospheric restaurant and cosy bar, both of which welcome families. Roaring fires provide welcome cheer in the colder, wetter months. Food is traditional pub grub but with local ingredients, including Welsh lamb, of course.

Felin Fach Griffin ⬦ eatdrinksleep.ltd.uk. North of Brecon, the Felin Fach is a renowned slow-food spot, serving up local beef, cheese, game and lamb. To reduce food miles, the owners grow much of the fresh produce on-site. Sunday lunch is a lavish affair, best saved for a treat – there's a kids' menu, too. The tables in the garden are ideal in summer.

Llanthony Priory Hotel

⟨⟩ llanthonyprioryhotel.co.uk. This tiny country inn, all dark panelled walls, worn cobblestones and roaring fires, is a brilliantly cosy place for lunch after a walk in the Vale of Ewyas in the east of the national park. The cellar bar is part of a hotel connected to the priory ruins; the whole place feels isolated and eerie, and kids will love soaking up the atmosphere.

BEFORE YOU GO

In 2017, the Welsh government launched a plan to revive the **Welsh language**, which UNESCO considered 'vulnerable to extinction'. Minority languages are under threat the world over, and it's always those that don't have economic or political clout that suffer the worst. Yet the Welsh language is an integral part of the country's heritage and culture – many legends and myths would have been lost had they not been passed down in the oral tradition. In 2021 there were just over 883,300 Welsh speakers; the plan is to have one million by 2050, and Welsh is becoming an official language in more and more education settings. So before visiting, why not swot up on a few words so you can impress new friends along the way. Take a look at ⟨⟩ learnwelsh.cymru and ⟨⟩ nantgwrtheyrn.org.

MORE INFO

Welsh Tourist Board ⟨⟩ visitwales.com

15
GWYNEDD: SNOWDONIA & THE COAST

Rugged peaks, disused quarries and sweeping sands provide a dramatic backdrop for year-round adventure.

TOP FAMILY EXPERIENCE

ECO EXPERIENCES AT THE CENTRE FOR ALTERNATIVE TECHNOLOGY, MACHYNLLETH

BEST FOR KIDS AGED: 6+

WHEN TO GO: February to November

INTREPID LEVEL: ①

ADDED ADVENTURE: Mountain hiking, climbing and biking, and mine castle explorations, adrenalin sports, wild nature

TIME: Two days to one week

ECO INNOVATION & NATURE REGENERATION IN A DISUSED QUARRY

Centre for Alternative Technology, Llwyngwcrn Quarry, Pantperthog, Machynlleth SY20 9AZ &cat.org.uk

'There's an old legend in Wales that anyone who can build a house in 24 hours can keep it,' Rob Bullen, our tour guide, explains as we step into a turf-roofed hut on the edge of a lake. The water shimmers with reflections of the hills above, laden with trees, moss, lichen and ferns. We later learn that this type of habitat is called Celtic rainforest, and that here it forms part of the Dyfi Biosphere, which runs from the high peat moorland of the Aran Fawddwy mountain down to the coast.

'George Clarke from *Amazing Spaces* [the Channel 4 show] took on that challenge, and this is what he created,' Rob continues as we admire the hut. 'I'd live here!' one of my boys chimes in, using a stray reed to pretend-fish from the lake.

'This lake is actually a reservoir, supplying the whole centre with drinking water,' Rob tells the boys, their brains visibly churning. 'Like a well,' the youngest adds. Just below the lake, a display demonstrates the system; the water passes through CAT creating electricity, providing drinking water and driving the cliff railway before it heads out to sea. A brick chamber below where we stand cleans it ready for drinking.

It's this mix of folly and purpose that makes the Centre of Alternative Technology (CAT) so unique, and ideal for families – there's something to captivate and inspire all imaginations. The boys bounce about like pinballs, ricocheting enthusiastically from one concept to another.

CAT's history, steeped in a commitment to the environment, is very much part of its appeal. The centre was started by a group of volunteers in the 1970s, keen to find solutions in response to the first inklings of the climate crisis. Their chosen location was a disused slate quarry near Machynlleth (still an eco-minded town, brimming with creativity), where they converted abandoned buildings into a visitor centre and began experimenting with renewable energy.

As those experiments grew more ambitious the centre attracted more skilled people, leading to a series of environmental wins: they created the first entirely solar-heated building and the largest PV roof (photovoltaic) in the UK. The most notable first is the water-balanced cliff railway, which is how visitors start their CAT journey – soaring up through the forest by the power of water.

Our visit kicks off with the family-friendly Quarry Trail, where we discover George Clarke's hut, the lake and the water system, but also get distracted by wildlife – the centre is home to dormice, pine marten, badger, tawny owls, pied flycatchers, ravens and many more (though you may not see them all!) – and the views; in the end it takes us over an hour to walk the two-mile trail.

The highlight, however, is the quarry itself. Almost entirely reclaimed by nature, it's like a forgotten kingdom. Relics of the region's industrial past – in the 19th century this part of Wales was home to numerous slate

◀ Centre for Alternative Technology.

quarries and railways to transport the mined goods – poke through the undergrowth. The rusty remains of a crane look incongruous in a sea of green, and a brick-weighing station is barely visible behind its walls of velvety moss. The place is a little eerie but also bursting with hope: nature will regenerate the moment it's given a chance.

Next, we head down to the main centre, where there are interactive displays on everything from compost bins to soil particles. I soon give up trying to follow the carefully laid out path, and enjoy dashing about with the boys as they pass a winter warm well – a hole that draws warm air up from underground – and through a human-size mole hole created by the centre for kids to experience subterranean life. Finally we sit down for a rest in a straw bale theatre.

The site is so packed with ideas, innovations and curious inventions that it's hard to take in in one visit and we struggle to tear ourselves away. Plotting a return trip helps – special family days include activities from pond dipping to planting, solar-boat making to willow weaving, and the centre also offers occasional wildlife-tracking experiences. Next time, we'll spend the night in one of the centre's eco huts for full off-grid immersion.

ADDED ADVENTURE: UNTAMED LANDSCAPES & INDUSTRIAL HERITAGE

The county of Gwynedd, in northern Wales, encompasses most of Snowdonia National Park and the beautiful Llŷn Peninsula. Its 979 square miles is home to castles, forests, Wales' highest peak (Snowdonia itself), and a 180-mile coastline.

Adventure here is hardier than in the south of Wales (page 219 and page 247); even the views, often half submerged in cloud or mist, demand your full attention. But among this raw landscape there's a mysticism and magic that draws you in. In the market town of Machynlleth, it comes from people's ingenuity and creativity; throughout the Dfyi Biosphere Reserve it feels as though fairies and sprites might make their home in the waterfalls, lichen, and bogs; and in the north, it tumbles down via castle ruins and draws pilgrims to offshore islands. Wherever you choose to explore, your senses will be overloaded and you'll be left wanting more.

SNOWDONIA NATIONAL PARK: MACHYNLLETH TO BARMOUTH

A myriad of ecosystems is home to a variety of wildlife at the southern end of **Snowdonia National Park** (⊘snowdonia.gov.wales), which straggles the Dyfi river valley and estuary and Wales' only biosphere reserve: the **UNESCO Dyfi Biosphere Reserve** (⊘ dyfibiosphere.wales; the status recognises and facilitates a meaningful connection between communities and nature). Look out for wildlife bridges across roads and pollinating planters throughout **Machynlleth**, an eco-minded town on the edge of the reserve with many intriguing and creative goings-on, particularly during the **Comedy Festival** every spring (⊘ machcomedyfest.co.uk).

A few miles south of Machynlleth, the **Dyfi Osprey Project** (⊘ dyfiospreyproject.com) has been running since 2009 and receives thousands of visitors a year eager to see an epic raptor in the wild. The project is run by and based in the **Dyfi Wildlife Centre**, which has a 360° observatory deck and other hides – there are year-round activities. Further downstream, the **RSPB Ynys-hir reserve** (⊘ rspb.org.uk) is another great place to immerse yourselves in nature – lapwings, redshanks and butterflies can be seen in the summer, and ducks and geese in the winter. On the coast, seven miles down the river, **Ynyslas National Nature Reserve** (⊘ naturalresources.wales) is a vast coastal area made up of dunes, wetlands, beaches and bogs. Kids will love the huge dunes at Ynyslas itself, on the south side of the estuary, where there's a visitor centre and a car park.

Heading 15 miles north, further into Snowdonia National Park, you come to **Cadair Idris** (the 'chair' of a giant called 'Idris', legend has it). At 2,930ft, Wales' second-highest mountain dominates the landscape, its craggy peak contrasting with the smooth hills below. While the hoards flock to climb Snowdon, summiting Cadair Idris is a good alternative for older kids (the hike, whichever path you take, is designated hard or strenuous). The **Minffordd Path** starts near the **Cadair Idris Visitor Centre and café** (⊘ visitsnowdonia.info), south of the peak, while the **Pony Path** starts nearer the riverside town of **Dolgellau,** north of the peak; allow at least five hours there and back for both routes.

There are less strenuous activities in this area, too. On the road between Machynlleth and Cadair you'll come to **Corris Craft Centre** (⊘ corriscraftcentre.co.uk) where you can watch artisans

"Downstream, RSPB Ynys-hir reserve is another great place to immerse yourselves in nature – lapwings, redshanks and butterflies can be seen in the summer, and ducks and geese in the winter."

leatherworking, gin distilling and candle-making, and the **Corris Mine Explorers** (⊘ corrismineexplorers.co.uk), a good rainy-day option that takes visitors into the old Braich Goch slate mine.

A three-mile footpath along the northern shore of **Tal-y-llyn**, a lake nestled beside steep-sided hills south of Cadair Idris, is ideal for younger kids, weaving past deserted farms, babbling streams and ancient oaks. Some brave souls swim in the lake year-round. A few miles away, at **Tywyn**, steam engines on the **Talyllyn Railway** (⊘ talyllyn.co.uk) take passengers the seven miles to Abergynolwyn, stopping at **Dolgoch Falls** en route.

Heading deeper into rural lanes and big-farm country, you'll find the remote remains of the 13th-century **Castell y Bere** (⊘ cadw.gov.wales), a few miles east of Tal-y-llyn. It's a perfect setting for make-believe games, with epic views over the **Dysynni Valley**. At the top of the valley is a memorial to Mary Jones, a 15-year-old girl who in 1800 walked 26 miles from the nearby hamlet of **Llanfihangel-y-Pennant** to Bala to buy a Welsh Bible, which were scarce in those days. It's also the start of a 28-mile walking trail connecting the valley with the market town of **Bala**, where there's a museum dedicated to her life and memory: **Mary Jones World** (⊘ bydmaryjonesworld.org.uk).

On the coast, about 15 miles from Tal-y-llyn, **Barmouth** is a popular beach resort with amusements, fish and chips, and a small pier to go crabbing from. A pleasant way to get there is along the **Mawddach Trail** (⊘ mawddachtrail.co.uk), a flat nine-mile cycling or walking path from Dolgellau.

SNOWDONIA NATIONAL PARK: COED Y BRENIN TO LLANDUDNO

The middle of Snowdonia National Park is dominated by the **Coed y Brenin Forest Park** (⊘ naturalresources.wales), Wales' first purpose-built **mountain-biking centre** (⊘ mbwales.com). Eight trails start from the visitor centre, with plenty for beginners as well as pros. Other activities in the forest park include walking, orienteering and geocaching, and there are a number of natural play areas. Twenty miles to the east, the **Canolfan Treweryn National Whitewater Centre**

◄ RSPB Ynys-hir reserve. **1** The remote remains of Castell y Bere. **2** The Minffordd Path, Cadair Idris, is suitable for older children. ◄

(⊘ nationalwhitewatercentre.co.uk) near Bala is a great place for kids over 12 to try whitewater rafting.

Fifteen miles north from Coed y Brenin, the old slate-mining town of **Blaenau Ffestiniog** is the quaint, bustling heart of Snowdonia – a hub of bunkhouses and outdoor shops. It gets very busy in peak season, partly thanks to attractions like **Zip World Llechwedd** (⊘ zipworld. co.uk), a huge, converted quarry with a museum, mine tours and the longest zip line in Britain. A little more off the beaten track is the **Cwmorthin Waterfall** (⊘ gps-routes.co.uk) in the heart of Snowdonia's slate and mining country. The waterfall is a short walk from an accessible car park, but the surrounding area – **Cwmorthian Slate Quarry and Lake** – offers a range of hiking options including a longer walk that leads to Llyn Cwmorthin (lake), a renowned wild swimming spot.

Between Coed y Brenin and Blaenau Fefestinog, younger kids may enjoy the more unusual activity of sheep walking at a family-run farm, **Sheep Walk Snowdonia** (⊘ sheepwalksnowdonia.wales), near **Trawsfynydd Lake** (⊘ trawslake.com).

The scenic 30-mile road from Blaenau Ffestiniog up to **Conwy**, a walled town on the Conwy estuary, passes through **Betws-y-Coed**, another great base for hiking and adventure, and **Adventure Parc Snowdonia** (⊘ adventureparcsnowdonia.com) where you can surf artificial waves in a disused reservoir and climb on a series of indoor climbing and adventure walls (there is something for all ages). There's heaps of fun to be had, although a large Hilton hotel makes the place feel more corporate than outdoorsy. Beyond Conwy, you come to the grand Victorian seaside town of **Llandudno** with its pier, cable car up to the wildlife-filled **Great Orme** headland, and quiet beach with spectacular sunsets.

THE NORTHWEST COAST

In northwest Gwynedd, just short of the Llŷn Peninsula, **Harlech Castle** (⊘ cadw.gov.wales) and Portmeirion are both popular with holidaymakers. The former, with Snowdonia's peaks in the background and the sea lapping at the dunes below, lords over the landscape like no other Welsh castle. Year-round events bring history and Welsh heritage

◀ **1** Harlech Castle. **2** Mountain-bike trail at Coed y Brenin Forest Park. **3** Canolfan Tryweryn National Whitewater Centre.

to life, including a summer holiday Knight School for over-fives brave enough to take the challenge.

Portmeirion (⊘ portmeirion.wales), on the River Dwyryd estuary around eight miles to the north, was the creative vision of Sir Clough Williams-Ellis who scoured the world for unwanted artefacts and endangered buildings to create a cluster of Italianate buildings in bright colours. Kids love the model-village feel of the place, although it's worth avoiding peak times.

SPLITTING ROCKS: THE NATIONAL SLATE MUSEUM WITH QUARRYMAN CARWYN PRICE

Parc Gwledig, Padarn Country Park, Llanberis LL55 4TY ⊘ museum.wales ; age: 3+; intrepid level: ①

'Chop, split, chop, split.' Silence falls over the audience as Carwyn Price splits slate. It should be impossible, but he's splitting rock like it's cheese. 'The better quality the slate, the thinner you can split it. The splitting is almost always still done by hand, but the trimming – or dressing, as it was traditionally called – although sometimes still done by hand, is now more often done by machine. And a machine can do almost four times as much in a day,' Carwyn tells us; all of us, kids and adults, mesmerised by the rhythmic splitting. 'This piece is about 530 million years old,' he continues, inviting the kids to have a closer look. 'The Victorians exploited this natural resource by blasting the sides of mountains, but humans have always used it. The Romans used slate for roofing.'

People often tell Carwyn that he's very young to have been a quarryman for more than 30 years, but that's because he started at the nearby Penrhyn Quarry straight from school – 'I started my apprenticeship at 16', he tells us. 'Did you ever get hurt?' the children ask, having seen the pictures of the quarry hospitals and men working with little safety equipment. 'A little, but the dust was the worst thing; some people died from inhaling too much,' he replies.

Carwyn now works at the National Slate Museum, part of Amgueddfa Cymru – National Museum Wales – demonstrating slate splitting and answering questions about what life was like as a quarryman. The museum sits below Dinorwic Quarry, which closed in 1969. Former workshops, which once fashioned wagons and forged rails, now tell the story of the slate industry. The whole place looks as if the engineers and quarrymen have just downed tools and gone home, and every demonstration is run by former quarrymen. History doesn't get much more interactive than this.

'I bet I can guess which one you'd most want to live in,' Wynford Hughes, another local museum guide, challenges the kids as we stand in front of Fron Haul, a collection of quarrymen's houses through the ages, each

For a quieter slice of coastal life, head over to the **Ll n Peninsula**, a 30 mile finger of land projecting into the Irish Sea. Its remoteness is its appeal; Welsh is more commonly spoken than English and tiny coastal villages have an old-world charm. **Porthdinllaen beach** (⊘ nationaltrust.org.uk) is a sandy haven for kids and adults alike; enjoy a pint and chips with your feet in the sand at the waterfront Ty Coch Inn. Further south, **Porthor** (⊘ nationaltrust.org.uk) is another favourite; the white sands are said to whistle in certain wind conditions

GAIL JOHNSON/S

dismantled and rebuilt for the museum. The kids race into the dwellings, which span the years from 1861, a golden era for the slate industry, to 1969, the last moments before the industry's collapse. Everything is exactly as it would have been when they were in use – right down to the original pop music posters up in the 1960s house.

We learn about the Bradwyr (traitor) during the 1900–03 strike in Bethesda, and how scarce food was at that time. Our explorations lead to a series of questions from the kids: 'Where's the sofa? Where's the bathroom? Where are the lights? Ooooh, a fire!' Wynford guesses right; the boys would most like to live in the 1960s house, because it's the only one with a TV. 'Every time,' he says.

I later ask Carwyn whether he prefers working in the museum to the quarry. 'There's so much more variety here, I get to meet people from all over. But best of all, even though there's loads to see and do, everyone wants to see slate splitting. We quarrymen like to think we're still the top of the bill.'

and caves add to the adventure. Wild camping is allowed at **Porth Iago**, a sheltered bay below an iron hillfort just north of Porthor.

   Aberdaron, on the far southern tip of the peninsula, makes a quieter base than the bustling tourist town of **Abersoch** to the east. Seasonal boat trips head over to **Bardsey Island** (⊘ bardsey.org), an important pilgrimage site home to a 1,500-year-old church and Manx shearwater colonies.

PRACTICALITIES

FAMILY-FRIENDLY SLEEPS

Eco Retreats ⊘ ecoretreats.co.uk. Twenty-five minutes from the nearest tarmacked road, this collection of five yurts and one tipi offers one of Wales' finest back-to-nature experiences without having to go back to basics. The accommodation is spread across 50 acres, so space and privacy are as bountiful as the forest and stars. There's even an outdoor wood-fired bathtub for each yurt so you can make the most of big sunsets and clear nights.

Rocks at Plas Curig ⊘ therockshostel. com. This family-run, upmarket hostel is in a hub of hiking bunkhouses surrounding Betws-y-Coed; an ideal location for central Snowdonia hiking and adventures. Communal spaces are stylish and snug, and there's an adjacent cottage for those looking for more privacy. The local 'Sherpa' bus service takes guests to town and hiking hotspots.

Ty Coch ⊘ red-welly.com. Big groups and extended families will love this trio of sustainably minded cottages (and a shepherd's hut), with ten acres and a private beach on the Llŷn Peninsula. The grounds have been thoughtfully rewilded with paths and campfire spots, electricity is 100% renewable, and there's an on-site pizza oven.

Tyn Y Cornel ⊘ tynycornel.co.uk. This lakeside hotel is a great base for families passing through southern Snowdonia for a night or two. While it doesn't offer much in terms of facilities, and is on a

TRASH FREE TRAILS

The **Trash Free Trails** charity hopes to reduce litter on the UK's trails by 75% by 2025. On the website (⊘ trashfreetrails.org), the charity outlines nine steps so we can all 'Do It Ourselves': recognise what needs to be done; plan a 'rubbish route'; rally others to join in; get out there and pick up the rubbish; record what's been collected; recycle what's possible; tell the world; reward yourself; and repeat. Take a look at the website for organised cleans and events in Snowdonia, where some of the Trash Free Trails team is based.

fairly busy road, it is just yards from Tal-y-llyn lake, has heaps of walking routes from the doorstep, serves up pizzas in a tipi shelter, and offers family rooms tucked away at the back.

KID-FRIENDLY EATS

Dylan's ⊘ dylansrestaurant.co.uk. Scattered throughout north Wales, this family of three restaurants – with branches at Llandudno and Criccieth (where Cardigan Bay meets the Llŷn Peninsula), and in Menai Bridge on Anglesey – all serve locally sourced produce and seafood in beautiful coastal settings. Kids will love the stone-baked pizzas, and grown-ups will love the cocktails. Perfect for a special occasion.

George III ⊘ georgethethird.pub. It's almost impossible to cycle or walk past George III without being tempted into its snug bar or to stop for refreshments on its riverside terrace. Overlooking the Mawddach Estuary and at the end of a car-free cycle trail (page 239), it's a peaceful spot, serving traditional pub nosh with an extensive all-day menu and plenty of kid-friendly choices.

Sblash Caban Pysgod (Fish Bar) ⦿. Fish and chips are a must on the Llŷn Peninsula, and eating them while watching the sun go down at Aberdaron is the perfect setting. Serving locally caught fish and crab cakes, this fish bar has a long communal table or you can take your feast straight to the beach.

BEFORE YOU GO

Weather and conditions can change quickly in Snowdonia, and lots of people get caught out every day taking on more than they can handle or misjudging conditions. Being properly prepared not only protects you, but also the local services that must come to your rescue if something goes wrong. **Adventure Smart** (⊘ adventuresmart. uk) provides advice for those looking to enjoy the great outdoors throughout the UK by asking three simple questions: Do I have the right gear? Do I know what the weather will be like? Am I confident I have the knowledge and skills for the day? You can find resources particular to Snowdonia on ⊘ adventuresmart. uk/wales.

MORE INFO

Snowdonia Tourist Board
⊘ visitsnowdonia.info
Welsh Tourist Board ⊘ visitwales.com

16
PEMBROKESHIRE

You're never far from the sea in Wales' wild southwest, home to an untameable rocky coast and more dolphins and puffins than anywhere else in Britain.

TOP FAMILY EXPERIENCE

COASTEERING NEAR THE PRESELI HILLS

BEST FOR KIDS AGED: 8+

WHEN TO GO: March to October

INTREPID LEVEL: ③

ADDED ADVENTURE: Boating, quaint harbour towns, epic coastal wildlife, infamous geology

TIME: Two days to one week

EARTH-GROUNDING IN THE WATER: A COASTEERING ADVENTURE

Preseli Venture, Parc-y-nole Fach, Mathry, Haverfordwest SA62 5HN ⬠ preseliventure.co.uk; five-day activity weeks also available (Mon–Fri) including two coasteering, two kayaking & two surfing sessions

'What first springs to mind when you think of coasteering?' Tommy Barthorpe, adventure instructor, asks, looking around at our group of ten, ages ranging from eight to 65. We're in Preseli Venture's 'adventure barn', surrounded by wetsuits, paddles, kayaks, ropes and helmets. Tommy's gentle giant demeanour instils instant trust, which is exactly what you want when you're about to follow someone off a cliff.

'Jumping off rocks,' a few of the kids reply enthusiastically in unison. Tommy continues, 'Well, that's what everyone thinks, but actually

---

◀ Coasteering the Welsh coastline.

coasteering is about more than big jumps. We're going to do lots of walking around the edge of rocks, a bit of climbing, floating, and swimming, too. The only thing you have to be up for is getting wet.' The relief in a few grown-up faces is palpable.

We've arrived at Preseli Venture, tucked away in the near-deserted coastal valley of Abermawr, eight miles north of St Davids, for a half-day coasteering session. There's a lodge for those on activity weeks next door, but there are sessions for non-residents, too. Our group has come from all over Pembrokeshire, lured by the fact that Preseli Venture has been running coasteering here for over 30 years.

Nick and Sophie Hurst set up the business in 1988, and soon gathered a team of adventurers similarly eager to help visitors engage more deeply with the natural world. They call the concept 'earth-grounding': moving away from screens, technology and busyness to get back to our roots. Each session is structured specifically for a group's needs and level of experience. Accessibility is a key part of Preseli Venture's appeal.

"We gather on the muddy shingle of the bay, a long inlet surrounded by idyllic coastal cottages and craggy cliffs."

After a briefing and kitting up (wetsuits, helmets, lifejackets, and there's even a shoe rack of leftover trainers if anyone doesn't have shoes suitable for the water) we head into the minibus. There's a ripple of excitement; the adventure begins. So perfect is the Pembrokeshire coast for coasteering that there are endless options for where to go. Locations are secret (to protect the ecosystem and local communities), but Tommy tells us about a remote beach a little to the north, with rocky edges, where legend has it a farmer once caught a mermaid, and an azure, blue lagoon – an extraordinary setting for epic jumps.

Since we're beginners, Tommy opts for a harbour just ten minutes down the road. 'The coast is quieter up here than in south Pembrokeshire, so we often have the place to ourselves,' he tells us as we gather on the muddy shingle of the bay, a long inlet surrounded by idyllic coastal cottages and craggy cliffs. It's low tide, so we've got a way to walk before reaching the water's edge.

'It's so squelchy,' one of the younger kids declares as we wade towards the rocky inlet edges, seaweed gathering around our ankles. 'It's amazing what's edible out here,' Tommy continues, picking up a clump of delicate weed. 'This is pepper dulse, and tastes like garlic and truffles.' Once up on the rocks, scrambling around the inlet, we heed Tommy's advice that barnacles make good grips for feet but not for hands or faces. We learn about limpets, which have the strongest tensile strength in the natural world, and admire brilliant green sea lettuce swirling in the undercurrents.

Once accustomed to the water, we swim out to a channel between a small rocky outcrop and the coast. 'Coasteering is about teamwork,' Tommy reminds us, asking us to always wait for the person behind to catch up and never overtake the person in front, and to look out for one another. It's amazing how quickly we gel as a group and heartening to see the kids muck in and help the adults out as much as vice versa. Around the other side of the rocky outcrop, it's time to try some jumps. A diagonal ledge seems to be designed just for this purpose, and we each choose our spot with our distance from the water ranging from one foot to eight feet.

'Woahhhhhhhh!' the first jumper cries, tumbling into the wash and emerging with a huge grin. It doesn't take long to realise how addictive the combination of sea water and adrenalin can be. Scrambling and traversing back around the rocks, we head back towards the bay through a cave, ducking at one point. 'It's like being a seal,' my eight-year-old observes as we swish about in the cave with our black, shiny helmets bobbing up and down. Nerves seem to dissipate thanks to Tommy's calm and reassuring manner, always checking everyone is comfortable.

As we emerge from the cave, Tommy gives us our next brief. 'We're going to really work as a team this time, swimming across the bay like a link chain, feet under armpits.' Much giggling and splashing ensues as two 'teams' swim and wiggle their way across the bay. Around the first headland, those that want to head to a higher ledge, while the rest of us practise some more medium jumps – leaping with one foot in front and looking forward, as instructed by Tommy. The kids charge up and leap back down over and over like lemmings. Some of the older kids work their way up to 20ft leaps.

Back at the minibus we get into dry clothes and warm up with hot chocolate. Little can be heard above the collective shivering, chatting and giggling. We sound more like a flock of gulls than humans, which I suppose means earth-grounding has been well and truly achieved.

ADDED ADVENTURE: FROM WILDLIFE-FILLED BAYS TO LEGEND-SHROUDED HILLS

Wales' southwestern county of Pembrokeshire has long been loved by families seeking back-of-beyond, slow beach holidays. Bordered by Carmarthenshire to the east and Ceredigion to the northeast, most of the county juts out into the sea. Its popularity has led to soaring visitor numbers in hotspots like St Davids in peak season, so it's worth considering an off-season visit, or heading to the north of the region, around Cardigan, where it tends to be a little less touristed.

The coast and its estuaries, meandering inland, lie largely within the **Pembrokeshire Coast National Park** (⊘ pembrokeshirecoast.wales), Britain's only coastal national park. And although it's also the smallest, at 243 square miles, it offers huge variety, criss-crossed by more than 600 miles of footpaths through wooded valleys, vast estuaries and beaches of every shape and size. Marine life thrives among the limestone stacks, cliffs and crannies perched above the sea, protected by centuries-old seafaring communities.

CARDIGAN & SURROUNDS

The northern Pembrokeshire coast is quieter than the south, ideal for hiking and adventure pursuits with fewer crowds. The pretty and bustling town of **Cardigan** sits on the edge of the county, straddling the **River Teifi** (hence the town's Welsh name, Aberteifi) moments from the sea. It's hard not to fall for Cardigan's creative buzz; introduce kids to upcycling at the treasure trove **New Life Community Project** and **The Eco Shop**. On the High Street, **Stiwdio 3** (⊘ makeitinwales.co.uk) is a café and local craft shop where 'Make it in Wales' courses cover everything from block printing to Welsh quilting.

Just below **Cardigan Castle** (⊘ cardigancastle.com), home to 900 years of history and a family-friendly Escape Room, **Prince Charles Quay** is a pleasant riverside place to perch; retired shellfish and salmon fisherman **Dai Crab Evans** (⊘ daicrabsboat.com) runs boat trips along the Teifi estuary on *Diana Ellen*.

---

1 Sea kayaking, Cardigan Bay. **2** Walking trails criss-cross the Pembrokeshire Coast National Park. **3** Sedate explorations of Teifi Marshes Nature Reserve. **4** National Coracle Centre. ▶

A couple of miles north of Cardigan, **Cardigan Island Coastal Farm Park** (⌾ cardiganisland.com) is run by fifth-generation farmers (it's been in the family since the 1600s) and provides hands-on encounters with farm animals and a clifftop nature trail with views across to tiny, uninhabited Cardigan Island. There's a play area and campsite, too. A few miles up the coast, the idyllic sandy cove of **Mwnt**, below Foel y Ment hill, is perfect for a walk with epic coastal views. Pop into the quaint 14th-century Church of the Holy Cross, which on a brisk day feels like it's at the edge of the world. It's best to visit Mwnt early in the morning to avoid crowds, or park further along the coast path and walk from there.

A few miles inland from Cardigan, the **Welsh Wildlife Centre** (⌾ welshwildlife.org) in **Teifi Marshes Nature Reserve** has an adventure playground and a giant willow badger to please the kids, and runs seasonal events including a geocaching trail. Based at the wildlife centre, **Heritage Canoes** (⌾ heritagecanoes.squarespace.com) offer guided trips into the Teifi Gorge from April to September. The more adventurous might prefer sea kayaking or whitewater rafting (ages ten and up) with **Cardigan Bay Active** (⌾ cardiganbayactive.co.uk), based in the middle of Cardigan town.

A quirky attraction eight miles inland from the Welsh Wildlife Centre is the **National Coracle Centre**, a museum housing the country's largest collection of coracles – oval boats traditionally made with willow and animal skins. In a beautiful setting beside the Cenarth falls and a 200-year-old bridge over the Teifi River, the centre is home to a café and 17th-century mill, too.

THE PRESELI HILLS, ST DAVIDS & SURROUNDS

Ancient legends shroud Pembrokeshire's highest spot: the **Preseli Hills**. Once home to the infamous **Stonehenge Bluestones**, which are believed to have been carried from Wales to Wiltshire thousands of years ago, the Preselis may not be that high at 2,000ft, but they're big on drama. On a clear day, it's possible to see Ireland from **Foel Eryr**, one of the most accessible 360° viewpoints. More avid hikers can traverse the spine of the hills on the **Golden Road**, a walking route that dates to the Neolithic period. The seven-mile west–east trail begins at Bwlch Gwynt, not far

1 Preseli Hills. **2** Newgale Beach. ▶

from Foel Eryr. Along the way, Iron Age hillforts and Bronze Age stone ramparts, including Foel Drygarn, offer wonderful natural playgrounds for all ages.

Further southwest, **St Davids**, Britain's smallest city, is the end of the line before **Ramsey Island** and the churning Atlantic beyond. The city springs to life in the summer months, so much so that the shoulder seasons are best if you want to avoid crowds. The **Oriel y Parc Visitor Centre** (⊘ pembrokeshirecoast.wales) in the heart of town is a good place to start. The living and breathing green building, made entirely from local materials, is a source of information for the whole national park. A gallery hosts local artists, and a Discovery Room often has interactive creative projects for kids. Look out for holiday activities at **St Davids Cathedral**, too. Older kids may enjoy some of the local guided or self-guided pilgrimages to the cathedral (⊘ stdavidscathedral. org.uk): so significant was this location that in 1123 Pope Callixtus II declared that two pilgrimages to the cathedral were equal to one journey to Rome.

Beyond the city is the sea. Outdoor outfit **TYF** (⊘ tyf.com) can organise pretty much every water-based activity for all abilities and ages from its base in St Davids. Just below the city, **Whitesands Bay** is a popular surfing beach year-round; **Ma Simes Surf School** (⊘ masimessurfschool. co.uk) has been providing lessons for children over eight years old for more than 30 years. Nature-lovers must pay a visit to **Ramsey Island** (⊘ thousandislands.co.uk) where guillemots, fulmars and kittiwakes nest in rocky ledges. South along the coast, **Newgale Beach's** two-mile stretch of soft sands, backing on to the National Trust's Southwood Estate, is a haven for families looking for a lazy day at the beach.

TENBY & THE SOUTHERN COAST

Southern Pembrokeshire is more populated than the north and might better suit those with younger children. **Tenby** is a colourful harbour town surrounded by beaches (Tenby North and Tenby South) and well served by buses; an ideal base for those that want everything on the doorstep. Offshore, **Caldey Island** (⊘ caldeyislandwales.com) is a fun day out (boats depart from Tenby harbour from April to October) with a chocolate factory, woodland walks, a museum covering the island's

1 Tenby. **2** Daugleddau estuary. ▶

A BAY TO REMEMBER: DOLPHIN SPOTTING IN CARDIGAN BAY

Patch beach, Gwbert, Cardigan SA43 1PP ⌀ baytoremember.co.uk ; age: 6+;
intrepid level: ②

'Few people realise it, but Cardigan Bay is a special area of conservation because it has Europe's largest population of resident bottlenose dolphins – there are about 600 residents here,' Tony, founder of A Bay to Remember, tells us as we head out of Gwbert beach on one of his two RIBs. The business is a family affair – Tony's son often skippers the other boat, and his daughter is one of the wildlife guides. An invisible line across the bay means we're technically in the county of Ceredigion, but we head south back into Pembrokeshire to cruise around headlands, explore caves and look out for wildlife.

'Everyone asks if they're guaranteed dolphin sightings, so we've worked out there's a six out of ten chance of seeing them, but this increases to nine out ten on our longer trips, which are two hours so mean we can head further afield.' Tony explains, before I ask the same question. The longer trips are best for older kids. Minimum age on the hour-long trip is four. He continues, 'We do always see seals, and kids often find them more interesting anyway.'

Sure enough, around the next headland, my youngest spots a couple of black heads popping up and down in the water. I dismiss them for lobster pot buoys, but as we get closer we see the unmistakable outline of a seal – a kind face with big eyes, just like a dog staring back at you, inviting you to play.

We could watch the seals all day, but move on to explore caves along the coast. 'Some people are nervous of the caves, but I can tell that you two are brave enough,' Tony jokes with the boys as a huge chasm in the cliffs provides the perfect boat shelter. We bob up and down for a while in what feels and sounds like an underwater kingdom.

'When the seals have pups, the tours avoid the caves altogether, to give the animals their space,' Tony explains. A Bay to Remember adheres to a code of conduct for operating close to wildlife and submits any sightings to the Sea Watch Foundation so conservationists can benefit from the trips. Sometimes volunteers come out to photo the creatures for identification.

'What's that?' one of the kids shouts as we leave the cave. A huge barrel jellyfish floats

history, and a priory. A few miles northwest of town, kids can drive mini 4x4s and experience a tree-top trail at **Heatherton World of Activities** (⌀ heatherton.co.uk).

Saundersfoot, three miles north of Tenby along the coast, is another accessible stretch of sand. At low tide it's possible to walk the few hundred yards to **Wisemans Bridge Beach** via Coppet Hall

just below the surface, and we all agree we're glad we didn't jump in for a swim. Tony tells us to look out for compass jellyfish, moon jellyfish and lion's mane jellyfish, all of which can be found in these waters. The kids toss and turn watching out for floating jellies below, 100% tuned into the big blue.

We then head across to Cardigan Island, which is owned by the Wildlife Trust and protected due to nesting lesser black-backed and great black-backed gulls. Although no-one can step foot on the island, it's possible to admire fulmar shags, cormorants and the odd peregrine falcon from the boat. 'Few people realise how many seabirds we have, and they're always surprised at how fascinating they are,' Tony explains once we head back to base at speed. We're sorry not to have seen any dolphins but pleased to have a reason to come back.

'People are really overwhelmed when they see them. Some have travelled all over the world to watch dolphins and can't believe they can see them so close to home,' Tony explains, persuading us to come back another time for a longer trip. 'It's a great reminder that we don't have to go far to enjoy the wonders of the natural world.'

PAUL QUAYLE/A

Beach, which are also linked by tunnels and a tramway. Cutting through rocky outcrops, the tunnels now form part of the coast path but were first used in 1842 by horse-drawn trains. **Coppet Hall Beach Centre** (⊘ hean-castle-estate.com) provides facilities and parking, alongside watersports outlets including **Good Trails Paddleboarding** (⊘ good-trails.com).

WELSH WOOLLEN TEXTILES

St Davids peninsula is home to the last remaining Welsh woollen textile producers, and paying them a visit is a great way to support local craft and heritage. Although the water mills no longer drive the looms in either of the remaining woollen mills, both offer visitors a chance to see the historic set-up and how that connects to modern-day weaving. Visitors to **Solva Woollen** **Mill** (⌀ solvawoollenmill.co.uk) can nose around the 19th-century weaving shed and sometimes see the looms in action. Family-run **Melin Tregwynt** (⌀ melintregwynt. co.uk) has been the site of a working mill since the 17th century. Today, the simple, whitewashed mill stocks everything from throws to bags, and there's a popular on-site café.

Nine miles inland, three rivers (Western and Eastern Cleddau, and the Carew and Cresswell) converge at the **Daugleddau estuary**, a hidden area of wooded valleys and tidal marshes. The pretty village of **Lawrenny**, surrounded by water and ancient oak woodland, is a great spot for families looking to immerse themselves in natural beauty. Here, the **Little Retreat** (⌀ littleretreats.co.uk; see opposite), offers everything from foraging to stargazing. Further south, the dramatic ruins of 2,000-year old **Carew Castle** are fun to explore; bring bikes to join the ten-mile **Cresswell Trail** (⌀ pembrokeshire.gov.uk) through nature reserves and tidal mills.

PRACTICALITIES

FAMILY-FRIENDLY SLEEPS

Bluestone ⌀ bluestonewales.com. Bluestone's 500-acre resort in southern Pembrokeshire is an all-singing, all-dancing holiday park with holiday cottages and lodges. There's an on-site waterpark and heaps of activities from archery to rock climbing. Open year-round, it has packages for all seasons, including a Winter Lights option that offers illuminated woodland walks, magic shows and winter wildlife trails.
Felin Fach ⌀ underthethatch.co.uk/ felinf. Just south of Cardigan, on a quiet country lane two miles inland from the coast, this is one of Under the Thatch's many idyllic spots for family gatherings. Sleeping nine, the house is ideal for two families and has rambling, wild gardens. It's attached to a smallholding, so also offers plenty of opportunities to get involved in farm life.
Fforest ⌀ coldatnight.co.uk. This collection of converted farm cottages, stables, croft houses and huts and domes of all shapes and sizes is an institution

when it comes to slow, eco, family-friendly fun, with heaps of activities on offer. There are three sites – self-catering apartments on the water's edge in Cardigan, a coastal camp walking distance from Penbryn beach, and the main site next to the Teifi Marshes Nature Reserve.

Harbour Beach View ⊘ sugarandloaf.com. This second-floor apartment in a grand row of Victorian houses overlooking Tenby's Harbour Beach has sweeping sea views from every window. The beach is just 100yds from the front door and, being situated in the heart of Tenby, with bus routes and many attractions on the doorstep, this makes a great base for a car-free break. The apartment sleeps four and welcomes dogs.

Little Retreat ⊘ littleretreats.co.uk. In the heart of Lawrenny village, Little Retreat's domes offer luxurious camping for families, including private bathrooms, kitchens and wood-fired hot tubs. In addition, 'Stargazer' tents come with private garden space and outdoor bathtubs – perfect for those evenings when Wales' dark skies come to life.

Oak Tree Cottage ⊘ welshwildlife.org/oak-tree-cottage-cwtch. This cosy stone cottage for four – nicknamed *The Cwtch* – is right in the heart of Teifi Marshes Nature Reserve. Guests benefit from early morning and dusk in the reserve and those lucky (and patient) enough might even spot otters and badgers. The Glasshouse Café next door can offer a take-away service. Profits go back to the Wildlife Trust's conservation projects.

Preseli Glamping and Camping ⊘ preseliglamping.co.uk. Fourteen pitches across a grassy, sheltered meadow, just a mile from Aberbach beach, ten miles up the coast from St Davids, providing campers with a great base to explore wilder parts of the north Pembrokeshire coast. Each pitch enjoys a firepit, cooking grill, and picnic table and benches. This site is run by neighbouring Preseli Ventures (page 247).

KID-FRIENDLY EATS

Crwst ⊘ crwst.cymru. Locally owned and run, Crwst serves wholesome cakes, pastries and lunches in a beautiful high-ceiled building just off Cardigan High Street. Ingredients are the best of Welsh. The loaded pancakes are a brunch favourite, with Pembrokeshire sea salted caramel sauce and hazelnut chocolate spread.

Grub Kitchen at The Bug Farm ⊘ thebugfarm.co.uk. This combination of visitor centre, farm, museum, trail network, walled garden, zoo and café just outside St Davids is all about bugs. The on-site Grub Kitchen is Britain's first edible insect restaurant (although you may be pleased to hear there are non-insect dishes, too).

Pizzatipi ⊘ pizzatipi.co.uk. Tucked away in the heart of Cardigan on Cambrian Quay, with a terrace jutting out over the river, this huge tipi serves handmade stone-baked pizzas, breads and sweet treats – ideal family nosh made with local ingredients.

Simply Seafoods f castlesquaretenby. This tiny fishmonger, perched on the harbour's edge in Tenby, serves up cracking crab sandwiches and pots of cockles for lunch alongside the daily catch and fresh, local lobster for those self-catering.

BEFORE YOU GO

Throughout Pembrokeshire, vending machines at dairy farm gates sell milk directly to consumers, cutting out the middleman and plastic waste, and sending 100% of the profits to farmers. If you're self-catering or camping, look out for the chance to buy this way; check ⊘ easyfarmshop.co.uk for a map of vending machines throughout the county. Some, like Little Hasguard Dairy, even offer flavoured milk, hot chocolate and milkshakes.

MORE INFO

Pembrokeshire Tourist Board
⊘ visitpembrokeshire.com
Welsh Tourist Board ⊘ visitwales.com

THE LITTLE RETREAT

Time to explore...

The Little Retreat is a feel-good location that restores the body, inspires the mind and energises the soul.

Reconnect with yourself, with the wild and with each other in our luxury glamping accommodation.

www.littleretreats.co.uk
Pembrokeshire, Wales

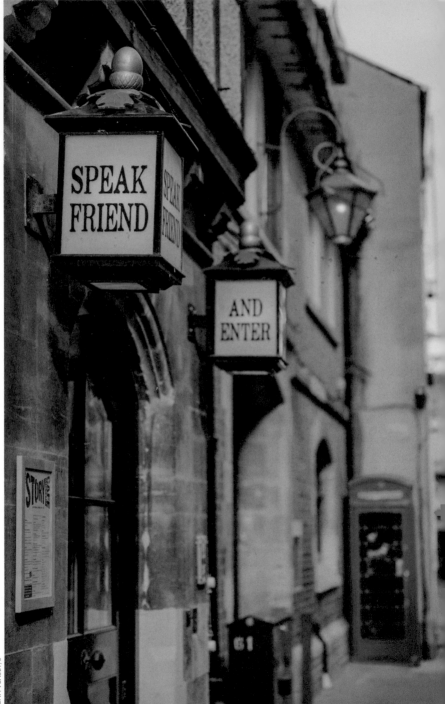

17
OXFORD

Let young imaginations run wild in the City of Spires.

TOP FAMILY EXPERIENCE

AN EXUBERANT JOURNEY THROUGH THE ART OF STORYTELLING AT THE STORY MUSEUM

BEST FOR KIDS AGED: 3+

WHEN TO GO: Year-round

INTREPID LEVEL: ①

ADDED ADVENTURE: Historic colleges, river adventures, literary attractions,
world-class museums

TIME: Two days

TALL TALES, MYTHS & MAKE-BELIEVE

The Story Museum, 42 Pembroke St, OX1 1BP ⊘ storymuseum.org.uk

'Buckle up, we're going to travel through thousands of years in the city of stories, through Wonderland, Middle-earth, Lyra's Oxford and back again,' the narrator booms as the ground shudders and silence falls. We're in a corner of The Story Museum, a telephone-exchange building on old-world Pembroke Street that's been cleverly converted into a literary adventure for kids of all ages (albeit probably best enjoyed by under tens). We've started our journey aboard the museum's 'Story Craft' to enjoy a film experience called The City of Stories.

For the next 25 minutes our 'flight' dodges mythical Welsh dragons fighting above medieval Oxford, watches Geoffrey of Monmouth composing the legends of King Arthur and passes Queen Matilda making a heroic dash for freedom from Oxford Castle one freezing December night. 'Always look up,' the narrator reminds the kids as we

---

◀ The Story Museum.

sweep past city gargoyles and spires that have stood through centuries, setting up our weekend of adventures around the city.

Blurry eyed, we return to the museum's colourful courtyard, where a café serves cakes labelled 'eat me' and other literature-themed snacks. There are touches of fun everywhere, from book extracts strung along staircases to the huge murals on the brick buildings. Fuelled up and ready for more, moments later we dive back into a land of imagination through the Portal, where the main museum experience begins. Here we travel in our minds beyond Oxford to experience stories from all over the world. The kids are handed wands and headsets to guide them through the Whispering Wood, where a twist or flick of the wand lights up tree trunks to reveal objects and audio relating to each story – a woven Ghanaian basket for the folk tale *Anansi and the Basket of Stories*, for example, or Norse gold for the Anglo-Saxon *The Treasures of the Gods*.

'If you don't know the trees, you are lost in the forest. If you don't know the stories, you are lost in life,' a Siberian proverb welcomes us as we follow a white hare's footprints through the darkened woodland. The hare stops at every tree inviting us to listen to myths and fables, and to join in; the kids muster all their strength to pull King Arthur's Sword from a stone, and tie a ribbon to a tree to make three wishes just like the man in the fable *The Old Man and the Sausage*.

Opposite the Whispering Wood, the Treasure Chamber is home to temporary displays; we catch *The Book of Hopes* exhibition, which brings alive a collection of writings by famous children's authors on the back of the Covid-19 pandemic. Although the exhibition is aimed at younger kids, the boys get stuck in, hosting their own puppet show, drawing pictures on a giant 'hope wall', and recording messages in huge flower heads.

A hop, skip and a jump and we're on to the next stage of the journey, the Enchanted Library. The kids dart between eight story-themed rooms while we adults meander around cabinets containing hundreds of literary memorabilia – books and props – tracing the last century or so of storytelling. 'Pooh sticks! Horrid Henry! What's this?' the kids holler across the museum (it's refreshing that such enthusiasm doesn't need to be hushed here). We play virtual Pooh sticks, shrink like Alice in Wonderland, and even sit on a whoopie cushion in the Horrid Henry room. There's plenty for adults and older kids, including an enchanted light installation depicting Narnia, and the chance to get up close to an alethiometer from Philip Pullman's *His Dark Materials* trilogy.

Back out in the fresh air of the courtyard, we fuel up with lunch before heading into the city to explore the literary references, myths and legends in real life. There's no better way to prep for exploring a city awash with stories.

ADDED ADVENTURE: COBBLED CLOISTERS, ANCIENT WATERWAYS & GREEN RETREATS

It may be best known for its venerable, world-class university, but look a little closer and eccentricity abounds in the City of Spires, from students wandering around in formal gowns to quirky gargoyles jutting out of centuries-old, hidden courtyards. Literary references fire up imaginations at every turn. From the pub where Tolkien plotted Middle-earth, and the dining halls that more recently hosted Harry Potter, storytelling seems to seep from every crevice. For a small city, Oxford also packs a punch when it comes to museums, and the ease of walking between them makes for a wonderful couple of days of culture.

CITY CENTRE

Oxford is best experienced on foot, meandering into whichever intriguing, cobbled squares, impressive cloisters or churches take your fancy.

Spreading in a triangular shape between the River Cherwell, the River Thames and **Christ Church College** of *Harry Potter* film fame (∂ chch. ox.ac.uk), **Christ Church Meadow** is a lovely spot for running off steam or having a picnic. The college, founded in 1525, is one of Oxford's grandest (alongside Magdalen) and is well worth a visit for those wanting to marvel at the film set and ancient dining hall, cloisters and chapel. At the far end of the meadow, **Oxford Botanic Garden** (∂ obga. ox.ac.uk) is the oldest in the country, celebrating 400 years in 2021, and home to over 5,000 plant species. The bite-size gardens and glasshouses, including creepy carnivores, are ideal for younger kids. Across the road, you can visit **Magdalen College** (∂ magd.ox.ac.uk) and wander along Addison's Walk, once a favourite footpath of Tolkien and C S Lewis, which meanders around a small island in the River Cherwell.

Back on the High Street, cobbled streets and winding lanes weave in all directions. Ditch the crowds and head down Queen's Lane (look out

for bikes) which leads to Hertford College's ornate bridge opposite the vast **Bodleian Library** (⊘ bodleian.ox.ac.uk). (The eagle-eyed will spot a secret alley to the Turf Tavern, one of the oldest in the city, under the bridge.) The Bodleian, one of Europe's oldest libraries, contains a copy of every book ever published in the UK, including four copies of the Magna Carta. Guided tours (suitable for kids aged seven plus) take visitors to the Divinity School (which stood in for the hospital in the first four *Harry Potter* films), and Duke Humfrey's Library, dating back to the 15th century. You can see here where the books were once chained to the wall – they were so valuable that it was forbidden to take them away. The Bodleian's most precious volumes are housed in the Weston Library on Broad Street, and are showcased during various exhibitions.

From the Bodleian head towards the High Street through the **Radcliffe Camera** square, and from here towards the **Covered Market** (⊘ oxford-coveredmarket.co.uk). Dating back to the 18th century, this maze of covered independent shops and cafés sells everything from designer hats to freshly shot pheasant. The hole-in-the-wall Ben's Cookies (now a nationwide chain) is a local institution. Kids will love spotting quirky items in the indie shops, and it's a great place to fuel up and rest the legs (especially if it's raining). Opposite the Covered Market, on the corner of Cornmarket Street, the 12th-century **Carfax Tower** (74ft) marks the original city centre and provides great city views (after climbing 99 steps).

From here it's a short walk to the **Ashmolean** (⊘ ashmolean.org), Oxford's largest museum and the first public museum in the world, with thousands of art and archaeological artefacts from around the world – it's widely considered to be one of the UK's most important collections. Families can book a digital Ashmolean Adventure trail where kids are handed an iPad to explore the collection and play interactive games at each stop; alternatively, follow the screen-free family trail that uncovers the most engaging exhibitions for kids. If you're short on time, plump for the Spotlight Trail, which highlights 12 key objects, from an Egyptian mummy to Alfred's Jewel, one of the finest examples of Anglo-Saxon jewellery ever discovered. The Rooftop Restaurant and Terrace has great views for lunch.

Further north – beyond the **Eagle and Child** pub, on St Giles' Street, where J R R Tolkien drank and plotted his epic tales – the **Pitt Rivers**

◀ **1** Bodleian Library. **2** City views from the top of Carfax Tower. **3** Oxford Botanic Garden greenhouse. **4** Covered Market. **5** Exhibit at the Ashmolean.

Museum of archaeology and anthropology (⊘ prm.ox.ac.uk) contains over half a million objects. It's accessed through the **Oxford University Museum of Natural History** (⊘ oumnh.ox.ac.uk) – the main atrium is a beautiful glass structure filled with skeletons and natural history exhibits, but that's just the beginning. Beyond, the Pitt Rivers rooms are packed with glass cabinets and drawers displaying items organised into curious categories like 'Magic' and 'Body Art', 2,000 of which are human remains. Behind the museum, **University Parks** (⊘ parks.ox.ac.uk) is a huge green space alongside the River Cherwell, where there's a bench to commemorate Tolkien, who liked to sit here.

SOUTH OF THE CENTRE

For some contemporary inspiration, head down to **Modern Art Oxford** (⊘ modernartoxford.org.uk), founded in 1965 and still occupying the former brewery building on Pembroke Street that it took over in 1966. Exhibitions are all temporary; when we visited, we saw evocative and unexpected works by sculptor/painter Anish Kapoor and multimedia artist Jesse Darling. The gallery's Creative Space hosts family events, designed to facilitate creative play, and at weekends curators run exhibition tours for kids.

Lesser known but wonderfully unique, the **Bate Collection** (⊘ bate. ox.ac.uk) holds more than 1,000 musical instruments from the Renaissance onwards. It's at the University's Faculty of Music on St Aldates and only open to the public during term time; tours can be booked in advance for a more interactive experience.

JERICHO & PORT MEADOW

When you've explored the centre, skip the more commercial part of town – except for maybe the legendary **Blackwells** bookshop on Broad Street – and head north towards the neighbourhood of **Jericho**, where hip Walton Street and Little Clarendon Street are lined with independent shops and cafés. The small **Oxford University Press Museum** (⊘ global.oup.com), in the OUP building on Great Clarendon Street, walks visitors through the history of printing and publishing from the 15th century to today – it's not designed with children in

1 Walton Steet in Jericho is lined with independent shops and businesses.
2 Modern Art Oxford. ▶

mind, but older kids interested in writing, stories and publishing will enjoy the in-depth exhibition.

A ten-minute walk from Jericho, **Port Meadow** is the largest green space in Oxford – surrounded by woodland, it feels more like countryside than town. You can take a nice three-mile circular walk along the west side of the river to explore the ruins of 12th-century **Godstow Abbey**, stop for lunch in **The Trout pub** (⊘ thetroutoxford.co.uk), and then walk back through the meadows on the other side of the river. The Thames here is a popular swimming spot in summer (although check conditions and pollution levels before plunging in).

PRACTICALITIES

FAMILY-FRIENDLY SLEEPS

Ethos Hotel ⊘ ethoshotels.co.uk. A hop, skip and a jump over the River Thames, in a suburban neighbourhood off the Abingdon Road, Ethos Hotel is in a peaceful spot moments from Christ Church Meadow, the river and the city centre. Rooms are ideal for families; larger than normal, with kitchenettes, sofa beds and connecting doorways.

Oxfordshire Narrowboats
⊘ oxfordshire-narrowboats.co.uk. Cruising into Oxford by boat, passing through Port Meadow and stopping off at riverside watering holes like The Perch, is an enchanting way to see the city. Heyford Wharf is one of the depots closest to the centre, from where you can pick up narrowboats of all sizes for an adventure lasting anything from one day to one week. Moorings on the Oxford Canal in Jericho are just a 20-minute walk from the city centre.

The Randolph ⊘ graduatehotels. com. Occupying an L-shaped building opposite The Ashmolean, well located for both Jericho and the town centre, The Randolph is an Oxford institution; it's been a hotel since 1866. More recent fame includes the filming of TV shows *Inspector Morse* and *Lewis*, and its rooms, restaurants and bars are adorned with images of Oxford's literary characters. Family suites are big and plush.

University Rooms ⊘ universityrooms. com. Oxford University terms last just eight weeks, so there's a considerable chunk of the year when college rooms are empty. Some colleges, like Wadham and Magdalen, jump at the chance to make a bit of extra money by renting rooms to visitors. Why simply visit the City of Spires when you can sleep in those spires, too? Some rooms are better set up for families, so book ahead to grab the best digs.

◀ Walking along the riverside through Port Meadow to The Trout.

TAKING A PUNT FROM MAGDALEN BRIDGE

Magdalen Bridge Boathouse, Magdalen Bridge, OX1 4AU ⏛ oxfordpunting.co.uk; age: 4+; intrepid level: ②

'We still race sometimes, but at the end of the season; it's packed out here in midsummer so there's definitely no room for racing,' Andrew tells us as we glide so slowly and silently along a foggy River Cherwell that it feels impossible to imagine busy, warm days. 'Do you ever crash?' the boys enquire, always eager to get to the drama. 'A little bit,' Andrew smirks. 'It's kinda part of the fun in summer, and most days someone falls in.'

The four of us – me, my partner and the two boys – are snuggled up under brightly coloured blankets in a punt, eye-level with the water, a bundle of pinks and reds in an otherwise pea souper of a day. Andrew grew up in Oxford and is making a bit of money leading punt tours before heading off to university. He's wearing a hoody rather than the more traditional boater and braces and seems to be enjoying the rhythmic clunk and glide of the pole pushing along the flat-bottomed wooden punt as much as we are.

It's the first weekend of the season, and while it doesn't look like punting weather, it's wonderfully atmospheric. We started our journey at Magdalen Bridge Boathouse, a small hut with hundreds of punts tucked beneath Magdalen Bridge. From here, the River Cherwell splits and divides around an island to one side of Magdalen College's wooded Addison Walk in one direction, and heads around the edge of the Botanic Garden towards Christ Church Meadow in the other. We head towards the meadow, hoping to get a glimpse of college spires despite the fog.

Talk of races stemmed from a discussion about the history of punting. Punts were used to transport fish and other goods until 1913, when John Anderezej Rivers organised the first punting race down the river. Novelist Aldous Huxley went on to organise the race for a couple of years, and after World War II Tolkien won five or six times. After a punting lull in the 1950s, the Royal Charter of Oxford Competition Punting was formed in 1960, and the competition grew from strength to strength throughout the 1970s and 80s. From then on, punting became a leisure activity.

'All sorts have a go. There's always a mix of students and tourists, all muddling and colliding down the river together,' Andrew tells us. Today, however, we have only ducks for company. One tries to jump on board,

KID-FRIENDLY EATS

Browns ⏛ browns-restaurants.co.uk. On the Woodstock Road moments from Jericho, the family-friendly chain brasserie Browns is a nice spot for brunch, but really comes to life on Friday and Saturday evenings, when it's awash with celebrations. The buzzy atmosphere is helped along by excellent service and a menu big enough to cater for the whole family. The building – a former museum and library, built in

and another swims within a few inches of the punt for several hundred yards. The boys look out for kingfishers, which are often spotted darting between the tree trunks and low-hanging branches along the river's edge.

After circling around Christ Church Meadow, spotting Christ Church's college tower soaring into the sky, we head back towards base. Longer tours, however, join the Isis (Oxford's name for the River Thames), where the river opens up and leaves the city behind. It's possible to hop off at the Isis River Farmhouse pub (⊘ theisisfarmhouse.co.uk) for a drink, or to prebook a picnic hamper.

Before returning to base, the boys are desperate to have a go. 'It looks so easy,' they declare confidently, making their way to the back of the boat. 'Well,' starts Andrew patiently, 'first you need to be able to stand up.' The youngest topples about all over the place and quickly sits back down, but the eldest manages to hold on to the pole for a few moments, before losing nerve. 'OK, it's not that easy,' they decide rather quickly. 'But let's try when we're bigger.'

DAISY DAISY/S

Venetian Gothic style in the 1870s, is impressive, too.

Thirsty Meeples ⊘ thirstymeeples. co.uk. Board games come first, tasty coffee and food second at this board-game café, which has a library of over 2,700 games, in the city centre. It's possible to while away hours here: a cover charge of £6 per adult and £5 per kid gives access to three hours of unlimited games.

Vaults & Garden

⊘ thevaultsandgarden.com. Hidden out

of sight, within 30yds of the Radcliffe Camera below the University Church of St Mary the Virgin, this organic and sustainably minded café has a pretty terrace for warmer days. Food is sourced from local farms, and cream teas come with a huge selection of homemade cakes. It's worth climbing the church tower for views across the spires.

BEFORE YOU GO

Kids may get more out of a trip to Oxford with some background knowledge of the city's literary greats. Recommended reads include Lewis Carroll's *Alice in Wonderland*, C S Lewis' *Chronicles of Narnia* and Philip Pullman's *His Dark Materials* trilogy.

MORE INFO

Oxfordshire Tourist Board
⟁ experienceoxfordshire.org

18
HEREFORDSHIRE

Explore England's borderlands, where old-world farmlands rub alongside creative enclaves and thronging market towns awash with local produce.

TOP FAMILY EXPERIENCE
CLAY MODELLING AT EASTNOR POTTERY, LEDBURY, FOLLOWED BY EXPLORATIONS OF
EASTNOR & THE MALVERNS

BEST FOR KIDS AGED: 5+
WHEN TO GO: Year-round
INTREPID LEVEL: ①
ADDED ADVENTURE: Wild hills, river adventures, upbeat market towns, arty enclaves,
                      farm experiences, orchard tours
TIME: Three days to one week

FROM PUMPKINS TO EARTHWORKS: POTTERING IN THE MALVERNS

Home Farm, Eastnor, Ledbury HR8 1RD ⬧ eastnorpottery.co.uk; enquire which sessions are best suited to children before you book

'Cor blimey, a five-eyed pumpkin!' potter Jon Williams exclaims, turning to my eldest, Wilf, as he carves the final eyeball into a slimy globe of clay. There's clay all over our hands, in our hair, and getting smudged pretty much everywhere as we (adults included) delve deeper into our creative hive minds. I've got a headphone-wearing pear to my right and an apple with a worm crawling through its brain to my left, and I wouldn't have it any other way. It's two days before Halloween, and the Eastnor Pottery clay modelling course theme is spooky or wacky fruits. Having spent the last week sipping apple juice (and cider) – Herefordshire's tipple of choice – direct from orchards, inspiration is plentiful.

The mess and imagination are what we came for, but we didn't anticipate how quickly we'd lose ourselves to such tactile pleasure. Jon and his partner Sarah Monk welcome the mêlée of mindful madness with pure delight. They exude such softness I start to wonder whether all potters are inherently gentle or whether the art form brings out the trait (Grayson Perry springs to mind). While the boys abandon all inhibition Jon and Sarah gently nudge us in the right direction, demonstrating how to make a hollow shape so that clay doesn't crack in the kiln, how to stick down shapes and get the moisture level just right.

'Time to paint,' Jon exclaims, revealing a wall of jars of washed-out colours with sponges and brushes to match. We splash and splatter different colours over our creations while Jon explains the kiln process. Our hardened and glossed fruits will arrive in the post in a month or so; anticipation is already sky-high. The painting part is harder than it looks. The pumpkin soon takes the form of an alien, and the apple morphs into a large pea, but this is no place for perfection; we're sitting together, concentrating and relishing in the same activity, which is magic alone.

Jon and Sarah have a combined 50 years of potting experience and, once our creations are complete, we get the chance to see some of their masterworks. Jugs, domes, instruments and various shapes and forms litter the room, in between other wacky fruits made during previous workshops. Jon is described as an 'artist potter', drawing on the sensory and interactive qualities of clay, while Sarah's work is more traditional; 'I make stuff you can use,' she says, with a mocking nudge at Jon. Captivated, the boys marvel at the intricate, bizarre and vibrant works. I wonder whether they're having a moment similar to one Jon describes experiencing at school: 'I met an art scholar and realised this fun stuff I do could be a job.'

They've certainly found an idyllic spot to do what they love. As we mould, paint and chat, the studio glows with warmth. Outside, the Eastnor Estate sprawls across nearly 500 acres of parkland at the foot of the undulating Area of Outstanding Natural Beauty, the Malvern Hills. After our pottery session, we find a footpath that weaves through woodland and a deer park and passes quaint 16th-century

◀ **1** Sarah and Jon, Eastnor Pottery. **2** Eastnor Castle. **3** Halloween creations at Eastnor. **4** Getting stuck in. **5** Walking trail in the Malvern Hills.

buildings before reaching **Eastnor Castle**. Having spent the morning contemplating colour and form, we all linger for longer than usual over the regal reflections in the estate's velvety-calm lake.

Although a mock 19th-century castle, it's a treasure trove of adventure for kids, hosting various activities throughout the year. Much to the boys' delight the Gothic details, turrets and medieval armoury look particularly eerie with the hanging bats, ghouls and lanterns that are up for Halloween. With zip wires, mazes, tree-top walkways, rope swings and even a Mini Land Rover experience (at extra cost), a quick stroll could turn into hours of fun.

But we're also on the lookout for wilder pursuits; some of the Malverns' most spectacular **walks and bike rides** are not far from Eastnor. With accessible walking paths and relatively quick climbs to the top of the Malvern spine, this is just the place for big views. On a clear day, it's possible to see across all of Herefordshire to the Black Mountains. The most popular chunk of the Malverns is the footpath that runs along the ridge from the **British Camp** (also known as the **Herefordshire Beacon**) Iron Age fort almost six miles to Great Malvern. On admiring the path meandering up towards the clouds we vow to come back for a longer hike, but for now we opt for an exploration of the 2nd-century BC earthworks at British Camp. The boys roll, jump and play-fight around the hillock while we admire kestrels hovering overhead with a flask of coffee and cake from one of Ledbury's many bakeries.

The sun soon makes its way down towards the Black Mountains, and a distinctively autumnal chill sweeps across the ridge. We usher the unnervingly quiet boys back to the path. 'Look what we've made!', Barney, my youngest, beckons. Tucked down one side of the earthworks, a heap of soggy mud, foraged sticks, stones and ferns looks like a mud-pie explosion. But perhaps us adults need more than one pottery class to fully ignite the imagination: 'They're mystical creatures, just like Jon's', Wilf proudly proclaims.

ADDED ADVENTURE: BOUNTIFUL BORDERLANDS

Some describe Herefordshire as the county that time has forgotten, but it is feistier, tastier and more creative than its reputation suggests. Yes, there are ancient farms that seep into the rolling countryside like they've always been there, but there are also makers, organic cider producers, funky burger joints, festoon-adorned riverside bars, fancy hotels and kayaking adventures.

HEREFORD

With its impressive cathedral and its leafy riverbanks, Herefordshire's capital, slap bang in the middle of the county, packs it in when it comes to culture, green spaces, food and drink. Best of all, it's small enough that you can stroll between the sights, making it an excellent car-free stopover. The generous square surrounding the **cathedral** (⊘ herefordcathedral.org) is a good spot for a picnic (pick up treats from the delis on East and Church streets nearby), but the real showstopper is the **Mappa Mundi** (⊘ themappamundi.co.uk) exhibition inside – the world's largest medieval map. Beyond the main chamber's medieval tombs and stained-glass windows (people have worshipped here since Saxon times), volunteers staff the ticketed exhibition and are more than happy to stir interest in little minds. The map of the world itself provides a curious social history of medieval society and sparks insights and questions well beyond straightforward geography.

Other museums worth a visit include the **Black and White House** (⊘ herefordshire.gov.uk), a well-preserved Jacobean building in pride of place in the market square, and the **Museum of Cider** (⊘ cidermuseum.co.uk), a short walk away, which showcases hundreds of apple varieties and the county's 'golden amber' traditions. Also in the middle of town, the **Courtyard Theatre** (⊘ thecourtyard.org.uk)

APPLES FOR AUTUMN

Owing to favourable soil conditions, throughout autumn Herefordshire is bursting with apples and pears. If you're visiting in October, check out the **Apples for Autumn initiative** (⊘ applesforautumn.co.uk), which helps restaurateurs to showcase this bounty and visitors to support local producers. Alongside tips for hotels and restaurants to help create apple-themed events and menus, Visit Herefordshire has created two cycling circuits so visitors can whizz between the orchards on two wheels. There are northern (49 miles) and southern (31.5 miles) circuits and, although both are fairly punchy distance wise, it's possible to choose a section to do with the kids. The website also lists those orchards, some of which are more than two centuries old, that are happy to welcome visitors, so there's no excuse not to pop into a few along the way.

is a hub of arts, dance and music, so it's worth checking listings that coincide with your visit.

Whatever the season, be sure to make time for a stroll down the footpaths that skirt both banks of the Wye, which pops with glowing hues in autumn and offers a welcome breeze in the height of summer. A good starting point is the **Castle Green**, where there's plenty of open space for kids to charge about. The green is surrounded by some of the city's grandest houses and leads to the ornate Victoria Bridge across the river. For those that would rather take to the water, **Left Bank Canoe Hire** (⌀ leftbankcanoehire.co.uk) runs kayak and canoe tours from the middle of the city.

WYE VALLEY

The **Wye Valley** Area of Outstanding Natural Beauty is cradled by Wales to the west and Gloucestershire to the east in the southernmost reaches of Herefordshire. It's probably the most visited part of the county, but that's no reason to shy away. The Wye's steep, wooded valley is arguably at its prettiest between **Symonds Yat** and Hereford.

It was here in the late 18th century that William Gilpin wrote *Observations on the River Wye*, which is thought to have marked the beginning of the Picturesque movement, giving a name to the appreciation of natural beauty for the first time. Nearly three centuries later, there are still plenty of opportunities to dive into the natural world. The valley's most famous viewpoint is atop **Yat Rock**, where the river meanders a giant U-shaped bend below. Nearby, the unspoilt **King Arthur's Cave** is believed to have been occupied by humans 2.5 million years ago.

Down on the river, short boat trips can be booked from the **Saracen's Head inn** (⌀ saracensheadinn.co.uk) at Symonds Yat, where you can also cross to the opposite bank on a traditional hand-pulled ferry. These are leisurely ways to explore the river if stand-up paddle-boarding, kayaking or canoeing are not an option. But if the latter sounds appealing, you're in the right place. **Canoe on the Wye** (⌀ canoethewye.co.uk) offers everything from half-day guided tours to two-day canoe and kit hire, so there's something for all ages. It's at

---

1 Canoeing on the River Wye. **2** Interactive displays at the Museum of Cider.
3 The Mappa Mundi in Hereford Cathedral is the world's largest medieval map. ▶

this level on the water that you're most likely to spot otters, kingfishers or even peregrine falcons.

A little further north there's the chance to get up close with wildlife at the **Wye Valley Butterfly Zoo** (⊘ butterflyzoo.co.uk), which not only has hundreds of species from all over the world but helps to protect what's left of the region's indigenous butterflies. The visitor centre has minigolf and a giant maze, too. Three miles north, **Goodrich Castle** (⊘ english-heritage.org.uk) is also worth a stop. The crumbling towers display some of the UK's best-preserved medieval stonework, although on a clear day the views of the Malverns might steal the show.

Almost exactly halfway up this section of the Wye is **Ross-on-Wye**, one of the county's prettiest market towns. While here it's worth paying a visit to the Market House, which dates back to the 17th century. Upstairs, the **Made in Ross** (⊘ madeinross.co.uk) arts and crafts market showcases local talent and curiosities, and there's a twice-weekly market that spills into the street.

SOUTHWESTERN HEREFORDSHIRE

In southwestern Herefordshire, the area around the **Golden Valley** – which stretches from the literary hub of **Hay-on-Wye** down to the village of Pentrilas – is where the wild things are. The landscape here feels older and more enchanting than other parts of the county. The **Black Mountains** loom in the distance across the border with Wales to the west, giant oaks carve up ancient farms, and the River Dore charges through the landscape, its speed dictated by rainfall in the mountains. The best place to take it all in is on a walk up **Black Hill** (known locally as Cat's Back, for its shape); there's a five-mile circular loop, or it's just over three miles up and down. The views from the ridge are mind-blowing, as can be the weather (it can be very windy!), so go prepared. Wild horses grazing on the slopes and merlins flying overhead make the whole experience particularly special.

Twenty minutes' drive north of the Cat's Back is **Drovers Rest** (⊘ droversrest.co.uk); a glamping site (page 286) and smallholding at the end of Watery Lane. Surrounded by woodlands, a heather-clad common and hills that drift into Wales, Drovers is all about getting families back to nature. Most activities are for guests, but it's possible to

---

1 Goodrich Castle. **2** Drovers Rest. ▶

ORCHARD TOUR WITH PAUL STEPHENS

Newton Court Cider, Newton, Leominster HR6 0PF ⊘ newtoncourtcider.com; age: 3+; intrepid level: ①

'Enjoy the orchard and make yourselves at home,' Paul yells from a forklift, after apologising that he'll be a little late for our tour. Two chunky spaniels bound up to the boys, and the four of them hurl through the warehouse into the dappled sunlight of the 50 or so fruit trees beyond. It's as bucolic as it gets, surrounded by fruit-laden trees that undulate into rolling hills beyond. The boys soon work out they can watch the forklift load apples on to a truck, which could probably stretch to hours' worth of entertainment.

We stomp between the bowing branches as Paul plucks different varieties of apples and pears. The taste is sharp, and the boys try to spit theirs out without anyone seeing. 'It's fine,' Paul chuckles, 'the drier and bittersweet or sharp varieties create deeper flavours in the cider – they're not really meant for eating.' Beyond the orchard, green pastures are home to Paul's cattle, sheep and more orchards. He explains, 'In the winter the cows will come into the orchard because they play a key role in fertilising the soil naturally and cleaning up fallen apples; that way we waste less and the apples taste better the next year.'

Paul's farm has been organic for 20 years, and he hopes soon to create a visitor centre to spread the word about wildlife-friendly farming. Thanks to his high standards, his apples (cider) and pears (perry) are in demand from cider makers all over the country (hence the truck). Herefordshire produces more than half of the UK's cider – the county is home to nearly 500 acres of orchards. When Magners started advertising cider in the 2000s demand shot up, but sadly it's now in decline again, although several boutique makers, like Paul, remain optimistic. 'More people want to buy local and organic, and so that's got to be a good thing for farmers like me,' Paul says. I drink cider every night of our trip from then on.

After touring the orchard we move into the warehouse, where the boys marvel at vats about ten times their size, and a complex new bottling plant. The adults taste cider and perry at different stages of the ageing and

book kids over ten on a 'day on the farm' experience where they learn to take care of the farm's residents – from the chickens to alpacas and stubborn Shetland ponies. The site also offers regular 'feasts' around rustic fire pits, on tables surrounded by haystacks or inside the snug dining barn and bar. Themes include Diwali, Mexican night, curries and pop-up supper clubs; everything revolves around local, organic and wildlife-friendly food and tastes as proper as it sounds.

For a more curated farm experience, head further north towards the market town of Kington to the **Small Breeds Farm Park and Owl**

fermenting process, to better understand what goes into finding the perfect palate; the boys, meanwhile, get to taste-test the non-fermented apple and pear juice, which keeps them engaged throughout. It's a treat to see the whole process from start to finish, from soil to apple to making and bottling.

Back in the tasting room, Paul proudly reveals his different labels and brands, including a new partnership with River Cottage and Gasping Goose (so-called because his grandfather once caught a goose drinking the cider). The focus is on heritage ciders; a homage to the centuries of cider-making in Herefordshire, and a nod to the fact that the traditional way of making things is usually the kindest to the environment and produces the most refined taste. After filling our bellies with the sweet amber samples, we pick up a crate of goods and leave happily, clinking along the bumpy country lanes.

HOLLY TUPPEN

Centre ($\mathcal{O}$ owlcentre.com), which has been run by Jay Brittain for some 30 years. Although the farm has been added to and adapted over the decades, the ethos has remained the same: to offer an up-close animal experience without distraction. Among goats, geese and red squirrels are more than 30 owl species.

Back down on the Wye, **Whitney-on-Wye's** toll bridge is one of the river's most unusual and impressive (younger kids might enjoy the novelty of handing over coins in order to cross). Further south, **Arthur's Stone** ($\mathcal{O}$ english-heritage.org.uk) is a Neolithic burial chamber which, according to legend, is where King Arthur slew a giant. There are expansive Golden Valley views from the surrounding footpaths, too.

Also tucked away in this part of the county is **Fair Oak Cider** (⌂ fairoakcider.co.uk) in the remote hamlet of Bacton. Here, the 17th-century stone mill is the only operating horse-drawn mill in the country that operates commercially – making Fair Oak the ultimate slow (and eco) cider.

PRACTICALITIES

FAMILY-FRIENDLY SLEEPS

Drovers Rest ⌂ droversrest.co.uk. In a remote spot between Hay-on-Wye and Dorstone, Drovers (page 282) is perhaps the poshest glamping site in all of England. It's the product of its owners' roots in South Africa, where warm hospitality is second nature. Huge safari tents, elegantly spaced throughout a field, come with two bedrooms, electric blankets, a makeshift kitchen, squidgy sofas and wood burners. Each tent gets a private bathroom in the washing block, with powerful showers and underfloor heating. There's a farm shop, daily farm tours, various outdoor activities and workshops, and regular food nights. Self-catering cottages are also available.

Green Dragon ⌂ greendragonhotel. com. Hereford's restored coaching inn is the grande dame of the city; its ornate Victorian façade is almost opposite the cathedral and overlooks trendy food and drink venue The Yard. For families, interconnecting rooms are vast, and there are a few apartments up for grabs, too. Locals visit for afternoon tea and special occasions, so while the whole place exudes indulgence it's relaxed enough to be suitable for kids.

Green Lane Carriage ⌂ airbnb.co.uk/ rooms/19044641. Just off the road between Hay-on-Wye and Hereford, near the pretty village of Eardisley, this beautifully cared for converted railway carriage is surrounded by orchards with Black Mountain views. It's ideal for a family of up to four, with a double bed and bunk beds, along with a comfortable kitchen, bathroom facilities and a small fenced garden with fields beyond. The award-winning Orgasmic Cider Company farm shop is just next door, too.

Perrycroft Holiday Cottages ⌂ perrycroftholidaycottages.co.uk. At the foot of the Malverns, surrounded by footpaths and wooded vales not far from Eastnor and Ledbury, Perrycroft has three cheerful self-catering cottages. Two are suitable for families – the Lodge, which sleeps six, and the Old Stables, which sleeps five. Interiors in the latter are upbeat, with mid-century furniture and splashes of 1970s hues (think orange, yellow, turquoise and bright green). Secluded patios and a sloping meadow come alive with wildflowers, birdsong and butterflies in spring.

White House Glamping

⌖ whitehouseonwye.co.uk. In the heart of the Wye Valley AONB, south of Hereford, five large tipis sleeping four or five share the shade of a riverside orchard that ambles down to a mile-long secluded stretch of river and a shallow pebble beach. Canoes and stand-up paddleboards aren't available to borrow, but visitors are welcome to bring their own or rent them nearby (the owner can offer advice). Special summer evenings feature a pop-up outdoor cinema.

KID-FRIENDLY EATS

Bridge Inn ⌖

thebridgeinnmichaelchurch.co.uk. Whatever weather greets you atop the Cat's Back, this riverside pub, in the village of Michael Church just below, has the terrace, pizza menu, roasts and fireside nooks for much-needed post-hike refreshments.

Burger Shop ⌖ burgershop.restaurant. Run by the Hereford-born and -bred

A Rule of Tum group of local chefs, producers and restaurateurs, Burger Shop takes all the good elements of fast food and waves goodbye to artificial ingredients, sweeteners and any other nasties. The burgers are stacked as high and juicy as can be (even the falafel). Slap bang in the middle of Hereford, the pretty courtyard garden is a convenient spot in which to refuel, too.

The Nest ⌖ nestledbury.co.uk. A few kilometres down the road from Ledbury, the village of Trumpet is home to a sprawling farm shop and café that celebrates cheesemakers, local farmers, butchers, crisp-makers, cider orchards and many other marvellous local producers. The centrepiece is the Scotch Egg Company's chiller that features over 30 varieties of the traditional snack.

MORE INFO

Herefordshire Tourist Board
⌖ visitherefordshire.co.uk
Walks & trails ⌖ herefordshire.gov.uk/walking-1/walks-trails
Wye Valley AONB ⌖ wyevalleyaonb.org.uk

19
THE PEAK DISTRICT

The Peak District is one of the UK's most visited national parks, but thanks to a patchwork of footpaths criss-crossing old-world farmland, rust-coloured streams and craggy peaks, you're never far from solitude.

TOP FAMILY EXPERIENCE
CYCLING THE MONSAL TRAIL
BEST FOR KIDS AGED: 3+
WHEN TO GO: Year-round
INTREPID LEVEL: ②
ADDED ADVENTURE: Accessible hiking and cycling trails, cave tours, a historic spa town, a sumptuous stately home, and bucolic farm visits
TIME: Three days to one week

TUNNELS & VIADUCTS: AN ENGINEERED CYCLE TRAIL

Hassop Station, Hassop Rd, Bakewell DE45 1NW ⊘ hassopstation.co.uk

'Again, again, again!', the boys demand, their squeals of delight echoing up the 100ft-or-so manmade gorge as our bikes screech to a halt. It's the fourth time we've pedalled through the Monsal Trail's epic Headstone Tunnel and we're all happy to go again. Such captivating thrills don't usually spring to mind when you think of a converted railway line, but the Monsal Trail is no ordinary cycle track.

Following an 8½-mile route between Blackwell Mill in Chee Dale and Coombs Road in Bakewell, the trail passes through four resurfaced and lit (in daylight hours) railway tunnels, previously closed to the

---

◀ Cycling the Monsal Trail.

public. The original track was built in 1863 by Midland Railway to link Manchester and London, and, given the area's natural beauty, was not popular with environmentalists at the time. Landowners dictated where the line went, following the Wye River Valley and dug into the hills to avoid disturbing Chatsworth and Haddon Hall's land and views. John Ruskin, who once said of the railway, '... you blasted its rocks away, heaped thousands of tons of shale into its lovely stream. The valley is gone, and the Gods with it,' might be pleased to see it being used in a more mindful way today, or at least happy to see the rewilded railway banks humming with bees and butterflies.

At about 1,312ft long, the tunnels are like no other cycling experience. Carving through some of the Peaks' most spectacular hills, the curved tunnels plunge us into near darkness as the temperature drops a few degrees and trickles of water seep down from the rocks above. 'Spoooookyyyyy,' shout the boys.

"Carving through some of the Peaks' most spectacular hills, the curved tunnels plunge us into near darkness."

Information boards pepper the route with facts, and one at the start of Headstone Tunnel tells us that the limestone rock cut into to create the railway was formed 350 million years ago. Once a tropical sea, the rock is full of fossils of shells and creatures that lived all those years ago. Moments later Wilf spots shales in the rocks above – wave formations created by sand when river deltas ploughed into that ancient sea.

Having started at Hassop Station, where we picked up hire bikes and crammed our rucksack with the most ridiculously stodgy and delicious Bakewell tarts and brownies, we got our first glimpse of the railway's mindboggling engineering at Headstone Tunnel. A little further beyond and now we're standing on another astonishing feat: the Headstone Viaduct, which soars 1,600ft into the sky above the Eden-like Monsal Valley where the River Wye gurgles through fields of grazing cattle and meadow flowers billow in the breeze.

Eager to fuel up on the cakes, we park the bikes and head out in search of an even more elevated view. The easy option is to scramble down to the river and look up, but more rewarding is the steep scramble up through the trees to Monsal Head where the hills, viaduct and valley spill out below. If you have the time, you could follow a two-mile walking route that takes in the bottom and the top.

Beyond Monsal Head, the trail follows the River Wye more closely. Between here and Wyedale there are eleven nature reserves, providing a nice contrast to the trail's industrial heritage. Some, like Deep Dale and Taddington Wood, require a half-hour or so detour on foot, while others, like Priestcliffe Lees and Ravenstor and Bellamy's Bank almost straddle the trail. In spring, the woods entice passers-by with pungent wild garlic smells and carpets of wood anemone; in summer they offer welcome shade.

After breezing along, all slightly in our own little worlds, from Monsal through Cressbrook and Litton tunnels, past Litton Mill and several lime kilns, we stumble upon Miller's Dale Quarry; a 59-acre bowl that has been left to nature since 1930. Having seen David Attenborough once hunt for fossils and wildflowers in a former quarry on TV, the boys get busy carefully lifting over rocks and logs in search of ancient life. Despite an unsuccessful fossil mission, I'm delighted to see my first ever wild orchid; an impossibly delicate early purple orchid that I usher the boys away from in case of trampling. After gazing at common blues fluttering between cowslips and wild strawberry flowers, and watching kestrels soar above, we drag ourselves away from the idyll to return to the trail.

By the time we reach Chee Dale, almost finishing the route, it's time to turn around to get our hire bikes back and reward ourselves with an ice cream before closing time. We had planned to divert off the trail into Chee Dale, one of the Peaks' less-known hiking gorges; here the Wye River babbles around impossibly high and craggy limestone cliffs, giving the impression (and probably reality, given the scrambling and stone stepping required) of total isolation. Time has run away with us, however. Momentarily regretful, we console ourselves with the thought that it's always good to leave something to come back for.

ADDED ADVENTURE: SLOW TRAVEL AT ITS PEAK

Slap bang in the middle of England, the Peak District – which stretches across the counties of Derbyshire, Yorkshire, Cheshire, Staffordshire and Greater Manchester – is not only accessible by train or car from most parts of the UK, but it also offers families endless opportunities to explore in as gentle or adrenalin-fuelled a way as they wish. Between the wild and more challenging terrain of the Dark Peak in the north and the gentle farmland and green valleys of the White Peak in the south, the region is more varied than first appearances may suggest. From strolling through astonishing stately homes to descending into mysterious limestone caverns, there's something to suit every slow traveller here.

BUXTON

Welcoming visitors for over 2,000 years, thanks to its world-renowned waters, **Buxton** comfortably rivals Bath (the only other Roman spa town in the UK) when it comes to spa-town splendour – the showpiece **Buxton Crescent**, now a luxury hotel, is the height of Georgian elegance. Nearby, **Buxton Pavilion Gardens** (⊘ parkwoodoutdoors. co.uk) has two big playgrounds and heaps of romping space; most interesting of all are its pretty Victorian pavilions, home to two cafés, and the Conservatory, which is filled with rare plants. The **Retail Arcade** (⊘ visitbuxton.co.uk) here sells goods from over 20 local producers. A good option for rainy days, **Buxton Museum and Art Gallery** (⊘ buxtonmuseumandartgallery.wordpress.com), a few minutes south, is packed with information on local geology and archaeology.

Buxton is often referred to as the gateway to the Peak District, and there are outdoor adventures aplenty on the doorstep. **Buxton Country Park's** trails, caves and **Go Ape** treetop adventure park (⊘ goape.co.uk; ages six and above) will entice the whole family into the great outdoors. The two-mile walk up to **Solomon's Temple**, a 19th-century tower atop a Neolithic burial mound, which looks out over the Peak District (on a clear day you can spot Mam Tor) and the town, is a must. Look out for wood carvings along the country park's various trails – there are walks of between 25 and 45 minutes, doable for all ages.

When you've walked to the top of a hill, it's worth heading in the opposite direction: deep underground. Most visitors to the Peak District make a beeline to better-known caverns in the north, but **Poole's Cavern** (⊘ poolescavern.co.uk), in the country park, is just as impressive. Guided tours run every 20 minutes and take visitors through the history and geological wonders of the 0.6-mile-deep cave. A whole series of limestone creations, including 'Poached Eggs', 'The Fitch of Bacon', 'Mary, Queen of Scots' Pillar' and the gushing source of

SAUCED HERE

One of the most positive ways we can impact on the places we travel to is to ensure our money stays in the destination. With that in mind, why not ditch the supermarket shop and stock up instead on local Peak District produce via **Sauced Here** (⊘ saucedhere.co.uk).

This online shopping and delivery service enables you to pick and choose everything from coffee to beer and bread to meat from more than 40 Peak District producers. For those celebrating a special occasion, Sauced Here organise catering with local chefs, too.

the River Wye, all come with enough tales and legends to occupy little imaginations for the rest of the day.

ILAM & THE MANIFOLD WAY

Home to Italian gardens, a Norman church, a riverside walk (aptly named Paradise Way) and Gothic **Ilam Hall**, framed by the dramatic peaks of Thorpe Cloud and Bunster Hill, **Ilam Park** (⊘ nationaltrust. org.uk) provides families of all ages with a wonderfully accessible slice of Peak District drama and beauty. A popular jaunt from the National Trust car park (with tea rooms, toilets and a secondhand bookshop) is the 1½-mile walk to **Dovedale Stepping Stones**, which have enabled people to hop, skip and jump across the Manifold River for more than 100 years. Along the way, it's possible to spot fossils in Dovedale Gorge's crumbling limestone walls.

The National Trust website lists longer hikes, including a challenging **10-mile walk** that follows the Manifold River valley to Wetton and Thor's Cave. Whether you hike or not, **Thor's Cave**, a 25ft-wide karst (limestone formation), is worth a visit. It's visible from the valley 260ft below, or you could climb a series of steps to enjoy views and marvel at it up close. The steps veer off the **Manifold Way** (⊘ letsgopeakdistrict.co.uk), an eight-mile tarmacked footpath and cycling track from Hulme End to Waterhouses that follows the disused Leek and Manifold Light Railway.

CHATSWORTH & SURROUNDS

It's not exactly off the beaten track, but **Chatsworth House** (⊘ chatsworth.org), home to the Duke and Duchess of Devonshire and their ancestors since the 1550s, has so much going on for kids and

Poole's Cavern. ▶

"A whole series of limestone creations, including 'Poached Eggs' and 'The Fitch of Bacon' that all come with enough tales and legends to occupy little imaginations for the rest of the day."

adults alike that it would be churlish not to mention it. The gardens are vast: you could easily spend a day meandering slowly around the kitchen gardens, Capability Brown landscape, cascade, rock gardens, and 500 years of sculpture. Inside, the sheer exuberance is a feast for the senses, from the Painted Hall to the Sketch Galleries with over 4,000 years' worth of art on display. Kids, however, will probably prefer to spend a good chunk of time in the wooded **Adventure Playground and Farmyard**, which has brilliant displays on the estate's farming history and the opportunity to get up close to the animals. Entrance is ticketed for the farmyard, playground, house and gardens but the public is free to roam the grounds and surrounding paths. A favourite for kids is the three-mile loop to the Chatsworth Hunting Tower, which lords over the estate from the edge of **Stand Wood**, home to Sowter Stone Waterfall and the Chatsworth Aqueduct.

Around four miles west of Chatsworth, **Bakewell** is the home of Derbyshire's most famous pudding, the Bakewell tart, and the **Old House Museum** (⊘ oldhousemuseum. org.uk), where 9,000 artefacts tell a 500-year history of the Peak District. From Bakewell, it's also possible to pick up the **Monsal Trail** (page 289). Another few miles south, where the River Wye meets the River Derwent, **Caudwell's Mill** (⊘ caudwellsmill.co.uk) is one of the region's finest examples of a historic water-powered flour mill. Today, the mill is on display thanks to a local charitable trust, and its courtyard is home to a vegetarian café and several local makers including a silversmith, printer and glass-blower. Across the road, families with older children can get stuck into a 24-hour Family Survival Course at the **Woodland Ways World of Bushcraft Centre** (⊘ woodland-ways.co.uk). Skills include shelter building, campfire cookery, tracking and lighting your own fire.

"Inside, the sheer exuberance is a feast for the senses, from the Painted Hall to the Sketch Galleries."

Younger families might prefer to head north towards **Thornbridge Hall Gardens** (⊘ thornbridgehall.co.uk) in Ashford-in-the-Water, which has 12 acres of quintessentially English gardens including paddling fountains and the chance to hook a rubber duck.

◀ **1** Hiking along the Great Ridge at Mam Tor. **2** Thor's Cave. **3** Climbing with Lost Earth Adventures. **4** Chatsworth House.

EGG-TEMPURA PAINTING WITH SUE PRINCE

Haybarn Gallery, Beechenhill Farm, Ilam, Ashbourne, Derbyshire DE6 2BD ⊘ sueprinceartist. co.uk; age: 6+; intrepid level: ①

'There are two things you need to be a good artist. Any ideas what they might be?' Sue asks, enthusiasm for her craft oozing out of every word; her energy is infectious. After a lot of suggestions covering everything from 'an iPad' to 'an imagination', my boys are stumped. Sue laughs. 'Kitchen roll – and never, ever leave the brushes in the water.' This simple mantra is wonderfully telling of Sue's approach to teaching. Despite being a world expert in folk art, having almost single-handedly revived the tradition of bonad painting (traditional painting with egg yolk and pigment) in Unnaryd, Sweden, and won several awards, Sue is all about accessibility and fun. The boys lap it up while I gawp at more than 50 of her paintings on display in the airy converted barn-cum-gallery.

The images vary in size but are all naïve or folk in style, framed by black writing. 'The words are often as important as the images,' Sue explains. Each is telling a story, marking a moment, or making a political or environmental gesture, just as bonad painting would have done hundreds of years ago. During the first Covid lockdown, Sue painted a scene every day; these have now been turned into two books called the *Isolation Chronicles*. For kids (and adults), they are a wonderful demonstration of how we can record things and express our feelings through creativity.

Sue paints using egg-tempura paint – earthy and natural pigments are mixed with egg yolk. The boys get stuck in mixing the powder with water on a special glass surface and dome, and then using a brush to add the yolk. Incredibly, the yolk doesn't leave a hint of yellow but does make the paint deliciously shiny and smooth. 'I'm obsessed!' exclaims Sue as the boys start to snake patterns around the paper with their paint creations.

'Now the paint is mixed, it's time to decide what you want to create,' Sue says, eager to

THE PENNINE WAY & CASTLETON

The northern Peak District is wilder than the south; up here it's all about hill walking, bogs, craggy peaks and caverns that plunge visitors into an underground world. For the last, the village of Castleton is a popular base for several caverns including **Speedwell**, which is one of the deepest and therefore most dramatic to visit. Guided tours descend 105 steps to an underground canal where boats glide through 200 years of mining history to the subterranean lake known as the Bottomless Pit.

Standing tall above Castleton, the ruined **Peveril Castle** (⊘ english-heritage.org.uk) is worth the climb for the views over Mam Tor and Hope Valley. **Mam Nick National Trust** car park is a good place to start the

hear what the little imaginations will come up with. Wilf opts for a Spitfire; Barney starts copying his brother but drifts into portraying a sea monster instead, creating something that we all confidently agree is entirely new to the world. What fun! Both are transfixed and I'm happily redundant as the three of them discuss brush styles, drawing techniques, writing in paint, and colour combinations. The result is two shiny, shimmering images that resemble something of a plane and a monster but, more importantly, a lot of imagination and commitment.

HOLLY TUPPEN

hike up **Mam Tor** (two hours; check ⊘ nationaltrust.org.uk for details); you come back down along the Broken Road, which has been damaged by landslides over the years (kids will love its dramatic appearance).

Below Mam Tor, the **Pennine Way** (⊘ nationaltrail.co.uk) starts in Edale and works its way 260 miles through the Yorkshire Dales and Northumberland National Park to just over the Scottish border in Kirk Yetholm. The Peak District's chunk passes by Kinder Downfall, a waterfall crashing down from the Kinder Scout plateau's wild moorland. For full immersion, outdoor activity experts **Lost Earth Adventures** (⊘ lostearthadventures.co.uk) organises guided hikes as well as scrambles, rock-climbing, abseiling and kayaking.

HIKING & CYCLING HOLIDAYS IN THE PEAKS

Thanks to its comprehensive walking and cycling trails, the Peak District is a great place to plan an A-to-B **hiking or biking expedition**. There's no better way to introduce kids to the concept of map reading and slow travel – they'll be amazed how far you can get under your own steam.

Several **tour companies** can help with the logistics, including Adventure Pedlars (🖉 adventurepedlars.com), Saddle Skedaddle (🖉 skedaddle.com/uk) and Macs Adventure (🖉 macsadventure.com). Bespoke trip planners at Live For The Hills (🖉 liveforthehills.com) can help with minibus transfers, too.

PRACTICALITIES

FAMILY-FRIENDLY SLEEPS

Bank House Farm Campsite
🖉 bankhousefarmcamping.co.uk. Right next to the Manifold Way and Manifold River, stumbling distance from a stream for playing and a pub for refuelling, Bank House is a carefully thought-out campsite with good facilities for families. Equidistant from Buxton and Ashbourne, in the hamlet of Hulme End, it's also a great position for exploring the southern Peak District.

Beechenhill Farm 🖉 beechenhill. co.uk. This beautiful, eco-minded family farm is in a surprisingly quiet pocket of Peak District countryside, close to popular Ilam Park. The 14th-century farmhouse, barns and outbuildings have been converted into three holiday cottages with a mix of private and shared outdoor space. Owner Alex lives on the property with her two boys, making it the perfect play space for kids — there's a treehouse, swing, 'mud pit', pond, plenty of space for football, and endless walks from the doorstep.

Hadden Grove Farm Cottages
🖉 haddongrovefarmcottages.co.uk. This enclave of ten cottages close to Bakewell, sleeping from two to ten, comes with ample outdoor space, old-world character, a games room, communal play areas and an indoor pool.

White Edge Lodge 🖉 nationaltrust.org. uk. If you're looking to get away from it all, this former gamekeeper's lodge sits in splendid isolation atop the Longshaw Estate in north Derbyshire, around eight miles north of Bakewell. Despite the dramatic exterior, surrounded by wild heathland, inside is cosy and civilised with an Aga, a wood stove and a fun attic room for kids.

YHA Ilam Hall 🖉 yha.org.uk. It's not every day that you get to bed down in a 17th-century Gothic manor with views over parkland and peaks like Thorpe Cloud. Ilam Hall youth hostel has 118 beds in total, and includes several private family rooms. There's a licensed bar and restaurant on site, and the Ilam Park National Trust tearooms are just across the yard.

KID-FRIENDLY EATS

Bluebells Dairy ⟡ bluebelldairy.co.uk. Family run since the 1950s, Bluebells Dairy diversified into ice cream in 2007 to keep the farm afloat. Today it offers visitors a play area, a chance to meet the animals, and 26 flavours of some of the finest artisan ice cream and sorbet around.

Royal Oak ⟡ peakpub.co.uk. A local venture through and through, the Royal Oak in Hurdlow, south of Buxton, supports a host of producers including the Peak District Dairy in Tideswell and Thornbridge Brewery in Bakewell. The menu suits every occasion, offering morning coffee, seasonal favourites, children's classics and loaded sandwiches. There's outdoor space and a self-catering barn and camping field for those that want to linger longer.

Yorkshire Bridge Inn ⟡ yorkshire-bridge.co.uk. Tucked into Hope Valley, close to the Ladybower Reservoir, with bike hire, fly fishing and riding on the doorstep (call for details), this is the kind of pub you may find difficult to leave. Luckily, there are 14 en-suite rooms for those that can extend their visit.

BEFORE YOU GO

After a surge in visitor numbers in 2021, the Peak District National Park launched the **#PeakDistrictProud** initiative to inform new and regular visitors how to better care for the national park. Tips include how to park, remove rubbish, prevent wildfires, support local businesses, and opt for car-free fun to protect the environment and local communities. Read the full list of advice before you go at ⟡ peakdistrictproud. co.uk. If you'd like to financially support the Peak District National Park and find out more about how it works to make the park more accessible to everyone, visit ⟡ peakdistrictfoundation.org.uk.

MORE INFO

Peak District Guide
⟡ letsgopeakdistrict.co.uk
Peak District Kids
⟡ peakdistrictkids.co.uk
Peak District Tourist Board
⟡ visitpeakdistrict.com

20
THE NATIONAL FOREST

An inspiring story of regeneration in Britain's youngest and fastest evolving forest.

TOP FAMILY EXPERIENCE
HONEYBEE HIVE TOUR WITH DAVE THE BEE FARMER

BEST FOR KIDS AGED:	7+
WHEN TO GO:	May to October
INTREPID LEVEL:	①
ADDED ADVENTURE:	Forest bathing, eco festivals, hi-ropes courses, woodcraft sessions, cycling trails, a woodland memorial
TIME:	A long weekend to a week

UNCOVER THE SECRET LIFE OF BEES WITH THE BEE FARMER

Cattows Farm, Sweptone Rd, Heather, Coalville LE67 2RF ⊘ thebeefarmer.co.uk; the two-hour visit to the honeybee hive is suitable for kids aged seven & above, while the more advanced introduction to beekeeping is best for 12 years & above

David McDowell, 'the Bee Farmer', greets us in his natty trilby at the entrance to Cattows Farm and its pick-your-own pumpkin fields. We're here with three other families to learn all about the secret life of bees, and there's certainly a buzz in the air as the kids' excitement levels are tinged with an edge of trepidation. 'What if we get stung?' is a major trope of the day, even though we're all big bee fans.

Dave eases us in gently with a spot of mindfulness, telling us that bees get giddy if you get giddy. 'Bees can fly at 15 miles per hour, faster than

◀ **1** A frame of bees from the hive. **2** Lighting the smoker.

Usain Bolt,' says Dave, 'so there's absolutely no point trying to run away from them. It's far better to stand still and be calm.'

He describes beekeeping as akin to life as a ninja, as it can involve handling up to a thousand bees at a time. We're all surprised to learn that there are just seven species of honeybee, but around 20,000 types of bees worldwide.

After a few necessary safety checks, Dave gives us an introduction to how bees and hives operate, and the various traditions of beekeeping. A lively discussion ensues about whether taking honey from the bees is theft, something that vegans believe, but Dave assures us that bees are overproducers and that the taking of honey is justified.

Once we're all at ease, we follow Dave over the fields to where his van is sitting near two green hives. He pulls open the back of the vehicle and hauls out a box stuffed with bee suits for every shape and size. There's something massively exciting and confidence boosting about putting them on and looking out through the gauze.

Dave gives the kids the chance to light a little fire inside the smoker. As soon as it starts to smoulder, there's great delight in pumping the smoke out. Dave tells us the reason you use smoke in the hive is to make the bees think their house is on fire, which leads them to gorge on the honey, leaving them less feisty. We have another good discussion about the ethics of this and also about how bees work together, and the lessons humans might learn from them. Dave describes all the different roles in the hive, from nurse bees to foraging bees, and the kids all wonder what kind of bee they'd like to be – the Queen obviously comes out tops.

Dave opens up a hive and pulls out a frame that is absolutely covered in bees. He shows us how to hold the wooden structure upright. It's thrilling to be so close to this moving mass of nature. Dave asks us to guess how many honeybees live in one hive in summer. Wild figures are plucked out of the air until we're told it's a mind-blowing 50,000.

Buzzards and yellowhammers fly over as Dave asks the children to think of as many things as they can that wax is used for. After candles, they come up with polishes, cheese wrapping and lip balm! We also hear that the reason some honey is runny and some is crystallised is all to do with the amount of glucose it contains.

As the hive is closed and we remove our bee suits we realise a couple of hours have flown by. No-one has been stung and we all have a new respect for these awe-inspiring creatures. We thank Dave and head off for high tea in Cattows Farm Café, where his honey is for sale. He tells me the honey is stocked there for free on this mixed-use farm because his bees pollinate the farm's pumpkins and fruit trees: everything working in a circular economy, just like the bees.

ADDED ADVENTURE: OUTDOOR LIVING & INNER CONTEMPLATION IN A THRILLING ECO WONDERLAND

If there's one part of the UK that captures the spirit of slow family travel, it's the **National Forest** (⊘ nationalforest.org), Britain's greatest story of regeneration and reforestation. This manmade, purposefully planted forest, spread across Derbyshire, Leicestershire and Staffordshire, has transformed 200 square miles of black coal mines, clay pits and heavy industry into a swathe of green. The word 'forest' is not describing an area entirely given over to trees, but used in the historic sense to mean a mixed mosaic of trees, wetlands and grasslands. The trees are important, though: over nine million have been planted since its conception 30 years ago, including birch, rowan, oak and lime. In 1991 the area had just 6% forest cover; it has now increased to 22%. New meadows and hedgerows are encouraged through funding, and when precious agricultural land can't be planted with trees the aim has been to create wildlife corridors. Many areas have been left wild to let nature restore itself. The aim is to reach 33% forest cover, linking the two ancient forests of Needwood in Staffordshire and Charnwood in Leicestershire. On top of all that, England's first new broadleaf forest in a thousand years, the National Forest has rebooted struggling Midlands communities by bringing in jobs in green pursuits and tourism, and improved the local quality of life.

Opportunities for outdoor learning abound – it's a truly inspiring place to visit with children, especially if they feel the weight of our climate crisis, as many young souls quite rightly do. Hundreds of miles of paths and trails criss-cross the forest, including the 75-mile-long **National Forest Way**, which links all the major attractions, making it easy to explore on foot or by bike. But more than that, the National Forest is a greenprint for the nation as the next 25 years, which will be a defining period in the history of our fragile planet, unfold.

THE WESTERN FOREST

Towards the western reaches of the National Forest, at Jackson's Bank in Needwood, Staffordshire, you can find one of the forest's six **Noon Columns** designed by sculptor David Nash. Slots cut into these 10ft-plus oak sculptures allow rays of sunshine through at 'true' noon – it's fun for kids to spot them and then, on fine days, to wait for the sunbeams. This particular example is made from a trunk of burr oak, the very essence of a mature tree that weathers and provides shelter and food for insects and birds.

Cycle or walk the eight miles south down the National Forest Way to the **National Memorial Arboretum** (⊘ thenma.org.uk). This may seem like a sombre place to head with children, but in reality it's a hugely rewarding experience, presenting young visitors with the question of how to remember people once they've passed away and how that helps the living, too. This former gravel works makes a major contribution to the greening of the National Forest, having seen 25,000 trees planted over its 20-year history. There's a lot to see, from the very grand Armed Forces Memorial, which is as impressive as anything you'll see in Washington DC, to the Royal National Lifeboat Institution garden. Kids can get an activity pack with stickers relating to eight memorials and there's also a Stick Man Trail, a sensory playground and a wonderful Children's Wood with a poignant bronze statue depicting the confusion of wartime evacuation. In summer there are outdoor escape room challenges that encourage children to look at memorials in a different way; in December the arboretum is illuminated and you can hang a bulb to remember a loved one. Next to the arboretum is **Croxall Lakes Nature Reserve** (⊘staffs-wildlife.org.uk), where you might be lucky enough to spot otters and kingfishers as well as another noon column.

To the north, there are a cluster of sights in the Burton upon Trent area. These include **National Forest Llama Treks** (⊘ nationalforestllamatreks. co.uk), and the **National Forest Adventure Farm** (⊘ adventurefarm. co.uk) where kids can get up close to farm animals and go on a tractor-and-trailer safari. In Burton itself, the **National Brewery Centre** (⊘ nationalbrewerycentre.co.uk) is a family-friendly attraction with shire horses and vintage steam engines and cars to admire.

---

1 Walking the National Forest Way. 2 One of the National Forest's Noon Columns.
3 National Memorial Arboretum. 4 Conkers is situated in the heart of the forest. ▶

DIANA JARVIS

NATIONAL MEMORIAL ARBORETUM

CHRISTOPHER BEECH

CONKERS/IAN KENNY

Rosliston Forestry Centre (⊘ roslistonforestrycentre.co.uk), on the National Forest Way, is a mix of woodland and meadow, ponds and play areas. It's a great place to hire bikes and explore or test your orienteering skills.

THE HEART OF THE FOREST

The central swathe of the National Forest, between Burton upon Trent in Staffordshire and Coalville in Leicestershire, is where the majority of the tree planting has taken place. Ashby-de-la-Zouch, of *Adrian Mole* fame – Sue Townsend's teenage diarist moved to the town from Leicester, and his girlfriend Pandora later became the local MP – makes a great base for exploring the region, as does the former mining town of Swadlincote.

Nearby, in the centre of the forest, is **Hicks Lodge: The National Forest Cycling Centre** (⊘ forestryengland.uk), which was an open-cast coal mining and clay extraction site up until the late 1990s. Today Hicks Lodge is the first part of the forest to have achieved about a third forest cover. It's a wonderful place to hire bikes and explore, and features walking and horseriding trails, natural play areas and an absorbing Superworm Trail, based on the much-loved book by Julia Donaldson and Axel Scheffler.

"Hicks Lodge is a wonderful place to hire bikes and explore, and features walking and horseriding trails."

If there's one National Forest attraction that gets the adrenalin flowing, it's the nearby **Conkers** (⊘ visitconkers.com), an outdoor and indoor play area that includes an obstacle course for teens, a barefoot walk – where kids delight in shedding their shoes and walking through squelchy mud, warm rocks, grass and soil among other things – and hi- and lo-ropes courses.

Feanedock, a 70-acre woodland site to the north of Conkers, is the location for the inspiring three-day **Timber Festival** (⊘ timberfestival. org.uk), a celebration of the forest with music, art, talks and workshops held at the beginning of July. Wild Rumpus are the creative geniuses behind this energising family event with its strong sustainability and arts theme. Festivalgoers of all ages, but especially families with children aged between eight and fourteen, enjoy trapeze artists high up in the

1 Cycling at Hicks Lodge. 2 Woodland workshop, Greenwood Days.
3 Feanedock's Timber Festival. ▶

trees, live music from up-and-coming performers, talks from the likes of the Green Party's Caroline Lucas and nature writer Robert MacFarlane, and all manner of eco-minded activities.

South of Conkers, **Moira Furnace Museum & Country Park** (⊘ moirafurnace.org) features an interesting small museum about this former iron furnace and is an easy, pram-friendly place to take a stroll in the country park or a boat trip on Ashby Canal. Hook up with Jodi and Becki from **Wild Minds** (⊘ wildmindsnature.co.uk) for a spot of forest bathing here, and learn about phytoncides – the essential oils given off by trees which are proven to lower heart rate and reduce stress – and the mycelium network whereby trees communicate. Wild Minds tours are all about slowing down in nature and taking time to hug a tree, to put your ear against its trunk to hear what's going on inside. Kids will find night-time sessions extra thrilling; if you're feeling really daring, book one of Jodi and Becki's wild forest sleepouts.

Crafts-loving kids will want to make a beeline for **Greenwood Days** (⊘ greenwooddays.co.uk) near the National Trust's Calke Abbey. Set up in the early days of the National Forest, this impressive canopied woodland workshop offers over 60 different courses in green woodworking – including willow weaving, basketry and spoon carving – using resources from the young woodlands . A family bonding experience might involve collaborating on making a three-legged stool from a chunk of greenwood, or building a much more elaborate Windsor chair – you get to take home what you make.

Learning about different types of wood, everyone also gets hands on with ancient techniques – such as pole-lathe turning, which goes back to Viking times, or using the shave horse – and little ones enjoy making flowers out of the wood shavings. It's immensely satisfying, and there's a brilliant sense of camaraderie, even at lunchtime, when families roll out dough and choose their toppings for a pizza that they can watch bubbling away in the wood-fired oven, and when blackened kettles over the open fire fuel endless cups of tea and coffee.

THE EASTERN FOREST

The eastern edge of the National Forest is bookmarked by the ancient **Charnwood Forest**, on the Leicester/Derbyshire border. With its stone-

▶ A fallow deer at Bradgate Park.

CANOEING ON THE RIVER TRENT

Trent Adventure, Poplars Farm, near Tywford DE73 7HJ ⬧ trentadventure.wixsite.com;
age: 6+ on canals or 8+ on river; intrepid level: ②

We can tell we've arrived at the right place by the colourful stacks of Canadian-style open canoes by the side of the River Trent. Owner/farmer Robin Raine and our canoeing expert Matt Thomas are ready and waiting by the side of the flowing water to kit us out in life jackets and give us a thorough briefing in canoeing know-how. As we stand on the pretty riverbank, we're shown how to hold the end of the paddle and dip it into the water to get a satisfying pull, and how to reverse. Soon we're clambering into our two-person canoes for a three-and-a-half mile taster session taking us from Twyford to Swarkestone – a leisurely hour-and-a-half outing.

You can take a self-guided canoe trip, but Matt is accompanying us today and using all his skills from his past life in the army, as a schoolteacher and as an activity leader. There's a wonderful sense of serenity on the water and bountiful birdlife from swans to herons and birds of prey. Matt tells us all about keeping safe and avoiding dangerous eddies under trees that overhang the banks. A highlight is a paddle up an inlet to Anchor Church, a series of ancient sandstone caves close to the village of Ingleby, with eerie doors and window holes that are thought to have housed a hermit in the 6th and 7th centuries.

We learn that flooding is a problem along these banks, and that wet grasslands have been created to combat this. There has also been an effort to bring otters back to the river with the creation of otter holts. Sadly we don't spot any of these playful creatures during our paddle, but my kids love messing about on the river and we promise ourselves a return visit, perhaps next time on the Trent and Mersey Canal so we can get up close to the colourful canal boats.

TRENT ADVENTURE

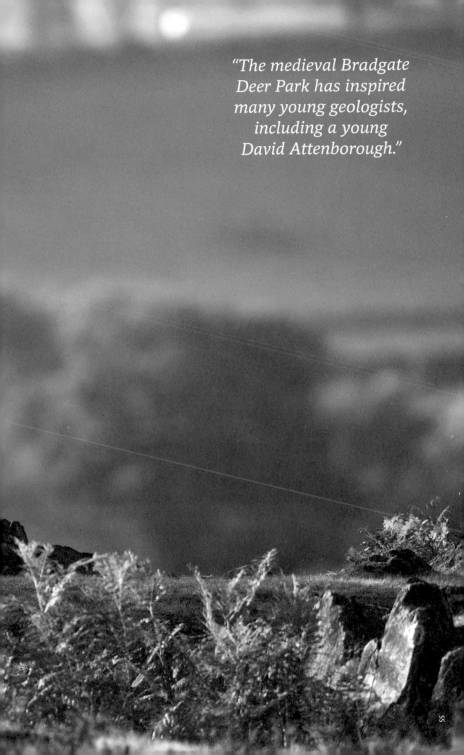

*"The medieval Bradgate
Deer Park has inspired
many young geologists,
including a young
David Attenborough."*

built houses and Swithland slate roofs Charnwood can sometimes feel a little like a mini Lake District – with no lake in sight, of course! For a spot of ancient forest exploration, take a family walk through the **Outwoods** to see the wet alder and dry oak and birch woodlands. Kids will love to clamber on the pre-Cambrian rocky outcrops.

Bradgate Park (⌂ bradgatepark.org) is a historic medieval deer park in the heart of Charnwood. Home to some of England's oldest rocks, it has inspired many young geologists, including a young David Attenborough.

Alternatively head for **Snibston Colliery Park** (⌂ leicscountryparks. org.uk), a former colliery spoil heap turned woodland and open grassland with a mountain-biking trail, nature reserve, heritage trail, café and play area.

Finally, for a different perspective on this region, stop by **Stoneywell** (⌂ nationaltrust.org.uk), a lasting homage to the British Arts and Crafts movement created by furniture designer and architect Ernest Gimson for his brother in 1898. Rather poignantly, Gimson was a great believer in the philosophy of John Ruskin and William Morris who abhorred the evils of mass industrialisation and machine production that so scarred this region.

PRACTICALITIES

FAMILY-FRIENDLY SLEEPS

The Boot ⌂ thebootatrepton.co.uk. This pretty boutique hotel, housed in a 17th-century coaching inn in the Derbyshire village of Repton, has nine rooms including doubles and twins, along with the Mercia Suite which sleeps four – perfect for families wanting a little more luxury. The restaurant is loved by locals, offering classic mains such as herb gnocchi and sea bass, a kids' menu and lavish afternoon teas.

Calke Abbey holiday cottages
⌂ nationaltrust.org.uk. There are five fairy-tale cottages, in typical National Trust chocolate-box style, in the grounds of Calke Abbey: a perfect little brick house with roses round the door, a mini Georgian mansion, two white gatehouse lodges and a vast thatched cottage. Sleeping between two and 14 people they are all tastefully and luxuriously decorated, with plump sofas, wood-burning stoves and private gardens.

Dandelion Hideaway
⌂ thedandelionhideaway.co.uk. On a working goat farm in the Leicestershire countryside, south of Charnwood, this glampsite offers six luxurious canvas cottages each sleeping six. Masses of

love and attention have been poured into making this a magical place for families to stay, with retro furniture, Roberts radios, gingham teddy bears and whistling kettles; the third bedroom sleeps two in a secret wooden cabin. There is also the Bluebells tent, which sleeps two but comes with its own treehouse where kids can sleep, and has an al-fresco wood-fired hot tub. Families can collect eggs from the hen coop, take a tour of the goat farm, groom a Shetland pony, badger-watch from the nature hide in the on-site Spinney Woods, tell stories round the campfire, and play table tennis and football.

Deerpark Lodge ⌂ ruralretreats.co.uk. This imposing A-frame lodge, made from local timber, is set in the grounds of the grand Staunton Harold Estate near Ashby-de-la-Zouch, and overlooks the parkland from its woodland clearing. It sleeps six, with three bedrooms and a comfortable open-plan lounge, dining area and kitchen that all let the light in. There's a log-burning stove to keep things cosy and lake fishing can be arranged for guests.

Fire & Stars ⌂ fireandstars.co.uk. Located at Nethercote Farm, just south of Conkers, this off-grid campsite offers authentic woodland camping in the National Forest. Generous pitches come with a wild woodland firepit and log packages can be pre-ordered. Showers are in the nearby Old Crown pub and portable toilets are dotted around the site.

Hastings Retreat ⌂ hastingsretreat. co.uk. Close to Ashby-de-la Zouch and next to Hicks Lodge Cycling Centre, this collection of four converted barns, sleeping between six and nine, offers slick yet homely self-catering stays for families; the larger barns have hot tubs on the decking along with firepits on the lawn. Guests also have use of a three-acre fishing lake with sunbathing platforms – book Lake View Barn for its wide terrace overlooking the water. It's worth taking the 50-minute woodland walk to the Bull & Lion pub in Packington.

Martin Green ⌂ canopyandstars. co.uk. A converted horsebox by the side of the River Trent at Twyford – where Trent Adventure (see box, page 311) frequently sets off on canoeing trips – ingeniously sleeps a family of four in its shabby chic interiors. Highlights include the sinks made from copper pans, the wood-burning stove, and the panoramic riverside views.

Springwood Fisheries
⌂ springwoodfisheries.com. This lake fishing site, near Greenwood Days and Calke Abbey, is home to a variety of waterside glamping options, including basic log pods where you bring your bed linen or sleeping bags and camping equipment, and standard pods which have a double futon and two camp beds, microwave and kettle. For more mod cons, book a deluxe pod; these come with kitchenette, en-suite shower and a small terrace with table and chairs for outdoor dining.

Upper Rectory Farm Cottages
⚮ upperrectoryfarmcottages.co.uk. These high-spec luxury cottages, just south of the forest near junction 11 of the M42, sleep between two and 22 when combined, making them ideal for extended family holidays or families travelling with other families and friends. The Byre is an accessible ground-floor cottage, sleeping between four and six, so perfect for a single family. Ashby Canal, good for scenic walks, is close by, as are a number of family attractions.

Wigwam Holidays ⚮ wigwamholidays. com. Stay in the depths of the ancient forest of Charnwood in one of six en-suite luxury cabins sitting around a wildlife pond. All sleep four and have private outdoor decks for al-fresco dining; three have wood-fired hot tubs, too. The nearest village is Newtown Linford, which has pubs, shops and tea rooms.

YHA National Forest ⚮ yha.org. uk. Conveniently located next door to Conkers, YHA National Forest is an affordable, eco-friendly place for families to stay in the heart of the forest. Rooms are clean, comfy and basic, with a choice of shared bunks or private en-suite rooms. The café serves breakfast to guests and is open to all in the early evening.

KID-FRIENDLY EATS

Cattows Farm ⚮ cattowsfarm.co.uk. Called a tea room, but more like a fully blown restaurant, Cattows Farm (page 303) is a winner for families on the lookout for a hearty meal or an afternoon tea; the children's menu features winners such as beans on toast and macaroni cheese. The farm shop is packed with local produce, and you can also book a bee experience, pick your own soft fruit, sunflowers or pumpkins, try the Corn Maze or wander along the Woodland Walk.

Curzon Arms ⚮ thecurzonarms.com. This pretty pub, just outside the forest but within Charnwood, is a classic for families looking for reliably good pub grub and has a gorgeous beer garden for outdoor dining when the sun shines. The menu features a 'For the little people' section with kids' classics including burgers and beans or vintage cheddar on toast.

Deer Park ⚮ deerpark.farm. In Hoar Cross, in the far west of the forest, this family-owned and -run farm shop, butcher and restaurant is a relaxing place to come with kids for a meal or to stock up on supplies. Café The Linhay is open for breakfast, lunch and afternoon tea and has a huge grassy field at the back for kids to run around on. A children's menu features crispy chicken skewers, fish-finger or cheese sandwiches, and soup.

Honey Pot Tea Rooms
⚮ thehoneypotcompany.co.uk. For a traditional English tea room, head to the Honey Pot at the Beehive Farm campsite and fishing lakes between Linton and Rosliston. Come for hearty breakfasts, lunches, afternoon teas or just a slice of cake – there's a comfort food kids' menu, too.

Park Kitchen & Deli ⊘ the-park. co.uk. With menus featuring locally sourced, homemade produce, this family restaurant in Newton Linford near Leicester is a fun and nutritious place to bring children. The dining area is spacious and relaxed, or you can take away for a picnic in Bradgate Park, opposite. For breakfast the kids' menu features a Deli Baby Breakfast and a tasty range of pancakes; lunch staples include sausages or pasta and a vast range of sandwiches.

BEFORE YOU GO

By making a monthly **donation** to the **National Forest** (⊘ nationalforest.org/donate/support-the-forest-monthly) you will help nurture young trees, create wildlife habitats and support volunteers. For a more hands-on approach, purchase a Plant a Tree gift to celebrate family holidays or to remember a loved one.

MORE INFO
The National Forest
⊘ nationalforest.org

21
LIVERPOOL

An industrious riverside city bursting with creativity.

TOP FAMILY EXPERIENCE
THE BEATLES STORY MUSEUM

BEST FOR KIDS AGED:	7+
WHEN TO GO:	Year-round
INTREPID LEVEL:	①
ADDED ADVENTURE:	Vibrant galleries, thought-provoking museums, living musical heritage, water-based fun
TIME:	Two days

WITH A LITTLE HELP FROM THEIR FRIENDS: THE BEATLES STORY

Britannia Vaults, Royal Albert Dock, L3 4AD ⊘ beatlesstory.com; Magical Mystery Tour ⊘ cavernclub.com

'Who are The Beatles?' my youngest asks as we descend the steps down to the Beatles Story. A reminder that it's always good to prep your kids before any cultural experience. 'The ones Granddad likes – you know, the old music,' the eldest retorts before I get a word in. My dad grew up in Liverpool and so The Beatles' songs are a family staple. Within moments of entering, we're thankfully all on board with who The Beatles are.

Inside, we pick up audio guides and the kids get activity packs. The museum funnels visitors through various interactive, life-size displays, including an aeroplane (to signify the band breaking America) and a yellow submarine. It's as captivating as it is surreal, which perhaps neatly sums up the Fab Four.

◀ **1** The Beatles statue. **2** Children enjoying educational activities in the 'Discovery Zone'.
3 Exhibit at the Beatles Story.

Audio tour on, and John Lennon's half-sister, Julia Baird, welcomes us on the journey. Throughout the next hour she's joined by Paul McCartney, Cynthia Lennon (John's first wife), and the band's producer, George Martin, often referred to as the 'fifth Beatle'. The commentary is interspersed with audio and video clips from every era, bringing each stage of the story to life. Within five minutes, everyone is happily absorbed in their own little Beatles world.

Halfway through the tour, we all welcome a sit down in the true-to-size mock-up of The Cavern Club, the music venue in Liverpool that 'broke' The Beatles. Chairs are arranged in front of a stage and music plays overhead. It's a good chance to remove headsets and chat about what we've seen so far. The boys ask if we can visit NEMS record store and Hessy's guitar shop, not realising they no longer exist. 'Can we go to the Cavern?' one of the boys asks, not put off by the descriptions of the dingy cellar with 'sweat pouring off the walls, mingled with disinfectant to get rid of the smell.'

We're already booked in for a visit later that day as part of another Beatles experience – the **Magical Mystery Tour**, which takes visitors to famous Beatles' landmarks around the city. It's a brilliant complement to the museum if you have the time for both. Nowadays, rather than sweat pouring from the walls, the Cavern Club welcomes families before 8pm. Live acts perform from 11.30am, so it's a good way for kids to get a sense of Liverpool's live-music culture.

Incredibly, given the youngest couldn't remember who The Beatles were an hour ago, enthusiasm lasts until the very end, including lots of questions around why John Lennon was shot. 'The kids always ask that,' Nick at the Discovery Centre comments, as I explain why we're talking about mental health. The Discovery Centre (only open in school holidays) is the finale of the museum, before the Fab Four diner-style café and shop, and the kids can't believe their luck. Nor can we.

'Look! Look!' we all cry, discovering the mini karaoke stage, the giant light-up step-on piano, and a mock record store and player where the kids can choose which records they want to play. At the art station, Nick asks the boys what they'd like to colour – Pop Art renditions of the Fab Four, or psychedelic album covers. Before long, the whole family is lost to mindful colouring.

Although the whole experience takes just two hours, it feels like it will have a lasting impression. Not only do we all know a lot more about the history of the city, eager now to find Penny Lane, Strawberry Fields and Walton Street, but the boys have a twinkle in their eye as they ask if they can buy some guitar music. Perhaps they no longer believe football is the only way to international stardom.

ADDED ADVENTURE: REINVENTION, REVITALISATION & RIVERSIDE JAUNTS

Since winning the title of Capital of Culture in 2008, Liverpool has continued to surprise and delight with its museums, galleries and music venues, reinventing and revitalising the city centre without losing touch with its industrial roots. The sense of history is tangible, and from the transatlantic slave trade to the Victorian penal system, much of it is heart-wrenching – with topical overtones. There are years' worth of stories to delve into, and institutions like Tate Liverpool and the Liverpool Museum do a good job at bringing it all to life. And it's by no means all museums, either: surrounded by a tidal river and the sea, the city offers plenty of scope for outdoor adventures.

At heart, of course, this is a music city. As journalist Paul du Noyer once wrote, 'Liverpool is a busker deep down... When all else fails... this city will sing for its supper.' Before you arrive, why not get the whole family fired up and enthused by listening to a soundtrack of Liverpool greats including The Beatles, Gerry and the Pacemakers, The Real Thing, The Lightning Seeds, The Coral and, for the pop fans, Atomic Kitten.

CITY CENTRE

If you're travelling by train, you'll most likely arrive in the heart of the city at Liverpool Lime Street. Opposite the station, the grand and slightly intimidating **St George's Hall** is home to the **History Whisperer** (see box, page 326); a little further north, the **World Museum** (⊘ liverpoolmuseums.org.uk) offers five floors of natural history and science, and has a planetarium. Nearby, the impressive **Central Library** (⊘ liverpool.gov.uk) features a huge kids' section, and the **Walker Art Gallery** (⊘ liverpoolmuseums.org.uk) is packed with works from Degas to Hockney.

Between Lime Street Station and the waterfront, **Liverpool ONE** (⊘ liverpool-one.com) is a huge shopping mall. Bypass the chain stores and head to the eastern side of the mall, where **St Johns Beacon Viewing Gallery** (stjohnsbeacon.co.uk), at the top of a 400ft-high 1960s radio tower, offers 360° views of the city and the Mersey. Moments from Liverpool Central Station, south of the mall, the **Bluecoat** (thebluecoat.org.uk) contemporary arts centre is housed in a beautiful 300-year-old building. There's plenty for families here: previous events have included Liverpool's first comedy club for kids and an exhibition on colonialism designed by young Liverpudlians.

Heading southeast, enter Liverpool's thriving **Chinatown** through the huge traditional arch adorned with dragons at the top of **Nelson Street**. This area was home to the first Chinese community in Europe, and although it is no longer the largest, its two streets are packed with highly regarded restaurants – Yuet Ben is recommended. Not far from here, to the south, the **Baltic Triangle** is mostly taken up by trendy late-night bars and markets, but kids will enjoy the huge murals and skateboarders along Jamaica Street. The Baltic Triangle is also the starting point for theatrical **Shiverpool ghost tours** (shiverpool.co.uk); these are best suited to kids over nine years old, depending on the child.

Further north, aptly named **Hope Street** links the city's two cathedrals, one Catholic and one Anglican (the largest Anglican cathedral in Britain), and is surrounded by attractive Georgian streets. On the third Sunday of every month, a **Makers Market** ( ) floods the streets with the best local traders.

A couple of miles from the city centre, **Sefton Park** (liverpool. gov.uk), covering 235 acres, is the best of Liverpool's Victorian parks. Here, the **Palm House** (palmhouse.org.uk) hosts the city's botanical collection, including 20 varieties of palm and 23 types of orchids. The park also has a boating lake and a 'fairy glen' – a series of waterfalls tucked away in the northeast corner.

THE WATERFRONT

Water creeps into the city from the Mersey in all directions, creating a grid of waterways and docks now packed with museums, galleries, historical buildings and restaurants, with ample space to run about. The city's Victorian docks and famous skyline earnt the city UNESCO World Heritage Status in 2004, a status that was controversially stripped

1 Chinatown, Nelson Street. **2** World Museum. **3** Walker Art Gallery. **4** Sefton Park. ▶

in 2021 after the UNESCO committee decided new development had destroyed the area's heritage – an interesting debate that makes visiting and contemplating the old and the new even more compelling.

Heading straight for the Mersey from Lime Street Station, you hit the **Royal Albert Dock** (⊘ albertdock.com). The converted warehouses here are mostly occupied now by restaurants and bars, but you'll also find **Tate Liverpool** (⊘ tate.org.uk) and the **Merseyside Maritime Museum** (⊘ liverpoolmuseums.org.uk) – both free to visitors. Exhibitions in the latter cover the building of the *Titanic*, the intriguing and sometimes bizarre history of smuggling, and stories from seafaring Liverpudlians throughout the ages. In the same building, the **International Slavery Museum** (⊘ liverpoolmuseums.org.uk) is an incredibly moving experience, recounting Liverpool's extensive role in the 18th- and 19th-century slave trade.

"Liverpool's marinas recently earnt Blue Flag status in part thanks to the work of the Canal and River Trust."

On the south side of the docks is the entrance to **The Beatles Story** (page 319) and **Wild Shore Liverpool** (⊘ wildshoreliverpool.co.uk), an inflatable aqua course along a canal. Further south, on Queen's Dock, the not-for-profit **Liverpool Watersports Centre** (⊘ liverpoolwatersports. org.uk) offers paddleboarding, open-water swimming, kayaking and canoeing for a wonderfully active way to explore the city's historic canals and docks (children – aged between five and 16 – must be accompanied by an adult). The centre also has one of the country's only wheelchair-accessible powerboats.

If you feel a little squeamish about leaping into city-centre waterways, be assured that Liverpool's marinas recently earnt Blue Flag status. This is partly thanks to the work of the Canal and River Trust (⊘ canalrivertrust.org.uk), whose website provides visitors with audio walks, maps and explorer packs to discover the **Liverpool Canal Link**, a 1.4 mile historical route from Albert Dock north to Stanley Dock.

The **Museum of Liverpool** (⊘ liverpoolmuseums.org.uk), north of Albert Dock, is an architectural showpiece between the Royal Liver Building (Europe's first skyscraper) and the waterfront. There's a play zone for under-six-year-olds, Little Liverpool, with an alphabet of Liverpool history and dock-themed water play. The Wondrous Place

---

1 Albert Dock. **2** Museum of Liverpool. **3** Black Pearl, New Brighton. ▶

GARETH JONES/MUSEUM OF LIVERPOOL

gallery showcases the city's cultural and creative history, from football rivalries to local celebrities. Footsteps away, you can hop on a 50-minute **River Explorer Cruise** (⊘ merseyferries.co.uk) to see the sights from the river. The ferry makes a stop at Woodside, so this a great way to head across to explore The Wirral (page 328).

THE HISTORY WHISPERER

St George's Hall, St George's Place, L1 1JJ ⊘ stgeorgeshallliverpool.co.uk; age: 8+; intrepid level: ②

'Just like our city, our History Whisperer, 12-year-old Livie, is full of heart, humour, emotion and dreams,' volunteer Paul Leach tells us as we enter Liverpool's huge Neoclassical St George's Hall via a nondescript side entrance. Before Livie transports us to Victorian Liverpool, recounting her family story via interactive audio and video, Paul tells us a little about the building's history.

With wealth pouring in from shipping and slavery in the 1700s, Liverpool was eager to rival London but was lacking two key buildings – a concert hall and a court. A young architect won a competition to build them both, but as funds ran low, they had to be merged into one site. Paul continues, 'Hence the staggering contrast of the splendour and glamour of a concert hall sitting above the horror and degradation of a penal court and cells.'

The experience kicks off with a film introducing us to Livie, a fictional character designed to bring the past to life, who will guide us through the cells and the courtroom. 'Dear Dad, dance wherever you are. They can never take the dance away. That's what you always said to me,' she writes, as we learn her father has been sent to Australia for stealing a blanket, and her mother has died of consumption. Soon her brother, Jack, is also arrested. The family came to Liverpool to escape the Irish famine, and dancing and her imagination keep Livie going despite falling victim to Victorian disease and injustice.

For the next hour, we follow Livie's journey as she takes food to her brother in the cells and attends his trial. As we walk quite literally through the original cells and courtroom, the walls tell stories with interactive videos and audio clips. 'What's this?' one of the kids asks, touching the spot where soot from a 19th-century gas lamp still stains the brick wall. 'Imagine how smoky the atmosphere would have been,' Paul adds, as he explains the horrific conditions the prisoners had to endure. We ponder whether the fact the cells were described as 'state of the art' was the first example of fake news.

The content is full on – death, disease, injustice – but the kids can choose what they linger over. An interactive timeline of St George's Hall and Liverpool's history offers a bit of respite from Livie's story.

'Park your cheeks, the judge is coming. Keep it down, keep it down!' bellows a voice across

BEYOND THE CITY

Four miles upstream, **Otterspool** (⌽ otterspooladventurecentre.co.uk) is a waterside park and promenade that offers all manner of kids' activites, from jumping pillows to adventure playgrounds and go-karting. For a more genteel experience, head six miles further on to **Speke Hall**

the courtroom as we move to the next part of the experience. The original courtroom remains so true to life that it's often used as a location in films and TV shows. We nervously sit up in the viewing pews, while Jack's trial unfolds on screens all around us. The youngest (aged six) nestles into my lap; the noise and scenes prove a bit overwhelming for younger kids.

The experience finishes in the Great Hall, so you can get a real sense of the contrast. Extravagance fills the air. Paul explains, 'The lower classes paid to sit in a gallery above the hall to watch the upper classes dance and

dine here, while the upper classes enjoyed watching the lower classes sentenced to death or Australian penal colonies in the court.' There's probably nowhere else that so neatly sums up the highs and lows of Victorian life.

As we leave blinking into sunshine, marvelling at the hall's great pillars and gardens, I realise we're so accustomed to seeing the architectural splendour of the Victorian era that it's refreshing, and incredibly moving, to hear, see and imagine life on the other side. As Livie says, 'We must never forget.'

(⊘ nationaltrust.org.uk), a huge Tudor mansion and gardens. Kids will love fossil hunting in the Great Hall's stone-flagged floor — home to 350 million year old belemnite fossils.

North of Liverpool, at **Crosby Coastal Park** and beach, Antony Gormley's **Another Place** (⊘ visitsouthport.com) is a surreal sight – 100 life-size, iron figures gazing out to sea dotted around the beautiful two-mile sandy stretch of beach between Waterloo and Blundellsands.

On the other side of the Mersey from the city itself (accessible by boat, train or ferry), beyond the town of Birkenhead, kids can run wild on expansive beaches backed by sand dunes throughout **The Wirral** – a seven-mile chunk of land sandwiched between the River Mersey and the River Dee. On the River Dee side, you can have a fun coastal adventure by crossing the sands at low tide from the small town of **West Kirby** to **Hilbre Island** (⊘ hilbreisland.info), which is home to a colony of grey seals.

On the Mersey side, the Victorian seaside resort of **New Brighton** is more developed; younger kids will love the **Black Pearl**, a pirate ship made entirely by driftwood on the beach. For anyone looking to stretch legs or hop on a bike, the 35-mile **Wirral Circular Trail** (⊘ visitwirral. com) starts and finishes at the Seacombe Ferry Terminal in Birkenhead.

PRACTICALITIES

FAMILY-FRIENDLY SLEEPS

Hope Street Hotel ⊘ hopestreethotel. co.uk. Occupying a Cheshire pink brick building in the city's Georgian Canning neighbourhood, Hope Street Hotel is an independent boutique hotel with heaps of style and character. It's near the Everyman theatre, known for innovative plays to suit all ages, and the Liverpool Philharmonic Hall. Toys, colouring kits and an in-house cinema help entertain the kids.

Pullman Hotel ⊘ pullman.com-liverpool.info. Chain hotels tend to feel a bit soulless, but the Pullman is in a great location: on the waterfront close enough to the action to enable you to hop in and out but far away enough not to suffer from noisy late-night bars. There are connecting rooms for families and a large lobby, bar and café space for downtime.

Titanic Hotel Liverpool ⊘ titanichotelliverpool.com. North of the centre, this converted warehouse may be less central than others, but makes up for that in terms of space and style. The 153-room hotel sits on the mouth of the Mersey in Stanley Dock, opposite vast abandoned warehouses including the

14-storey Tobacco Warehouse. Families love the generous rooms and the river or port views.

KID-FRIENDLY EATS

The Bagelry 🔲. Rainbow bagels, vegan bagels, chocolate-cake-topped bagels and donut bagels; bagels come in all shapes and sizes at this cute café in Chinatown, which also serves good coffee. There are tables inside, or get a take-away and head down to the docks to enjoy eating on the Mersey.

Duke Street Market
⚘ dukestreetmarket.com. This lovely indoor market, conveniently located in a converted 100-year-old building on Duke Street near the city centre, provides plenty of options for weary, footsore sightseers. Vendors and restaurants include Barnacle (⚘ barnacleliverpool. co.uk), a 'Scouse brasserie' serving Merseyside produce.

Homebaked Bakery 🔲 HomebakedA. After the famous Mitchell's Bakery in the Liverpool suburb of Anfield was forced to closed in 2011 due to regeneration plans, the community rallied to save their beloved pie shop and Homebaked Bakery was born. Today, it's possible to grab one of their famous Scouse (beef stew) pies from a second base in St George's Hall opposite Lime Street Station: a cavernous café that is dark but homely with high chairs and colouring kits for kids.

MerseyMade ⚘ merseymade.uk. A haven for all things local in a central location between Duke Street and Albert Dock, MerseyMade is home to ten open artists' studios, a shop selling local crafts and art, and the homely and welcoming Gordon Smith Café, celebrating the best of local produce. The menu includes build-your-own breakfasts and toasties, burgers, loaded fries and mounds of baked goods.

Yard & Coop ⚘ yardandcoop.com. This small chain on Hanover Street (there are restaurants in Manchester and Leeds, too) knows a thing or two about chicken. The owners have experimented to create the perfect buttermilk fried chicken and serve it in every shape and form possible. Kids' menus, including main and dessert, are just £5 – and look out for deals where kids eat for free.

MORE INFO

Liverpool Museums
⚘ liverpoolmuseums.org.uk
Liverpool Tourist Board
⚘ visitliverpool.com
Wirral Tourist Board ⚘ visitwirral.com

22
THE LAKE DISTRICT

*Whether it's poetry or paddleboarding on your
family agenda, the wild beauty of the Cumbrian
lakes and mountains will inspire you.*

TOP FAMILY EXPERIENCE
WALKING WITH FELL PONIES THROUGH GRIZEDALE FOREST

BEST FOR KIDS AGED:	10+
WHEN TO GO:	May to September
INTREPID LEVEL:	②
ADDED ADVENTURE:	Literary trails, watersports, family bushcamps, lake cruises, wild swims, adventure playgrounds, hill walking, quaint villages
TIME:	A long weekend to two weeks

WILD PONIES & SECRET SCULPTURES

Main car park, Grizedale Visitors Centre, LA22 0QJ (🖉 forestryengland.uk/grizedale);
🖉 fellpony.co.uk; day treks around the forest, guided day-long walks around Windermere &
one-, three- or four-night wild camping trips (May–Sept only) are available.

As my ten-year-old son holds out an apple on his upturned hand,
as instructed, Fay the fell pony performs a dexterous hoovering-
up manoeuvre followed by much pleasurable crunching, her soft
nuzzle nudging Fin for more. My child giggles with the sheer joy
of the connection, and whispers to me that he's sure this glorious
creature of palest grey, accompanying us through the forest with our
picnic lunch in her panniers, is a unicorn in disguise. And I have to
admit that standing here under the coniferous trees, by a lily-pad-
covered Grizedale Tarn in the heart of the Lake District, this notion

---

◀ Fell Pony Adventures.

doesn't feel entirely implausible. Such is the magic created by Fell Pony Adventures.

We met Fay and her chestnutty brown half-sister Pansy a couple of hours earlier by their natty horse truck in Grizedale Visitors Centre car park, with guardian Tom Lloyd patiently chatting and attending to his two companions. Giving us a warm welcome, Tom's emphasis is on putting us at ease as much as the ponies, inviting Fin and I to go ahead and stroke, pat and generally get acquainted with our new equine friends.

Before setting off, Tom explains that fell ponies have been here in Cumbria since at least Roman times but that these days there are less than 200 'wild' or 'semi-feral' ponies left. Historically fell ponies were bred as pack ponies for their stamina and surefootedness even in rough terrain, and back in the 1850s around 300 a day would leave nearby Kendal laden with wool and slate.

Tom grew up around horses and, after a career in film, having inherited his father's Hades Hill herd of 35 mostly unhandled semi-feral fell ponies, he realised that getting off-road with ponies up into the Cumbrian Fells was a life-enhancing experience, and one that he'd love to share. He was also spurred on by the fact that his dad had started to write a book about pack saddles and had left Tom many old maps of the area with routes marked out for fell pony adventures.

'Working ponies thrive out on the fells,' Tom tells us. 'They love a sense of purpose just like we do, and are hardy and courageous. You have a different connection with a pony when walking as opposed to riding. They are full of heart and character and once you have gained their trust they will do almost anything you ask.'

Our fell-walking adventure is pleasingly hands-on and Tom encourages us to help him put on the ponies' pack saddles and bridles, being careful to make the straps comfortable under their bellies and magnificent tails. The saddles have a clever metal frame on each side for hanging a pannier, preferably weighted the same on both sides. 'The point is to take all the weight off the spine,' says Tom. 'A fell pony can carry 20% of its own body weight comfortably. And you can tell a pony is happy if his ears are forward. If you want to work with the pony

---

The Fell Pony Adventure experience: from a sculpture trail to picnicking among the trees with Tom Lloyd. ▶

in partnership, you have to be calm. Then you can connect in quite a profound way.'

Tom uses a traditional rope halter and tells Fin how to hold the rope close to Fay's head at first, giving the command to 'walk on', gradually releasing rope as they both get used to one another. Tom says he's happy to take children under ten, though in those cases the route may be shortened and he will have a double rope halter on either side of the pony's head so the child can hold one side and the other is held by an adult. Other useful commands include 'Steady' for slow down, 'Whoa' for stop and 'Stand' for stay. Fin learns about horses being measured in hands and that the tallest fell ponies are just 14 hands high.

"We're climbing a cobbled path with the sunlight pouring through the trees. It's thrilling to feel the power of the ponies."

Tom also tells us that ponies are very cheap to feed, costing about £1 per week in hay during the winter. It's the weekly shoeing that costs money, at about £10 a week per pony.

Soon we're off, climbing up a cobbled path with the sunlight pouring through the trees. It's thrilling to feel the power of the ponies and to believe that you can work with them, even command them, though I'm never really sure who is in control. On narrower stretches I'm constantly being yanked back as Pansy stops for a mouthful of lush grass. And who can blame her? It's incredible to witness how skilled they are at climbing uneven steps and navigating narrow paths – you just have to be sure to walk in front, letting out more rope so you don't get bumped out of the way by pony or pannier. We emerge at the top of the hill where Fin lets out an excited yell: 'fox!' He's caught sight of the first of several forest sculptures on our route, *Red Sandstone Fox* by Gordon Young. It's a childlike version of the creature we're used to seeing on our city streets, in giant proportions and practically irresistible to kids. Fin leaps on its back, and I wonder if our ponies give the fox a sympathetic nod.

After a little more walking along the forest path, Tom instructs us to leave the ponies with him and head up a dirt trail between the trees to spot another manmade creation. This time we encounter an alien-looking creature fanning out above us in a lush dell. *Some Fern* by Kerry Morrison is a towering oak sculpture made up of 18 mighty carved fronds, bringing attention to this wondrous plant that's often taken for granted.

Back with our ponies, the walk offers glimpses of the incredible Lakeland landscape. At times we can gaze out over hill and vale as far as Morecambe Bay, which Tom reminds us is the largest expanse of intertidal mudflats and sand in the UK. Like the Lake District, it's a designated World Heritage Site.

At our scenic lunch stop by Grizedale Tarn, we help Tom unload the panniers and unsaddle the ponies who watch as he creates something of a gourmet picnic on a soft rug. We even have cushions, for goodness sake. There are two types of bread, with a cranberry and balsamic dip, local Garstang brie, lime and coriander hummus, grapes and olives. A mini stove magically appears to heat the leek and potato soup Tom made last night.

With the day's magical mix of fairy-tale forest and mysterious sculptures – our favourite is Andy Goldsworthy's *Taking a Wall for a Walk*, an awesome winding drystone wall tucked between trees, part forest snake, part swirling, moss-covered boundary – and the deep connection we've made with these gentle, wise animals, it feels as though Fin and I have tapped into some supernatural Lakeland energy. I gratefully memory bank it as one of those precious mother-and-son bonding experiences, which ultimately is what slow family travel is all about.

ADDED ADVENTURE: ULLSWATER, GRASMERE & WINDERMERE

Take your kids to the Lake District, which was awarded UNESCO World Heritage Status in July 2017, and you're stepping into a destination on a par with some of the most sought-after places in the world. Sprawling across northwest England, the UK's second largest national park after the Cairngorms offers 912 square miles of awesome lakes scooped out by glaciers in the last Ice Age and mountains that inspired the 19th-century Romantic poets – this sublime landscape will remind your children of just how mighty nature can be.

The Lakes are wildly popular these days, but plan well and you'll find a slow family treasure bursting with memorable experiences – from hearty hiking to luxury adventure playgrounds, active watersports to literary attractions.

Ullswater. ▶

"This sublime landscape will remind your children of just how mighty nature can be."

ULLSWATER

Long and skinny at 7½ miles long and less than a mile across, Ullswater is the second-largest lake in England. For a classic family day out, take a mini voyage with **Ullswater Steamers** (⊘ ullswater-steamers.co.uk). Board the *Western Belle* and stay on deck to see the district's highest mountains, including Helvellyn at 3,117ft, or head down below to the snug with its tiny café and old-school copies of *The Ullswater Times* which look like something out of a Wes Anderson movie. Disembark at **Aira Force** (⊘ nationaltrust.org.uk) for the pretty woodland walk to the 65ft waterfall; this could take up to an hour with ambling children in tow.

If you fancy a family lake swim but need a bit of support to do so, contact cold-water expert Colin Hill of **Chill Swim** (⊘ chillswim.com). Colin, who is a super guide, and his team take families with children over 11 out on the lake and even offer stargazing night swims under the light of the Milky Way, accompanied by the soft glow of your light-up tow float. If an SUP session is more up your street, check out Adrian Bacon, whose **Ullswater Paddleboarding** (⊘ ullswaterpaddleboarding. co.uk) gets all ages up on boards and exploring the lake.

Back on dry land, **Lowther Castle** (⊘ lowthercastle.org), about two miles east of the top of Ullswater Lake, is well worth a visit. Families can learn about this 19th-century pile's quirky ancestry, but it's the gardens that will delight. Discover fairy-tale follies and the incredible avenue of yew trees where red squirrels appear for the eagle eyed. Let kids stumble upon the Lost Castle, a vast mock wooden castle that echoes the real thing, at the heart of one of the UK's largest adventure playgrounds. Children can lose themselves charging around the battlements, hurtling down slides and shooting along zip lines. There's a stylish café to check out after all the fun, and a cycle hub from where you can explore estate trails on all-terrain or electric bikes.

Thacka Beck Nature Reserve (⊘ cumbriawildlifetrust.org.uk), further north, is an easy place to introduce children to birdlife, from mallards and moorhens in winter to swallows, house martins and swifts in summer. Its hay meadows, wet grassland, scrub, hedges, ponds and the beck create flood protection for Penrith, so it provides a good lesson in habitat preservation. Check out their family conservation days.

---

1 Ullswater Steamers. **2** The Lost Castle, Lowther Castle. **3** Splashing about in the lake. **4** Aira Force. ▶

GRASMERE

William Wordsworth believed poetry was the shortcut to the human soul. Nowhere will you be able to give your kids a greater understanding of this Romantic poet and his forward-thinking views on art and nature than at **Dove Cottage** (⌀ wordsworth.org.uk) in the quintessentially Lakeland village of Grasmere. Wordsworth moved into this modest little white house in 1799 when he was just 29, with his sister Dorothy and later his wife Mary, dwelling here for eight and a half years. It was here that he wrote what became his guide to the Lakes and some of his most influential poetry, while his sister wrote her now famous journal. He was also one of the pioneers of the National Trust and an early proponent of the region becoming designated a national park, calling for the Lake District to become 'a sort of national property'. In 2020, on the 250th anniversary of his birth, the house was reconfigured as a home rather than a museum to give visitors a better understanding of how the Wordsworths would have existed according to their philosophy of 'plain living and high thinking'.

In the drawing room, tea cups are laid out for afternoon tea beside the original grandfather clock, and mixing bowls and a recipe for gingerbread stand ready and waiting in the kitchen. One of the most intriguing spaces is Dorothy's bedroom, lined with old copies of *The Times* for insulation from the damp coming up below from the buttery. Children are encouraged to have a hands-on experience, trying out the beds and using baskets to pick up old-fashioned household objects such as socks and playing cards, engaging with how life must have been back then, way before our digital age.

Next door to the cottage is a state-of-the-art museum all about the Wordsworths. Here younger visitors can raid the art cart, full of inventive suggestions: they might pick up a charade card inviting them to 'pretend to compose a poem out loud while pacing up and down', or illustrate a passage from Dorothy's journal with coloured pencils and card. There's even a Minecraft Dove Cottage on an iPad, depicting moments from Wordsworth's long poem, *The Prelude*.

Outside, there's a short woodland orchard trail and a moss hut in the sensory garden that hosts 'Little Wanderers' sessions for under-fives with crafts, sing-songs, story time and bug-hotel explorations.

Step outside the museum and you immediately see why the Wordsworths were so inspired by nature. Helm Crag lies to the north, towering over Grasmere at an elevation of 1,329ft. Ask your children if they can spot the shapes of a lion and a lamb in the rocks.

Less than a mile away across the river, Wordsworth's later home, **Allan Bank** (⊘ nationaltrust.org.uk), is a relaxed place to visit with kids. This former home of National Trust co-founder Canon Rawnsley has beautiful views of Grasmere Lake and fells from its woodland grounds, home to red squirrels and pretty picnic spots.

It's well worth spending some time in the village of Grasmere itself, which Wordsworth called 'the loveliest spot that man hath ever found'. A favourite destination is **Grasmere Gingerbread** (⊘ grasmeregingerbread.co.uk) which celebrates Victorian cook Sarah Nelson's spicy take on that very British sweet treat. Blow your children's minds by informing them that this tiny shop was built in 1630 as the village school – and that Wordsworth taught here.

WINDERMERE

Lake Windermere, the largest lake in England, a mighty 11 miles from north to south, is a force of nature that once seen no child will ever forget. Surrounded by mountain peaks and pretty villages, it may be on a well-trodden tourist path, but that doesn't mean it's not worth taking the slow approach. The north end is the most commercialised, and the southern end less developed. A good way to orientate yourself is with a lake cruise. **Windermere Lake Cruises** (⊘ windermere-lakecruises.co.uk) offers old-fashioned cruiser sailings from 45 minutes to four hours, sailing between Ambleside in the north, Bowness halfway down and Lakeside in the south. If you prefer a greener approach, hire yourself a new electric Fantail boat with **Windermere Boat Hire** (⊘ windermere-boat-hire.co.uk). Kids will love the little FM radio and Bluetooth stereo speakers and central table with cup holders. These covered boats are perfect for rainy weather as you can see out through the transparent sides. Give the children a map of the lake and go explore.

On the southwest side of the lake, the mighty Graythwaite Estate is the headquarters for **Graythwaite Adventure** (⊘ graythwaiteadventure. co.uk). Slow, experiential travel is at the heart of what this enthusiastic young team offers, including outdoor survival courses in the grounds of the grand private estate. Depending on the age and attention span of your children, bushcraft sessions can last anything from an hour to a full day, teaching the joys of outdoor living, respecting and harnessing

nature through a variety of ancient skills. Typically these include friction fire-lighting, open-fire cooking, shelter building, wood carving and weapon making. During the day you may spot ospreys, golden eagles or peregrine falcons wheeling overhead, plus red squirrels and pine martens on the ground, and otters in the water. Another highlight is an off-road adventure in a Land Rover Defender. With an instructor in the vehicle, you negotiate steep inclines, epic leans and water crossings, catching stunning views of Lake Windermere. And if you want to combine bushcraft or 4x4 adventures with a host of other activities, including archery, axe throwing, stand-up paddleboarding, canoeing and a RIB ride around the lake, a full- or half-day of family fun can be tailor-made with an ice-cream stop in Bowness thrown in for good measure.

"Children can meet a boat builder and learn about traditional craft skills or sail their own model boat."

Bowness gets extremely crowded in summer, but there is one attraction that's well worth a look, especially on a rainy day. The **Windermere Jetty Museum** (⊘ windermerejetty.org) is a collection of vast modern boatshed spaces dedicated to the vessels and people that make this area so special. It's all about storytelling here, via multimedia displays and an impressive collection of motorboats, steam launches, sailing yachts and record-breaking speed boats in the interactive galleries built right over the water, essentially making the lake part of the museum. Children can meet a real-life boat builder and learn about traditional craft skills, take a cruise on a restored Edwardian launch or sail their own model boat on an outdoor boating pond. The museum could also provide your child's introduction to the world of Arthur Ransome's *Swallows and Amazons* as they watch an animation of the adventures of John, Susan, Titty and Roger, and view some of the author's real-life illustrations and manuscripts.

The other great children's author and illustrator inspired by the Lake District was, of course, Beatrix Potter, who was also one of our earliest conservationists. Her creativity and exuberance for the Lakes and all its creatures comes through loud and clear on a visit to her beloved farmhouse **Hill Top** (⊘ nationaltrust.org.uk), a couple of miles west of Windermere towards Esthwaite Water, which she bequeathed to

◄ **1** Traversing Lake Windermere with Windermere Lake Cruises. **2** Kayaking on Lake Windermere. **3** Wordsworth's Dove Cottage, Grasmere.

FAMILY BUSHCAMP WITH WOODMATTERS

Footprint Building, Patterdale Rd, Windermere LA23 1NH ⊘ woodmatters.org.uk; age: all ages; intrepid level: ②; groups of about six families per camp; held in May & October

My kids and I arrive with just a sleeping bag and a mat each. Our first task of the weekend is to build our own shelter out of sticks and tarpaulin, no tents or electricity in sight. Luckily we have the very lovely Ro and Gareth Thomas, who have lived in the Lake District for 22 years, to lead the way. Their Woodmatters family bushcamps are run in partnership with the National Trust from Footprint, a beautiful canopied woodland camp in Windermere. They also find time to run community wood-share schemes, make charcoal and firewood, and carry out conservation work in the woods. 'Everything we do centres around positive human connections with local woodlands and the emotional and physical benefits of that deepening connection to the natural world around us,' Ro tells me as her two children, Orin, 13 and Maya, 11, lend a hand. 'It's a very supportive, nurturing environment and having our two children assisting gives families the confidence to come,' she adds.

The whole weekend is based around living comfortably in the woodland. A key element entails building a fire to cook on, be that with traditional flint and steel or friction firelighting with a bow drill. My kids and I learn how to use different tools safely, including saws and whittling tools, and even make string out of leaves which is immensely satisfying.

'We look at the ways humans have interacted with all these primitive skills over the centuries,' says Ro. 'We teach lots of different wildlife-tracking skills so you can understand all the different flora and fauna in the woodland. We look for clues, like poo or nibbled nuts, to see where badgers, foxes and squirrels might have been and where they are going.'

the National Trust. Wandering around her house and garden is like stepping into the pages of *The Tale of Peter Rabbit* or *Mrs. Tiggy-Winkle*. It's wonderful to stroll through the pretty village of **Near Sawrey** where Potter found much inspiration, and just up from Hill Top is **Eccles Tarn**, where she often went rowing and sketching with her husband. Alternatively, head a mile downhill and you'll reach **Esthwaite Water**, Potter's favourite lake and home of Jeremy Fisher.

At the **Beatrix Potter Gallery** in Hawkshead (⊘ nationaltrust.org.uk), north of Esthwaite Water, budding artists will be inspired by her original artworks and illustrations. Hawkshead is also home to the **Children's Chocolate Factory** (⊘ chocolatefactoryhawkshead.co.uk), where kids can create their very own chocolate bar or animal.

There's much camaraderie in the camp and all ages help one another. 'It's not a kids' camp that the adults come along on,' says Ro. 'It's for every single person in the family and each time it's slightly different, depending on whether you come with a three-year-old or a 16-year-old.'

After surviving two nights under canvas and communing with the sounds and smells of the forest, we're all feeling the benefits of getting closer to nature. With no phone signal or charging points, everyone is truly present and we all naturally start to tell stories round the fire in the evening and sing songs. As we pack up to go and return to the so-called comforts of modern living – from central heating to mobiles, we're so very much richer for our forest time together, and feel fortified by the knowledge that we could just about survive in a woodland setting.

ROMAN SAMBORSKYI/S

The south end of Windermere offers the gentlest of walks for families. Make your way up to **Gummer's How**, an easy 1.4-mile walk, with awe-inspiring 360° views down the full length of Windermere and the Old Man of Coniston, one of the best-loved fells in the region. Alternatively, you could pay the admission charge to explore **Fell Foot** (⚲ nationaltrust.org.uk), where a lowland lakeshore walk has the added appeal of a playground and easy family watersports including rowboat hire, kayaking and paddleboarding. Close by is the **Lakeside & Haverthwaite Railway** (⚲ lakesiderailway.co.uk) where you can hop on a steam train for the 18-minute ride between the villages of Haverthwaite and Lakeside. Kids will also love the engine shed and woodland playground with zip wire.

PRACTICALITIES

FAMILY-FRIENDLY SLEEPS

Another Place ⟨⟩ another.place. At this five-star hotel on the shores of Ullswater it's all about getting out on to the lakes and mountains, with kayaking, archery by the water, night walks, ghyll scrambling, rock climbing and overnight camping on the lake shore. Parents can borrow off-road Micralite strollers to get out and about. The hotel is a delight, with beautiful interconnecting rooms, complimentary Tunnock's teacakes, relaxed restaurants and an OFSTED-registered kids' space with wood cabin, safari tent and woodland area; supervised sessions here include forest skills. There's a heated indoor pool, too, with dedicated family swim times.

Edenhall Estate ⟨⟩ edenhallestate.com. This grand family-owned estate in the Eden Valley, north of Lake Windermere, offers a range of self-catering accommodation. Family-friendly options include Sala Cottage, a beautifully designed space sleeping six.

Glamping at Graythwaite
⟨⟩ graythwaiteadventure.co.uk. From July to September, this innovative activity company (page 341), based on the shores of Lake Windermere, hosts a pop-up glamping site. There are 40 sturdy bell tents, a chill-out glamping hut featuring table football and music, a volleyball court, an on-site shop for essentials and weekly visits from a pizza van.

Hinterlandes ⟨⟩ hinterlandes. com. Luxurious yet quirky off-grid accommodation in the spirit of the Tiny House Movement. The converted bus, cabin, hidden hut and Airstream all move to different Lakeland locations every 56 days, leaving no footprint. The large black cabin is ideal for families and sleeps two adults and two children.

Into the Woods
⟨⟩ intothewoodscumbria.co.uk. This family-run farm in the Eden Valley offers a range of woodland accommodation including the Tree House, which sleeps six, with stylish interiors, hot tub, wood burner, underfloor heating and ping-pong table.

Lake District Farm ⟨⟩ featherdown. co.uk. Stay on the Stobart family's sheep and cattle farm near the village of Hesket Newmarket, north of Ullswater, in one of two safari tents sleeping up to six. Children can help out on the farm and feed the lambs in lambing season.

The Quiet Site ⟨⟩ thequietsite.co.uk. This award-winning eco holiday park overlooking Ullswater offers luxury glamping cabins, timber camping pods, underground Hobbit Holes and self-catering cottages, as well as all-weather tent pitches and hardstanding pitches for caravans and motorhomes. New sustainable 'Gingerbread Houses' sleep two adults and up to four kids. The Quiet Bite is a take-away coffee and pizza hut, and there's also a campers' kitchen, children's games room, dog and boot wash room, laundry room and bike store.

The Samling ⌂ thesamlinghotel.co.uk. This upmarket hotel on the shores of Lake Windermere offers plush accommodation including cottages suitable for families with kids over eight. Foodie families will love the seasonal menu by Chef Robby Jenks. Wilderness Adventure by The Samling, meanwhile, takes the hotel's luxury outdoors, into a hillside meadow setting where 'prospector tents' sleeping four come with a personal butler and chef.

Storrs Hall ⌂ storrshall.com. Storrs Hall is a luxurious Georgian mansion hotel with a glorious setting right on the southeastern side of Lake Windermere. Enormous high-ceilinged bedrooms are large enough for a huge double plus a sofa bed and Z-beds, and bathrooms have waterfall showers and TVs. A Tiny Tots Afternoon Tea features Beatrix Potter crockery and tiny cake stands with bunny-shaped sandwiches.

Victorian House Hotel
⌂ victorianhousehotel.co.uk. This Grasmere village B&B is perfectly placed to explore the area. The largest suite comes with a double bed and sofa bed plus cots if required; you can even set up a playful wigwam. A cute shepherd's hut at the bottom of the garden by the river suits teens or a single parent and child.

The Yan ⌂ theyan.co.uk. Just outside Grasmere, this stone-built boutique hotel is a great base for foodie families, with a renowned bistro serving hearty seasonal dishes perfect for satisfying broods who've been out all day in the fresh air. The ultra-modern rooms sleep up to four, and some are dog friendly.

KID-FRIENDLY EATS

Grasmere Pizza Co. ⌂ grasmerepizza. co.uk. A little artisanal pizza shack in the village, where inventive toppings include Oink Oink (tomato, locally sourced salami, cheddar and mozzarella). Eat in or take-away.

Lakeland Farm Kitchen
⌂ lakelandfarmvisitorcentre.co.uk. Rock up for breakfast, lunch or Sunday roast at this welcoming restaurant between Windermere and Staveley on the A591. The L'al Farmer's menu for kids features staples such as cheese and tomato omelette with chips and salad. Take the opportunity to learn more about traditional farming methods with sheepdog demonstrations and sheep shearing, drystone walling and wool spinning.

Lakeshore Café at Windermere Jetty Museum ⌂ lakelandarts.org.uk. Built into the modern museum on the lake shore in Bowness, this café has an impressive outdoor terrace right on the lake with oversized tables perfect for family gatherings. The Little Skippers menu features easy pleasers such as creamy macaroni with ham and peas.

Low Sizergh Barn ⌂ lowsizerghbarn. co.uk. This beautiful farm near Kendal is home to a daytime café serving great pizzas (which you can also take-away) and a farm shop where you can take your own bottles to fill with organic raw milk and buy produce from the on-site market garden. There's camping too, if you fancy.

Old Hall Farm ⬧ oldhallfarmbouth. com. Jersey ice-cream parlour between the southern tip of Lake Windermere and Coniston, where kids can meet the Jersey cows and build their own ice-cream sundaes or waffles. Shire horses, steam engines and tractor-driving experiences all add to the fun.

Tweedies ⬧ tweediesgrasmere.com. This friendly pub-style restaurant in Grasmere is a good choice for a relaxed meal. Burgers and craft beer top the list for grown-ups, while fish and chips, chicken goujons and macaroni cheese feature on the kids' menu.

BEFORE YOU GO

Check the erratic weather and go prepared for rain or shine, taking a good look at the advice from the national park authority (⬧ lakedistrict.gov.uk/ visiting/plan-your-visit). The website also includes 50 suggested 'Miles without Stiles' routes across the national park suitable for those with mobility issues, including families with pushchairs and wheelchair users.

MORE INFO

Cumbria Tourism ⬧ golakes.co.uk
Lake District National Park
⬧ lakedistrict.gov.uk

23
NORTH YORKSHIRE

God's Own Country delivers world-class family adventures from York via the moors to the fossil-rich coastline.

TOP FAMILY EXPERIENCE
FOSSIL HUNTING ON WHITBY BEACH WITH HIDDEN HORIZONS

BEST FOR KIDS AGED: 5–12
WHEN TO GO: Year-round, but winter weather brings more fossils ashore
INTREPID LEVEL: ②
ADDED ADVENTURE: Viking history, chocolate making, adventure cycling, steam trains, cooking classes, ghost tours, stargazing, treetop trails
TIME: One to two weeks

JURASSIC PARK: AN AMMONITE ADVENTURE

A good meeting point is at the foot of 199 Steps, Whitby YO22 4DF ⏣ hiddenhorizons.co.uk; two-hour fossil-hunting trips are available year-round, & are in fact better in winter when stormy seas bring in more rocks. Wellies or stout footwear are recommended, & a bucket to put your finds in. Hidden Horizons also offers coastal foraging/fossil-hunting combination trips; their fossil shop in Scarborough is well worth a look, too.

'Essentially what we've got is 50 million years of earth history laid out in front of us,' exclaims fossil expert and Hidden Horizons founder Will Watts enthusiastically. My kids gaze up at the mighty cliffs rising up from Whitby Beach, the harbour behind us and the famous Gothic abbey tucked up on the headland. I can sense their minds whirring, as is mine, trying to put an impossible timeline in place.

'If we start at the top of the cliff,' Will continues, 'it's made of those big blocky layers of yellow rock. That's sandstone, formed on the banks of a Mississippi-scale river that flowed north to south about 165

million years ago, which makes them Middle Jurassic. Those rivers were surrounded by forests and very lush vegetation, where dinosaurs roamed. If we're lucky we might find a block of sandstone with a dinosaur footprint in it!'

There are gasps of excitement all round as we walk further along the beach and Will encapsulates in a nutshell what we're here to find.

'As we come down the cliff, we go through some multicoloured layers of greys and browns and oranges – they are essentially mud stones formed on the bottom of oceans. At the bottom are grey rocks which are 200 million years old – the Lower Jurassic. Those oceans were 330ft deep and anoxic – which means there was no oxygen there most of the time. Things at the surface died, sank to the seabed and weren't eaten by large creatures, so they had a good chance of turning into fossils. They became buried by mud and sand, then crushed, pressurised, heated up and baked. A process otherwise known as digenesis.

'And for the last 60 million years or so they've been coming back up to the surface. It is pure fluke that we have these rocks at sea level today. They are nothing to do with the North Sea. That's a completely different environment. We were roughly where Morocco was on the planet when these rocks were formed. And we were under water!'

Will admits that all of this information is a bit of a brain melt, and hard for an adult to get a handle on, never mind a child, but it's certainly exciting and the basis of what we're about to discover. Will asks us all to find three interesting stones. My kids and I pick up what turns out to be a piece of sandstone, and a piece of quartz from Scotland which could be two billion years old. So far, so epic.

What we're really looking for, though, are grey sedimentary rocks with a telltale fault line that could mark the edge of an ammonite. Will describes it as resembling a burger in a bun or a tractor-tyre mark. He soon finds a rock the size of his palm that he thinks looks promising, reaches into his rucksack for a hammer and starts tapping away at the fault line. Suddenly the rock gives way, half of it shearing off dramatically, and inside is the most incredible ammonite.

'You are the first living creatures to see that for 185 million years,' Will says, handing the two sides to each of my children, which they repeatedly slot back together and open again, as if to recapture that

◄ Fossil hunting on the beach with Will Watts.

moment of discovery. Still giddy from this find, we pick up stones that look like fossilised shells. Will tells us they are Devil's Toenails – Jurassic oysters about two million years old.

'It's all about looking with your eyes, being outside and finding the slow adventures,' he says. With 185 million years in our pockets, we can only agree.

ADDED ADVENTURE: FROM VIKINGS TO VAMPIRES

North Yorkshire offers the perfect multi-centre holiday: an ancient city, epic rolling countryside and a dramatic coast, with as many highlights as you want to pack in. York is one of the country's great cities, with a palpable sense of history that is made very accessible for children of all ages. It's fun, for example, to follow the story of our railways and to carry the theme beyond the city – admiring Stephenson's *Rocket* at the National Railway Museum and then jumping aboard a real-life steam train and chugging through the valleys of the Yorkshire moors to a quaint seaside railway station. There's more history – and splendid watersports – on the coast, where Whitby makes a fabulous, atmospheric base, while out on the vast moors you'll find a genuine, and precious, sense of remoteness. It's enough to make your children want to pen a poem or, at the very least, run wild!

YORK

The ancient city of **York** is the perfect, walkable metropolis to explore with kids, its cobbled streets excelling in child-friendly attractions. A good place to start is **York Minster** (*⊘* yorkminster.org), a building so imposing that even the most jaded teenager can't fail to look up in awe. Ask children to imagine a time before digital devices, and to feel what it must have been like to gaze up at those vast stained-glass windows, showering down rainbows of light brighter than any computer screen. Just wandering around you'll find quirky religious objects such as the extraordinary box for formal church capes, shaped like an enormous piece of cheese. There's also a creepy crypt to explore and a museum holding the remains of Roman barracks, You can climb the 275 steps to the top of the Central Tower (for ages eight and above), contending with medieval and Gothic gargoyles, for panoramic city views.

For a touch of time travel, your next stop should be the **JORVIK Viking Centre** (⊘ jorvikvikingcentre.co.uk), a few minutes' walk to the south. The centre opened in 1984, following a five-year archaeological excavation that uncovered over 40,000 artefacts from the 10th century onwards. Today families board an open carriage to be transported back more than a thousand years for a nosy around Coppergate street in AD960. It turns out that it's a hive of activity and small industry – carving antlers, dying wool, working with leather. Fishermen sit next to their barrels full of squirming eels and couples argue in Old Norse while a priest administers last rites. With earthy smells to complete the sensory experience, and plenty of Vikings around to ask questions about how they lived, this is a historical experience like no other.

Carry on your exploration of York with a free, self-guided **Little Vikings I Spy Trail** (⊘ little-vikings.co.uk). The circular trail starts and ends at the Visit York Information Centre on Museum Street, where you can pick up the map (also available to download from the website); there are 22 things to discover en route, and you're sent down atmospheric streets such as The Shambles where children really will think they've stepped into Diagon Alley. Depending on what you want to linger over, it could take between a couple of hours and a full day.

A highlight on the route is the **National Railway Museum** (⊘ railwaymuseum.org.uk) where you can see all manner of classic locomotives including the revolutionary Stephenson's *Rocket*. This superb museum can't fail but fire the kids' enthusiasm for what we now regard as our greatest method of slow travel.

Another recommended stop on the trail is **York's Chocolate Story** (⊘ yorkschocolatestory.com), which teaches families about the importance of chocolate in the history of the city – Terry's, Cravens and Rowntree's all had their factories here. You're invited to step back in time once again with the reconstruction of a historic sweet shop, dating back to 1862 when Henry Isaac Rowntree, a visionary Quaker businessman and social reformer, founded his confectionery company. Learn about iconic products, including Terry's Chocolate Orange, which was brought out in 1932 originally as an apple, and observe how modern marketing was born with branding for Smarties, Polos (where marketers were effectively selling a hole!), Black Magic chocolates and the famous Kit Kat, with one of the most memorable marketing slogans of them all: 'Have a Break, Have A Kit Kat'. At the end of the tour, you can all get

DAVID IONUT/S

NATIONAL RAILWAY MUSEUM

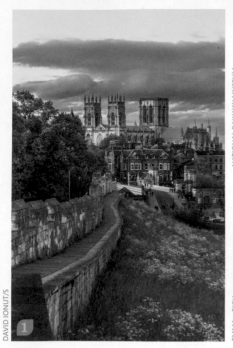

EMMA + RICH

CKTRAVELS.COM/S

MANOR PHOTOGRAPHY/A

JANE ANDERSON

hands on and create your own chocolate lollies, not to mention eat an awful lot of sweet stuff.

If that has budding chefs wanting more, check out the parent-and-child cooking sessions at the **Grand Cookery School** (∂ thegrandyork. co.uk). This state-of-the-art school, around the back of York's five-star railway hotel (page 366), gives children a taste of what it's like to be a professional chef. There's no expense spared on top-notch equipment, and the atmosphere is one of friendly professionalism as chef Andrew guides children aged seven to 14 through how to make fresh ravioli, meatballs, cupcakes, biscuits and chocolate bars; over-14s can progress to kormas and spectacular pork pies. As well as taking home the recipes and the life skills, you also get to sit down and eat your creations for lunch.

A great way to end a visit to York is with a ghost tour. **The Deathly Dark Tours** (∂ doriandeathly.co.uk) is one of the best, Dorian's wit and delivery making children giggle and shift nervously as they hear all about the dark side of this incredible city. It's best suited to children aged eight and up; during the summer Dorian presents 'The Grimly Gross Tour', tailored to younger audiences, with water-pistol duels and an exploration of Viking poo.

THE NORTH YORK MOORS
The **North York Moors National Park** (∂ northyorkmoors.org.uk), north of York and covering 554 square miles out to the coast, may not be one of our most famous national parks, but it's one of the best for family adventures. Encompassing ancient, heather-covered moorland, forest, dales and a phenomenal Jurassic coast, this is the place to slow down and take a few nights to reset and enjoy one another's company.

A wonderful way to experience the varied beauty of the North York Moors while getting your hearts pumping is to cycle. The knowledgeable staff at **Sutton Bank Bikes** (∂ suttonbankbikes.co.uk), at **Sutton Bank National Park Centre** on the western edge of the park, between Thirsk and Helmsley, will kit you all out with the right size and type of bike and advise which of Sutton Bank's five interlinked trails to take. These include an exciting pump track on which kids can learn how to use suspension

◀ **1** City walls and York Minster. **2** The National Railway Museum. **3** The Deathly Dark Tour of York. **4** York's Chocolate Story. **5** Immersive fun at JORVIK. **6** Pie making at the Grand Cookery School.

"Encompassing ancient, heather-covered moorland, forest, dales and a phenomenal Jurassic coast, the North York Moors National Park is the place to slow down and take a few nights to reset and enjoy one another's company."

HELEN HOTSON/S

and take turns, and Cyclo Cross, an exhilarating 1½-mile race course which kids love tearing around. The three-mile cliff trail is suitable for beginners and young children, but for a longer ride with children who are competent cyclists, the 5½-mile green/blue Fort Trail and the fuller seven-mile full blue Fort Trail take you through deep forest, hurtling round the edges of wheat fields, the corn whipping against your legs, and along undulating paths with incredible escarpment views. In spring and summer, watch out for skylarks, house martins and butterflies along the way.

Sutton Bank is part of the **Dark Skies park** (⊘ northyorkmoors.org. uk/darkskiesfriendly); ask at the Sutton Bank National Park Centre about night cycle rides, stargazing, space-related crafting sessions, night navigation and nocturnal wildlife tracking. The **North York Moors Dark Skies Festival** (⊘ darkskiesnationalparks.org.uk), in February and October, includes twilight mindfulness walks run by **Adventures of the Soul** (⊘ adventuresforthesoul.co.uk), stargazing and more.

If your kids are up for a walk, choose a bite-sized piece of the 109-mile **Cleveland Way National Trail** (⊘ nationaltrail.co.uk), which crosses from the western side of the moors at Helmsley right over to Saltburn-by-the-Sea (page 365).

For a memorable day out, **Castle Howard** (⊘ castlehoward.co.uk) in the Howardian Hills in the south of the national park, is one of the UK's grandest country piles, home to the Howard family for over 300 years. Older parents and grandparents will forever associate it with the 1980s TV series, *Brideshead Revisited*. Make sure you drive or cycle down the Avenue, a pin-straight, tree-lined road that runs south to north for five miles past obelisks and beneath pyramid arches. The gardens are as big an attraction as the house, especially for children, who will love exploring the follies and the woodland nature trails in Ray Wood, and picnicking by the lake. There's an even bigger treat in store in the shape of **Skelf Island Adventure Playground**, a treetop adventure that invites children to explore nest structures in the trees, connected by exciting rope bridges strung over the lake, along with slides, zip wires, tunnels and nets. There are elusive 'skelves' to spot along the way, along with rabbits, butterflies, hedgehogs and toadstools.

◀ The North York Moors National Park, looking out across Robin Hood's Bay. **1** Cycle trail at Sutton Bank. **2** North Yorkshire Moors Railway. **3** Exploring the grounds of Castle Howard. ▶

North of Castle Howard, **Dalby Forest** (⊘ forestryengland.uk) has 43 miles of cycle trails through forest and moorlands, and features a Zog the Dragon Trail and a Gruffalo orienteering map-reading challenge for little ones. Older children and adults can take part in tree climbing, paint balling and outdoor laser combat at the **Dalby Activity Centre** (⊘ dalbyactivitycentre.co.uk) or swoop along high rope walkways, Tarzan swings and zip lines at **Go Ape** (⊘ goape.co.uk).

Finally, take the weight off your feet and recreate the heady days of steam locomotives with a trip on the **North Yorkshire Moors Railway** (⊘ nymr.co.uk), which cuts a picturesque swathe through the wooded valleys of the moors from Pickering to Whitby. Kids will love boarding the train at the pretty station of Grosmont and travelling in an old-fashioned carriage with an old-fashioned paper ticket for the 20-minute ride to Goathland, which stood in for Hogsmeade Station in the first *Harry Potter* film. It makes a neat round trip to walk back along the Rail Trail from Goathland to Grosmont (1hr 30mins), a woodland path that's suitable for buggies, passing derelict iron works and the chocolate-coloured Murk Esk tributary along the way.

WHITBY & THE NORTH YORKSHIRE COAST

Whitby, at the mouth of River Esk where the North York Moors meet the North Sea, is an ancient harbour town that has ignited the imaginations of storytellers and explorers over its long history. There's a sense of intrigue here that's hard to put your finger on: children's imaginations will certainly be set alight by the ghostly shape of the Gothic abbey, which looms high on the headland. Whether you arrive by steam train on the North Yorkshire Moors Railway (page 367), or have made the spectacular drive over the moors, this coastal town has a distinct aura.

Down by the harbour, there's old-fashioned seaside fun to be had with fish 'n' chip kiosks, amusement arcades and sweet shops selling rainbow-coloured rock. The working swing bridge is well worth a look and if you walk out to the end of the pier there's a good chance you'll spot bottlenose dolphin playing in the waves. In September, **Whitby Whale Watching** (⊘ whitbywhalewatching.net) boats head out from the harbour into the North Sea to spot minke, fin, sei and

---

1 Climb Whitby's 199 steps to reach Whitby Abbey. **2** Learn to surf at Saltburn-by-the-Sea's surf school. ▶

ALPACA WALK & FARM TOUR

The Private Hill, Thrussendale Farm, Acklam YO17 9RG ⊘ theprivatehill.co.uk; 📷 @theprivatehill; age: 8+ or 12+ to lead an alpaca; intrepid level: ①

If there's one thing you should know about alpacas, it's that they have the softest wool in the world, especially the extra thick bun between their ears, sometimes called a topknot and guaranteed to make your children oooh and aaah. My two certainly did when they first met Renoir, Perseus and Ziggy at The Private Hill, a glampsite on the edge of the North Yorkshire Wolds that forms part of Thrussendale Farm, a diversified working farm business.

However much they may look like oversized fluffy toys, alpacas are hardcore, having originated in the high Andes of South America. They may be pack animals but they all have distinct personalities, as our walking guide Charlie, who helps out on the farm and grew up nearby, is keen to point out to us.

'Renoir is very nice natured and probably the best to walk with. Perseus (Percy to his friends) is big and cuddly and Ziggy is very vocal,' he tells us as we stand by The Private Hill's impressive geodomes getting acquainted. With a bit of encouragement from Charlie, we're able to stroke them and take hold of their simple rope harnesses for our walk around Thrussendale's farmland, which has panoramic views west across the Yorkshire Wolds, with Leeds and York in the far, far distance.

It's soon clear who's in charge, as Renoir, Percy and Ziggy will only walk in a caravan formation with Renoir out front as the dominant male. Charlie tells us that in the wild alpacas move around in herds of up to 100. 'I think of them a bit like a hybrid of many other animals,' he says. 'They move a bit like deer, they have rabbit-like noses, two-toed feet like camels and make a sound like Chewbacca from *Star Wars*!'

They may have originated in the Andes, but Renoir, Percy and Ziggy seem pretty happy here in North Yorkshire and now that everyone's got to know one another my children love walking beside them, giggling when they veer off to do some grass nibbling or to occasionally stop stubbornly by an open gate refusing to go through.

Charlie explains that alpaca wool or fibre is especially warm when knitted, making it superb for jumpers, scarves, gloves and blankets. 'It's odd to think that an animal coat is something we end up wearing,' comments my son, quite rightly. Charlie explains that unlike sheep, alpacas have no lanolin in their fleeces, and so if they get wet the water penetrates down to their skin and they can easily catch pneumonia, which is why they have a field shelter for spring and summer, and are housed indoors in the wet winter weather.

humpback whales; even outside whale season, in summer or in other autumn months, it's worth heading out for a scenic cruise – vast shoals of herring attract sharks, seals and seabirds including gannets,

As we stroll, Charlie chats about the grassland farm where sheep are grazed and haylage and silage is made. The farm is part of a Countryside Stewardship scheme, with plans to increase wildlife and nature habitats. He points out the important wildlife corridors, created to to enhance ponds, woodland and hedgerows and to attract wildflowers, birds, insects and pollinators. We see a field full of clovers, vetches and sainfoin, all great for attracting insects.

'The ongoing programme of hedgerow planting helps to create safe nesting cover for birds and a diet of berries in the autumn,' explains Charlie. He tells us that curlews have returned. 'We also have foxes, badgers and bluebells in our ancient woodland at the north end of the farm, along with a resident barn owls.' Diversifying into tourism – in which the alpacas play an important part – has meant that this small farm is more able to create a sustainable future for itself.

At the end of our ninety-minute stroll, we return the alpacas to their their smart wooden shelter filled with fresh hay and right next door to the chickens. My kids give them a final tickle of their topknots before we head off to the on-site café for homemade alpaca-shaped biscuits, leaving Renoir, Percy and Ziggy to munch their hay.

JANE ANDERSON

guillemots, razorbills, puffins, fulmar, kittiwake and cormorants. The wide, sandy stretch of the beach north of the harbour is great for beach games and swimming.

MICRO-VOLUNTEERING IN THE NATIONAL PARK

The **North York Moors National Park** is full of opportunities for family micro-volunteering adventures, from joining a two-minute beach clean to downloading the **iNaturalist** app and contributing to the National Parks UK **Look Wild** project. The app helps children and adults alike to identify the local wildlife; the idea is that you then upload photos of interesting animals or plants that you encounter on the North York Moors and the project team record what's out there.

Back on dry land, families can delve into the history of jet, a black, semi-precious stone made from fossilised monkey puzzle trees preserved in Jurassic rocks. Whitby jet is said to be some of the highest quality in the world and was beloved by the Victorians who crafted it into all manner of jewellery. At the **Whitby Jet Heritage Centre** (⊘ whitbyjet.co.uk) you can see the historic machinery from a Victorian jet workshop and a contemporary jet jeweller at work.

Nearby are the 199 well-trodden steps leading up to **St Mary's Church** and the mighty **Whitby Abbey** (⊘ english-heritage.org.uk). Challenge your children to climb the steps and count them. Kids' brows may furrow as they're told that this splendid ruin was the inspiration for the story of *Dracula*. Author Bram Stoker went on holiday to Whitby back in 1890 and came across tales of Vlad Dracul, the original story of Count Dracula, in the town library. He also drew inspiration from local legends of a ghostly black dog and the shipwreck of the *Dmitri*. In his famous novel, the eponymous vampire first enters England on a boat at Whitby. In the abbey's exhibition space, you can see a first edition of *Dracula* signed by Stoker in 1901, on sale at the time for six shillings. How far from our digital world this old book seems and yet how powerful still is the impact of the story.

Another famous figure associated with this atmospheric town is explorer Captain James Cook: you can visit his former home on Grape Lane, where he lodged as a seaman's apprentice, and which is now the **Captain Cook Memorial Museum** (⊘ cookmuseumwhitby.co.uk). If this captures your kids' imaginations, head on to the life-sized replica of Cook's ship, the HM *Bark Endeavour* (⊘ hmbarkendeavour.co.uk), moored at Whitby Harbour.

This part of the North Yorkshire coast is a boon for fossil hunters of all ages (page 349), with ammonites galore washing up on the shore. **Whitby Museum**, up the hill from town in Pannett Park (⌀ whitbymuseum.org.uk), is well worth a visit for its incredible fossil finds including ammonites bigger than your head and a mighty ichthyosaurus crassimanus found nearby.

North of Whitby, kids will delight in dam building and surfing at **Sandsend** and rock pooling at **Runswick Bay**. The stretch of coast by the quaint town of **Saltburn-by-the-Sea** is renowned as a great surf spot, with board hire and lessons at Saltburn Surf School (⌀ saltburn-surf.co.uk) – and don't miss the Victorian funicular that takes you up and down the cliff.

"To the south of Whitby is the pretty fishing village of Robin Hood's Bay with its quaint streets."

To the south of Whitby is the pretty fishing village of **Robin Hood's Bay** with its quaint streets and **Old Coastguard Station** (⌀ nationaltrust.org.uk), originally built to combat smuggling along the Yorkshire coast. Here children can discover how the forces of nature have shaped the bay.

Further south again, **Scarborough** is a famous holiday resort favoured by Victorians for its spa waters and fresh sea air. Children will love the Hidden Horizons **Fossil Shop** (⌀ thefossilshop.co.uk; page 349). It's also worth tackling the steep climb up to the ruins of the 12th-century **Scarborough Castle** (⌀ english-heritage.org.uk), with views over the town's two bays, before heading down for some local fish and chips.

Not quite as firmly placed on Scarborough's tourist trail, but equally fascinating for families, is England's first commercial seaweed farm, **SeaGrown Centre** (⌀ seagrown.co.uk). It's owned by Wave Crookes, whose background in the British Navy, deep-sea diving on oil rigs and captaining British Antarctic missions led him ultimately to the harnessing the power of seaweed. You can board his working ship, moored in Whitby Harbour, which has a bespoke area for children to learn about seaweed farming.

A great way to explore the coast on two wheels is along the **Cinder Track**, a 21-mile route that follows the old railway line between Whitby and Scarborough, passing Robin Hood's Bay, Ravenscar and Cloughton along the way. Hire bikes at Hawsker from **Trailways** (⌀ trailways.info), directly on the trail at the top of Robin Hood's Bay, or in Scarborough from **Bayhire** (⌀ bayhire.co.uk).

PRACTICALITIES

FAMILY-FRIENDLY SLEEPS

Alice Hawthorn ⚘ thealicehawthorn.
com. This beautiful pub with rooms,
in Nun Monkton, halfway between
Harrogate and York, is a great one for
families with older kids looking for a
bit of local luxury. The beer garden is a
relaxed setting for family meals, too.

Camp Kátur ⚘ campkatur.com.
Geodomes, bell tents, hobbit pods and
lodges between the Yorkshire Dales
National Park and the North York Moors
National Park, near Thirsk. A host of
outdoor family experiences includes
foraging, bushcraft and den building,
stargazing and wild cooking. In a 'wild
wonder' workshop you will learn how
to identify flora and fauna and track a
roe deer through the woods, and play
woodland games. The on-site restaurant
serves seasonal family food including
stonebaked, wood-fired pizzas.

Cayton Village ⚘ experiencefreedom.
co.uk. Four miles south of Scarborough,
this glamping and camping site is great
for exploring the north Yorkshire coast
and moors. Fully accessible glamping
pods and cabins are available, along with
yurts and tent pitches. There's also a play
area on-site.

Farndale Cottages ⚘ farndalecottages.
co.uk. Self-catering cottages in the heart
of the North York Moors National Park, all
with extensive gardens for kids to play
out in and for stargazing at night. Barn
conversion West Steading, which sleeps
four plus a baby (baby gear is supplied if
required), has a log burner and flagstone
floors with underfloor heating.

Forest Holidays ⚘ forestholidays.co.uk.
Forest Holidays has two North Yorkshire
sites, at Cropton and Keldy in the middle
of the North York Moors National Park.
Cabins and lodges come with hot tubs,
log-burning stoves, gas BBQs and
hammocks. The Keldy site also has a
330ft zip-wire experience.

Grand Hotel ⚘ thegrandyork.co.uk. If
you're looking for a luxury family stay
in York, this five-star Victorian railway
hotel does the job nicely, with the
fragrance of fresh flowers to welcome
you and smiley staff to guide you.
There's no end to the family extras,
including goody bags, babysitting,
children's menus, interconnecting
rooms, spa slots and cookery classes
(page 355).

Humble Bee Farm ⚘ humblebeefarm.
co.uk. Yurts, bells tents and spacious
wigwam cabins give families the chance
to experience life on a working farm as
part of a luxury glamping trip. Just 15
minutes' drive from the seaside town
of Filey, with its five-mile beach, the
farm comes alive in the spring with the
lambing season and kids can also get
involved in egg collecting and wildlife
walks. They can meet the ducks, pigs,
cows and dogs and follow interactive
nature trails; there is also a playground
and a sports field.

Holiday at Home ⊘ holidayathome. co.uk. This collection of North Yorkshire holiday cottages, farmhouses, lodges and apartments aims to offer all the pluses of a boutique hotel but with the independence of self-catering. They're located either in the countryside or in pretty towns, and include larger houses for multi-gen gatherings and dog-friendly places.

Jollydays ⊘ jollydaysglamping.co.uk. You won't find anything as entrancing as Jollydays' four cabins, set in 200 acres of woodland just east of York near Stamford Bridge. Queen Mab, Queen Titania, King Auberon and the Magician's Bothy take their inspiration from the Victorians' love of faeries, with hand-painted magical scenes adding to the atmosphere. Each sleeps up to six and has a wood-burning stove, small kitchen and bathroom with a rolltop bath. Kids can explore the incredible woods, the magical Northwood Fairy Trail and the on-site Fairy Museum and Café.

La Rosa Hotel ⊘ larosa.co.uk. A Whitby B&B full of imagination and fantasy, La Rosa is a good choice for families with older children. It's in a towering townhouse on West Cliff, offering epic views across the bay to the abbey, and all rooms are themed – including 'Lewis', named after the *Alice in Wonderland* author who stayed here during his numerous visits to the town.

Lobster Pot Beach House
⊘ sykescottages.co.uk. There's no mistaking you're near the seaside in this beach-hut-styled house at The Bay Coastal Holiday Village near Filey. It's perfect for a family of four, with an outdoor terrace and dining table, a full kitchen, and use of the on-site swimming pool. Children will adore the curios, from telescopes to china teacups by the bed.

Middlethorpe Hall & Spa
⊘ middlethorpe.com. This William III country house near York has vast manicured gardens and parkland for kids to explore, including an arboretum and roaming roe deer; you can also take enjoyable tours of the walled garden with the head gardener. The hotel is great for gathering families as it offers varied accommodation including two-bedroom cottage suites. Middlethorpe Hall only welcomes families with children over the age of six years in the hotel, but the cottage suites are open to all ages.

No.1 by GuestHouse
⊘ guesthousehotels.co.uk. Housed in a handsome Regency Georgian building just a ten-minute walk from York Minster, this new 39-room hotel offers families a relaxed boutique experience. The designer interiors may be swanky, but you can help yourselves to goodies in the pantry kitchens and spin a disc on the vinyl record-player in your room.

North Yorkshire Moors Railway
⊘ nymr.co.uk. For children who are nuts about trains, book a stay in one of two camping coaches fashioned from former steam-train coaches on the rail line at Levisham and Goathland stations (each sleeps four), or in the beautifully restored

Station Cottage at Grosmont (sleeps five). All are available for a minimum of seven nights; rates include unlimited travel on the heritage railway.

Private Hill ⊘ theprivatehill.co.uk. Four smart geodesic domes at the top of a long grassy climb, overlooking the expansive landscape of the north Yorkshire Wolds. Each comes with real beds, hot shower, flushing toilet and small kitchenette along with a wood-burning stove, and are suitable for a family of four. A communal terrace has an impressive outdoor fire for gatherings. And you can book an alpaca walking experience (see box, page 362) right from your front door!

Raithwaite Sandsend Hotel
⊘ raithwaitesandsend.co.uk. Set between Sandsend Beach and the North York Moors just outside Whitby, this family-friendly hotel has a two-bedroom family suite and a relaxed restaurant. The hotel strives for sustainability and has recently planted a forest garden to promote biodiversity.

Wild Woods Camp
⊘ coastandcamplight.co.uk. Leave your car in a nearby field and go off-grid at this safari-style camp at Stainsacre, near the coast at Whitby. Styled with vintage and upcycled furniture, including double beds and bunk beds, each safari tent has a log burner, wide decking, a covered galley kitchen, a bathroom, hammocks and a firepit. Woodland walks, den making and paddling in the beck are right on your doorstep.

KID-FRIENDLY EATS

Balloon Tree Farmshop & Café
⊘ theballoontree.co.uk. Just outside York, this farm shop and café is all about local produce, serving seasonal home-cooked dishes. Come in summer and pick your own strawberries.

Bettys Cafe Tea Rooms ⊘ bettys.co.uk. Bettys, in St Helen's Square in York, is a Yorkshire institution – and a bit of a treat with its comfy but posh interiors inspired by *The Queen Mary* ocean liner, and enough tea and cakes to sink a battleship. Kids will delight in the Yorkshire tradition of calling a fruit scone a fat rascal. Bettys cookery school in Harrogate offers a day course in showstopper baking skills for eight- to 14-year-olds.

High Paradise Farm ⊘ highparadise. co.uk. This traditional moorland farmhouse, on the Cleveland Way near Boltby Bank, is the perfect pit stop for cyclists taking the Drovers Trail from Sutton Bank Bikes (page 355) or families exploring the moors who need to refuel with tea and cake or wood-fired pizza. It's only accessible by foot, bike or horse!

Los Moros ⊘ losmorosyork.co.uk. Right in the centre of York, this independent restaurant serves modern North African food; many ingredients, including the pickled cabbage and sausages, are made on-site using local suppliers. Children will love the bright interiors, and there's a pretty paved courtyard out back for outdoor dining.

Old School Coffee House
⊘ grosmontcoffeeshop.co.uk. After

the walk from Goathland to Grosmont, reward yourselves with a hearty sandwich and a local Yorvale ice cream at this former school house right by the station.

Quayside ⊘ quaysidewhitby.co.uk. A no-brainer in Whitby for families in search of local fish and chips, with gorgeous views of the abbey too. Children's meals feature cod fish bites and Whitby scampi and there's an even smaller menu for toddlers.

Star Inn The Harbour
⊘ starinntheharbour.co.uk. This friendly, nautically themed Whitby restaurant is owned by celebrated chef Andrew Pern who grew up around here. Dishes reflect the bounty of the coast and the moors, featuring local seafood, meat and game. The Starlet's menu, for tiddlers ten and under, is more inventive than most kids'

menus, featuring such dishes as little prawn cocktails and garlic mushrooms on toast.

The Talbot ⊘ talbotmalton.co.uk. The foodie town of Malton just outside the North York Moors National Park, east of Castle Howard, is the place to head to buy local produce; one of the best places to eat here is the Talbot, a 17th-century coaching inn with seasonal menus. There are lovely outdoor tables in summer, with gardens for kids to run around. Afternoon tea is a great family treat and dogs are very welcome, too.

MORE INFO

Discover Yorkshire Coast
⊘ discoveryorkshirecoast.com
Visit York ⊘ visityork.org
Yorkshire Tourist Board
⊘ yorkshire.com

RISKA PARAKEET/S

...N/A

SCARLETT TOOZE

COLIN SEDDON/S

24
NORTHUMBERLAND

*Discover white-sand beaches, ancient castles,
starry forests and the Galápagos of the north
in this beautiful northeastern county.*

TOP FAMILY EXPERIENCE
SEABIRD SAFARI, FARNE ISLANDS

BEST FOR KIDS AGED: 4+ years
WHEN TO GO: May to October
INTREPID LEVEL: ②
ADDED ADVENTURE: Beach school, ancient castles, broomstick riding, stargazing,
a poison garden, kipper suppers
TIME: A week to a fortnight

A WILDLIFE WONDERLAND

⌖ nationaltrust.org.uk/farne-islands; private boats to the Farne Islands leave from
Seahouses – companies include Serenity Farne Islands Boat Tours (⌖ farneislandstours.
co.uk) & Billy Shiel's Boat Trips (⌖ farne-islands.com); advance booking recommended,
especially in summer.

My eight-year-old daughter Scarlett lies belly down on the cliff edge, my
SLR camera slung around her neck. It looks massive in her grasp. The
guano-clad igneous rocks plunge down into the frothy North Sea. I'm
wedged next to her on the scrubby grass in that excruciating parental
dilemma – how to allow your kids a bit of danger and excitement
while also ensuring their utmost safety. We're perched prone together
on Inner Farne, one of the Farne Islands, a haven for seabirds, seals
and nature lovers. Scarlett has recently discovered cameras that don't

---

◀ **1** Children and adults alike cannot help but be charmed by Atlantic puffins. **2** Taking the
boat to Inner Farne. **3** One of Scarlett's prized photos. **4** Grey seals.

BEACH SCHOOL WITH JANE LANCASTER

Various sites, from Druridge Bay to Berwick ⊘ rangerjane.co.uk; age: 3+; intrepid level ①

There's an otherworldliness to sand dunes, I've always thought. These fragile ecosystems that hold shifting sands in place – their undulations and hollows so organic and playful. We're lucky enough to be on the edge of Bamburgh dunes, where the beach is so white and long it takes your breath away, not to mention the sight of the castle up on the promontory. It feels like we're on a film set – and indeed this is a vista familiar from numerous movies, not least the fifth *Indiana Jones* picture.

I'm here with my daughter Scarlett and the inspiring Jane Lancaster, a former Northumberland National Trust coastal ranger and ex coastguard rescue officer who now runs her very own Beach School where families can learn about the sea life on our shores via educational activities and beach safaris.

Our task today is to construct a beach shelter in the dunes that will stand up to all the North Sea elements. Soon we're hands on, involve learning knots, teamwork, communication and mindfulness. Jane talks to the children about how the sand dunes form, with the help of lyme and marram grasses, pioneering species that help the sand to stabilise and stop the wind from taking it as easily. We anchor a tarpaulin in a hollow which feels wonderfully sheltered and secure.

We learn how to light a fire without matches, using fire strikers and cotton wool in a scallop shell. Jane also shows us how to use a telescope and binoculars to look for passing bottle-nosed dolphins, regularly seen around the Farne Island trip boats.

Jane's beach safaris also explore Northumberland's many rock pools, teaching care and compassion for the creatures that live there. The habitat of a rock pool is a special environment where, she explains, every stone acts as a house with a roof. The roof protects the creature that lives underneath it from sunshine and all the elements, but keeps it wet so that it can survive.

involve a phone and is keen to capture a bird up close in order to enter a wildlife photography competition. We've come to the right place. Guillemots and kittiwakes wheel overhead, but it's the nesting shag just a few feet in front of us, seemingly oblivious to our clumsy mother-daughter shenanigans, that she has in her lens. Unbelievably there are newborn chicks in the nest, guarded by their formidable mum who still has the look of her dinosaur ancestors about her. If you want to give your children an unfair advantage in the wildlife photography stakes, these islands, the Galápagos of the north, are your best bet. Shutter shut, we edge back on our tummies away from the cliff edge, grinning with elation as we huddle over the camera to see what she's captured.

We round off our beach activities with a mindful beach clear-up, removing small pieces of plastic washed up from the sea that won't degrade naturally and which are harmful to marine wildlife (such as puffins and seals) that often mistake plastic as food, and end up trying to digest it.

All in all, it's been an enlightening day thanks to Jane's coastal knowledge and infectious enthusiasm. We leave the beach with a renewed respect for our fragile marine environment and far more aware of how much we humans need to do to halt further damage.

FACEBOOK: RANGER JANE BEACH SCHOOL

Much of my childhood was spent living on the northeast coast of England; that stretch of wild North Sea from the mouth of the River Tyne up into Northumberland. Last stop before the Scottish Borders. Most summers, we'd have a family day out to the Farne Islands. We'd jump in the car and drive an hour or so up the coast to a little harbour town called Seahouses, a hub of fish 'n' chip shops and amusement arcades, and an impressive fleet of sightseeing boats to the Farnes, a cluster of offshore islands that seemed incredibly exotic, visible from the harbour on a clear day. These trips were my first sea voyages, not to mention my first encounter with properly wild wildlife. The toy-like puffins and sleek grey seals stand out in my memory. Of course, I took the longevity of all this for granted. In the 1970s and 80s, there was little talk of climate change, overfishing, plastic pollution or endangered species. With oil drilling in the North Sea, there was always the threat of a spill following the SS *Torrey Canyon* disaster off the western coast of Cornwall in 1967, but as a rule, the North Sea felt like an indomitable force of nature. Surely it was in charge of its own destiny? It just seemed so vast and powerful to me as a child. I never doubted it could look after itself.

And thankfully, returning to the Farne Islands almost 45 years later (where does the time go?) with my own children – the generation brought up under the shadow of global warming – these islands remain a nirvana for 23 species of seabirds and a sprawling colony of grey seals, with more than 1,000 pups born every autumn. And although rising sea temperatures have depleted stocks of sand eels, the puffin's favourite food, these hardy fellows remain a force. In 1925 the National Trust bought the islands for £800 from the industrialist William Armstrong. And wow, what a bargain! Because of this purchase, millions have shared in this gold standard of conservation, a favourite of naturalist Sir David Attenborough. Every day, National Trust rangers, in permanent residence, balance conservation with a desire to educate the public about these island gems. Visitor numbers have been strictly limited since 1971, and just 400 privileged humans make it to the islands daily during the high season.

On our family visit, we head to Seahouses harbour to find the Serenity Farne Island Boat Tours kiosk, where two smiley Geordie women hand over our pre-booked tickets with a 'There you go, pet!' We board our sturdy Serenity vessel for the voyage, packed lunches in our rucksacks. (You won't find anything as disruptive as a café on these protected islands.) The sun bursts from behind the clouds and we enjoy the mesmerising view back to the coast with the mighty Bamburgh Castle and the Cheviot Hills behind. We head across Staple Sound to Staple Island and The Pinnacles. At the height of the breeding season, 1,000 guillemots can be seen on each pinnacle, isolated rock stacks that protrude 65ft above the water. The on-board guide tells us how the eggs jockey for space on the tiny ledges, which is why they are pointy at one end, so if knocked they will spin in a circle rather than roll off the edge.

The water is darkly sparkling and clear, an inspiring example of how exotic and wondrous the seas around our own island can be. Who would think the North Sea would offer such impressive wildlife at close quarters? Puffins are an attention-grabbing sight here, especially for children, with their cute plump bodies and striped beaks. The Farnes are their summer breeding ground before they depart in early August toward the north coast of Scotland, then on to Iceland for nine months.

As we continue our sail, my kids squeal with delight as they spy grey and common seals sunbathing on the rocks. Our guide tells us scuba divers come to dive with the seals, which can hold their breath for over 30 minutes and plummet to depths of 250ft. Visibility can be up to 65ft, and the seals love divers to scratch them.

We arrive at Inner Farne, where Scarlett captures her wildlife shots and we experience the close proximity to nature that makes the islands so thrilling. It's a voyage that has remained vivid in her memory and her photos remain a source of pride – if that's not a successful family day out, I don't know what is.

ADDED ADVENTURE: CASTLES OF SAND & STONE

To say the Northumbrian coast is a treasure trove for families is an understatement. With immense stretches of fine sand beaches, barely populated even in summer, and ancient castles to ignite children's imaginations, it's an easy win for families looking for a slower pace of holiday. Take your time to walk or cycle the **Northumberland Coast Path** (⊘ northumberlandcoastpath.org). It's easy to pick a section and make it as long or short as you like depending on the age and stamina of your kids. There's no-one rushing you here.

BAMBURGH & ITS CASTLE

For the ultimate seaside fortification, **Bamburgh Castle** (⊘ bamburghcastle.com), just north of the village of Seahouses and south of **Lindisfarne Nature Reserve** (⊘ lindisfarne.org.uk), trumps most. Towering over its eponymous village on one side, it boasts a vast sweep of powder-fine sand on the other side that wouldn't look out of place in Australia, and epic dunes to the south. In holiday seasons, the castle organises carriage rides, alpaca walks, outdoor cinema and singalongs. The dunes are a relaxing place to wonder at the beauty of the coast, play hide and seek or roll down – you could even build a shelter in one of the hollows and have a picnic (see box, page 372).

The pretty village of **Bamburgh** is worth a stroll with children. There's a vast green in front of the castle just made for playing tag. And don't miss the **RNLI Grace Darling Museum** (⊘ rnli.org/gracedarling) to get a good dose of female empowerment as your kids learn about the heroism of local girl Grace – the daughter of a lighthouse keeper who risked her life to rescue others from certain death in a terrible sea storm back in 1838.

ALNWICK

About 15 miles south of Seahouses and slightly inland, 35 miles north of Newcastle, Alnwick Castle (⊘ alnwickcastle.com) is a must-see. The second-largest inhabited castle in the UK, Alnwick has been home to the Duke of Northumberland's family, the Percys, for over 700 years. Looking around the vast rooms, it's thrilling for kids to spy real family photos next to grand portraits. Who would have thought you could actually live in a castle? It also has the immense attraction of being the location for scenes from the *Harry Potter and the Philosopher's Stone* and *Harry Potter and the Chamber of Secrets* films: Harry learned the rules of Quidditch in the Outer Bailey, where he and his fellow students also learned to fly broomsticks with Madam Hooch. If that isn't enough of a boon for Potter fans, they can also take part in broomstick tutorials, complete with flying and levitating.

Next to the castle, **Alnwick Garden** (⊘ alnwickgarden.com) is a wonder in its own right, with a spectacular multi-level fountain, the Grand Cascade, that kids can play in, collecting and dumping water in mini trucks. Heaven on earth for toddlers! The highlight for many, though, is the Poison Garden. Visitors must only enter this garden with a guide, as 90% of the plants here can kill, so it's definitely not for toddlers with wandering hands but exciting for children who are a bit older. Droll but dedicated guides bring to light alarming facts. Did you know that rhubarb and dock leaves are poisonous, that you can eat nettles despite their sting… and that three berries of deadly nightshade are enough to kill a child?

If you've time to spare after the excitement of Harry Potter, cascades and poisons, take young bookworms to **Barter Books** (⊘ barterbooks.

---

1 Bamburgh Castle. 2 Barter Books, Alnwick. 3 The Northumberland Coast Path.
4 Learning to ride a broom at Alnwick Castle. ▶

GARY LAWSON/BAMBURGH CASTLE

Rise up, my love, my fair one, and come away.

For lo, the winter is past the rain is over and gone

The flowers appear on the earth:
the time of the singing of birds is come

PSYCHOLOGY POLITICS ROMANCES MINING ENGINEERING RELIGION PHILOSOPHY

LONTANO/S

D K GROVE/S

ALNWICK CASTLE

co.uk), in Alnwick village station, just around the corner from the castle and gardens. This massive secondhand bookshop has a cosy café, sofas by an open fire and a little elevated train that runs around the shop.

FROM AMBLE TO NEWTON-BY-THE-SEA

South of Alnwick but still north of Newcastle, plenty of lesser-known coastal spots are worth exploring. The little coastal town of **Amble** is home to the **Northumberland Seafood Centre** (⬦ northumberlandseafood. co.uk) lobster hatchery – not an immediately obvious draw for kids, perhaps, but actually a fascinating insight into the life cycle of lobsters. There will be oohs and aahs when they learn that a female lobster can carry 20,000 eggs under her body for over nine months, but that after all that effort the chances are only one egg will survive into adulthood.

A little further north is **Alnmouth**, a beautiful sweep of beach and river inlet. When the tide is out, stride over the low sands to the opposite bank and walk around the grounded fishing boats.

Head a little further up the coast to the fishing town of **Craster**, where you can follow the scent of woodsmoke to **L. Robson and Sons Ltd** (⬦ kipper.co.uk), a family smokery and shop famous for its kippers. If this is the first time your children have encountered a smoked mackerel, it could be one of those holiday memories that stay with them forever – good or bad! Craster harbour is a great place for crabbing, or you can head north along the grassy headland where it meets the sea (or if the tide is out, along the impressive rocks with their multitude of rock pools) to the impressive ruins of **Dunstanburgh Castle** (⬦ english-heritage. org.uk). In contrast to the intact Bamburgh Castle, Dunstanburgh is a fine example of a castle twice besieged during the Wars of the Roses and left in ruins. It's fun to ask children to imagine how it would have looked in all its glory.

Continue a little further north to **Embleton Beach**, an under-the-radar, beautiful and family-friendly strand, and **Newton-by-the-Sea**, a tucked-away hamlet at the start of another vast stretch of beach backed by impressive dunes. Whitewashed 18th-century fishermen's cottages surround the village green, and at its corner is the **Ship Inn** (⬦ shipinnnewton.co.uk), a flagstoned pub and micro-brewery that serves the best crab sandwiches around. Lie on the green in the sunshine

---

1 Family-friendly Embleton Beach. **2** Crabbing in Craster. ▶

to eat your sarnies and sip a local Dolly Daydream bitter while the kids enjoy a lemonade.

Just north of Newton-by-the-Sea at Beadnell Bay, **KA Adventure Sports** (⊘ kitesurfinglessons.co.uk) runs watersport activities for kids aged six and up, including coasteering, cliff traversing, rock scrambling, rock pooling and cliff jumping – all exhilarating ways to experience the dramatic Northumberland coastline.

KIELDER WATER & FOREST PARK

If time allows or you're planning a two-centre holiday of coast and countryside, head inland for the two-hour drive from the Bamburgh coast to **Kielder Water and Forest Park** (⊘ visitkielder.com), home to the biggest manmade lake in northern Europe and the largest working forest in England. It's well known for its dark skies, and is perfect for stargazing fans. At the **Kielder Observatory** (⊘ kielderobservatory.org) children can learn about the night sky and use the powerful telescopes, meet real-life astronomers and learn how to take photos of distant objects in the universe. Right in the heart of the forest, you can pick up bikes from **The Bike Place** (⊘ thebikeplace.co.uk) to explore round the lake and discover surprises such as *The Head*, an awesome sculpture resembling a giant's head emerging from the ground. Kids can scramble inside the skull and run upstairs to hang out of his eyes! After you've dropped off your bikes, stroll to the nearby **Kielder Castle Café** for a much-needed cuppa and the opportunity to watch a live feed of an osprey's nest.

PRACTICALITIES

FAMILY-FRIENDLY SLEEPS

Castle View Cottage ⊘ joiners-arms. com. High-end self-catering cottage which sleeps four adults and two children in the pretty hamlet of Newton-by-the-Sea, with a spacious garden and countryside views, just minutes from the beach. It's managed by The Joiners Arms gastropub, which is two minutes' walk away.

Coastal Retreats ⊘ coastalretreats. co.uk. This upmarket collection of self-catering places to stay around Northumberland and the Scottish Borders

---

◀ **1** One of Kielder's many sculptures. **2** Dark skies over Kielder Observatory. **3** Kielder is the perfect place to explore on bike.

SEVEN STORIES: A SIDE TRIP TO NEWCASTLE

If you want to combine the Northumberland coast and countryside with a day or two in the city, Newcastle is well worth a trip. Chief among its attractions is the outstanding **Seven Stories** (⊘ sevenstories.org.uk), the National Centre for Children's Books, which always has something creative going on based around children's literature. Another good stop is the **Baltic Centre for Contemporary Art** (⊘ baltic.art) right on the River Tyne; both have family-friendly cafés. **Motel One Newcastle** is a value-for-money place to stay just south of the river; children up to 12 years old stay free in their parents' room.

stands out from the crowd. Particularly family-friendly accommodation includes Bamburgh Beach House, just across the road from the eponymous beach, with views of the castle from the front and a garden with play equipment. The Moo House is a former cow byre in the coastal hamlet of Tughall Steads, just south of Seahouses, with a separate games room called 'The Cow Shed' and two gardens, one for dining and one with swings, football and table tennis.

Coquet Cottages ⊘ coquetcottages. co.uk. A great selection of self-catering accommodation. Options include Lyndhurst Cottage near Alnmouth, which sleeps up to eight adults, two children and two babies, so is perfect for large or multi-gen family holidays, and The Penthouse apartment which sleeps eight and has panoramic views over Amble Marina and the North Sea.

Crabtree & Crabtree

⊘ crabtreeandcrabtree.com. This collection of upmarket self-catering accommodation across Northumberland has a selection of family-friendly holiday cottages with enclosed gardens, convivial kitchens and games rooms. Babysitting and activity recommendations are offered, too.

Emble Coastal Farm Stays ⊘ emble. org. On a working farm just outside Seahouses, these off-grid safari-style cabins sleep six. You'll have hot water showers and flushing loos, and can enjoy your own wild cooking on a wood-burning stove, campfire, BBQ or gas rings. Cots and high chairs are provided on request. Guy, the owner, will give you a tour of the farm, and also hosts pizza evenings around the wood-fired oven next to the honesty shop.

Huts in the Hills ⊘ hutsinthehills.co.uk. Jamie and Nicola, parents to three girls, offer four beautiful shepherd's huts on Prendwick Farm in the countryside about ten miles inland from Alnwick. Facilities include cute bunks for kids, power showers, a fridge, oven and hob, a wood burner and a flushing toilet. Some even have outdoor bathtubs for starbathing.

Northumberland Farm

⊘ featherdown.co.uk. A member of the Feather Down group of upmarket farm stays, this glamping spot is less than a mile from the beach and a 15-minute walk to Seahouses. As well as luxury family glamping, the site offers kids the opportunity to learn about traditional farming and biodiversity.

Springhill Farm Cottages
⌀ springhill-farm.co.uk. Located between Seahouses and Bamburgh, Springhill Farm offers a selection of cottages, caravan and camping pitches, wigwams and bunkhouse accommodation, with plenty of outdoor space for kids to enjoy.

KID-FRIENDLY EATS

Copper Kettle
⌀ copperkettlebamburgh.co.uk. Cosy café on Bamburgh's little high street, within walking distance of the castle, serving seasonal food including a 'Little Rascals Platter' of ham, cheese, raisins, cucumber, crisps, a soft roll and a drink, and for adults a Seahouses kipper in a bun.

Jolly Fisherman
⌀ thejollyfishermancraster.co.uk. Fabulous gastropub with sea views over Craster, serving locally sourced food including sandwiches, crab soup and Craster kippers.

Lord Crewe ⌀ lord-crewe.co.uk. This restaurant with rooms in Bamburgh is all Farrow and Balled and serves hearty food in a gastropub atmosphere that welcomes kids.

Riley's Fish Shack ⌀ rileysfishshack. com. It's worth making the effort to drive south to the mouth of the Tyne and walk down into King Edward's Bay to reach this award-winning fish restaurant right on the beach. Sit in deckchairs around a firepit while the kids play.

Treehouse ⌀ alnwickgarden.com. Your children will not believe their eyes when you take them to this restaurant, which is literally in a treehouse in the Alnwick Garden. Kids' menus feature Northumberland sausages and other reliable British staples.

BEFORE YOU GO

Guy Douglas from Emble Coastal Farm Stays (see opposite) has launched a string of free **mini 'libraries'** along the coast in locations such as the Shoreside camping huts in Alnmouth (⌀ alnmouthhuts. com). Each 'branch' has an array of books for children and young readers. Discover their exact locations on ⌀ emble.org/ books-by-the-sea, and leave a few kids' books in return if you can.

MORE INFO

Northumberland Tourist Board
⌀ visitnorthumberland.com

KITCHEN COOS & EWES

25
DUMFRIES & GALLOWAY

Lower profile than the Highlands, but just as beguiling, Dumfries & Galloway is Scotland's slow family travel secret.

TOP FAMILY EXPERIENCE
GUIDED HIGHLAND COW SAFARI WITH KITCHEN EWES & COOS

BEST FOR KIDS AGED: 2–16
WHEN TO GO: May to October
INTREPID LEVEL: ①
ADDED ADVENTURE: A Peter Pan house, mighty forests, galaxy gazing, cycling trails, wild, sandy beaches, towns arty & bookish
TIME: One to two weeks

FACE TO FACE WITH A HIGHLAND COO

Airyolland Farm, High Arrioland, Newton Stewart DG8 0AU ⬦ kitchencoosandewes.com; in addition to the half-day safari they also offer a full-day 'Haute Coo Tour' that includes sheep-shearing demonstrations.

As my 17- and 14-year olds lock eyes with Eve, a shaggy white Highland coo (Scottish vernacular for cow!) and cover star of *Hello!* magazine, there's an air of unadulterated joy that you don't often get with teens on tour. These majestic bovine creatures, such a symbol of Scotland, metaphorically lock horns with my two in the most positive of ways.

If you've always hankered after taking your children on safari, but the expense and carbon miles of getting to Africa are just too much

◄ Highland cow safari.

to stomach, Kitchen Coos & Ewes is your slow travel alternative. This hands-on, farmer-led Highland cow safari allows you to get up close to these beasts, gaining a sense of their strong personalities. And this intimate encounter with such sentient animals will definitely make you think twice about eating meat.

Arriving at Airyolland Farm, eight miles east of Stranraer in the scenic Luce Valley, we're greeted by the smiling faces of Neale and Janet McQuistin. Coming from generations of local farmers, they proudly tell us they have 108 years of farming experience between them in the Galloway and Southern Ayrshire UNESCO Biosphere (∂ gsabiosphere. org.uk). This forward-thinking couple made the decision a decade ago to farm for the environment rather than for food production, and now make a living from the coo safaris and the sale of their high-value flock of stocky Beltex sheep – highly prized for mating with ewes to produce lambs for meat. As we board the impressive farm-tour trailer, with its padded seats and covered roof, Neale takes the wheel of the tractor up front and Janet jumps in the back to provide the expert commentary.

It's immediately obvious how passionate Janet is about this Scottish lowlands landscape and the life it supports. As we head out to the high ground to find the coos, she describes having created the pond to our right which now attracts otters, and fires up our appreciation for this delicate ecosystem where everything has a role in supporting something else. The nettles are the preferred food of caterpillars – known locally as 'granny moolies' – while the tall marsh thistles are a favourite for flocks of goldfinch. We also have a new respect for bogs, which Janet tells us are massive carbon stores.

My daughter Scarlett leans over the trailer and a beautiful red coo nudges her hand with her wet nose while Janet explains that Highland cows are slow growing and have an efficient double coat to combat the cold. She also tells us that they are especially good for rewilding because they don't require high-grade grasses and plants to eat and consequently don't affect local biodiversity. What's more, coo poo is a highly effective fertilizer. As Neale tells us, each coo makes eight cow pats a day which attract egg-laying insects, which hatch into grubs – a rich source of food for birds such as curlews and golden plovers. Who needs the African savanna, I think – though in typical Scottish fashion, it's lashing down.

Scarlett meeting Hector Hamish. ▶

We're nicely sheltered, though: Neale is constantly shielding us from the elements by pulling down the awnings or angling the trailer.

The cows are undeterred by the wind and the rain, and very vocal. Their strong moos are glorious to hear, especially when the excitement rises as Janet gets out a massive scoop and a bag of feed which she shovels out over the back as we're driven along. The protein in the feed comes from pulp from sugar beet and rejected peas. It's quite a sight to see 30 coos jostling close to the trailer; Janet points out the pecking order of who gets to eat first.

Further on, we pass the Beltex sheep, which remind me of school bullies with their hard faces and muscular bodies. Janet has named each one in this herd after pop stars, so we say hi to Madonna and Avril Lavigne, and marvel that they sell for £18,000 each.

Post safari, we're invited in the cosy farmhouse kitchen, where an impressive spread of sandwiches, scones, lemon drizzle cakes and Highland coo-shaped shortbread is laid out for us – all home baked by Janet. Huge china teapots appear on the table and by that stage we feel like we've known these hospitable farmers for years.

There's one more treat in store. After tea we head into one of the tall barns to meet Hector Hamish, a four-month-old red coo being hand reared, having had trouble feeding from his mum. Scarlett and Fin crouch down among the straw for a cuddle and just about manage to see his big brown eyes through his impressive dawson (the shaggy hair on his head). We're all reminded of *Hamish the Highland Cow*, a favourite children's book. I get a nostalgic rush back to when my children were little ones, along with a surge of happiness at spending this exciting and educational day out with them as teens in the company of these beautiful coos and ewes.

ADDED ADVENTURE: REACH FOR THE STARS

Southwest Scotland may not have the reputation of its show-stopping northern cousin the Highlands, but what it lacks in Munros it makes up for in laid-back lowland style. In this corner of the country, Dumfries and Galloway (⊘ visitsouthwestscotland.com) has a coastline dotted with sandy beaches and coves, mighty forests – including the Galloway Forest Park, a Dark Sky Park where cycling and celestial adventures are waiting to happen – and something around every bonny bend in the road, be it an ice-cream-making dairy farm, a town dedicated to books, a botanic garden or the home of J M Barrie, creator of *Peter Pan*.

DUMFRIES & THE FOREST OF AE

The historic market town of **Dumfries** is where many families will begin their exploration of southwest Scotland, especially if they arrive by train. Nicknamed the Queen of the South, this former home of Scottish poet Robert Burns has an elegant air with its wide streets and stone houses. Tucked away beside a kink in the River Nith, on one of the town's oldest streets, you can immerse yourself in the magical world of *Peter Pan*. **Moat Brae** (⊘ moatbrae.org) was the grand house of its author, J M Barrie, from 1860 to 1937, where he wrote the story of the Lost Boys. Now the **National Centre for Children's Literature and Storytelling**, the house has been reborn as a place for families to not only discover more about Peter Pan but also to inspire children about reading and literature in general.

Entering via an impressive modern side extension, you are instructed to pass through a 'magic door' and nose around the house as if you were visiting a beloved relative. Before entering, everyone measures themselves against a wall chart to see how 'grown down' they are. Toddlers might match up with Nana, while teens could be Mrs Darling, and tall parents possibly Captain Hook!

With three floors of grand rooms to investigate there are plenty of interactive surprises along the way, including leather chairs with ear-level story-telling speakers, Peter Pan's shadow hidden in a drawer, and Nana's kennel, through which kids can crawl into Neverland. There's the grandest dolls' house you're likely to see, art installations, reading wigwams, dressing-up boxes and whole rooms dedicated to flopping down and enjoying a good book. As it says on the stair walls: 'Do you know why swallows build in the eaves of houses? It is to listen to the stories.'

History recounts that J M Barrie was inspired to write *Peter Pan* after playing in the garden behind Moat Brae. Now named the Neverland Discovery Garden, it's an enchanting place for kids to let off steam. There are characters to spot hidden in the trees, a Wendy house to explore, Captain Hook talking to you from the bushes and a Jolly Roger pirate ship to invade. You'll leave with a fuller understanding of this enigmatic writer and his unforgettable characters.

"Galloway Forest Park: a Dark Sky Park where cycling and celestial adventures are waiting to happen."

DOUBLECLIX/S

As a good contrast to a day immersed in literature, spend some time in the **Forest of Ae** (⌁ forestryandland.gov.scot) which lies directly north of Dumfries just 12 miles up the A701. This working forest, planted with commercial Norway spruce that is used to produce paper and house-building materials, is one of the largest forests in the UK – about the size of 10,000 football pitches. Just north of **Ae** village, created for forest workers, lies the **Ae Café and Bike Shop** (⌁ aebikeshopandcafe.co.uk), the HQ for the Ae Forest branch of 7Stanes, a network of mountain biking centres and trails across Scotland. Book ahead and you'll be kitted out with mountain bikes or e-bikes, with child seats or trailers if required. The most family friendly of the five routes is the 5½-mile **Ae Valley Route**, an easy single-track forest road with just one sharp climb and epic views of the Water of Ae, a tributary of the River Annan. If you want something more challenging for older kids, take the 8½-mile **Larch View Route**, on which a steep climb and thrilling downhill chicanes give way to a scenic cycle back by the Water of Ae. A paddle in its peaty shallows followed by a picnic by the rocky banks makes a slow day of it.

KIRKCUDBRIGHT & GATEHOUSE OF FLEET

Head southwest of Dumfries along the A75 and down to the coast, passing Castle Douglas, and you'll reach **Kirkcudbright** at the mouth of the River Dee, a town whose written name will provoke a family game of 'how on earth do you pronounce that?' The answer is 'kir-coo-bree', otherwise known as 'Artists Town' for its profusion of creative endeavours. Come in late July and early August and you'll catch the **Kirkcudbright Art & Crafts Trail** (⌁ artandcraftstrail.com) – a great way to explore the town and get children all fired up about art.

One of the newest family attractions here is the **Dark Space Planetarium** (⌁ darkspaceplanetarium.org). You would never guess that inside this traditional Victorian school building is a world of astronauts, moons and galaxies far, far away. The intimate space has been ingeniously used and isn't overwhelming for younger kids like some vast science museums can be. There are plenty of fun, hands-on exhibits to get minds whirring. Pick up a tin of beans on Earth, the moon or Saturn,

1 & **2** Exploring the Forest of Ae on foot and by bike. **3** National Centre for Children's Literature and Storytelling. ▶

and discover how gravity affects weight. Find out if you have what it takes to be an astronaut, and take a heat-sensor selfie. The domed planetarium shows a selection of short films, some exploring life on other planets and moons, taking you soaring above the oceans of Europa.

Heading down the old school corridor from the planetarium brings you to the **Wee Pottery** (⏁ theweepottery.co.uk) where children can paint their own pots, and next door, the **Dark Art Distillery** (⏁ darkartdistillery.com) where grown-ups might like to buy a bottle of Sky Garden Gin, inspired by the clear night skies above the nearby Galloway Forest Park and its woodland botanicals.

En route to the pretty town of **Gatehouse of Fleet**, an eight-mile drive from Kirkcudbright, make a stop at **Cream o' Galloway** (⏁ creamogalloway.co.uk), an organic dairy farm famous for its ice cream. Families can don blue hairnets and create their very own flavour and brand. My kids came up with 'Freeze Ma...' in cocoa flavour. There's also a farm tour and a farmer-led sustainable food tour.

"One of the great joys of this area is its coastline. You'll find one of the best family-friendly beaches at Mossyard."

One of the great joys of this area is its pretty coastline. You'll find one of the best family-friendly beaches at **Mossyard**. There's a sandy bay here and, when the tide is in, safe paddling and swimming. Slightly inland and up the hillside is the holiday village of **Laggan**, home to the wonderful Gather restaurant (page 400) with awesome views over the bay.

WIGTOWN TO THE MULL OF GALLOWAY

Families who love to get lost in a book can literally lose themselves in **Wigtown** (⏁ wigtown-booktown.co.uk), west of Gatehouse of Fleet, which has around 16 bookshops. The most labyrinthine is **The Old Bank Bookshop** (⏁ oldbankbookshop.co.uk), which feels like something out of a *Harry Potter* movie with its towering corridors of tomes. As it says on a pebble by the entrance, 'Books are dreams you hold in your hands'. **Byre Books** (⏁ byrebooks.co.uk) is entered through a tangle of overhanging trees and for little ones **Foggie Toddle Books** (⏁ foggietoddlebooks.co.uk) is the place to head. Needless to say,

---

1 Mossyard Beach. 2 Dark Space Planetarium. 3 A sculpture in Kirkcudbright.
4 Walled Garden Pond, Logan Botanic Garden. ▶

STARGAZING AT GALLOWAY FOREST PARK

Kirroughtree Visitors Centre, Forest Drive, Newton Stewart DG8 7BE ⌖ forestryandland.gov.
scot; age: 6+; intrepid level: ①; late August to mid May; book a private family stargazing
experience or join one of the public events based around the expectation of meteor showers
or the northern lights.

Nightfall in Galloway Forest Park, a designated Dark Sky Park that occupies much of the central inland region of Dumfries and Galloway, west of Dumfries, has a fairy-tale quality. On a cloudless night, the stars really do come out in force. Up to 3,000 twinkling lights are visible with the naked eye according to Dark Sky Ranger Matthew McFadzean, due to the lack of light pollution. 'Look up,' he says, 'and there's a palpable sense of being part of something immense – bigger than any of us could ever imagine.'

Matthew meets us in the forest just as the sun is setting and starts with some experiments to help us get an idea of the size of our night sky. 'When you start talking in billions and trillions people can't conceive it,' he explains. So we set about creating a scale model of the solar system using tea lights and a 0.4-inch diameter marble to represent a scale model of the sun. We place the sun at the centre and walk out along a path, putting down tea lights at the various points where the planets sit in the solar system. We light them all and head out to the furthest point, looking back at the tiny little dot of our sun.

It's mind-blowing to conceive just how big the solar system is.

'Our sun, which is ridiculously huge, is tiny in comparison to the supergiant stars in our galaxy. If you were to fly a jumbo jet at 600 miles per hour around the outside of giant star UY Scuti, it would take you 1,500 years to get round it!'

Matthew encourages families to spot which stars come out first in the sky and, with the help of a set of powerful binoculars on a tripod, everyone is able to see Jupiter and its moons. We also look at Saturn – you can actually see the moons and rings going around it.

'When the Orion constellation starts to be more visible,' Matthew says, 'we look at Orion's Sword, which is actually a nebula, where stars are being born all the time – another mind-blowing concept.'

My kids love it when Matthew shows us how to navigate the night sky using true north and working from there: 'To find the North Star, also called Polaris, we use the Big Dipper, also called the Plough, to navigate us there. Then we use the constellation of Cassiopeia to find

Wigtown has a much celebrated **Book Festival** (⌖ wigtownbookfestival. com), in early autumn, with literary events throughout Dumfries and Galloway.

Heading south to the seaside town of **Isle of Whithorn**, you will find many family-friendly cycling routes. Carry on around the scenic **Luce**

the Andromeda Galaxy, which is our nearest galaxy and the furthest thing in the night sky that you can see with the naked eye.' Through our binoculars we can see its spiral arm galaxy, a patch of light filled with swirls, which contains around 200 billion stars. We are also lucky enough to catch sight of the International Space Station, to much whooping.

Matthew lights a firepit for us to sit around and we chat about local myths and legends and historic figures like Robert the Bruce, one time king of Scotland, who passed through here. We're glad of our extra layers of clothes, our hot drinks and our snacks in the chilly night air, made all the colder by those awesome cloudless skies.

'Looking at the night sky really does broaden your horizons,' Matthew muses. 'It has transformative qualities and connects us with our ancestors as well as nature.' As my kids crane their necks to take in as much of the night sky as possible, and start downloading constellation apps, it's clear this star-gazing experience has fired their imaginations and set them on a path to discovering more about our dark skies.

BEN BUSH/VISIT SOUTH WEST SCOTLAND

Bay and you'll come to the port town of **Stranraer** where ferries leave for Larne and Belfast. Further down the region's westernmost peninsula, the Rhinns of Galloway, lies the **Logan Botanic Garden** (⌀ rbge.org. uk) where kids will feel like the Borrowers as they wander through the giant rhubarb-like gunnera. It's fascinating to learn that Logan has an almost subtropical climate, due to Gulf Stream warming, which makes it possible for exotic plants to thrive.

If you make it down right to the tip of this narrow peninsula, you'll be rewarded with the **Mull of Galloway RSPB Reserve** (⌀ rspb.org.uk) with its clifftop grassland and heath. Guided walks help you spot colonies of guillemots, razorbills, kittiwakes, shags and black guillemots, and enjoy awesome views over to the Isle of Man and England's Lake District.

PRACTICALITIES

FAMILY-FRIENDLY SLEEPS

Balnab Farm ⌀ featherdown.co.uk. This working dairy farm near the Isle of Whithorn offers families the opportunity to meet cows, sheep and goats. You can help groom the ponies and even hire your own hen coop next to your safari-style tent. Farmers' football matches, tractor rides and pizza nights all add to the fun. The canvas lodges have outdoor showers and sleep up to six. Kids love the cupboard bed with its heart-shaped peepholes.

Barend Holiday Lodges ⌀ barendholidaylodges.uk. You might be forgiven for thinking you'd arrived in the Swiss Alps when you see the Toblerone-shaped lodges at this family-friendly holiday park, in the quiet countryside near the town of Dalbeattie, southwest of Dumfries. Sleeping between six and eight people, they're perfect for larger families. The indoor swimming pool, and the nearby loch and Sandyhills Beach are major pluses.

Brighouse Bay Holiday Park ⌀ brighousebayholidaypark.co.uk. Close to the pretty beaches and wildlife of Brighouse Bay, just south of Kirkcubbright, this easy-going, affordable holiday park offers lodges, cottages and holiday-home caravans. Old Mill Cottage and its garden is great for a multi-gen stay or two families travelling together. The park offers a leisure centre with heated indoor pool and toddler pool, coastal pony treks, mountain-biking trails and a pump track.

Ken Bridge Hotel ⌀ kenbridgehotel.co.uk. This hotel, by the Ken Bridge and the Water of Ken, on the eastern edge of Galloway Forest Park, offers lodgings in the Georgian coaching inn, a camp by the riverside and Rowan Cottage, created from a barn, stable and byre, which sleeps six. There's a beer garden for relaxed dining after a spot of family fishing in the river; you might even spot a red squirrel or the occasional otter.

Laggan ⌀ lagganlife.co.uk. Families of four can book the chic, comfy Seaview Snugs on the heather-covered hillside at Laggan, with panoramic views over the coastal bay known as Big Water of Fleet. Convenient extras include Alexa and a fine pair of binoculars. Dine on-site at Gather (page 400). You can also self-cater here, at Cairnharrow Cottage (sleeping four), which has its own enclosed garden, and Laggan Behind, a spacious three-bedroom house sleeping seven with everything from a pizza oven on the outdoor decking to a children's playground.

Loch Ken Eco Bothies ⚭ lochken.co.uk. These four luxury bothies sleep between two and eight guests and are perfect for off-grid family holidays with no TV or Wi-Fi. Set by the shores of Loch Ken, north of Kirkcudbright, each comes with its own log-burning hot tub and one or two kayaks and buoyancy aids. The Osprey is the largest, and has a mezzanine level perfect for spotting red kites, deer and ospreys. The Galloway Activity Centre is on the doorstep with archery, sailing, windsurfing, SUPs, a wobbly waterpark, mountain biking and a climbing tower.

Mossyard ⚭ mossyard.co.uk. Set just above one of the best family beaches in Dumfries and Galloway, with the Galloway Hills behind, Mossyard, four miles west of Gatehouse of Fleet, offers a collection of beautiful self-catering cottages and lodges with sea views and enclosed gardens, and a caravan park from April to October – all dog-friendly, too.

Mull of Galloway Lighthouse Cottages ⚭ lighthouseholidaycottages. co.uk. Lighthouses have a magical quality to them and, at the 19th-century Mull of Galloway lighthouse, which marks the southernmost point of Scotland, kids will

be excited to stay in the very cottages where the lighthouse keepers used to live. Sleeping between four and six, these high-spec refurbished cottages include access to picnic tables and a summer house within the lighthouse walls, plus free entry to the lighthouse itself. Dogs are welcome.

Trigony House Hotel ⚭ trigonyhotel. co.uk. This independently owned country house hotel, just north of Dumfries, offers families and dogs a warm welcome. There are gardens and woodland to explore, pretty rooms with quality camp beds added for children, rustic meals with a kids' menu – or the option for them to have half portions – and an organic garden spa. Cycle hire, horseriding and falconry displays can all be arranged. Free electric car charging for guests.

Woodpecker Cottage ⚭ woodpecker-cottage.co.uk. In the small conservation village of Bladnoch, just a mile from bookish Wigtown, this 19th-century cottage (sleeping six) is perfect for families, with an inner courtyard garden and larger back garden. Kids also love the games room with table tennis and pool table.

KID-FRIENDLY EATS
Castle Street Bistro
⚭ castlestreetbistro.co.uk. Directly opposite MacLellan Castle in Kirkcudbright, this family-owned bistro is great for children, offering pleasing pizzas and pastas made with fresh local ingredients.

Gallie Craig ⊘ galliecraig.co.uk. This family-run café, with its award-winning turf roof, teeters on the Mull of Galloway clifftop and offers epic views. Tasty dishes include steak pie made with local farm produce.

Galloway Lodge Café
⊘ gallowaylodge.co.uk. Right on the High Street in Gatehouse of Fleet, this roomy café serves hearty, family-friendly meals — some, such as the haggis and chilli melt, with a Scottish twist. There's a tasty children's menu and Cream O' Galloway ice cream and milkshakes for dessert. The shop at the front specialises in local preserves and chutneys.

Gather ⊘ lagganlife.co.uk. Up on the hillside, with sweeping views out over Big Water of Fleet, Gather is a super-stylish yet family-friendly glass-fronted bistro with plenty of outdoor seating. Brunch is a particular treat here, with fresh pancakes and waffles, while hearty dishes for lunch and dinner include fried chicken and Scotch beef burgers.

Kings Coffee & Books ⊘ kings-online.co.uk. For a cosy family pit stop in Dumfries, Kings serves yummy things on sourdough toast that kids will devour, plus toasties, scones and all kinds of cakes. A wide range of milkshakes go down a treat too, from caramel to banana.

Lost Boys Bistro at Moat Brae
⊘ moatbrae.org. Choose from tasty child-friendly menus, listing classics from hearty burgers to scones and jam, in this light-filled café overlooking the gardens at Moat Brae.

Mr Pook's Kitchen ⊘ mrpooks.co.uk. For a gourmet meal with slightly older children, Mr Pook's, in the foodie town of Castle Douglas, southwest of Dumfries on the A75, stands out for its creative use of local and foraged ingredients. Kids' menus are available.

Potting Shed Bistro ⊘ rbge.org.uk. The bistro at Logan Botanic Gardens is the kind of restaurant where parents breathe a sigh of relief knowing their kids will wolf down what's on offer, from tasty soups and sandwiches to Mull of Galloway crab salads and Cream O'Galloway ice cream to finish.

Selkirk Arms Hotel Restaurant
⊘ selkirkarmshotel.co.uk. This hotel restaurant in Kirkcudbright is one of the best in the area, using local produce to cook up a Mediterranean-influenced menu. There's a wood-fired outdoor pizza oven, serving at weekends in summer.

MORE INFO

South West Scotland Tourist Board
⊘ visitsouthwestscotland.com
Visit Scotland ⊘ visitscotland.com

26
EDINBURGH

From volanocoes to Voldemort, Scotland's gloriously walkable capital is a vibrant slow adventure hotspot.

TOP FAMILY EXPERIENCE
EDINBURGH INTERNATIONAL FILM FESTIVAL

BEST FOR KIDS AGED: 8–16
WHEN TO GO: August
INTREPID LEVEL: ①
ADDED ADVENTURE: An atmospheric castle, an urban volcano, a botanical garden, festivals galore, intriguing museums, beaches
TIME: Three days to a week

FOR THE LOVE OF FILM

Various venues across Edinburgh, including the Festival Theatre; festival HQ is at the Centre for the Moving Image, 88 Lothian Rd, EH3 9BZ ⌔ edfilmfest.org.uk

Everyone has heard of the Edinburgh Fringe Festival and all the joy it brings, the streets literally coming alive every summer. My dad was from Edinburgh and I grew up with regular visits to my grandma's house in Colinton. Every August we'd go and see the Royal Edinburgh Military Tattoo, my grandma bringing her Anderson tartan blanket along with her for our knees – even in summer you might need it on an Edinburgh night. In my late teens and 20s I started exploring the Fringe and, once I had kids, made sure I took them along with me too. Performances that stick in my childrens' memories include John Hegley reciting his wonderfully poignant dog poems and a show about Marvel comics in which the presenter wore underpants over his trousers and made us all stand up every time American comic book maestro Stan Lee was mentioned.

Of course Edinburgh doesn't just host one festival, but an impre 11 every year, bringing together artists, audiences and thinkers fro

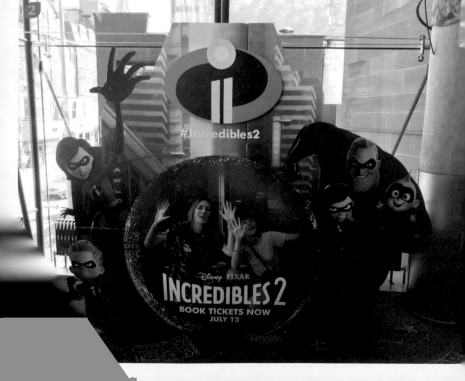

70 countries to its medieval closes, cobbled streets, underground vaults and grand Georgian terraces. The original festival was conceived in 1947 as a platform to celebrate art and culture and to bring nations together following the devastation of World War II; today the festival calendar celebrates everything from Scottish storytelling to jazz and blues.

Though there's an International Children's Festival during the May half term, top of my list for slightly older kids (nine upwards) is the Edinburgh International Film Festival, the longest continuously running film festival in the world. It's particularly exciting when the star-studded premiere is a family movie – *E.T. the Extra-Terrestrial* and *Back to the Future* were both given their first UK screenings here.

My kids have grown up loving film. Now in their teens, they're adamant they have lived through a golden era for kids' movies. It can't be denied that the art form has excelled itself in this period, with gems coming from sources as diverse as Studio Ghibli, Aardman Animations and Pixar. *The Incredibles* was released the year my daughter was born, 2004, and when I took them to the film festival 14 years later, Scarlett and her brother Fin, 11, were excited to see the premiere of *Incredibles 2*, which sees everybody's favourite superhero family slip back into their super-suits. Other recent highlights have included a preview screening of *Toy Story 4*, and quirky family offerings such as *UglyDolls*.

As we approached the premiere, held at the **Festival Theatre** (⊘ capitaltheatres.com), the atmosphere was buzzing. My kids and other young moviegoers met the 'real' Mr and Mrs Incredible in full 'supers' style, posing on the stairs for photos with fans, face painters on hand to create the iconic black masks on young wannabe superheroes. The free ice cream and balloon folding added some good old-fashioned fun. And once everyone was seated, Disney animator Fran Kalal – in essence, the real Edna Mode – took to the stage to chat about designing the super-costumes. Getting to see the people behind the scenes was a total eye-opener for my children and inspired them to see film as something that begins with ideas and sketches – all things totally within their reach.

The festival doesn't just champion the A-list movies, either. My kids loved *Vitello*, a gentle animation about an energetic young boy who lives alone with his mother, that originated in Denmark but involved a Scottish

◀ **1** A screening of *Everybody's Talking About Jamie*. **2** Jane and family making the most of the *Incredibles 2* promotional backdrops.

crew to bring it to the screen. As we arrived to watch it at the modern **Cineworld** (⊘ cineworld.co.uk) in Fountain Park, we were allowed to walk the red carpet and pose like movie stars, and after the show we were treated to a talk by the director, Dorte Bengtson, and four of the English-speaking cast, three of whom are kids. Hearing from the children who voiced the characters gave an inspiring insight into what it's like being involved in a movie production – and as soon as we got home my daughter immediately set to collaborating on a short film with a friend.

For any young person interested in working in cinema, the festival is a dream. The **EIFF Youth** programme, aimed at 15- to 25-year-olds, offers an array of cutting-edge screenings, special events, talks and masterclasses for young audiences, and even the opportunity to influence the festival screenings. At its HQ in the **Cornerstone Centre** on Princes Street (⊘ cornerstonecentrestjohns.org.uk), workshops include film acting, script writing, camera work, scoring and film journalism. My kids and I were treated to a first screening of a clever short about bullying, created by and starring some of the city's underprivileged young residents who gave a passionate group talk at the end. As Janine Koppe, EIFF Youth Events Manager, says, 'It's thrilling for young people to be trusted to make big decisions in film-making and at the festival, deciding which films to screen.'

My daughter Scarlett, having since completed her short film with her friend, would agree. 'We had such a laugh making it, and it gave us both a lot more confidence,' she says. 'I can definitely see now how empowering film-making can be.'

ADDED ADVENTURE: NEW FUN IN AULD REEKIE

Edinburgh is such a complete destination. I would put it at the top of my list for walkable city breaks for families. It has everything you need: history that's easily accessible and fun, culture around every corner, unique outdoor spaces, and even a seaside enclave. And, of course, the Scottish capital was doing festivals before festivals became a thing.

In reality, Edinburgh is a tale of two cities – the Old Town and the New Town –which meet in the middle at Princes Street Gardens, a valley-like divide. To the south is the Old Town, cut through by a majestic cobbled thoroughfare called The Royal Mile – which, just to confuse kids, is slightly over a mile long (perhaps a Scottish mile?) and surrounded by labyrinthine medieval streets. Edinburgh Castle sits at one end and Holyrood Palace at the other, just before the towering Arthur's Seat. To the north of Princes Street Gardens is the New Town, with its wide boulevards leading back to trendy Leith and the Firth of Forth waterfront. Together these areas cover only a couple of miles, but are packed full of enough history and intrigue to qualify them for UNESCO World Heritage status.

Quite apart from all the big sights, the great thing about Edinburgh is that no matter where you wander with your kids you'll stumble of something of interest, be it a monument to a faithful dog, an independent art gallery, or a stunning botanic garden.

ARTHUR'S SEAT

Tell your kids they're about to climb the back of a mighty lion that's actually an extinct volcano, 820ft above sea level, and a family walk up a hill turns into a daring adventure – some might even say a quest. What makes climbing **Arthur's Seat** even more remarkable is its location in the heart of the city, bumping up against the mighty **Holyrood Park** (⊘ historicenvironment.scot), home to everything from Iron Age forts to a loch, and located just opposite the Scottish Parliament and the **Palace of Holyroodhouse** (⊘ rct.uk), the monarch's official residence in the city.

It's actually nuts when you think about it: right in the centre of the Scottish capital, just a stone's throw from the busy Waverley Train Station and Edinburgh Castle, is a mini mountain with an ascent that really puts children to the test and rewards them with incredible 360° views.

Families can take a choice of trails and don't necessarily have to conquer the summit to have a great walk. Some are suitable for all abilities, including the trail to **St Margaret's Loch**, which takes approximately 10 minutes walking from the Palace of Holyroodhouse and is both wheelchair and buggy accessible. It's also the site of a well-preserved fort, one of four hillforts around Arthur's Seat dating from around 2,000 years ago.

The views from the top are a geography lesson in themselves. Bring a picnic of local Scottish food and take in the vista. As you gaze out over the city to the east there's a clear view of majestic Edinburgh Castle, perched high on its own lump of rock – a perfect illustration of how castles were built on high land for defence purposes. Gazing over the

town, you can easily spot a clear division between the mass of curving and tightly knit streets of the medieval Old Town (page 407) and the neat grid system of the New Town, which was built in stages from the late 18th to the mid-19th century (page 409).

The vista continues, sweeping out to the Pentland Hills, to suburbs like Colinton (where my own dad grew up) and round to the Firth of Forth and the mighty Forth Bridge with its distinct red oxide paint. I remember my dad telling me that it took so long to paint this behemoth that as soon as they'd finished the job they had to start all over again to keep it fresh.

Most surprising, perhaps, is the view out to sea. Few really think of Edinburgh as a coastal capital, but the North Sea coast is just a couple of miles to the west with suburbs such as Portobello (page 411) great places to head for a paddle and an ice cream.

Once you're back in Holyrood Park, take a look at the 15th-century ruins of **St Anthony's Chapel** and, at the other side of the park, **Duddingston Loch** (scottishwildlifetrust.org.uk), a freshwater loch rich in birdlife. If you're lucky, you might even spot an otter.

Before leaving this area, make sure you visit **Dynamic Earth** (dynamicearth.co.uk), an attraction consistently voted the number one attraction in Edinburgh for children, with its emphasis on the scientific wonders of our planet from the aurora borealis to deep ocean life.

THE OLD TOWN

Edinburgh's **Old Town** is teeming with family-friendly things to see and do. Along the **Royal Mile** with its ancient closes, you can catch street performers such as Super Scot, a comedic escapologist who's been performing since the age of ten. Down the steeply curved, otherworldly **Victoria Street**, allegedly the blueprint for J K Rowling's Diagon Alley, don't miss a look around one of the many Harry Potter shops that rub shoulders with whisky and tartan houses.

Situated just before you reach Edinburgh Castle at the top of the historic Royal Mile, **Camera Obscura & World of Illusions** (camera-obscura.co.uk) is one of those attractions that go the extra mile. Spread across five floors, it features more than a hundred

◀ **1** Arthur's Seat and city views. **2** Climbing the trail. **3** St Margaret's Loch.

GREYFRIARS BOBBY

interactive, hands-on exhibits and mind-bending illusions, and culminates with a camera obscura right at the top where you can tour Edinburgh's streets without moving – before stepping outside on the terrace to see the real thing. Children are particularly enthralled by the mind-boggling, tummy-turning Vortex Tunnel, finding themselves lost within the never-ending Mirror Maze, and seeing themselves bigger than their parents in the forced perspective of the Ames Room. Each space provokes thought and discussion on science and the wonders of the world.

Practically next door, **Edinburgh Castle** (⊘ edinburghcastle.scot) is more fortified village than standalone castle, sitting majestically on its great granite rock. Kids will learn about how the castle was built in 1103, and that it has been home to kings and queens including Mary, Queen of Scots, who gave birth here to James VI of Scotland/James I of England in 1566. Don't miss the dog cemetery, the Great Hall, the National War Museum and the Redcoat Café with its panoramic views over Princes Street and the New Town. On our visit, hard-hatted workfolk were hard at it constructing the seating for the epic **Military Tattoo** (⊘ edintattoo.com), part of the Edinburgh Festival in August. Booking in advance is strongly recommended for this Scottish spectacle.

Another gem for families, the **National Museum of Scotland** (⊘ nms.ac.uk) features interactive areas for kids covering everything from meteorites to monsters from the deep. It's perfect for a rainy day. Opposite the museum on George IV bridge, say hello to the city's iconic **Greyfriars Bobby** statue, the epitome of doggie devotion.

THE NEW TOWN & LEITH

Given that the area was designed in 1767, the notion of the **New Town** being 'new' could well be confusing for kids. Set upon a grid system, it offers interesting insights into early town planning. The most famous thoroughfare is **Princes Street**, with Edinburgh's original railway hotel – now The Balmoral – at the east end and the Waldorf Astoria at its west end. Both offer epic castle views (no need to step inside). It's fun to take a tram ride around the New Town or, for a bird's-eye

◀ **1** Colourful Victoria Street, Old Town. **2** Edinbugh Castle. **3** Greyfriars Bobby. **4** The Infinity Corridor at Camera Obscura & World of Illusions.

view of Edinburgh, to climb the 287 tight spiral steps within the **Scott Monument** (⊘ edinburghmuseums.org.uk), built in honour of the novelist Sir Walter Scott and one of the largest monuments dedicated to a writer anywhere in the world.

Head to the east end of Princes Street and take the long straight walk into the increasingly trendy neighbourhood of **Leith** – about a two-mile stretch – or catch 16 or 35 bus. The tram from St Andrew's Square is set to start by summer 2023 (⊘ edinburghtrams.com). Once in Leith, make sure to explore The Shore area, now home to the **Royal Yacht Britannia** (⊘ royalyachtbritannia.co.uk), the Queen's former floating palace for over 40 years. Visitors can look around the Admiral's Quarters, the Crew's Quarters, The Royal Deck Tearoom, the State Apartments and The Bridge. Cream tea in the tea room on the Royal Deck is a cool family treat.

It's also fun to walk to Leith along the surprisingly rural-feeling **Water of Leith** (⊘ waterofleith.org.uk); the stretch of the river from the Pentland Hills to the Leith Docks is a designated urban wildlife site. The walk takes you through the very pretty Dean village, home to the **Scottish National Gallery of Modern Art** (⊘ nationalgalleries. org), which has a wonderful trail in its extensive grounds where you can discover local art and make your own. Carry on along the Water of Leith to **Stockbridge** (just under a mile), another hip and happening neighbourhood, and the **Royal Botanic Garden** a further half mile from Stockbridge (⊘ rbge.org.uk; page 414).

FURTHER AFIELD

You can take a fun family day out via a 45-minute train journey from Waverley Station to the pretty shore district of **South Queensferry** to check out the **Forth bridges** (⊘ theforthbridges.org). The **Maid of the Forth** (⊘ maidoftheforth.co.uk) offers a 1½-hour sightseeing trip by boat to see all three bridges, and a three-hour trip on which you land at **Inchcolm Island** and explore its abbey, wildlife and beaches.

Not many people associate Edinburgh with the seaside, but it's just a 25-minute train ride from Waverley Station east to **Portobello Beach**, where Georgian architecture bumps up against two miles of Scottish sand. If you're in the mood for a walk, you can do it from town – it takes

◀ **1** The Scott Monument. **2** Royal Yacht Britannia. **3** Scottish National Gallery of Modern Art.

about 90 minutes. Take a bucket and spade, have a paddle in the sea and be sure to have a meal at the Beach House café (page 415).

Two other satellite attractions – both about an hour from the centre by bus or train – are well worth visiting. To the southeast, **Dalkeith Country Park** (⏀ dalkeithcountrypark.co.uk) has a fantastic adventure playground, great woodland walks, a Go Ape outlet (⏀ goape.co.uk) and the pretty Restoration Yard for food and a spot of shopping for the parents, while **Jupiter Artland** (⏀ jupiterartland.org), southwest, is an extraordinary outdoor wonderland of art and sculpture, with creative workshops for children during school holidays and a lovely café.

PRACTICALITIES

FAMILY-FRIENDLY SLEEPS

Adagio Aparthotel ⏀ adagio-city.com. With its central location, Adagio Aparthotel, just down the road from Edinburgh Castle and around the corner from Waverley train station, is a real find, combining the essentials of a hotel with apartment-style stays. The downstairs communal living space has blue velvet sofas and table football. There's a basket of free fruit and croissants, and cooked and Continental help-yourself breakfast is served daily. If you want a quick dinner, you can buy DIY fast food at reception; all the apartments come with fully fitted kitchens.

The Balmoral ⏀ roccofortehotels.com. If you have a healthy budget, you won't regret splashing out for a night or two at this majestic five-star, built as a grand railway hotel in 1902, but now a pleasing combo of ancient and modern. Kids will love the fact there's a J K Rowling suite, where the famous Scottish author stayed to finish *Harry Potter & the Deathly Hallows*. Vast, high-ceilinged interconnecting suites are best for families; kids under 13 are greeted in the room by a Bonnie the Owl soft toy (the hotel's mascot), a thoughtful selection of comics, sweet treats and a personalised passport to be stamped around the hotel.

Fingal ⏀ fingal.co.uk. Edinburgh's first floating hotel, the Fingal started life as a Northern Lighthouse Board ship. Now permanently moored in Leith next to the Royal Yacht Britannia, the vessel is an exciting treat for families, with 23 luxury cabins – some of them interconnecting – all named after Stevenson lighthouses.

McCraes B&B ⏀ mccraes.co.uk. This eco-conscious, family-run townhouse B&B in the New Town does its best to keep its carbon footprint low. There's a large family room, which sleeps up to five and has a bath; a cot and baby blankets

◀ **1** Portobello Beach. **2** Jupiter Artland. **3** Dalkeith Country Park.

THE POWER OF PLANTS: ROYAL BOTANIC GARDEN EDINBURGH

Arboretum Place, EH3 5NZ ✍ rbge.org.uk; age: all; intrepid level: ①; before your visit, check the website to see what special trails, events & exhibitions are on for families & to find online resources for children

Coming to a capital city, you might not expect to go on a world expedition, but here at Edinburgh's Royal Botanic Garden, children have access to over 8,000 exotic plans from around the globe, explains marketing officer Sandra Donnelly as she shows us around. Each of the ten glasshouses has a different climatic zone so you can experience the hot and steamy rainforest and see giant Amazonian waterlilies, follow dinosaur footprints through the lush, cool tree fern forest, and wander among cacti and succulents in the desert.

'The garden has seasonal trails aimed at young visitors,' Sandra says. 'The popular Easter and Halloween trails are a highlight of the events calendar. Apart from being immense fun, these are a way to engage young audiences and get them thinking about the natural environment.'

Each year, the garden participates in the Edinburgh Science Festival, organising a two-week summer programme for primary-aged children packed with educational activities and hands-on experiences to raise awareness of the importance of plants and why it is crucial to conserve them and our natural world.

Sandra advises families to keep their eyes open for the many creatures that live in the garden, be it a bright blue flash of kingfisher at the pond, the still, statue-like grey heron looking for fish, grey squirrels jumping from branch to branch, or woodpeckers tapping on the trees. 'Look carefully for the mini beasts that live in secret hidey-holes and under logs. Spot pollinators like bees, hoverflies and butterflies flitting from flower to flower helping the plants make seed. And feel like a Borrower in the giant redwood grove.'

are available free of charge. Babysitting is available for a fee, and there's also bike storage.

Norton House Hotel & Spa
✍ handpickedhotels.co.uk. If you fancy getting out of the city centre, check out this country house hotel near the Jupiter Artland contemporary sculpture park. Children under three stay and dine for free and there are discounts for guests

aged 12 to 18 sharing a room with their parents. The hotel also has a large swimming pool.

Rutland Hotel ✍ therutlandhotel. com. This West End hotel has 12 boutique bedrooms, but it's the serviced two-bedroom apartments with their own garden that are perfect for families. Cots and folding beds are available, plus toy boxes and Nintendo Wiis.

Children can also try and spot Marley, the garden cat, who loves to wander through the glasshouses.

Young children will enjoy a walk around the Demonstration Garden to see how many vegetables they recognise in the veg plots and say hi to the scarecrow. And best of all is the climb up the Chinese Hillside to look for bamboo, when you're rewarded with an amazing view of the Edinburgh skyline.

ROYAL BOTANIC GARDEN EDINBURGH

KID-FRIENDLY EATS

Alby's ⚲ albysleith.co.uk. Not your average sandwich shop, this is the Leith home of 'Big Hot Sandwiches', with a rotating menu offering delicious fillings between large wedges of soft focaccia.

Badger & Co ⚲ badgerandco.com. This lively restaurant with Edinburgh Castle views is housed in the former home of *Wind in the Willows* author Kenneth Grahame; kids will recognise the riverbank characters in the paintings on the wall. Serving hearty comfort food, from burgers to apple tarts, it has a pretty courtyard for al-fresco drinks and dining in the summer, and 'Kids eat Free' offers during the school holidays.

Beach House ⚲ thebeachhousecafe. co.uk. Down on the Portobello seafront, this is the perfect family pit stop for breakfast, lunch or supper by the beach, with organic and locally sourced food and tasty homemade ice cream.

Bonnie & Wild

⊘ bonnieandwildmarket.com. Edinburgh's first food hall, in the new St James Quarter at the east end of the New Town, Bonnie & Wild features some of Scotland's best independent food and drink producers. Families with diverse tastes will find what they're looking for – from fresh seafood to Hong Kong-style street snacks – in its range of stalls, shops and bars. It's a great place to stock up for picnics for the walk up Arthur's Seat.

Edinburgh Farmers' Market

⊘ edinburghfarmersmarket.co.uk. Held on Castle Terrace every Saturday, with stunning views of the castle and only a hop, skip and a jump from the Royal Mile, this splendid market is a renowned foodie haven, showcasing the very best of Scottish produce. If you're self-catering, it's the perfect place to catch the highest quality local ingredients – fresh scallops, smoked salmon, venison, cheese, seasonal fruit and vegetables, and more.

Howies Restaurant ⊘ howies. uk.com. Seasonal and cosy, Howies is a great place to take the family for tasty Scottish cuisine. Kid-friendly classics include cullen skink (creamy smoked fish and potato stew), haggis, neeps and tatties, and smoked salmon. There are two historic venues to choose from,

one in Waterloo Place and the other on Victoria Street.

Makars Gourmet Mash Bar

⊘ makarsmash.com. Offering hearty crowd-pleasing Scottish favourites, including haggis, neeps and tatties, this friendly restaurant also has a committed plant menu that features veggie haggis and roast vegetable bakes. Child portions of anything on the menu cost £5.

Mary's Milk Bar ⊘ marysmilkbar. com. This marvellously modern milk bar in Edinburgh's historic Grassmarket, in the Old Town, serves handmade gelato and chocolates, presenting weird and wonderful seasonal flavour combinations like toast and marmalade or goats cheese and figs, along with favourites like salted caramel.

Tani Modi ⊘ tanimodi.co. In a child-friendly setting in the centre of the New Town, this family-run brunch house, serving hearty pancakes and fry-ups, is a great stop for sightseeing families.

BEFORE YOU GO

Booking Royal Edinburgh Tickets (⊘ edinburghtour.com) gives you 48 hours' access to three city bus tours, Edinburgh Castle, the Palace of Holyroodhouse and the Royal Yacht Britannia.

MORE INFO

Edinburgh Festivals
⊘ edinburghfestivalcity.com
Visit Scotland ⊘ visitscotland.com

27
THE CAIRNGORMS

*The Arctic of the British Isles is a
wild Scottish playground.*

TOP FAMILY EXPERIENCE
BESPOKE TOUR WITH BRAEMAR HIGHLAND EXPERIENCE

BEST FOR KIDS AGED: 5–15

WHEN TO GO: Year-round; particularly good times include May, when things
are relatively quiet and the weather is generally great,
and September, when the Braemar Gathering takes place

INTREPID LEVEL: ②

ADDED ADVENTURE: Skiing, steam trains, foraging, fairy-tale castles, reindeer spotting,
loch adventures, Highland Games

TIME: One to two weeks

WILD TREASURES & COSY DENS

Various meeting points within the national park ⊘ bhe.scot; although pricier than other
options, bespoke family tours are well worth the extra cost. Tours are more difficult with a
pushchair, so it's better to carry small children on your back if they can't walk far.

My son is getting muddy, on his hands and knees, studying the leaf litter
out in the wilds of the Cairngorms National Park, having just learnt the
most effective way to pace out 100m, and how to wield a compass to
find true north. Could this be the same child who I prise off his Xbox at
home to come for a park stroll?

We're in the middle of a very special treasure hunt that's loosely
based around the theme of *Treasure Island*, tying in with the fact that
Robert Louis Stevenson wrote the first five chapters of the book here
in the Cairngorms. We're here to decipher a treasure map and delve
into some historic parts of Braemar before heading off into Creag
Choinnich Woods to learn more about the art of navigation. I marvel

at the knowledge and enthusiasm of our guide, Katy Fennema, whose ancestors were local shepherds and blacksmiths.

The Braemar Highland Experience is all about slowing down, truly observing the surrounding landscape and looking at the details. You could sign up for a mountain climb, or a personalised farm tour meeting reindeer, red and roe deer and rare-breed sheep, or even simply take a half-mile walk, gazing at the lichens growing on the trees. Our day is kept to the treasure hunt and a spot of den building in a birch wood with Katy and her husband Julian, a member of the mountain-rescue team.

As we press on, we feel like Highland detectives as we stride through the purple and white heather of a remote glen (Scottish access laws allow you to go off track), and discover ruined bothies. Katy encourages us to build a picture of how these dwellings would have looked in the past, and how the people living in these wild spots would have cooked and farmed. It's a history lesson all wrapped up in adventure.

My son gasps at the sight of a golden eagle overhead and Katy tells us it's rare to come out and not spot this bird of prey, or perhaps a sea eagle. What a different world this is to our urban dwelling. Yet is this all entirely as nature intended? As we encounter the denuded, but profoundly epic, landscape, Katy encourages us all to think about whether what we're looking at is natural.

As she tells me, 'We go into a lot of detail about the landscape and land management, and about how what you're looking at in the Highlands often isn't its natural state. Children find this fascinating and it's something that's massively misunderstood by all ages. You drive up to Braemar over the highest through-road in the UK at Glenshee. Families generally think they are in an entirely natural landscape, which couldn't be further from the truth as this area was once covered in native trees. So it's important to explain what's going on and why it's happening.'

Katy asks my son how else he thinks we could use the land, and he immediately answers that we should plant more trees for the environment and bring in some wolves. It's a contentious and interesting conversation, and one that many people in the Highlands are now invested in. Fin is excited by the idea of living alongside wild animals and realises that we've

◀ On a treasure hunt through the Cairngorms with Braemar Highland Experience.

created a world where human needs have been prioritised over those of every other species. He thinks that maybe it's time to redress the balance.

Our adventure ends with a spot of den building. We drag wood into a clearing and assemble a very satisfying structure with the help of Katy and Julian's know-how. We then sit down and light a fire using natural materials and flint, which is pretty empowering – Fin instantly suggests he should get a flint for his next birthday. Magically, a pan of milk appears, along with hot-chocolate powder, and we're sitting in our cosy den, warmed by a steaming cup of cocoa, my son grinning wildly.

ADDED ADVENTURE: MOUNTAINS, MUNROS & LOCHS

The **Cairngorms** mountain range, in northeast Scotland, is a beguiling land of superlatives. Not least in its weather conditions: enduring the UK's lowest recorded temperatures – in 1982 it reached -27.2°C in Braemar – the region can also reach a balmy 18°C in August. Covering a colossal 1,500 square miles, the **Cairngorms National Park** (⊘ cairngorms.co.uk) is twice the size of its better-known cousin, the Lake District, and is home to five of the UK's six highest mountains – not to mention its 55 Munros (mountains over 3,000ft).

Coming here with urban children is like entering another dimension, or at least a living geography lesson: along with the mighty peaks, you will encounter ancient native trees, waterfalls, lochs and exotic wildlife. Children will feel like they're in a foreign land, one inhabited by creatures with such exotic names as ptarmigan and capercaillie. The park is home to a quarter of the UK's threatened bird, animal and plant species, including mountain hares, snow bunting, golden eagles, red squirrels, red deer and black grouse. Bonus points for spotting the forest-skulking pine marten and bonus points with bells on if you see a wildcat.

For any non Scots, even the language is alien, with the 'Munros' and the 'lochs' and the prospect of getting a 'drookit' (a drenching) or eating a 'clootie' (a spicy dumpling dessert). All you need to do is get your kids to read a Rabbie Burns poem and they'll think they're tackling a foreign language.

---

1 Strathspey Steam Railway. **2** Ospreys flourish at Loch Garten Nature Reserve.
3 Horseriding through Cairngorms National Park. ▶

AVIEMORE & SURROUNDS

In winter, the Cairngorms offer families an alternative to the Alps, with a ski season centred on the town of **Aviemore**. There are so many Landrover tracks that when they are covered with snow you have ready-made cross-country skiing across the region. Although these days, with changing weather patterns, locals would advise families never to pre-book a ski holiday here, when the conditions are right you will find the best skiing anywhere in Scotland at **Glenshee**. If snow is forecast and it's a good snow year, then definitely get yourselves up there as fast as you can. You can check conditions on the **Snowgate webcam** set up near the village of Braemar (⊘ braemarscotland.co.uk).

In summer this is a region of adrenalin-fueled outdoor pursuits, from mountain-bike trails to pony treks. There are numerous walking trails suitable for families in the national park. Even the 4,081ft summit of **Cairngorm** (⊘ cairngormmountain.org) itself is within reach of outdoorsy children thanks to the steep, well-marked **Coire Cas Loop** that snakes up the mountain for just under a mile from the base station of the funicular railway. And, of course, the big incentive for tackling this mighty Munro on foot is that you can take the mountain train back down again.

> "The big incentive for tackling this mighty Munro on foot is that you can take the mountain train back down again."

Cairngorm may be the crowning glory of many a family hike in the national park, but there are other less lofty options, too: weaving through forest, perhaps, or looping around lochs. Call in at a visitor centre – in Ballater or Aviemore, for example – where rangers can advise you on the most appropriate trail.

If you're not in the mood for walking, you could take a step back in time instead with a ride on the **Strathspey Steam Railway** (⊘ strathspeyrailway.co.uk). From Aviemore, the western terminus, you can catch the train the six miles to the village of Boat of Garten, where ospreys flourish at the famous **Loch Garten Nature Reserve** (⊘ rspb. org.uk).

It's a short drive southeast from Aviemore to **Loch Morlich**, where you can amaze your children with a golden sand beach 40 miles from the sea. The **watersports centre** (⊘ lochmorlich.com) offers stand-up

◀ **1** Paddleboarding on Loch Morlich. **2** Feeding reindeer at Glenmore.

paddleboarding, kayaking, canoeing and mountain biking for families (minimum age depends on activity). Nearby, make sure to visit the UK's only free-grazing reindeer herd at **Glen More** (∂ cairngormreindeer. co.uk). It's only when you hand-feed a reindeer that you realise just how soft and velvety their muzzles are. The Cairngorm herd numbers around 150 and the opportunity to feed and pet them is a dream come true for most children.

Loch an Eilein (∂ rothiemurchus.net), around five miles south of Aviemore, is another magical find – with a 13th-century castle perched on an island in the centre, it's the stuff of fairy tales and a favourite with picnickers. Further to the southwest, **Loch Insh** (∂ lochinsh.com) has the added bonus of three children's adventure play areas plus an activity centre offering everything from archery to stand-up paddleboarding (five years and above; other age restrictions vary).

Head another few miles southwest to the **Highland Wildlife Park** (∂ highlandwildlifepark.org), near the small town of Kingussie, for your very own safari. Don't miss the drive-through reserve, where you can spot European bison, yak, Tibetan wild ass, mouflon and red deer from your car. Then it's on foot to see more mountain wildlife from red pandas and Japanese macaques to wolves and the highly endangered Amur tiger.

If you're after a taste of local culture, check out the nearby **Highland Folk Museum** (∂ highlandfolk.com), an open-air museum that uses historic buildings and costumed actors to portray rural Highlands life from the early 1700s to the mid 1900s. Structures include a reconstruction of part of the medieval township of Easter Raitts, with its turf-walled, heather-thatched dwellings; a 1930s farm with a wartime kitchen where children can learn about rationing; and a railway halt, post office, shepherd's bothy and clockmaker's workshop all linked by a vintage bus ride. Don't forget to enrol the kids for a 1930s-style lesson at the tin-walled school. Summer events include baking and basket weaving.

BRAEMAR

Braemar, a pretty Cairngorms village with the River Dee coursing through, is most notorious for its Highland Games, the **Braemar**

◄ **1** Highland Folk Museum. **2** Tossing the caber, Braemar Gathering.

"Loch an Eilein is another magical find – with a 13th-century castle perched on an island in the centre, it's the stuff of fairy tales and a favourite with picnickers."

WOODLAND FORAGING FOR FAMILIES

Fife Arms, Braemar AB35 5YN ⊘ gatheringnature.com; age: 5–18; intrepid level: ①

Forager and medical herbalist Natasha Lloyd, and her dog Rosie, meet us in the lobby of Braemar's Fife Arms for our immersive foraging experience. She begins by telling us the rules of foraging: 'Never take more than a third of a patch and never eat anything you're not 100% certain is edible.'

We set off up the high street and past the Braemar Highland Games Centre, along the river and finally into the woods. There, Natasha introduces us to an astonishing array of plants and their properties – including limeflower, daisy, mullein, selfheal, rosebay willow herb, rosehips, common and wood sorrel, hawthorn and nettle – never dumbing down the information and helping the kids to really look to see what's growing wild around them.

She tells us about the plants and trees that grow in mountainous areas coursed through by large rivers – heather, rowan tree, meadowsweet, blueberry, birch tree, pine tree and Douglas fir. We try and spot them all en route as she explains how the Douglas fir was brought to Braemar by botanist David Douglas in 1827. The needles are foraged and used in Douglas Fir bitters, served in the Fife Arms bar (page 430).

When it comes to nettles, Natasha challenges us to collect and eat the raw leaves, which she describes as 'nature's multivitamin pill'. She encourages us to get over our fear of the sting, and if we do get stung to turn to the plantain leaves sprouting nearby, which contain serotonin to alleviate the pain. It's heady stuff.

Natasha is also keen to show us the mycelium network in action. She explains, 'This information highway known as the world-wide-wood (www) lies hidden beneath

Gathering (⊘ braemargathering.org), held on the first Saturday of September. The gathering was regularly attended by Queen Victoria and is still a must for members of the Royal Family. For children who have never have heard of tossing the caber, seen Scottish dancing or heard the full force of a pipe band, it's a revelation. Make the experience even more child-friendly by coming in July for the **Junior Highland Games** (⊘ braemarjuniorgames.com).

Another must-see for families is **Braemar Castle** (⊘ braemarcastle. co.uk), the only castle in the UK that's leased to the local community. Run by volunteers and fundraisers, it has a relaxed feel. The castle is steeped in tales of Jacobites, Redcoats and Victorian derring do, and for younger children there's a teddy-bear trail. The bottleneck dungeon is popular with older children, while the labyrinth in the garden is a hit with all ages.

our feet and allows plants to communicate.' She brings the concept to life by showing us a tree that has a chaga mushroom growing on it. This mushroom provides extra nutrients and is something the tree has sent a signal out for in order to help it repair itself.

By the time we head back, we've experienced a whole lot of new flavours. We love the taste of sorrel, with its lemony or green-apple-peel tang. Apparently it contains oxalic acid which also gives rhubarb its tartness. Natasha recommends we take home some meadowsweet to make ice cream with, along with valerian, lady's bedstraw and roses.

At the end of her tour, Natasha takes us to the Fife Arms and brings out her range of homemade wild condiments, including rose-petal salt, nettle salt, yarrow vinegar and strawberries pickled in apple cider vinegar. They're all a fabulous game of dare for our palates.

JANE ANDERSON

Braemar is also the starting point for the very accessible four-mile **Creag Choinnich** nature trail, perfect for small children who aren't up for more challenging walks. Climbing this little hill to the east of the village, through the pinewoods, you can teach your kids the Scots word for pinecones: yowies. For a glossary of interesting Scottish words, invest in a copy of *The Living Mountain* by Nan Shepherd. Her descriptions of hill walking in the Cairngorms are so evocative.

For a treat, take the time to pop into the **Fife Arms**, the village's former coaching inn (page 430), for its theatricality and extraordinary art, care of its creators, Iwan and Manuela Wirth of acclaimed art gallery Hauser & Wirth. Enjoy afternoon tea in the drawing room with a Picasso on the wall, or dine in the Flying Stag Restaurant, where a taxidermied stag flies over the bar with cherubic wings – or just peep into the hallway to see literally hundreds of mounted animal heads in a crazy formation.

PRACTICALITIES

FAMILY-FRIENDLY SLEEPS

Coylumbridge Hotel

⊘ coylumbridgeaviemorehotel.co.uk. This crisp, modern hotel, just a few minutes south of Aviemore, has family rooms with two double beds and space for a baby too. Kids will adore the three-floor Fun House with its soft-play area with ball pit, slides and tunnels – the Kids Club offers free supervised evening play sessions here for over-fives, great if parents fancy dinner on their own for a change! There is also an Outdoor Discovery Centre, where kids can let off steam on trampolines and a climbing wall, plus cycle and ski hire including tag-a-longs and tow-carts.

Cranford Cottage

⊘ unique-cottages.co.uk. Cranford Cottage is a new build, wood-clad cottage on the outskirts of Braemar, perfect for a family of four and their dog. The open-plan downstairs makes for a relaxed stay, with French doors opening to an enclosed garden.

Eriskay B&B and Glamping

⊘ eriskay-aviemore.co.uk. This smart and friendly guesthouse, right in the centre of Aviemore, has a family room, a double room and one twin room, or you can book one of four glamping pods in the garden.

Fife Arms

⊘ thefifearms.com. Occupying a coaching inn dating back to 1856, this extraordinary five-star hotel, brought to you by the owners of fine art gallery Hauser & Wirth, oozes creativity and local colour from every nook and cranny (page 429). The lavish rooms include four interconnecting family suites. The playroom is cosy and stylish, with table football, books, films and a joyful jungle-themed loo, and young guests are gifted a beautifully designed booklet called *The Great Braemar Beast Gathering* which invites them to track down beasts around the hotel and draw them.

Glenmore Campsite

⊘ campingintheforest.co.uk. Near Aviemore, Glenmore is a tried-and-tested favourite for family campers, with uplifting mountain views and access to the beaches and watersports of Loch Morlich.

Glenshee Glamping

⊘ glensheeglamping.co.uk. This collection of off-grid glamping options, just a short drive from the Glenshee snowsports centre, is open year-round and includes family-friendly pods, shepherd's huts, cabins and tent pitches, plus a fully restored 1940s railway goods wagon. Many have wood-fired hot tubs to add to the fun. Kids will love meeting the llamas, donkeys, goats and chickens.

Hillgoers

⊘ hillgoers.com. Mountain leader Garry Cormack and his team offer families guided or self-guided wild-camping trips in the Cairngorms, offering camping cooking tips, camp craft sessions, navigation training and qualifications. They will also assist if your teenagers (age 14+) want to tackle camping on their own.

Lazy Duck ⏒ lazyduck.co.uk. Adventurous, eco-conscious families will love the The Lazy Duck, just 20 minutes by road from Aviemore but a whole world away. Stay in luxurious eco huts or the bunkhouse hostel, or on the intimate campsite, and round off your day with a session in the wood-fired hot tub or infrared sauna. Yoga and massage are also on offer.

Macdonald Hotels ⏒ macdonaldhotels. co.uk. Macdonald Hotels & Resorts has five family-friendly four-star resorts in the Cairngorms in and around Aviemore. Macdonald Aviemore is one of the most family friendly, with rooms to accommodate up to five and its own lagoon-pool complex and soft-play centre.

Woodland Cottages ⏒ kiphideaways. com. Kit Hideaways' tagline is 'small places with soul', which is certainly true of this pair of stunning three-bedroom cottages on a private estate in the national park. Kids will find lovely books in the twin bedrooms and rope swings in the garden, not to mention pretty hammocks and lanterns between the trees in the extensive grounds.

KID-FRIENDLY EATS

Boat Country Inn & Restaurant
⏒ boathotel.co.uk. This Boat of Garten restaurant serves hearty pub-style cuisine. The Wee Rascals kids' menu offers reliable staples including steak pie, macaroni cheese and fish fingers,

with Highland-themed colouring-in and quizzes on the menu itself.

Boathouse Café ⏒ lochmorlich.com. Upstairs at the Loch Morloch watersports centre, this cosy café with scenic views over the loch and beach serves up soups, paninis, rolls and an array of tasty home-baked cakes.

Boathouse Restaurant ⏒ lochinsh. com. This family-owned and -run restaurant on the shores of Loch Insh offers home-cooked dishes using locally sourced ingredients, all served with incredible loch views. Don't miss the legendary carrot cake.

Cairngorm Café
⏒ cairngormmountain.co.uk. For a meal on Cairngorm Mountain, this wood-clad café, on level two of the Day Lodge, serves seasonal dishes from soups to venison pie. Kids' portions are available.

Chaplin's Coffee House & Ice Cream Parlour ⏒ chaplinsgrantown.co.uk. Twelve miles northeast of Aviemore, this unassuming little coffee house on Grantown on Spey's High Street is a bustle of breakfasts, lunches and afternoon teas.

Rothiemurchus ⏒ rothiemurchus.net. This café and farm shop on a working farm near Loch an Eilein serves up soups, sandwiches, stews, cakes and coffee in relaxed surroundings for families. Take-aways available, too.

Route 7 Café ⏒ route7.co.uk. Taking its name from one of the routes on the National Cycle Network, this Aviemore café at the Highland Home Centre serves hearty soups, sandwiches, burgers and potato skins along with a vegan menu and Scottish favourites such as Cullen Skink.

BEFORE YOU GO

Because family holidays in the Cairngorms are so steeped in nature, it's good to check out these environmental groups before you go:

NatureScot ✐ nature.scot, **OneKind** ✐ onekind.scot and the **Scottish Wildlife Trust** ✐ swt.org.uk.

MORE INFO

Go Rural Scotland
✐ goruralscotland.com
Majestic Aberdeenshire
✐ visitabdn.com
Visit Scotland ✐ visitscotland.com

28
ISLE OF LEWIS

Nature, ancient history and crofting crafts are all writ large on this wild Outer Hebridean isle.

TOP FAMILY EXPERIENCE

WHALE- & DOLPHIN-WATCHING LIVEABOARD CRUISE WITH HEBRIDEAN ADVENTURES

BEST FOR KIDS AGED: 8+

WHEN TO GO: May to September

INTREPID LEVEL: ②

ADDED ADVENTURE: Wild swimming & surfing, 12th-century chessmen, historic crofting villages, standing stones, pony trekking, white-sand beaches

TIME: One to two weeks

WHERE THE WILD THINGS ARE: A HEBRIDEAN VOYAGE

Stornoway harbour, HS1 2XS ⊘ hebrideanadventures.co.uk; sailings last between one & six days

As our sturdy MV *Monadhliath* confidently cuts through the opaque waters of the Minch (the stretch of the North Atlantic Ocean between Stornoway and the Scottish mainland), a summer fog rolls in around us. My children and I stand steadfast on the upper viewing deck, binoculars rendered useless in the eerie mist. Our cool and dependable Hebridean skipper Tony cuts the engine as Muriel, our on-board whale watcher and wildlife expert, beckons us to stay silent and listen out for the sound of whales.

'There! Can you hear that rumble? It's the minke whales feeding,' she exclaims, just as we see a pointy grey nose rising out of the water, tantalisingly close to our boat. Binoculars fly up to eyes and we're all rapt, but the best is yet to come as two minkes sweep right beneath the hull in a balletic flow, their white tummies and fins translucent

turquoise and ethereal beneath the clear Scottish water. They disappear into the depths then reappear, diving under the boat again, playing with us, our hearts and minds racing at being so close to these mighty creatures.

My kids career from one side of the platform to the other as the boat bobs and the minkes switch sides. Involuntary whoops of delight slip out. I wonder if the whales sense our excitement. Muriel says they are intelligent enough to differentiate between the boats that are friendly and those that might be a threat, such as ferries that won't stop. 'Minkes are very inquisitive and know our boat,' she tells us. She advises us to download the Hebridean Whale & Dolphin Trust (⊘ hwdt.org) app called Whale Track (search 'HWDT') on to our mobiles so we can actively take part in recording whale and dolphin sightings – which all helps in efforts to protect these precious creatures. This gets an excited thumbs-up from the kids.

The minkes head off as quickly as they appeared and Tony restarts the engine only for us to be joined by a pod of energetic, short-beaked common dolphin, jumping and racing close to the bow. It's thrilling for my kids to be this close to such an abundance of marine life, with diving guillemots, soaring kittiwakes and bobbing puffins adding to the party.

We joined our Hebridean Adventures boat, docked in the pretty harbour in Stornoway, the previous day. It was a thrill to explore this modest converted fishing boat, a world away from a flashy cruise liner, which was to be our home for the next three days. With just five snug, windowless cabins below deck sleeping between one and three people, it takes a maximum of just nine passengers – perfect for an extended family takeover. There's plenty of communal space to relax, and the tiniest of swaying kitchens where chef Aaron, our third and final crew member, whips up incredible three-course meals worthy of any fancy restaurant – pan-grilled mackerel with leafy kimchi, soy and apple sauce, anyone?

We're all on a Hebridean high after our first full day. Tony explains that we'll overnight in Loch Erisort, a safe haven from any bad weather. As we manoeuvre through the inlet, the water turns a deep jade green. We spot a sea eagle wheeling overhead and seals pop up to see who's arrived. The children are delighted when one of the other passengers

◀ Whale- and dolphin-watching cruises with Hebridean Adventures from Stornoway.

produces a fishing rod and starts pulling in silvery, flapping mackerel. Aaron has no hesitation in gutting the fish at the back of the boat – another life lesson for the kids.

Night seems to fall heavier over the loch due to the lack of light pollution and my kids dare themselves to go on deck, the intense dark blue of the sky matching the inky blue of the loch, a sliver of low hills all round us reflected in the still water. It feels gloriously remote, like we've journeyed around the world, yet here we are in Scotland.

After a peaceful night in our three-person cabin, I stir the kids early for a pre-sail dip in the sea loch. There are moans and groans, of course, but once we have our wetsuits on and plunge in, whooping as we do, the invigoration sets us up for the day. There's nothing like bobbing at head height with a seal and her pups before breakfast to raise your spirits.

Back on board, Tony briefs us about today's mission to see a group of three remote islands called the Shiants (pronounced 'shants' and meaning holy or enchanted islands), five miles off the east coast of southern Lewis.

We dock in the concave curve of the islands, the water alive with razorbills, guillemots and shags enjoying a noisy bath. Muriel tells us the Shiants are home to 200 pairs of storm petrels and together form a breeding site for thousands of seabirds. The children are most excited about the puffins. Dinghied across to the pebbly beach at the foot of a cliff face, we are within feet of them as they emerge comically from their cubbyholes, hopping from grassy ledge to rock and launching off like mini skydivers down to the water.

Once back on the boat we motor slowly past some of the most awesome sheer cliffs I've ever seen – 500ft of black columnar basalt rising vertically out of the sea – to the third Shiant island, home to the trio's only manmade structure, a humble bothy. Even with the dinghy to take us to the water's edge, it's touch and go as to whether we can scramble ashore over yards of slippery kelp-laden rocks. The kids relish the hint of danger and are soon on shore heading for the solitary bothy – like a fairy-tale shack with a weathered door that magically opens to reveal a fireplace, a basic kitchen with tins of food, and four bunk beds.

Aaron doubles up as our guide here, telling us the Shiants were once home to a settlement of 40 people and pointing out the 'lazy beds' – small undulating lines in the grass where beds were ploughed for Highland farming. As we scramble up the hill behind the bothy, where bracken, reeds and wildflowers thrive, he tells about the Shiants Isles Recovery Programme, which involved eradicating the rats that were eating the birds' eggs. A lively discussion ensues about invasive species and human intervention. More questions arise when my children hear that the islands are the subject of a memoir called *Sea Room*, written by Adam Nicolson, who inherited the Shiants from his father and handed them over to his own son: how can you own an island and all the wildlife on it?

Finally we arrive at an ancient monolith, with epic views towards the isles of Harris and Skye, the MV *Monadhliath* looking like a toy boat beneath us. We all agree that the Outer Hebrides is one of the most special places on earth and experiencing it from the ocean in the company of cetaceans has been an utter privilege.

ADDED ADVENTURE: MYSTERIOUS ISLAND – FROM CHESSMEN TO CROFTS

The Isle of Lewis sits at the northwest corner of the Outer Hebrides, otherwise known as the Western Isles, otherwise known as The Long Islands because they stretch for hundreds of miles. The Isle of Lewis and Isle of Harris share the same island, but tend to be referred to as two separate places, split in name by ancient clans.

If ever there was a time to buy an old-school OS map and lay it out on the table for your kids to ponder over where exactly you are, it's now. Archipelagos have a real power to capture children's imaginations – which will be even more fired up when you tell them that Lewisian gneiss rock is some of the oldest in Britain at three billion years, that the island's ancient sights include standing stones to rival Stonehenge, and that there's a stunning dose of Viking heritage, too. That's not even to mention the beaches, which rival anything you'll see in the Indian Ocean in terms of white sand and azure-blue seas, and the added intrigue that people on Lewis speak the ancient language of Gaelic.

At just 36 miles by 12 miles, Lewis is easy to navigate by car or bike along the Hebridean Way (sustrans.org.uk), which segues into Harris in the south.

Seilebost Beach, Isle of Harris. ▶

"That's not even to mention the beaches which rival anything you'll see in the Indian Ocean in terms of white sand and azure-blue seas."

STORNOWAY & SURROUNDS

The compact harbour town of **Stornoway** is a gentle place to stroll around with children. At the outer harbour you can see the Caledonian MacBrayne ferries coming and going from Ullapool on the mainland and further round there's another busy harbour where sightseeing and fishing boats come and go.

Dating back to 1844, **Lews Castle** (⊘ lews-castle.co.uk) overlooks Stornoway Harbour from behind its wooded grounds. It's an exciting place to visit for any young chess fans; some of the **Lewis Chessmen** are on display in the adjoining **Museum nan Eilean**. These exquisite figures, carved from walrus ivory and sperm-whale tooth, full of detail and character, date back to the late 12th century and were found in 1831 on Uig beach on Lewis's west coast. We particularly like the warder biting his shield like a Viking berserker and the knight on horseback, very low to the ground. My children think it's cool that chess was played 900 years ago.

There's a cute outdoor play park with wooden climbing frames and forest shade next to the café (page 450), and the wooded grounds are great for a cycle. You can hire bikes from **Bespoke** (⊘ bespokebicycles. co.uk) on Willowglen Road or order bikes to be delivered to your island location.

Over in the main part of town, among the Harris Tweed and whisky shops, the **An Lanntair Arts Centre** (⊘ lanntair.com) is a great place to head with youngsters for local contemporary art exhibitions, kids' film screenings and workshops – past events have included a two-day workshop creating figures from natural clay deposits found on Lewis's Barvas Moor, then firing them on a local beach. In summer there's often live music outside and a couple of food trucks.

To get a bit closer to island life, take your kids to see a game of **shinty** – a Highland version of hockey. Check out match times at ⊘ camanachdleodhais.com/youth-shinty. You can also head way up to Ness to meet local celebrity **Sweeny** (Donald Macsween) who hosts the *An Lot* ('The Croft') programme on BBC Alba and featured in *The Misadventures of Romesh Ranganathan* TV series. Sweeny takes visitors on a tour around his croft and regales them with great stories of life on Lewis (⊘ airanlot.com).

---

1 Stornoway. **2** An Lanntair Arts Centre. ▶

From their base in Sandwick just outside Stornoway, **SurfLewis** (⏣ surflewis.com) offers surfing, stand-up paddleboarding and wild swimming at various locations around Lewis (children must be 12 or over for all activities). According to founder Rodney Jamieson, known as Cheggs, the Hebrides are in the perfect location to catch the swell (waves) heading to the mainland, and while other UK surf hotspots get crowded in summer, you'll always find a fairly deserted beach here. When one side of the island is too crashy for surf lessons, the other side is usually perfect, with the added advantage of spectacular scenery just about everywhere.

THE WEST COAST

On Lewis's west coast, the **Calanais Standing Stones** (Callanish when anglicised; ⏣ calanais.org) present a 5,000-year-old mystery just waiting for families to unlock. Walking up to the stones from the informative visitor centre, children will learn that they are looking at a landscape of lochs, drowned valleys and hills formed after the last Ice Age, 14,000 years ago. There are stunning views over Loch Roag and it's fun to spot the shape of a reclining figure in the hills named 'The Old Woman of the Moors'. Perhaps she's a giant who could rise at any time, or maybe Mother Nature herself?

At the top of a curving climb, the stones rise up before you and, unlike at more heavily visited sites like Stonehenge, you are free to walk right up to these towering monoliths and even touch them. Any parents who have watched the popular TV series *Outlander* might be tempted to lay a hand on them to transport themselves to another time! There's undoubtedly a magic about the stones, felt especially if you visit at sunrise or sunset; they're said to be oriented perfectly for midwinter sunrise and sunsets.

For children there are big questions to be answered. How did they get here and why were they erected? It's certainly a testament to the skill and determination of the people who lived here 5,000 years ago, who probably used rollers, wooden frames and brute strength.

Closer inspection will reveal that the stones don't actually form a simple circle, but a cruciform – a shape similar to a Celtic cross. Evidence of a small burial chamber in the centre of the circle suggests that this

---

◀ **1** Calanais Standing Stones. **2** Gearrannan Blackhouse Village. **3** Watersports fans can seek out one of several local businesses offering a full range of water-based activities.

PONY TREKKING ON THE SANDS WITH LEIGH MINION

Traigh Mhòr Pony Trekking, 15 New Tolsta, HS2 0NN ⌀ tolsta41.com; age: five & over for beach rides; younger children can go on village rides; intrepid level: ②

We first glimpse the powerhouse that is Leigh Minion handing out riding hats and politely but firmly assigning riders to ponies and guides. It comes as no surprise that this multitasker not only set up Traigh Mhòr riding school with her husband Gavin, she's also a science teacher in a Lewis secondary school. So far, so impressive. When we show up, Leigh immediately assesses me and my kids as amateurs and guides us to her gentlest, most steadfast ponies!

I'm offered Woody, a traditional Gypsy Vanner Cob, while my son rides Six, a Quarter Horse gelding. Leigh tells us that he was orphaned at six weeks old and loves being around people. As Fin stands in front of him Six somehow manages to get hold of his coat zip and pulls it down. Hilarity ensues. My daughter, meanwhile, has fallen in love with Dee, a Connemara cross gelding.

We head off in a group, down a beautiful rural road that curves downhill towards the ocean, each with a helper guiding our ponies. Leigh employs local youngsters, giving them job opportunities, life skills and work experience for Duke of Edinburgh qualifications. All in all, we feel she's a bit of a local hero.

As we descend, the awesome Traigh Mhòr (Gaelic for 'Big Beach)' gradually reveals itself, unfolding its mile of palest yellow sand and rolling white breakers on a turquoise sea. It's easily as beautiful as the Caribbean with cliffs, stacks and vast caves at either end. It's a huge thrill and a wonderful sense of freedom to be up high on a pony, taking in the views

was once a place of ritual and worship. Others believe the stones were an astronomical observatory or a place to exercise civil liberties. Locally the stones are called Na Fir Brighe, 'The False Men' – giants who were turned into stone for refusing to convert to Christianity, a powerful image for children. Whatever version your children choose to believe, it's fascinating to discuss what might have happened all those years ago. In effect, you have all become time travellers.

For a bit of fun after the intensity of the stones, head to the nearby **Callanish Alpacas** (⬛) where you can drop in and see alpacas, Hebridean sheep, Kunekune pigs, Indian Runner ducks and a whole squad of unusual chickens. Or for something more learned, book a Gaelic lesson for all the family with **Magaidh Smith** (⌀ magaidhsmith. co.uk), a native-speaking Gaelic tutor who lives in a croft just ten minutes from the stones.

and the salty sea air, especially when having come from city life.

A more experienced rider in our group has a canter along the full length of the beach, making us all want to learn to ride and be able to experience that level of freedom, splashing through the surf.

'Riding is extremely therapeutic for children,' says Leigh. 'We provide a sense of safe adventure. We often take out children with special needs, which is a very positive experience. It's also great exercise in the fresh air. People often think that you just sit on a horse, but you are in fact activating the core, even just by walking.'

The combination of learning a new skill, interacting with these intelligent creatures and being out in this stunning natural environment make this a slow family experience we'll all cherish for years. What's more, I don't think my son Fin will ever forget the day a pony helped him to get dressed!

JANE ANDERSON

Gearrannan Blackhouse Village (⊘ gearrannan.com), on the coast some nine miles north of the stones, offers unmissable insights into crofting life going right back to the 17th century. These longhouses made from drystone walls topped with turf, and impressive thatched roofs held secure by long ropes anchored with heavy stones, were home to an ageing local community as recently at 1974. Take a stroll around a working house, reconstructed as it would have been in the 1950s. Kids will be struck by the alarming slope on the floor and the soot-blackened ceiling; before the fireplace and chimney were installed, the fire would have been in the middle of the floor (hence the name blackhouse) – which at least killed off the bugs in the thatch! In the rear of the house is a 120-year-old Hattersley loom, which you may see being worked by one of only 200 Harris Tweed weavers still alive today. On our visit the weaver invited us to look at his weaving template and told us that punch cards like these paved the way for early computer codes. As he clacked away on the loom we learned about the warp and the weft and the fact it takes one hour to weave 3ft of his green tweed, with its smart red fleck – 'If I'm not talking!' he winked.

In the next house a video shows how peat is made – there's a massive pile of it outside – and explains more about the looms. The village offers accommodation, too, in blackhouses right by a little beach (page 449).

From Gearrannan there's a stunning four-mile waymarked coastal walk east to the beaches at **Dalmore** and **Dalbeg**. For another option, head west along the coast to Laimishader Lighthouse on the headland at the mouth of Loch Carloway. Both walks can take up to three hours one way over rugged terrain and are suitable for confident walkers and children aged eight and over.

Further south lies **Uig Bay**, where the famous 12th-century chessmen were discovered; wild and expansive with fine white sand, it's a lovely place to take a bucket and spade to do your own digging.

If wild swimming is more your thing, contact **Immerse Hebrides** ($\oslash$ immersehebrides.com), based in Stornoway. Options include gentle swims off **Bosta Beach** and **Reef Beach**, keeping within everyone's depth and close to rocks and seaweed in order to spot the most marine life, or wild-swimming boat tours, which depart from **Breasclete Pier** to a number of uninhabited islands. Children five years and over can come on the boat, but you must be at least 12 years old to swim.

INTO HARRIS

For smaller children, the **Aline Community Woodland** ($\oslash$ alinewoodland.org), 20 miles south of Stornoway, has a wonderfully remote play park surrounded by woodland, with accessible boardwalks, tracks, and tables for picnics.

Some four miles further south, in Harris, the **Scaladale Centre** ($\oslash$ scaladale-centre.co.uk) offers on-site abseiling, archery and bushcraft tours and will take families rock climbing, sea kayaking, coasteering, gorge scrambling and loch kayaking around Harris and Lewis.

Nearby is the **Ardvourlie Nature Observatory**, run by the North Harris Trust ($\oslash$ north-harris.org) and set in a woodland that has been

1, **2** & **3** The Scaladale Centre offers a variety of activities on both Harris and Lewis. **4** Visit the North Harris Eagle Observatory to be in with a chance of spotting golden eagles. ▶

COMMUNITY EVENTS AT EOROPIE PLAY PARK

Well worth a visit for kids who need to let off steam, the play park at **Eoropie Beach** (⊘ eoropiedunespark.co.uk) is set on the natural machair (grassland) and dunes near Port of Ness in the far north of Lewis. It's right next to Traigh Shanndaigh, one of the best beaches on the island, so you can combine a visit with playing in the sand and a cold water swim. The park hosts many community events that benefit local youngsters. Park entry is free but visitors can show their support by donating via the website, or in donation boxes on-site.

planted with birch, rowan, alder, willow holly and juniper trees over the last twenty or so years. Look out for golden eagles soaring above; this is some of the best eagle habitat in Europe. For more of these magnificent birds of prey, head west across Harris to the **North Harris Eagle Observatory,** seven miles northwest of Tarbert, Harris's main town. Families must walk the two miles up the track from the car park to the viewpoint, which is open year-round, to catch sight of the birds.

PRACTICALITIES

GETTING THERE

The greenest way to get to the Isle of Lewis is by Calmac ferry (⊘ calmac.co.uk), which sails from Ullapool to Stornoway, Uig (on Skye) to Tarbert and Lochmaddy (North Uist) and Oban to Castlebay (Barra) and Lochboisdale (South Uist). Calmac also run a ferry service between Bernerary and Leverburgh (Harris).

FAMILY-FRIENDLY SLEEPS

Borve House Hotel
⊘ borvehousehotel.co.uk. Located on the west coast of the Isle of Lewis this friendly hotel has nine bedrooms including a family suite, and four self-catering chalets sleeping up to six.
Broad Bay House B&B
⊘ broadbayhouse.co.uk. Best suited for families with older children, this contemporary, family-run B&B just a few miles north of Stornoway – with views over the Minch – offers four immaculate luxury suites and the use of a laundry and study with PC, local guidebooks, maps, DVDs and novels. Three-course meals or sharing platters can be booked on certain evenings.
Dragonfly B&B ⊘ the-dragonfly-bed-breakfast-stornoway.hotelmix.co.uk. This smart B&B in central Stornoway is a great base for families. Book the large top room with en-suite bathroom for great views out over the rooftops towards the harbour. The owner is a music teacher, and the breakfast room is full of guitars. There are also board games, including a chess board with replicas of the Lewis chessmen.

Gearrannan Blackhouse Village

⊘ gearrannan.com. Staying in an authentic blackhouse village (page 445) gives children a taste of what life must have been like for islanders hundreds of years ago. Though these self-catering cottages – right by a small beach, with access to wonderful coastal walks – now have electricity and modern furniture, the on-site museum reveals the tough living conditions in the days of old. There is also a more basic bunkhouse which sleeps 14.

Heather Isle Chalets

⊘ heatherislechalets.com. Perfect for a wilderness getaway, the Erisort and Orisaigh self-catering chalets, built from Siberian larch, have the most wonderful views over sea lochs and hills in the small village of Leurbost just south of Stornoway. Each sleeps a family of four; pets are welcome.

Laxdale Holiday Park

⊘ laxdaleholidaypark.com. This intimate family-run holiday park just outside Stornoway offers wigwam pods, luxury caravans, self-catering lodges and a modern bunkhouse, or you can bring your own tent or campervan.

Lews Castle ⊘ lews-castle.co.uk. Kids

will be excited to hear they are staying in a real-life castle (page 440) – the apartments, however, on the extensive upper floors, are modern, with upscale furnishings and scenic island views. They sleep up to six.

Moorpark Cottages

⊘ moorparkcottages.co.uk. Set on the west side of Lewis in Barvas, an old crofting community, these attractive larch-and-slate cottages each sleep a family of four.

Uig Camping ⊘ visituig.co.uk/camping. The stunning beach at Uig makes this an attractive place to set up camp. Two community campsites are available: Kneep Campsite on the Bhaltos Peninsula and Ardroil Sands Campsite near vast Uig Beach, both on the west coast.

KID-FRIENDLY EATS

An Lanntair Café Bar ⊘ lanntair. com/cafebar. This lively and attractive modern café-bar, on the first floor of the An Lanntair Arts Centre in Stornoway, is an uplifting place for a family meal or snack, with fresh organic food and a children's menu featuring breakfast pancakes, homemade macaroni cheese and tasty sandwiches.

Blue Lobster

⊡ @thebluelobsterstornoway. This pretty café and gift shop overlooks Stornoway harbour and the turrets of Lews Castle from its large picture windows, or you can sit outside on the terrace, lit with fairylights in winter. They serve seriously good coffee and cakes, plus sandwiches and seafood.

Boatshed Restaurant

⊘ royalstornoway.co.uk. Located in the Royal Stornoway Hotel, this upscale restaurant is a favourite with islanders and serves local seafood. Encourage your children to try hand-dived scallops, mussels and sustainable creel-caught langoustine. A take-away menu is also available, good for self-catering stays.

Crown Inn ⌂ crownhotelstornoway. com. This friendly Stornoway restaurant offers an extensive menu of seafood, burgers (with local venison or haggis and black pudding) and pizzas. The Wee Ones' options offer smaller dishes with a free fruit juice, cordial or milk.

Hub Café ⌂ bespokebicycles.co.uk. Run by the bike-mad team behind Bespoke Bicycles in Stornoway, this welcoming café serves sandwiches, soups, filled bagels and cakes from local suppliers. Dogs are welcome.

Storehouse Café ⌂ lews-castle.co.uk. On the ground floor of Lews Castle, this opulent café serves hearty full Scottish breakfasts featuring Stornoway black pudding, plus paninis, smoked-salmon platters with island oatcakes, and pizzas – or you could just come for coffee and cake.

Uig Sands Restaurant ⌂ uigsands. co.uk. This place is all about the staggering views across Uig Beach, the bay and mountains beyond. Quite frankly, they could dish up anything here and you'd be happy, but luckily the food is great, from the seaweed and potato cakes with poached eggs and wilted greens to Carloway lobster. While there's no kids' menu, just smaller portions, children are very welcome and high chairs are available if you book in advance.

Woodlands Café ⏹. Set in the wooded grounds of Lews Castle, this modern but cosy café serves tasty sandwiches, toasties and paninis, baked potatoes and burgers. The kids' menu features a half sandwich, dried apple, raisins, yoghurt and juice.

MORE INFO

Isle of Lewis Tourist Board
⌂ isle-of-lewis.com
Visit Outer Hebrides
⌂ visitouterhebrides.co.uk
Visit Scotland ⌂ visitscotland.com

INDEX

INDEX OF ADVERTISERS